BY ADAM MAKOS

A Higher Call

Voices of the Pacific

Devotion

Spearhead

Tidal Wave

FOR KIDS

Spearhead (Adapted for Young Readers)

Devotion (Adapted for Young Readers)

TIDAL WAVE

A R C T
PYRENEES
Madrid
Barcelona
Marseille
Gulf of Lions
Turin
Milan
CORSICA
SARDINIA
I T A L Y
Rome
Naples
TYRRHENIAN
SEA
YUGOS
ADRIATIC SEA
M E D I T E R
IONIAN
SEA
Longitude West of Greenwich
Longitude East of Greenwich

TIDAL WAVE

THE PILOTS, THE PRINCESS, AND THE ENEMY ACE—A TRUE STORY OF COURAGE AND SURVIVAL IN WWII

ADAM MAKOS

BALLANTINE BOOKS
NEW YORK

Ballantine Books
An imprint of Random House
A division of Penguin Random House LLC
1745 Broadway, New York, NY 10019
randomhousebooks.com
penguinrandomhouse.com

All interior maps by Bryan Makos of Valor Studios, Inc.

Photo credits can be found on page 425–26.

Hardcover ISBN 9780593725276
Ebook ISBN 9780593725283

Printed in the United States of America

1st Printing

FIRST EDITION

Book Team: production editor: *Evan Camfield* • managing editor: *Danielle Maldonado* • production manager: *Angela McNally* • copy editor: *Jolanta Benal* • proofreaders: *Michael Burke, Martin Schneider*

Book design by Barbara M. Bachman

The authorized representative in the EU for product safety and compliance is Penguin Random House Ireland, Morrison Chambers, 32 Nassau Street, Dublin D02 YH68, Ireland. https://eu-contact.penguin.ie

To Frederick W. Smith—
and the brave young American fliers of Operation Tidal Wave,
whom we set out to honor.

CONTENTS

INTRODUCTION

SOME STORIES FIND YOU WHEN YOU LEAST EXPECT THEM.

It was a Monday evening in July 2018 when I was waiting nervously in the lobby of a hotel in Memphis. Businesspeople clustered around tables, laughing over drinks, while others rolled their suitcases toward the front desk. Most wore some variation of the same logo—a flash of purple, orange, and white. FedEx. The company's airport hub lay only a few miles away.

I was at the hotel to meet someone they all surely knew—their boss, Mr. Fred Smith.

The name sounds ordinary. The man was anything but. He was the founder of FedEx, one of America's great business successes, and a tremendous champion of our nation's veterans.

When he entered the hotel, I was surprised. No entourage. No bodyguards. Just Mr. Smith. He was of medium height, with a round, robust face framed by white hair. Strapped to his wrist was a simple Casio. His clothes were neat but unpretentious: business attire with an open collar and plain black shoes. He radiated Southern friendliness and greeted me with a handshake that felt like a big warm paw.

I had seen the endless purple tails of his planes as I flew into Tennessee that afternoon, and I was already a bit awed. Not only was he overseeing more than 425,000 employees as CEO, but he carried another level of distinction.

Before he built his company, Mr. Smith had been a Marine officer in Vietnam. He'd commanded K-Company, 3rd Battalion, 5th Marines, the storied unit that fought its way across the Pacific in World War II.

Mr. Smith had earned the Silver Star, the Bronze Star, and two Purple Hearts. When he came home from Vietnam, he rolled up his sleeves and put the lessons of military leadership—vision, discipline, logistics—to work. Out of them, he built FedEx.

That war, and the hard-felt losses he carried from it, left him with a lifelong reverence for service and sacrifice. He'd even chaired the fundraising for the World War II Memorial in Washington and the National Museum of the Marine Corps.

At the time I met him, he was helping bring my book *Devotion* to the big screen. The next morning, we were bound for Hattiesburg, Mississippi, to meet the daughter of Jesse Brown, a hero from that story and the upcoming film.

But that night at dinner, there was another story on Mr. Smith's mind: Operation Tidal Wave. Arguably the most daring bomber raid of World War II, it was born of an audacious gamble—when the Army Air Forces gathered every available B-24 bomber in the Libyan desert for a nearly unthinkable mission: a low-level surprise attack on Hitler's most vital asset—the oil refineries of Ploesti, Romania.

Mr. Smith had a personal connection to the raid. His early legal counsel, a man named Ramsay Potts, had flown that mission and earned the Distinguished Service Cross.

I acknowledged that I knew the story. Any aviation buff does. B-24s flying low and fast like fighters, skimming the treetops, through fire and flak, over refineries ready to explode beneath them. It's a mission etched in legend, written about many times.

But not *this* part, Mr. Smith said. He'd zeroed in on a remarkable thread: one American bomber that was shot down during the attack and crash-landed in the last place its crew ever imagined: on the estate of a Romanian princess. By nationality, she was their enemy. The Americans had just bombed her homeland. Yet what she did next defied every expectation.

Mr. Smith said the princess was an integral part of the story, and that around that moment lay an even larger story still waiting to be told, one of intense action and adventure set in a little-known arena of World War II, where Germans, Romanians, Americans, Britons, and Russians all converged to slug it out.

He urged me to investigate.

I took his advice and began to dig deeper. The story started to show itself. Not only was there a princess walking a perilous line between loyalty to her country and quiet defiance, there was a Romanian fighter ace flying a Messerschmitt 109, reluctantly, for the other side. A twenty-one-year-old king desperate to pull his nation from Hitler's grip. A Nazi-backed dictator working against him. And a Great Escape by American fliers—unfolding right under the noses of the Germans. How had we never heard this before? Blame the communists. At the end of World War II, Romania—and the stories of what had happened there—was sealed behind the Iron Curtain.

Yet even during the conflict, Romania was a mystery to most Americans. "Romania, are they even in the war?" more than one American flier wondered when he first learned of their faraway target. Even all these years later, Romania remained, to me, little more than a name on the map of Europe, wedged between the Balkans and the Black Sea. I pictured dark-haired, sharp-featured people, somehow mixed up with the Romani. Their Latin-based language, I would learn, sounded remarkably like Italian. And apparently, at one point, this small country was swimming in oil—black gold that had drawn the attention of Hitler himself.

There was a more immediate obstacle. After seventy-five years, was anyone still alive to tell this story firsthand? Out of 178 crews—more than 1,700 men—who'd flown the Ploesti raid, I needed to locate the men of the one plane that went down on the princess's estate: *Chattanooga Choo Choo.* Ten men total. Ploesti had happened a lifetime ago. Any man who had flown that mission would now be nearly one hundred years old.

My research team started digging anyway. We were looking for a needle in a haystack. Then came a lead: a single name in an online news article. A man was still alive from Tidal Wave.

Ernie Poulson.

He was an officer. And what the article said about him made my jaw fall. He'd been the copilot of *Chattanooga Choo Choo,* the bomber that crash-landed on the princess's estate in 1943 . . . the very crew at the heart of Mr. Smith's story.

We sent him a letter. A shot in the dark. Then we made a follow-up call. At his home in Utah, Ernie Poulson answered.

He was ninety-seven. Remarkably fit. Sharp-minded, direct, precise. Former Air Force colonel. Ex-POW. In a recent photograph, he was still handsome, like an actor cast to play a veteran in a film. He was, it turned out, the last living survivor of his crew, and likely of the raid itself. Locked inside his memory lay the eyewitness experience of one of the great untold stories of World War II.

We explained what we hoped to do. We wanted to write an immersive, richly detailed book about him and his crew and their paradoxical enemy, the Romanians whose lives became entangled with theirs.

Ernie confirmed the story was all true. He still thought about those people and places every night before bed, every morning when he woke.

But he hesitated. He had lived through this incredible adventure once, and that was enough for him.

Then something caught his ear.

"This book won't be just about you," we told him. "It'll be about *all* the guys."

Ernie's demeanor softened. He knew what was at stake. The story of 1,700 brave Americans was about to fade away, its best part untold. It was about bringing the Ploesti raid to life for those who never knew what those young Americans endured. The Air Force colonel and former POW felt he had a duty as possibly the last survivor.

"My door is open," he said. "Come on out."

AT HIS HOME, ERNIE showed us a copy of the diary he'd secretly kept as a POW. He handed over a memoir he'd written for his family decades earlier.

Using those sources, we sat down with Ernie, interviewing him multiple times in person, then countless times by phone. He connected us with the families of his crewmates, who opened their collections of letters and old interviews. Ernie's navigator had even written and self-published a book of his own.

And then there was "The Crew Diary." Hidden for decades in an attic, it was a loose set of pages written by Ernie and his men during the war. In the fall of 1944 and early 1945, each of the nine surviving airmen had sat down with pen and paper to record what they'd seen, said, and done. It was unheard-of.

Nine men chronicling the story of one mission together.

In *wartime.*

Edited into a single narrative, it became the best-documented bomber crew account I'd ever read.

From there, our research stretched across America and Europe. We dug through six U.S. archives and an equal number of Romanian repositories.

Our research team even plunged into the shadowy hollows of Transylvania in search of the final clues to this epic adventure that once shaped the outcome of the European war.

PREPARE FOR FLIGHT.

In the pages ahead, you'll ride along with Ernie and his crew, twentysomethings brought to the desert on a secret mission. You'll see Operation Tidal Wave through their eyes, from cockpit to captivity, and meet the Romanians whose lives collided with theirs: "Buzz" Cantacuzino, Princess Catherine Caradja, and King Michael.

But this is not a tale of grand strategy, mission statistics, or royal intrigue. It's a story of humanity, of people with the trappings stripped away, of courage, survival, and ultimately a revelation about the person we call the enemy.

Mr. Fred Smith saw it first. This is the story he urged us to chase—the one he believed the world needed to know. It's the saga that would define our friend Ernie Poulson for the rest of his life.

The props are clear. The bomber's fueled. The course is set.

Ahead lies a mission no one expected to survive.

Our destination?

Libya, 1943.

TIDAL WAVE

CHAPTER 1

THE NEW ARRIVALS

JULY 3, 1943
North Africa

THE AIR BASE WASN'T WHERE IT WAS SUPPOSED TO BE.

In the right seat of a B-24, the copilot leaned forward and strained to see ahead as the bomber hugged the desert coastline of Libya, flying at a thousand feet.

The four-engine "Liberator" was a boxy brute of a machine with a glass-plated nose, slab-sided fuselage, and long, slender wings set high on its frame. And the trademark of the design from Consolidated Aircraft: twin tails spaced apart like rudders on a catamaran.

The B-24 "Liberator" bomber

Beyond the bomber's left wing, the Mediterranean unfurled to the horizon like a giant sapphire lake. Off the right wing and in front of the plane, the desert stretched flat and red beneath an unflinching blue sky. The terrain was "shimmering in the clear, dry air."

Where are you? wondered Second Lieutenant Ernie Poulson. The longer he searched, the tighter the knot in his stomach grew. There was no sign of an air base, anywhere.

Thoroughly perplexed, Ernie sat back in his seat and flipped open a pad to review his notes from the preflight briefing. Beneath his green crush cap with its brown leather brim, Ernie's appearance reflected his Swedish roots. Twenty-two, blond and blue eyed, with a prominent, square jawline, Ernie was a dead ringer for the future movie star Marlon Brando. He stood five feet ten inches tall when not crammed into the seat of a B-24, and he had a weightlifter's upper physique, but his muscles came from a rugged outdoor upbringing in Utah's Sanpete Valley rather than gym workouts.

Ernie Poulson

It was around 2 P.M. and the white-hot North African sun bored through the glass plates in the ceiling. The Plexiglas side windows were open, letting in a rush of hot air and propeller drone. It made little difference. The cockpit smelled of gasoline and hot oil.

There was something else about Ernie, something curious. Even now, near the end of a long journey, his tie was cinched tight and hardly a hair was out of place. Wherever he was, Ernie always tried to look his best. His officer's file noticed this "quiet, unassuming, pleasant" young man was "unusually neat." It was not for vanity's sake that he took immense pride in his uniform; Ernie came from a family that barely scraped by. He was proud of the uniform because of everything it stood for. His country. And what the Army Air Forces did for him. The first time he put on the uniform was the first time in his life he felt important.

Now, after flying for eight hours across the coast of North Africa, and nine hours before that to reach North Africa from England, Ernie just wanted to put the plane down, get his feet back on solid ground, and find out what the heck they were doing here.

A week ago, his outfit, the 389th Bomb Group, had reported to their fog-shrouded base in England, ready to fly high-altitude bombing raids over Hitler's Germany. But they were told by the 8th Air Force not to unpack. Plans had changed. Then three days later they had been sent here, to the middle of nowhere, for detached service with the 9th Air Force. "Liberators are needed in the Middle East" was all they'd been told.

Their cryptic orders were to report to a former Luftwaffe air base called Berka 4, somewhere along the Libyan coast—but finding it would be another matter. Even the intel boys couldn't say exactly where the new base lay. For some reason it didn't appear on any American maps.

When Ernie envisioned their new desert home, he pictured something out of the airport scene in *Casablanca:* colonial-era hangars and palm trees and a tower with a searchlight beaming through the fog at night. Now, motoring through the desert sky, he was no longer sure what to expect.

Ernie turned to the pilot in the seat beside him, the aircraft commander, twenty-four-year-old First Lieutenant Bob O'Reilly. The pilot's attention was fixed on the controls, making small corrections as he guided the big B-24 through the air.

Bob was a sandy-haired Irish American with a square face and hazel eyes that were always brimming with humor. Average in build, he made up for it in scrappiness and charm—it was said he'd "never met a stranger." Unlike Ernie, Bob wasn't fastidious about his appearance. His shirt looked slept in, and his tattered brown shoes were "on the verge of falling apart." What few of the crew knew—and Bob never let slip—was that he hailed from St. Louis high society. Back home in the leafy streets of Westminster Park, his neighbors didn't call him Bob at all. To them, he was R. J. O'Reilly III.

Ernie triggered the intercom by pressing the button on the yoke in front of him. "Bob, am I cracking up? I don't see a thing out there."

Bob craned his neck to see for himself.

Both men could spot the port city of Benghazi coming up on the left side of the plane, its whitewashed buildings scorched and scarred, its harbor clogged by sunken Axis transport ships. The fighting in North Africa was over. Aided by an infusion of American manpower, the British had driven

Rommel and the German Afrika Korps from the continent just two months earlier.

"About ten miles south of Benghazi," Ernie said, reciting what he'd written in his notes from the preflight briefing. "That's where we're supposed to go."

Both men looked ahead and a little to the right, where the base should be. "I'll be damned," Bob said, seeing nothing. "You're right."

There was nothing out there but red, hard-packed desert.

Ernie knew something was wrong—an air base shouldn't be this hard to find. He offered a solution.

Ernie suggested they fly up to Benghazi and ask for directions. The British were there. Supposedly, a number of American units too. Find a field, radio their tower, and get some bearings.

"I bet we're not the first crew that needs directions," he said.

Bob looked like someone had spat in his coffee. Directions? No way were they asking for directions.

Before Ernie could lodge a further protest, Bob put the bomber in a holding pattern and called for their navigator, Britt, to come up to the flight deck—and to bring one of their useless maps.

Ernie conceded defeat. What else could he do? For the last twelve hundred miles they'd alternated who flew the plane. But at the end of the day, Bob was the aircraft commander.

The crew's navigator, Second Lieutenant Richard Britt, twenty-one, emerged from the nose of the plane. Standing a lanky six foot one, he had to squeeze up and onto the flight deck behind Ernie and Bob. Britt had tight-set blue eyes and a thick chin; he projected a precise but friendly demeanor. Back home in Chicago's suburbs, Britt had set an "enviable" record at his high school. He'd missed only two days of school in four years—and went "0 times tardy."

Britt plugged in to the intercom system and unfolded his map. He had an idea about how to find their base: good old-fashioned pilotage. He motioned to his map and explained that they were coming up on a narrow-gauge railroad that ran south from Benghazi into the desert.

"Now, if I was a German building an airfield that needs a regular resupply of fuel from Benghazi, where would I put it?" He tapped the map. "Somewhere near a railway."

Richard Britt and Bob O'Reilly

He told Bob to follow that railroad south. "Sooner or later, we're bound to find Berka 4."

"Or we can use the radio," Ernie reminded his friends.

Never! Bob grinned. Where was the fun in that?

And besides, Britt had his reputation going for him. Barely a week before this, he had successfully navigated them from the United States across the frigid black Atlantic, alone, at night, relying on just the stars to reach England.

Ernie and Britt felt the plane turning beneath them as Bob wheeled the bomber south.

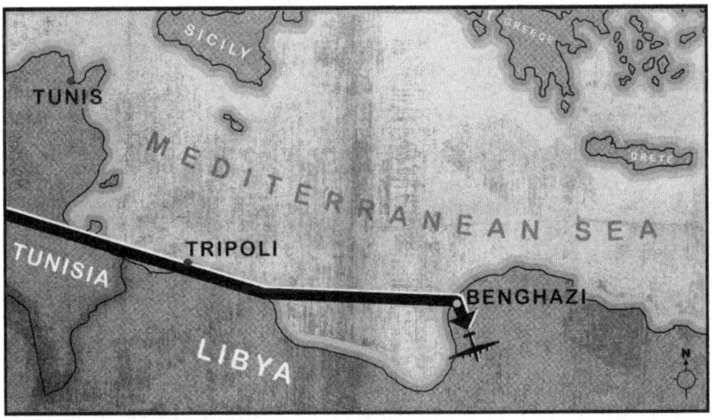

The patched and bomb-scarred railroad tracks weren't hard to follow. With their backs toward civilization, the crew flew into the blinding sun.

Below on the ground, there was nothing in the Libyan outback except British recovery crews towing back their knocked-out tanks to repair them for the next battle, or hauling in wrecked German and Italian planes for salvage.

Some thought the war would have been ended by the combat here in North Africa. Hitler had lost boundless "Iron Treasure" and more than 600,000 men. Yet the Nazi war machine shrugged off its losses and kept fighting on all fronts, walking away with an aura of invincibility.

Minutes and miles flew by with no sign of anything.

The crew almost flew past it.

On the left side of the plane, Ernie, Bob, and Britt looked down on a distinct ribbon of dirt in the scorched desert—tractors had scraped out a runway, with a smaller taxiway running perpendicular to it. Piles of tents and crates were dumped on the ground and a swarm of soldiers moved among them.

Someone was making a bomber base in the desert.

By God, Britt was right, thought Ernie. That was why they couldn't see Berka 4 from the air. It was nothing but a scratch on the sand.

Further east, on the fringe of the airfield, Ernie and his friends could make out a half dozen B-24s, factory fresh with dark green bodies, sky-gray bellies, and white American stars on the fuselage and wings. They were 389th planes all right, the other early arrivals from their outfit. There would be thirty planes and crews by the time everyone was here.

Ernie and his friends were in disbelief.

"This can't be it?" Bob said. Ernie withheld judgment. It was hard to argue with the facts. Wherever they were, it was nothing like he saw in *Casablanca.*

The radio popped with static. "B-24, we have you in sight. Runway is clear. Come on down." There was no tower to make the call. It was a fellow pilot, calling them on the group channel from the radio in his plane.

Bob cringed. This was the place. Ernie shut the cockpit window on his side as Bob began their descent. Things were about to get dusty.

ON THE GROUND AFTER landing, Bob steered the bomber off the taxiway to park in the rough desert. The B-24 taxied to a halt.

Through his side window, Ernie glimpsed a squad of British soldiers digging in an anti-aircraft gun on the perimeter of the airfield. They were filling sandbags, kicking up a tornado of dust. Beneath their flat-brimmed helmets they wore gas masks so they could breathe. Other British gun crews were settling in around the field.

Ernie was shocked to see the gunners. Wasn't the fighting in North Africa supposed to be over?

The new arrivals would soon learn that the Luftwaffe could, in fact, send a surprise air raid from Sicily, Greece, or mainland Italy at any time. And two weeks earlier, German paratroopers had raided American and British air bases at Benghazi, killing two American airmen and sabotaging two British bombers that later "blew up on takeoff," slaughtering their entire crews. The Libyan desert was still very much a war zone.

THE B-24'S BOMB BAY doors slid up and alongside the fuselage, and a hatch opened beneath the tail. Ernie, Bob, and half the crew began exiting the plane via the bomb bay, while the others dropped down from the hatch.

Emblazoned on the copilot's side of the fuselage was the bomber's name, *Pistol Packin' Mama,* inspired by a radio hit of the day, and its nose art: a pinup of a nude blonde woman suggestively throwing back her hair. Ernie had had no hand in the artwork; it was all Bob. He had named the plane and designed the nose art, a woman so voluptuous that the men who painted her waited until he had left, then retouched the work to make the gal more modest.

Pistol Packin' Mama's crew of ten men—four officers and six sergeants—stepped out under the North African sun. Immediately they all threw on their wire-rimmed sunglasses to shield their eyes against the intense brightness. It felt like someone had opened a blast furnace. With an average daily temperature of 125 degrees Fahrenheit, "it was hotter than the hinges of hell." The heat literally took your breath away.

Other B-24s were parked haphazardly in the desert around them. Ernie identified some familiar nose art. *H for Harry. Blond's Away.* The other ships were the latest D-models like theirs, each with a ball turret slung under the belly and extra fuel tanks tucked in the wings. But no two Liberators were pointed in the same direction. With no aircraft marshals to direct them, the exhausted young pilots had parked every which way.

It was a fitting start to their desert adventure. From the get-go, little of this mission had made sense.

Officially, they'd been sent here to support an invasion of Sicily. But that was just a cover story. The 389th hadn't been briefed about bombing Sicily or Italy; there was no mention of it whatsoever. However, before the crews of the 389th departed for North Africa, word reached them of a significant development: two veteran B-24 groups—the 44th Bomb Group, the Flying Eight Balls, and the 93rd Bomb Group, the Traveling Circus—had already left England bound for Benghazi, four days before theirs. Together, the three groups and their ninety-odd bombers represented all the Liberators in the 8th Air Force.

Rumors of a secret mission ran through the ranks. Supposedly they were headed to Africa to run "a great raid" against a target deep behind enemy lines. Where, exactly? No one knew. Not at their level. It was still classified. But the men spreading the rumors were certain: This would be a highly dangerous "medal raid," guaranteeing that "anyone who participated could be sure he would get at least the Silver Star."* Ernie put little stock in the scuttlebutt. And yet—three bomb groups had been pulled from the air war over Hitler's Reich. Something was afoot.

Dust whisked in front of the men like restless spirits as Ernie and the crew took stock of their surroundings. The terrain beneath their feet was surprisingly hard, just a thin layer of red sand over rock. Their eyes were drawn to activity at the western end of the airfield, where a service company of GIs from Benghazi was putting up mess tents and Quonset huts and unloading trucks, while the other early arrivals from the bomb group were pitching sleeping tents. There was no welcome. No direction. And no shade in sight.

The only signs that the Germans had ever used this patch of dirt were a few leftover slit trenches and piles of small, empty fuel drums, their white paint faded by the sun.

The truth dawned on Ernie, Bob, and the crew. Berka 4 had never been a full-fledged Luftwaffe air base. It was most likely a satellite strip, a temporary staging ground for enemy aircraft after their bases at Benghazi had been bombed. Suddenly it made sense why nobody could find Berka 4 on an American map. It was an airfield in name only.

"It's austere," Ernie said. It was all he could come up with.

* As for the rumors of a raid so great that every man would receive a medal, Captain Philip Ardery, a 389th pilot, would later write, "It was funny how great the percentage of truth in that one turned out to be."

Bob thought that was putting it mildly. He was perturbed. They'd traded their mess hall with cutlery, and their officers club, and English pubs for this? A patch of dirt?

Back home in St. Louis, Bob had grown up in the lap of luxury. His father was an architect. Their home was a Georgian Revival mansion with a seamstress and cook on staff, and Bob and his sisters had a nanny when they were young. Before the war, Bob was a regular at "dances and debut parties." He knew he'd be roughing it in the Army, but not like this.

Ernie, meanwhile, never had a problem when it came to the great outdoors. He had practically been raised in the saddle with a rifle across his lap. His father, Lester, made his living as a professional hunter and trapper. The local farmers and shepherds called upon him whenever predators slinked into the valley and killed their livestock.

Lester would ride deep into the snowcapped Rockies to hunt wolves, coyotes, or mountain lions, often bringing Ernie, who rode an old blue mare, as his helper. By day they'd ride the trails; by night they pitched camp beside a spring and baked sourdough biscuits over the campfire. Ernie's dad didn't talk much. And he was gruff with the horses. A cigarette always dangled from his lips—he'd been smoking since he was twelve—and he'd never finished tenth grade. "Son, these sons-a-bitches are killing me," Lester would mutter as he lit another cigarette. Ernie vowed at an early age "to avoid use of vulgar and irreverent language," like the words he heard from his dad. Sometimes Ernie envied his friends, other boys his age who had shiny new bicycles. "But then I had a horse and saddle which they envied," he recalled, "and I was the first to get a caliber 22 rifle."

Ernie never particularly enjoyed killing animals, but with the farmers' livelihood at stake, he learned to do it well. He trapped his first coyote at age eight. He shot his first mountain lion at twelve.

Now, standing in the barren Libyan desert, Ernie wasn't entirely out of his element. He felt most at home in wide-open spaces. But he had also thought those days were behind him. This was supposed to be the Army *Air Forces.*

Uncharacteristically, Ernie loosened his tie, unbuttoned his dark green shirt, and rolled up his sleeves. All around him, Bob, Britt, and the crew were doing the same. They tugged at their thick brown slacks to try to let the cloth breathe. This was the desert in July, and they were still wearing their wool uniforms from England, the heavy-duty attire suitable for a cool northern climate. They had nothing else to change into.

FOR YOUNG MEN WHO envisioned themselves as highly trained professionals, who were used to pampering their state-of-the-art planes, everything about Berka 4 came as a bitter pill to swallow. Ernie wasn't about to complain about their situation in front of his men, although he would later admit in his diary: "The mid-summer daytime desert heat almost did us in."

The crew looked longingly to distant Benghazi. The former Italian colony was said to be "the most bombed and shelled" city on the planet. It looked like paradise.

The crew's laments were interrupted when a British soldier approached them from one of the anti-aircraft positions. He wore a flat-brimmed helmet and a gas mask, and had his rifle slung over his shoulder. He removed his gas mask as he approached.

The allies exchanged greetings. The British soldier had a cheerful, toothy, working-class face and a deep tan. He carried himself with sharp military bearing despite having been in the desert for who knew how long.

"Is this Berka 4?" one of the crew called out.

"It most certainly is," the British soldier said. The men of *Pistol Packin' Mama* groaned.

"Sorry, chaps," the soldier added with an apologetic grin. He assured the Yanks that a truck would be along for them shortly. Out here in the desert, the British were handling most of the logistics for their American allies.

As Bob and the crew retreated to the bomber to grab their bags, Ernie glanced back at the other men of the 389th pitching tents. Something didn't add up about their purpose here. They were Uncle Sam's freshest and best-trained aircrews, armed with the most advanced bombers in the world, and yet the Army had quietly brought them to this patch of sand, in the middle of nowhere, under obviously false guises.

Why would the brass send anyone to a place like this?

Alarm bells were ringing in Ernie's mind. He felt a tinge of nervous energy. There was more to this mission than met the eye.

CHAPTER 2

UNDER A DESERT SUN

THE NEXT MORNING
Berka 4

BY MID-MORNING ERNIE AND BOB WERE STRUGGLING. BARE-CHESTED, wearing wool pants and ankle-height Brazil boots, they hauled a GI footlocker containing personal effects from their plane.

Perspiration trickled down Ernie's back. On the footlocker's other end, Bob wrestled with his share of the weight as he side-pedaled through the dust, cursing the desert under his breath. The temperature was 120 degrees and it wasn't even 10 A.M. Their shoulders and necks already showed the red glow of sunburn.

Behind them, a flight line of a dozen B-24s stood against the shimmering horizon—the other early arrivals. Ernie, Bob, and the other pilots had re-parked their bombers in neat intervals, and British troops now paced along the line, guarding the aircraft. So far, about a third of the 389th had made it to Berka 4. The rest of the planes were still en route somewhere between England and Benghazi.

Ernie, out of habit, had shaved earlier that morning and attempted to style his hair using water from his canteen. He wanted to present himself well even here, although there had been no briefings or even roll call yet. But as the workday progressed, Ernie realized that trying to look presentable was a losing battle.

He and Bob and the other men who were unloading their planes were covered in a thin layer of the "all-pervasive" red dust. It settled into a man's hair and stuck to his sweaty back. Ernie itched all over. Inside his socks, he could feel a gritty layer of sand caked between his toes, a staple of life in North Africa.

There would be no showers any time soon. British soldiers sweated knee deep in the sand, digging a new well. Word had it that the rickety Italian pump powering the old one was on its last legs, and the secondary well would not be running for a few days. Until then, water was being rationed.

Huffing and puffing, Ernie and Bob reached the crew encampment, a sea of thirty khaki tents pitched on the north side of the field. Around them, their fellow officers and airmen were working to make Berka 4 livable. They'd ringed the latrine with palm fronds for privacy, and men in sweat-soaked wool were now digging trenches where they could hide during an air raid. At present, Berka 4 looked, "at best, like a very primitive Boy Scout camp." Still, a youthful spirit of decency and optimism prevailed in the rookie bomb group despite the challenges around them.

That was, until they dug a little deeper. One after another, pockets of men tossed away their shovels and ran for their lives after they unearthed "a few" venomous snakes and "a great many" scorpions. The British gunners who guarded the base had ambled over earlier and warned the newcomers to beware of a nasty variety of scorpion nicknamed the Deathstalker, with a waxy yellow body and a potent stinger in its tail.

"But don't worry," one British gunner said as he flashed a grin, "the sting only kills children and old-timers."

Were the "Limey gunners" joking? None of the rookie Americans wanted to find out. As one airman put it: "One quickly develops a healthy respect for the desert."

Ernie and Bob returned to their tent, a British design, the type that rolled up from the bottom on all four sides, safari-style. The flaps were all raised, and from inside came the steady clink of a hammer. Britt was at work, stripped to the waist, sweat dripping from his nose. Beside him, the crew's little bombardier, Lieutenant Romano, crouched low, holding planks steady. Britt, who had studied architecture in college, had noticed a pile of discarded packing crates piling up behind the newly built mess tents. An architectural idea had taken shape. He was laying a wooden floor for their tent.

The footlocker hit the ground in a puff of dust. Ernie and Bob shook out their stinging hands, pausing to catch their breath before hiking back for another load.

There was still plenty to haul: helmets; duffels stuffed with fleece-lined pants and flying boots for the cold at altitude. Kit bags packed with gloves and goggles. And the parachutes, oxygen masks, and Mae Wests—life preservers—that they'd normally pick up at a Nissen hut back in England? Not here. Everything was going into their tent for now—four officers' worth of gear. Ernie shrugged off the discomfort. The heat and dust didn't matter. He would see the job through. That was something he had learned from his father.

Back home, even when their family had little, Ernie and his dad helped others, cutting wood for widows, delivering it to the elderly. Ernie had spent "hundreds of hours on the opposite end of a crosscut saw" from his dad, cutting logs until his arms gave out.

When the local farmers' crops fell under siege by "an over-population of rabbits," Ernie and his dad joined the great community rabbit hunts.

And then there was a night Ernie never forgot. He and his dad were camped near the Seeley Creek ranger station when a fierce storm swept in. Lightning cracked overhead and hail pelted down; their horses reared in the dark. Ernie lay awake, "wondering if our tent would withstand the hail and wind." At first light, his father slipped out of their tent, then returned with a cigarette hanging from his lips and grim news: A shepherd needed their help.

Ernie's dad,
Lester Poulson

Ernie followed his dad up to a pasture and stopped cold. Before him lay the gruesome sight of more than a hundred dead sheep, eyes bulging, struck down by the storm. Ernie recoiled, stomach turning. He wanted to leave. He was only eight. Instead, his father handed him a knife.

"The man's only hope is to salvage the hides," his father said, gesturing to the "frantic" shepherd. "And it's got to be done now."

Ernie hesitated.

"You've seen me do it," his father reminded him.

Ernie nodded.

And so, he worked. All day Ernie was arms-deep in dead sheep, slicing and tugging hides, his small hands slippery with blood and sinew. Side by side, he and his dad helped the shepherd, a total stranger, skin every one of the carcasses. More than a hundred sheep.

The lesson etched itself deep: Sometimes you have to roll up your sleeves and get the job done—even if it's the last thing you want to do.

AS MORE BAGGAGE PILED up around the tent and Britt's floor inched closer to completion, it looked as if no relief was in sight.

There were no flights scheduled that morning, no escape into the cooler air at altitude. They would need to wait until the rest of the bomb group arrived.

Ernie pitied Bob, Britt, and the other city boys. Even for him, who'd grown up outdoors, this was miserable. And it was only day one.

Then came the call, the sweetest words they'd heard since leaving England: "Heading for the beach—all bathers get with the program!"

The 389th was giving them the day off.

A CARAVAN OF JEEPS and trucks skidded to a halt near the Libyan coast. Ernie, Bob, Britt, and assorted aircrews came tumbling out. Men whose uniform normally included pressed pants and ties looked like castaways, wearing only boxers and boots. The officers kept their crush caps on to shield them from the sun. Many of the men carried canteens full of powdered lemonade.

A line of palm trees separated them from the beach. Ernie and his friends ran through the groves like lost explorers who'd found an oasis. On the other side came a tantalizing sight: the soft white sand of an immaculate beach, and beyond that, the Mediterranean with its gentle but "delicious looking" waves.

The water gleamed with such beauty and allure that it seemed like a mirage. On their left, the war-ravaged city of Benghazi lay within walking distance down the coast to the west. About thirty-five barrage balloons hovered over its harbor. This was the land where ruins of ancient temples still stood overlooking the sea, relics of the days when Libya was a Roman province called Cyrenaica.

On a sunny Mediterranean morning, the men of the 389th had stumbled upon an unspoiled desert paradise all their own. Except for one problem: They didn't have the place to themselves.

Up the beach in the opposite direction from Benghazi, the area was "covered with bathers—all male." Men emerged from the tree line sipping beverages. They entered the water and floated, talking loudly.

Bob looked as if he'd bitten a lemon. "Who are these jokers?"

Ernie shrugged. They didn't look like locals. Soon enough, the groups shuffled closer to each other out of mutual curiosity. The strangers were all young, like the men of the 389th, and all wore dog tags, but they weren't pale enough to have just flown in from England. These fliers wore deep tans from long months of desert life. The groups exchanged greetings, and a number of men recognized old friends from flight school. A flurry of handshakes and hearty backslaps ensued.

The "strangers" were from the battle-hardened 376th Bomb Group, the core unit of the 9th Air Force. These were the most seasoned B-24 flyers in the Army Air Forces. Not only had they had a hand in driving Rommel out of North Africa, many of their planes and crews had participated in the first American bombing raid over Europe, back in June 1942. By now, they had been in the desert for a full year, first in Egypt, now in Libya. They called themselves the Liberandos—a Mediterranean-inspired nickname loosely meaning "those who liberate." Their encampment was established about a hundred yards inland, close enough to permit swimming on moonlit nights.

The boys from the 9th Air Force were not on vacation, even if they looked like it. They had been busy flying missions to soften up Sicily, the locale next in line for an Allied invasion. But they were enjoying a "quiet" morning because that day's particular mission had been scrubbed.

The Liberandos informed Ernie and his friends that still another B-24 group from the 9th Air Force, the 98th, had set up shop at Benghazi. Nicknamed the Pyramiders, they, too, had done a tour in the Egyptian desert like the Liberandos.

Suddenly it made sense to Ernie why the 389th had been given a desolate field in the middle of nowhere. All the other aircrews in Benghazi were seasoned veterans. Where else would you stick the rookies?

The groups tied in together on the beach, as men threw towels and canteens down in the shadows of palms. Some men from the 389th went with their friends to tour the Liberandos' camp. Others dived into the clear azure water. The water was perfect, surprisingly cool. They felt safe, knowing that British anti-aircraft crews in Benghazi were constantly scanning the skies.

Ernie, Bob, and Britt kicked around on the sand at the water's edge, talking among themselves, trying to process the news that five bomb groups had come to the region—the Traveling Circus, the Flying Eight Balls, and them from the 8th Air Force, plus on top of that the Liberandos and Pyramiders from the 9th.

Standing on a beach in North Africa, in the company of a veteran bomb group, Ernie, who had discounted the rumors of a Great Raid, was beginning to rethink his previous stance.

Their orders had said, "Liberators are needed in the Middle East."

But every last aircraft?

The five bomb groups comprised all the B-24s in England and Africa. Suddenly and inexplicably, they'd all been brought to Benghazi. It was a lot of hardware in one place. Heck, these were all the Liberators on this side of the Atlantic.

Why?

None of the men on the beach seemed overly concerned. But Ernie was convinced: There was something to the rumors after all. This could be bigger than anyone knew.

FOR SOME TIME, all that could be heard was the shouting and laughter on the beach. Ernie and his friends were standing knee deep in the surf when they detected a sound and looked east. They saw it coming from far away. A bomber, but this one was a faded pink color. It was flying far too low for comfort, almost like it was making a strafing run. And it was coming straight toward them.

"What the hell?" Bob said.

"Let's get out of here!" Ernie said.

Men from the 389th scrambled out of the water and sprinted toward the relative safety of the beach, where they waited, dripping wet, with Ernie and his friends.

The bomber tore down the surf toward them, roaring over the wet sand at the water's edge, her four huge Pratt & Whitney R-1830 radial engines growling angrily.

The pink B-24 descended lower. Even lower still. It came "barreling down the beach only about ten or fifteen feet above the sand," with a wingspan so wide it extended partly over the men in the water and partly over Ernie and the others on shore. It shook the beach with a deafening roar and left a spray of water behind it as it buzzed by. The old-timers from the Liberandos waved and cheered from the surf.

The rookies of the 389th were surprised to see the veterans laughing and hooting like this was all a big lark. The bomber was one of theirs.

The Africa-based bombers had been in the desert so long that the scorching sun had oxidized their tan camouflage paint, breaking down its yellow pigment and leaving only pink. The transformation would lead the England-based groups to jokingly refer to these B-24s as Pink Pigs.

Bob admired the gutsy flyby, but Ernie and Britt weren't as impressed. Flying low over a populated area? It was downright risky for the aircraft's crew and everyone on the ground.

"He could lose his wings for that," Ernie muttered.

Back in the States, bomber pilots were strictly forbidden from buzzing because so many young men had crashed and even killed themselves while pretending their heavy bomber was as nimble as a fighter. The hard truth was that heavies weren't built for low-level flight. A machine that big had slow control responses—the time needed for input on the controls to take effect. Even if a pilot was quick to react, there was no guarantee that the ailerons, elevators, and rudders would respond in time.

Still, none of the veteran crews seemed bothered by the display. The rookies of the 389th were left to scratch their heads. "Maybe this was just the natural thing in the combat zone?" wondered one pilot.

After buzzing the beach, the bomber pitched out to land at the Liberandos' airfield nearby, just inland. The men from that group left the water in an obvious hurry and congregated by the tree line, almost as if the plane had crash-landed. But nobody seemed alarmed. In fact, the mood was the opposite. Festive.

Ernie grabbed one of the passersby. "What's the story?"

"Cold drinks!" came the answer.

Cold drinks?

It seemed that the Liberandos had perfected the ultimate desert survival technique. They'd send bombers up under the guise of a test hop or training flight, but the planes didn't fly empty: The fuselage would be loaded with half-gallon cans of fruit juice and crate upon crate of bottled beer. The pilots would go up to about ten thousand feet, open the bomb bay and let the cold air rush in, chilling the beverages, then quickly head back down again. The drinks would be swiftly unloaded into jeeps and hauled straight to the beach. To make ice, the crews going aloft would fill ammo cans with water and go up higher where it was colder.

Ernie, Bob, and Britt looked at one another and grinned. Ernie didn't drink alcohol—his dad was a hard drinker, so he avoided the stuff. But Britt downed the occasional alcoholic beverage, and Bob loved beer. Ernie and his friends rushed over to join the fast-forming lineup of officers and airmen. In no time at all they were floating in the shallows, Ernie with a canteen cup of ice-cold grapefruit juice and Britt and Bob sipping frosty beers.

The bomb groups must have been thirsty, because seemingly "every few minutes" a regular string of B-24s zipped over the men on the beach. Ernie and Bob and the others couldn't help but wave at the planes as they went by, their shadows rippling over them.

All the rest of that long sun-kissed day, they swam and floated in the translucent water, sipping cold drinks with their fellow Americans far from home, with no enemy in sight. They took turns leaving the sea to fetch cold drinks for their pals, feeling like they'd been sent to the desert for R&R.

As Ernie hiked back from a drink run, carrying more beer for Bob and Britt and another juice for himself, the so-called Great Raid felt far away. Ernie had always wanted to go somewhere in his life, to escape the Sanpete Valley, to get out and make his mark on the world. Maybe this was his chance? And who knew, this new mission of theirs might even be fun.

He handed the beers to Bob and Britt, finished his juice, and dove in.

CHAPTER 3

THE MILK RUN

FIVE DAYS LATER, JULY 9, 1943

Berka 4

AT AROUND 4 P.M., THE TELLTALE OUTLINES OF B-24S APPEARED through the red haze as the bombers rolled along the taxiway from the runway. Landing lights projected fuzzy halos from the wings.

The dust had been stirred at Berka 4. What looked like faint ground fog when one or two planes were taxiing had become a total red-out when the bomb group returned all at once. Only the bombers' noses were easily visible before their fuselages faded away.

About halfway down the line of the bombers, *Pistol Packin' Mama* bobbed on its nose gear as it crawled along the uneven terrain. The bomber was running on three engines instead of all four. The outboard engine on Bob's side of the plane was shut down, and a red-tinged fluid coming from the bomb bay streaked the aircraft's belly.

Inside the cockpit, Ernie and Bob coughed and squinted to see forward through the dust. They were weighed down by gear—thick leather jackets, harnesses, and bulky Mae Wests. Red grooves lined their skin, impressions from the goggles and oxygen masks they'd been wearing for hours. And there was something else different about them. Both faces carried unmistakable signs of strain.

The group had just come back from their first mission of the war. The 9th Air Force had a surprise in store for the rookie B-24 outfit, to welcome them to the theater: real-world combat.

At first, the assignment made no sense to young aircrews who had visions of a Great Raid dancing in their heads. In their minds, they were ready for something big. The reality was that the 9th Air Force wasn't about to send the 389th on any mission of consequence before they had some experience under their belts. So the 9th ordered a series of "break-in" raids against lightly defended targets to give the rookies a taste of the action to come.

Now, as the B-24s rolled back to the parking area, it was obvious that their warm-up mission had gone awry. *Pistol Packin' Mama*'s brakes squealed as Bob followed the stop-and-go traffic. The planes ahead moved more slowly than usual, because their pilots were exhausted.

Crew chiefs covered their faces with handkerchiefs as they waved the returning Liberators into their parking spots.

Blinded by the red desert fog, the pilot of one B-24 in the front missed his turn entirely and rolled right past the crew chief. Hoping to correct his mistake, the pilot pulled a U-turn on the desert floor, but he became disoriented and didn't see a slit trench left behind by the Germans. In one swift motion, the B-24's big balloon tire plunged into the trench. The landing gear slammed up and into its shock-absorbing strut. The plane came to rest with its propellers whirling just inches from the sand. Quickly, the pilot cut his engines before the plane could sink any further and cause a propeller strike.

Ground crewmen rushed to the scene. The plane's crew inside were unhurt, but their bomber hadn't fared as well. The accident fractured the plane's wing.

Ernie and Bob never even saw the accident. Too many big machines with whirling propellers were in front of them, and the dust was too thick.

Arriving at their designated desert roost, Bob swung the bomber around. The world outside momentarily disappeared in the dust before he cut the engines. The three still-functioning Pratt & Whitneys wheezed with relief as they wound down to a stop.

The bomb bay doors were stuck shut by battle damage, so Ernie followed Bob, Britt, and the bombardier out of the plane by squeezing through the wheel well in the nose. The men peeled off their jackets but kept on their blue electrically heated "bunny suits" and fleece-lined leather pants.

Ernie stood on wobbly legs in the desert heat, his hair matted with sweat.

A discernible shakiness was felt up and down the entire flight line. The returning crews looked distressed. Whatever had happened up there had left the group "greatly affected."

Clutching his ears, Ernie slipped away from the crew and took a knee. Berka 4 spun in his vision. The hot engines ticked and pinged nearby, but Ernie couldn't hear a thing. His ears were ringing like crazy.

Britt rushed to Ernie's side. "You okay?"

Ernie pointed to his ears. He needed a moment. He'd only fully noticed the issue after the engines were off and he tried to stand on his own two feet. Maybe it was vertigo? Luckily, the problem was gradually wearing off.

Soon enough, Ernie straightened and stood. He made his way toward the left wing, where Bob and others were gathered beneath the battle damage. Along the way, he spotted the top turret gunner, Tech Sergeant Clell Riffle, who was giving him a wide berth. A skinny, jug-eared Southerner with shy eyes and an overbite, Riffle obviously felt guilty over what had happened in the air. Riffle was the reason Ernie's world was spinning.

Clell Riffle

What was supposed to be a "milk run"—as safe as a milkman's early morning deliveries—had played out differently than anyone in the 389th had expected. For their first target, the higher-ups had picked the Germans' Maleme aerodrome, a sleepy backwater garrison on the Greek island of Crete. The strike was meant as a feint, a distraction to draw enemy eyes away from the upcoming invasion of Sicily. The intel boys predicted light opposition.

When the group showed up at 21,000 feet over Maleme, however, the Germans were ready. The B-24s had just dropped their bombs and were turning for home when a dozen German Messerschmitt Me-109s pounced on them from out of the sun. In an instant, the 389th's "rather ordinary" mission turned "a bit more scary" than anyone had bargained for.

Across the bomber formation, the novice American crews panicked. The primary radio channel became "filled with blurred voices, shouting and swearing in English," while "trigger happy" gunners burned through their ammunition.

When an Me-109 came at *Pistol Packin' Mama* from one o'clock, Riffle brought his twin .50 caliber machine guns around to meet the threat. The gunner had been jittery just thinking about combat—now with a '109 charging directly at him, he was scared out of his mind.

Riffle aimed. The muzzles of his guns hovered almost directly over Ernie's head. Only the cockpit's glass ceiling separated them. Then Riffle opened fire.

The earsplitting roar of his guns tore through the glass. There was no escaping it. The sound knifed straight through Ernie's headphones and into his eardrums.

Every gunner was trained to fire in short, controlled bursts. "Accuracy, not volume," their instructors had hammered into them.

But Riffle forgot all that.

The terrified airman clutched his triggers and held on. Ernie swore the invisible shockwaves from the sustained firing were going to jar his teeth loose. Either that, or Riffle would melt his guns outright.

The '109 fired a short burst into *Pistol Packin' Mama* before diving between their bomber and the three-ship flight ahead. Only then did the noise stop pouring from Riffle's muzzles.

Pistol Packin' Mama took more hits in the ensuing melee, but others had it worse. When a bomber behind them was hit and the rookie crew bailed out, one man made a tragic mistake—the straps on his parachute harness were too loose. He slipped through the webbing and fell to his death in view of almost everyone.

Their first mission had been anything but a milk run. It was a horror show.

When Ernie approached Riffle afterward, the gunner shrank back, bracing for a tongue-lashing. Everyone knew he had panicked.

Ernie saw the shame in his eyes and softened. "It's all right, Clell," he said. "You're supposed to shoot at them."

Riffle cracked a weak, relieved smile.

Privately, Ernie had already vowed to bring cotton balls for his ears the next time. But that wasn't what he wanted to talk to Riffle about. Ernie had more serious concerns. "Do we know who went down?" The bomber they had lost was behind them in the formation. Ernie and Bob hadn't been able to see a thing from up front.

Riffle, who doubled as their radio operator, had no idea. He said the radio channel was too jammed with voices.

Ernie joined Bob, Britt, and other members of the crew beneath their inoperative engine. *Pistol Packin' Mama* had been beaten up. Black oil pooled on the sand, and the inside of the engine cowling was pitted with bullet holes.

Bob had to shout so Ernie could hear him. "Supercharger got knocked out. Oil regulator, too." Somehow the engine had held together, allowing them to fly back with the group. It had only given out moments before they landed. "Close one, huh?"

Ernie nodded. Too close.

The rest of the crew had gathered at the root of the wing to examine the damage to the bomb bay. The red-tinged liquid that covered the aircraft's belly was hydraulic fluid that had leaked out during flight. The crew's flight engineer, a mechanic by training, was cranking open the bomb bay doors from inside.

"Lieutenants, you gotta see this."

One of the crew led Ernie and Bob to the site of the latest commotion. The others had the bomb bay opened and were gawking at something inside.

Ernie and Bob looked for themselves. Daylight streamed into the bomb bay. A fist-sized hole in the ceiling marked where a 20mm shell had penetrated the fuselage and knocked out the bomb bay doors' hydraulics. The crew exchanged uneasy looks. There'd been twelve 500-pound bombs in the bay moments before the 20mm hit—but what if they hadn't been dropped yet?

It was way too close.

AS ERNIE AND THE crew left the flight line and rode back to the HQ area in a truck, their silence spoke volumes. Each man harbored serious doubts about their future. Their break-in raid nearly did them in. And something else plagued their minds.

Britt opened his navigator's log and checked his notes. The lost bomber had gone down about twenty-five miles from Crete. "Maybe some of them will make it ashore?" he said. He looked to Ernie and Bob for confirmation.

An uneasy silence fell over the group. They would learn soon in the debrief that the missing bomber was *Stella*—Lieutenant Scates's ship. The plane's pilot, First Lieutenant Arthur Scates, was twenty-three, with a cleft chin and eyes that always looked deep in thought. Ernie didn't know him well; he was in another squadron.

Scates had named his bomber after his mother, Stella, a single woman who raised eight kids after her husband left. During his last visit home, Arthur had prepared his mother for the possibility of his being shot down in combat. "Don't worry if you get word that I am missing," he told her. "Don't give me up for five years—I'm a good jumper."

What was Ernie supposed to say? He feared mightily for the lost crew. "It'll all come down to the tides," he said to Britt's question. The thought of floating at night in the Mediterranean made him shiver.

In the weeks to come, word that Scates had been shot down would reach his hometown in Union City, Tennessee, and a local reporter would interview his mother. She was holding on to hope. "I am doing just what my son told me," she told the writer. "I believe he is alive and that I will soon hear about him." Despite her son's optimism, none of *Stella*'s crew would ever be seen again.

The 389th had lost their first bomber in combat and another to a slit trench, not to mention ten good men. And what did they have to show for it? The debrief would reveal that all the group's bombs were seen falling harmlessly on both sides of the Germans' runway, or splashing into the sea.

Ernie was full of misgivings as the truck carried him away from his wounded bomber. The rigors of combat were the only test that mattered, and the whole group of rookies had botched it. His ringing ears wouldn't let him forget. Suddenly their Liberators "did not seem invincible."

The run to Crete was a wake-up call for Ernie and the young aircrews of the 389th. Whatever mission had brought them to the desert, they now knew they weren't ready for it.

The enemy had made sure of that.

CHAPTER 4

THE OLD HANDS

TEN DAYS EARLIER, JUNE 29, 1943
Southeastern Ukraine

WITH THE FIRST GLIMMER OF DAWN, A SMALL AXIS AIRSTRIP ON THE Eastern Front stirred to life. Ground crewmen peeled the dew-soaked covers from the canopies of sleek Messerschmitt 109 fighters, and Opel blitz trucks ran deliveries.

A tall, broad-shouldered Romanian officer pedaled his bicycle up to the front gate of Mariupol-West, a run-down formerly Soviet airfield in the coastal grasslands near the port city of Mariupol. A frontline station of the Royal Romanian Air Force, the 7th Fighter Group (Grupul 7 Vânătoare), three squadrons strong, operated from this ramshackle base.

Romanian soldiers in brown uniforms with ankle wraps waited in the early morning shadows to check the papers of anyone seeking admission.

The gate guards immediately recognized the man on the bicycle: Lieutenant Constantin Cantacuzino, leader of the 58th Squadron. Bâzu, as he was known—in English, it would be "Buzz"—carried himself differently from the other officers. He was thirty-eight, with a strong nose and black hair slicked back from a sharp widow's peak. His posture was squared, his gaze steady and reflective. His brown eyes took in not just his surroundings, but the weight of responsibility that came with leading a fighter squadron.

Buzz was a celebrity on any Romanian airfield. He had personally shot down four enemy aircraft, but that was not the only reason he was the object of attention everywhere he went.

He was a prince.

His family, the Cantacuzinos, traced their roots to the twelfth century and had held power in Romania on and off since the 1500s, and in modern times had grown fabulously wealthy from oil. Buzz had earned his nickname as a boy when he'd run through his grandfather's castle while imitating the sound of an airplane engine.

There was something else in his lineage. Through centuries of intermarriage, Buzz had inherited some of medieval Romania's oldest dynastic bloodlines—including the Basarabs, the dynasty that produced Vlad III, the fifteenth-century Romanian prince the world had come to know as Dracula.

Now Buzz wore the uniform of a Romanian Air Force lieutenant: a robin's-egg-blue tunic and trousers, a crisp shirt with a black tic, and a small, tentlike overseas cap. A lifelong sportsman—he had even captained the national hockey team before the war—Buzz preferred to ride his bicycle to work rather than take a car.

Buzz in 1937 and during wartime

A sergeant barked orders. A soldier lifted the gate. Other guards snapped to attention and proudly held their salutes. Buzz offered a sincere wave and pedaled past the men and onto the grass airfield, heading toward the lone hangar.

As Buzz biked along the flight line, everyone he encountered stopped to greet him. Armorers with heavy belts of ammo over their shoulders nodded and smiled. Mechanics in baggy gray coveralls set down their tool boxes and saluted. Everyone stood a little straighter in his presence. Buzz handled the admiration with a statesman's grace.

The ground crewmen would be the first to tell you: "Anyone who knows him, loves him." In an era when 75 percent of Romanian enlisted men were illiterate peasants who'd been drafted from agricultural work, Buzz was known to exhibit "the warmest behavior" toward even the lowliest mechanic. "The prince was one of the few aviators who didn't know how to curse, let alone behave poorly toward those of lower rank."

The rank-and-file troops had heard stories about Buzz and looked at him with awe. They were still trying to fathom how common men such as themselves could be serving alongside a national figurehead. At times, they outright questioned his presence in the ranks. This was a man who had attended boarding school in Switzerland and held two university degrees—one in business law from the University of Strasbourg, the other in literature from the Sorbonne in Paris. In addition to elegant apartments in Bucharest, he owned five country estates, holdings spanning more than twelve thousand acres. His family had practically founded Romania's oil industry.*

A prince didn't have to fight. Why would anyone choose to be here?

For Buzz, it was a matter of duty.

Before the war, he'd enjoyed the luxury of being a civilian pilot. This was the golden age of aviation, and he'd earned his license when he was twenty-seven, becoming the fifty-eighth private pilot in the nation. Flying was more than a pastime to him—it became an obsession. He even took a side job with the national airline, flying commercial routes. "He couldn't bear sitting behind a desk in the palace," a relative remembered.

On Sundays, Buzz took to the skies and flew in air shows, looping and rolling before cheering crowds across Romania. In short order, the prince became the nation's most celebrated aerobatic pilot.

The Romanian upper crust was shocked. A Cantacuzino hauling passengers? Flying stunts?

But Buzz wasn't finished surprising his social class. In 1938, with war clouds gathering over Europe, he began his mandatory military service in the reserves like everybody else. Instead of seeking an exemption or a cushy desk job, the prince made headlines when he became a fighter pilot, entering

* The only time Buzz's pilots caught a glimpse of his wealth was when they played poker for money. If Buzz lost, he could always buy his way back in.

service with four thousand civilian flight hours, far more stick time than the average military flyer.

Three years later, when the reservists were called up to fight for Romania, his family name could have secured him safer duty anywhere but the "anti-Soviet" front. Instead, Buzz voluntarily presented himself to his squadron. A loyal Romanian who loved his country, he believed royalty should be the first to serve.

And now, driven by duty, one of Romania's best pilots found himself here at the Eastern Front, where the stakes were particularly dire.

In the nearly two years since Romania's iron-fisted dictator, ex-General Ion Antonescu, had marched their small country's military east to join Hitler's crusade, morale in the ranks had steadily waned. Most Romanian servicemen wished they were anywhere else. The Soviets, resurgent after their January victory at Stalingrad, had the Axis outnumbered and on the back foot, erasing any ground they'd gained. Russian factories in the Urals were cranking out planes and tanks, bolstered by Lend-Lease from the Western allies, aid on a scale Hitler could never match. The writing was on the wall, and you could feel it in the air. Romania was trapped in an unwinnable war.

BY 7 A.M., BUZZ and the other eight pilots of his squadron exited the hangar with their life preservers tossed over their shoulders. The day's work was about to begin.

"Alex" Moldoveanu

At Buzz's side was his wingman, Staff Sergeant Alexandru Moldoveanu. Thirty-two, Alex had a broad face with striking features, a long nose and wide chin that became even more pronounced when he smiled. The look was so exaggerated that he hardly fit the dashing image of a fighter pilot. "Experienced, modest, and brave," Alex was an "old hand" with three victories over enemy aircraft.

When Buzz, Alex, and the other pilots reached their planes, Romanian ground crewmen had finished servicing the lineup of Messerschmitt 109G-4 fighters. The German-built planes were sleek and gray, with a sharklike silhouette broken only by a boxy canopy.

But the fighters weren't German—at least in heart. Large yellow pointy-edged crosses adorned the planes' flanks and wings. The sharp-edged cross—formed from four Ms arranged to match the four points of the compass—was called the Michael's Cross in honor of the twenty-one-year-old king of Romania.

The fighters had come as a form of payment. Three months earlier, the Germans had equipped the 7th Fighter Group with forty of their mainstay fighters as token compensation for helping themselves to the nation's petroleum resources.

Buzz and his comrades affectionately called the aircraft the *Messer.* The prince wasn't about to complain about taking charity from their uneasy allies. The aircraft was far superior to the British Hawker Hurricanes he'd flown during his first tour in 1941—leftovers from when Romania and England had been allies.

Buzz bikes up to an Me-109 in Romanian markings

It was time to go to work. Buzz wished Alex well before he and his wingman parted ways. There was little to be cheerful about, but that didn't prevent an occasional display of gallows humor.

Zbor plăcut! *Have a nice flight!*

Alex and the other pilots drew confidence from Buzz's quiet steadiness—his uncomplaining, even-tempered, matter-of-fact outlook. He often stood with a relaxed slouch as if saving his energy for when it mattered, and behaved as if their life-threatening situation was a minor inconvenience. In doing so, he made them feel they could survive whatever the war threw at them.

Still, an air of mystery surrounded the prince, and the old hands like Alex understood it better than most. Rumors had dogged Buzz ever since his first deployment in 1941. The stories involved a common thread: sightings of a beautiful auburn-haired young woman who had followed him off to war. Some say the couple had run afoul of Antonescu's authoritarian government. Others whispered that State Security got involved, something about the prince violating race laws. Whatever had happened, it was serious enough that the authorities yanked him from his fighter between sorties and sent him home as punishment, back to the national airlines for nearly two years. Only recently had they allowed his return, because the situation at the front had worsened. And this time, they went from punishing him to giving him his own squadron.

Two years—then back again as if nothing happened. It raised a lot of questions. What could provoke Antonescu's government so fiercely that they would pull a skilled pilot, a Romanian prince, from the cockpit? Only veterans such as Alex knew the real story—but good luck prying it out of them. Alex's lips were sealed.

Buzz climbed aboard his plane, a Messer with a white number 4 on its flanks—"White 4." Four hashmarks painted on the rudder marked his victories over enemy aircraft, all from his first deployment in 1941. With any luck, today he'd hit a milestone. One more, and the prince would become an ace.

Buzz stepped into the cockpit, always with his right foot first, never his left—an unexplained superstition among Romanian pilots. He had to turn his shoulders to squeeze inside. He lowered the side-hinged canopy and closed himself in. The Messer was notoriously snug, leading German engineers to joke that the plane was supposed to be built with the pilot already inside. The cabin smelled of fuel, cordite, and sweat.

In the solitude of the cockpit, Buzz could let his countenance fall. Around his pilots and the ground crews, he always put on a brave face. But tightly wrapped in his aluminum-and-steel cocoon, he didn't have to hide his concern. The skies he was returning to were more terrifying than the ones he'd faced in 1941.

Over the two years since Antonescu's alliance with Hitler had plunged them into war with the world, the situation facing a Romanian fighting man had turned grim. Romania's small military had been ravaged by the fighting on the Eastern Front. Only about half of the 500,000 troops that they had committed to the war remained. The rest were wounded, captured, or dead.*

Half the Romanian army—gone. And Buzz's 7th Fighter Group was the only active fighter group at full strength. Aside from a squadron at Crimea, the others were licking their wounds or defending the homeland. About forty Romanian fighter pilots remained on the Eastern Front. That was all.

Now, with the fighter group 450 miles from home and fighting a losing battle, the bloodletting was far from over. Today, Buzz and Alex would be escorting bombers and could expect typical Eastern Front odds: They'd be outnumbered in the air by "three to five" enemy fighters for every one of theirs. Privately, Buzz would have given anything to fly one more air show performance in skies where no one was trying to kill you. But the odds of ever doing that again weren't looking good.

It was nearly takeoff time, 7:30 A.M. Buzz put on his tan fabric helmet, then slid into place the round German-issued goggles. Before pulling the starter to bring the Messer's engine to life, Buzz checked the floor of the cockpit around his boots. When stationed in the coastal grasslands, it was common to find a mouse.

Buzz wouldn't have harmed the little stowaway. These days, as the Eastern Front was ever shifting in the Russians' favor, Buzz and the Romanian pilots were quartered in the neighboring villages. There, they stayed "in abandoned rooms, destroyed and dirty, in improvised barracks or huts," where fearless mice stole food straight from their tables. On cold nights, when the men slept on hay-filled sacks, the mice would work their way

* Romanian soldiers and civilians alike "were now angry and bitter about the catastrophic losses they had suffered." The casualties from Stalingrad "increased the unpopularity of the war in Romania and exacerbated the already strained relations between the Romanian and German militaries." One Romanian officer, taken prisoner, told the Russians interrogating him "that his troops despised Antonescu for 'having sold their motherland to Germany.'"

through the bedding, looking to curl up against "the warmest parts of the human body." Buzz and his comrades forged a sympathetic attachment to the rodents. The mice were alone, against the world. Just like them.

The same mice that shared their beds sometimes found their way into the planes. In mid-air, Romanian pilots would often see a mouse scamper across their instrument panels or feel its tiny feet as it ran up one side of a pilot's back and across his neck. Buzz would have had a message for the little mouse if he found one now.

Get out while you still can.

CHAPTER 5

THE JOUST

THIRTY MINUTES LATER
At 5,000 feet

TO SOME, IT MUST HAVE LOOKED LIKE MADNESS. TWO MESSERSCHMITTS slicing through the sky, banking hard and sharp, without an enemy in sight. From inside his cockpit, Buzz wrenched his trusty Messer into another sharp bank while Alex fought hard to hold formation on his right wing. Just when it looked like Alex had caught up to the prince, Buzz snapped back in the opposite direction, testing his wingman's limits in the process.

Below the fighters, three friendly Junkers Ju-88 bombers, pencil-thin with stubby glass noses, flew straight and steady in the sharp morning light. The small formation cruised east along the inky blue water of the Black Sea toward territory controlled by the Soviet Red Army. The Ju-88s that Buzz and Alex were escorting were German planes like their Messers, another gift from their "protectors," although crewed by Romanians.

It was the usual desperate situation at the front. Buzz's squadron was spread thin. More targets existed than there were planes available, so the squadron operated in pairs to meet demands, leaving just Buzz and Alex to protect the flight of bombers. The trouble was that the Eastern Front was too broad. It ran some 750 miles all the way to the Gulf of Finland in the north. Mariupol marked the southern end of the line.

From his perch above the planes, Buzz scanned the skies for enemy activity as he and Alex cut back and forth in quick, tight arcs. Mile by mile, they raced closer to the front lines. The sun was rising in front of them, sending dazzling light through the bulletproof glass of Buzz's windscreen. Overhead, wispy blue coastal clouds drifted lazily against the morning sky.

The prince's chaotic flying style would have put any wingman to the test.

Buzz never flew in the same direction for more than a few seconds. The "continuous undulating maneuvers" reminded one wingman of the "flight of a butterfly." He recalled that after just an hour of flying with Buzz he landed drenched in sweat. Others shied away from flying with Buzz altogether because the pace was so exhausting. Alex was one of the few pilots who could keep up with him in the air.

There was a method to Buzz's madness. He'd learned the tactic of erratic flight by studying the French ace Guynemer who flew in the First World War. It was Guynemer who postulated that if you never fly in a straight line, it's much harder for the enemy to shoot you down.

THE SMALL ROMANIAN FORMATION—two fighters and three bombers—left friendly territory, soaring over the front lines. Below them, the coastal Ukrainian landscape was pitted with shell craters and dotted with charred tanks. Wisps of smoke rose from the ground, marking where German troops, who shouldered the bulk of the fighting, were engaged in skirmishes with the Russians.

The bombers were not far from their target now. It was just behind the Russian front lines. *Take them there, and bring them back alive.* That was the Romanians' mission. It wouldn't be easy. Buzz scanned the skies, looking for the unmistakable markings of Russian fighters—red stars on green fuselages.

Sure enough, other aircraft emerged "from the thinning clouds" in the distance, higher than the Romanians and directly in front of them. Enemy fighters. Buzz counted six in total—four sleek inline-engined Yak-3s and two powerful stub-nosed LaGG-5s with radial engines. The Soviets had been lurking, waiting for the exact moment to strike. They were heading straight for the Romanian bombers, and they were spoiling for a fight.

Alone, the bombers would have stood no chance against so many Soviet fighters. But with Buzz and Alex guarding them, this would be a two-sided fight. From a safe distance above the bombers, Buzz assessed the situation. Compared to the Messerschmitts, all the Russian planes were less powerful but more agile. Six against two, though, wasn't great odds.

Normally, entering into heavy-G "turning combat"—dogfighting—in a Messer wasn't encouraged if a pilot wanted to live long. The opponent could almost always outmaneuver the German plane. The Messer's strength lay in vertical combat, where it could dive in for an attack then rapidly climb to evade the enemy. But Buzz's mission this morning left him with no choice.

To keep the Russians off the bombers, he and Alex needed to fight from a disadvantage. That meant dogfighting.*

Buzz led Alex in a quick, steep climb, then charged headfirst toward the Russians. Below, the bombers lumbered onward to their target. The Russians spotted the fighters, sized up their opposition, then shifted course away from the bombers and aimed their noses at the two Romanian Messerschmitts.

In a blur of green and gray, the two formations met and tangled. Eight planes looped and spiraled after each other, roaring across the horizon in a deadly game of cat and mouse. Amid the sudden melee, Alex glimpsed a Russian fighter hurtling straight toward him. There was no time to react. The Russian's wing sliced through Alex's right wingtip. The impact sent them both into a spin, like tops out of control, plummeting toward the earth.

Buzz was locked on an enemy when he saw pieces of aircraft "projected" through the sky. He took to the radio. *Alex?*

The only reply was static.

Alex and his Russian adversary fell violently in parallel spins, a hundred yards away from each other. Alex fought to regain control, each revolution making his stomach lurch. After five spins, he managed to recover, but level flight was hard to achieve. His fighter yawed and pitched unpredictably. He checked the altimeter: 3,000 feet. His opponent wasn't so lucky. The other plane, completely wingless on the right side, kept spinning until it hit the ground. When Alex looked out his side window, he realized he'd won the joust. But a huge chunk of his right wing was missing.

"Atenție! Atenție!" Alex radioed to Buzz, his voice tight. "Lieutenant, I've been hit. My right wing is shattered. I have no stability." After a strained pause he added: "Please allow me to leave the fight."

Buzz told Alex he could go—"I'll remain with the bombers." He knew that if Alex tried to keep fighting in a compromised plane, he would almost certainly get killed.

Alex apologized, broke course, and limped back toward friendly lines.

The prince returned to the frenzy, flying one way then reversing course and cutting back the other direction, trading shots with the five remaining Russians. The Messer flew stiffly. It was built for straight speed, not the tight

* Some said aerial combat was, for Buzz, the ultimate form of competition: "I don't think he intended to kill people," a wingman would recall, "but with a great sporting passion he wanted to shoot down planes."

turns required for a twisting dogfight. It took all Buzz's strength to pull the hard turns. Green fuselages with red stars flashed everywhere. He couldn't hold out much longer. But Buzz realized his enemies' persistence was working in his favor. The Romanian Ju-88s were making their bomb run. In their dogged pursuit of him, the Russian pilots had forgotten about the bombers. To them, the lone Romanian fighter was the prize.

Buzz's plane was rocked by cannon shells, larger projectiles designed to detonate upon impact. Machine-gun slugs rapped his fighter's skin. Buzz could hear and feel every staccato strike. Even he was surprised that his Messer was somehow still responding to his commands. But the longer he could keep flying, the more time he could buy the bombers.

Finally, Buzz's earphones crackled with a voice. The leader of the bomber flight radioed to say they were coming back. Buzz's tenacity had paid off. They'd hit their target. Their mission was complete.

From his position north of the bombers, Buzz saw the small formation making a desperate dash for friendly territory, at least as fast as bombers could manage. He also saw that the odds had just tipped decidedly in the enemy's favor. The bombers were being followed by four fresh Russian fighters that had arrived on the scene. Buzz knew the bombers' fate was sealed unless he acted, and fast.

He pushed the throttle forward. The Daimler-Benz motor roared, RPMs building force. Power coursed through the control stick in his hands. As the supercharger kicked into a higher setting the Messer leapt forward with a sudden burst of thrust. Buzz broke off from the dogfight, racing to intercept this new threat.

Buzz scanned his distant foe, trying to size up the new enemy planes. They were flying in pairs, two by two, but something different about their outlines caught his attention. As he drew closer, Buzz's eyes widened in disbelief. The wings were elliptical.

Spitfires!

He was staring down the Messer's nose at the best of Britain's frontline fighters. The Spitfire had it all: blistering speed, unmatched maneuverability, a powerful Rolls-Royce Merlin engine that could climb out of any tight situation. But Britain's pilots weren't behind the yoke. Churchill had provided the planes to Stalin's boys as Lend-Lease. Buzz had never encountered Spitfires in combat, but knew their reputation. They were far more formidable than anything he'd ever faced.

The Romanian bomber crews spotted the Spitfires too. They radioed Buzz, desperate for assistance.

Buzz's mind turned "feverishly." Four Spitfires lay ahead. Five Yak-3s and LaGG-5s lay behind. Instead of charging straight at the Spitfires, which might betray his presence too soon, Buzz swooped up to a position above and behind them. For a few moments Buzz shadowed them, flying in the same direction as he planned his attack. His only chance was to play to his aircraft's strengths.

Having gained sufficient height over the Spitfires, Buzz pushed his plane over into a steep dive.

The speed was ferocious.

As he narrowed the gap with the Spitfires, luck was on his side. The four planes were still tightly bunched, flying two by two, straight and level. And he had another advantage—they were so focused on the bombers they didn't see him.

Buzz set his sights on the Spitfire on the left-hand side of the trailing flight. He would only get one gun pass before his momentum carried him past the targets. He needed to use it wisely.

Closer he drew. Closer still. The Spitfire came into sharp focus. He could make out the pale-gray and green camouflage punctuated by a red star. He saw the shimmer from the Perspex canopy, the whirling propeller. The instant the Spitfire's elliptical wings filled his illuminated gunsight, Buzz leveled out and mashed his triggers.

Fire spat from the nose cannon and the machine guns in the wings. The Messer's bullets tore into the Spitfire. Sparks and shredded metal filled the slipstream. Buzz knew he'd scored hits.

Using the speed generated by the dive, Buzz zoomed over the wounded Spitfire, settled his gunsight on the one flying in front of it, and squeezed the trigger again, firing "almost simultaneously" into his second target. This Spitfire gave a burst of smoke, a telltale sign of serious damage. Pulling into the clear, Buzz looked behind his tail and saw both damaged Spitfires peeling down from the sky trailing smoke and flames. He'd shot down two Spitfires in one pass! Normally he would call "Victorie! l-am doborât!"—I shot it down! But Alex wasn't there to hear, and there was no time to admire his marksmanship. The remaining Spitfires were breathing down his neck.

"Strike and (get) out!" was an Me-109 pilot's rule. Buzz gave his plane all the throttle he could and hauled back on the stick. The Messer bolted up and away. Heavy G forces shoved Buzz back into his seat, but he held his steep climb as his Messer clawed higher toward the wispy clouds. Nothing could climb like an Me-109—it "rose like an elevator," recalled one pilot.

Buzz checked his tail to see if the Spitfires had kept pace. They weren't behind him. But he was met instead by an equally troubling sight. The two Spitfires had shifted focus, hunting easier prey. They were targeting the Romanian bombers now—and worse, the lead Spitfire was within shooting range. A smutty trail of gun smoke poured from behind its wings as it fired at the Ju-88 on the left side of the Romanian formation.

Buzz broke from his climb and winged over into a dive to save the bomber. Plummeting from the heavens once again, Buzz hovered his thumb over the trigger. He had the leading Spitfire in his sights. It was almost in reach. Suddenly, he saw a fiery stream of cannon shells burst from somewhere on his right flank. One found its mark and slammed into the nose of his Messer. The explosion tossed Buzz's plane to the left like a car hit broadside in an intersection.

He glanced overhead just in time to see the gray bellies of two Russian fighters zipping over him. Fear coursed through Buzz. The Russian Yaks and LaGGs had caught up. Blinded by his desire to save the Ju-88s, Buzz had nearly forgotten about the other five enemy fighters.

Cutting loose from his attack on the Spitfires, Buzz steered west in the direction of friendly lines. He knew when he was beat. His engine shook in its mounts. Dark smoke poured into the narrow cockpit, thick and choking. Buzz gasped for air, trying to swat away the acrid smoke, unable to draw a breath as the air grew heavier. The wave of Russian Yaks and LaGGs made a gun run. More enemy shells tore into his plane, knocking off his canopy and tossing Buzz forward against his straps. He heard the roar of their propellers and felt the turbulent wake as they flew past.

With his canopy ripped away, a torrent of wind pushed out the smoke but buffeted his face. At least he could breathe again. Buzz took stock of his situation. Bullet and shell holes filled White 4 from nose to tail. He felt tempted to bail out, but what would the Russians do to him if they got their hands on a Romanian squadron commander? And a royal, no less.

Buzz decided to stay with his plane. He took evasive maneuvers while working his way west, trailing smoke as he went. His only mission now was survival. Buzz checked his position relative to the sea beyond his left wing. The German front lines had to be close. That was the finish line, where antiaircraft guns on the ground would be able to protect him.

Tracers came from behind Buzz and whizzed past his cockpit. He looked behind him and saw two Russian planes firing furiously from the cannons in their red spinners. The enemy smelled blood in the water. Buzz glanced at his plane's instruments. The gauges ticked backward. White 4 was bleeding oil pressure.

Just as the German front lines came into view ahead of his wings, Buzz's engine seized tight with a jolt. Not now! The propeller blades windmilled to a stop, further slowing the plane. He tried to awaken the engine without success.

More bullets nipped at Buzz's tail. Without power, using only his rudder and all his strength, Buzz dodged a knockout blow. His airspeed was dropping. The ground crept closer. Behind him, the enemy fighters sliced side to side, trying to line up a kill shot. He could feel their gunsights trained on his back. Buzz pitched forward to gain speed, urging White 4 to keep flying.

Just when it looked like he was finished, the firing inexplicably stopped. Buzz spotted a zigzag of trenches and log bunkers beneath his wings. He'd passed the German front lines and was back in friendly territory. The Russians gave up and turned around.

He was still not in the clear. Without an operable engine, his Messer was an 8,000-pound glider soaring "gently, surrounded by strips of blue clouds like waves of fairies." The whispers of wind across the propeller blades filled the cockpit. If these were his last moments, they were beautiful.

Buzz snapped out of any reverie. He was still going down. He searched the undulating coastal landscape for a flat spot and identified one that seemed as good as any. Buzz eased the plane down, pulling up slightly at the last moment to slow his speed. He crash-landed the dying plane on its belly. A whirlwind of seagrass and sandy soil rushed past his canopy rails. At last, the Messer skidded to a stop.

The engine was sizzling as Buzz leapt to a wing and ran from the plane, fearing an explosion. He tore off his helmet. His initial steps felt unnatural, as if he was learning how to walk for the first time.* A fellow Romanian pilot would later describe the feeling he had after being shot down: "I breathe a sigh of relief. Large drops of sweat cover my forehead; my back is a pool of water. Then, from within, like a huge river, an indescribable joy grows, spreading over the edges, the joy of someone who can still see the sky, the sun, the grass. The wind blows gently like a caress. Great God, how beautiful life is when it rises from the ground, from the fragments!"

* Of the two Spitfires he would claim as victories, Buzz would write in his encounter report: "I declare on my word of honor, man and military, and on my conscience, that both planes were shot down. —Lt. Av. C. Cantacuzino."

As Buzz grasped his own safety, he remembered: the bombers!

Buzz began scaling the nearest bluff in great strides, hoping to see farther into the distance. Reaching the crest, he spotted two plumes of smoke rising about two miles to the north, right around where he had last seen the Ju-88s.

Buzz felt a pang of fear for his countrymen. He didn't need to be told what had happened. He would later confirm that in the brief time it took him to escape, all three Ju-88s had been shot down. Of the nine crewmen aboard the Romanian planes, only one bombardier and a gunner managed to bail out. Everyone else died.

Buzz was deeply upset by the downed planes and his inability to prevent the losses. He might have just become an ace, but he didn't care. Every day Romanians were dying on Ukrainian soil. It was abhorrent to him.

As Buzz lingered on the crest of the bluff, staring at the smoke, soldiers with faded gray uniforms and sunburned faces gathered below. They were German troops sent to rescue him. Buzz came down the bluff to meet his uneasy allies. He and his fellow Romanian fighting men adopted a pragmatic approach in dealing with their German counterparts. Both sides were facing the same relentless enemy and were locked in the same day-to-day struggle for survival. They needed each other. The partnership was that simple. Besides, the average German soldier didn't want to be here any more than he did.

A German captain saluted Buzz. "Hauptmann Schultz," he said, introducing himself. "Panzergrenadiere."

"Oberleutnant Cantacuzino," Buzz replied. He had learned to speak perfect German at boarding school in Geneva, Switzerland.

A Romanian war correspondent recorded what transpired next: "A hand reaches out to him with a canister, a voice whispers something that sounds like it's torn from an angelic choir: 'Bitte trinken.'"

The prince understood the words: "Have a drink." Buzz knew that he, Alex, and their countrymen were pawns fighting and dying in droves for Hitler and Antonescu. But what could one man possibly do about it?

Buzz took the canteen cup from the German soldier and drank.

CHAPTER 6

IT MUST BE DONE

JULY 20, 1943, ELEVEN DAYS AFTER THE CRETE RAID
Libya

IN A DUSTY COMPOUND ON THE SOUTH SIDE OF BENGHAZI, WHERE THE city ended and the desert began, the commanders of all five B-24 groups and their deputies waited at the door of the ramshackle headquarters of 9th Air Force Bomber Command. They'd been summoned for a highly classified briefing. American MPs scrutinized the officers' papers and made them take an oath of secrecy before they let them in, while armed guards stood by the door.

Known informally as the Green Hut, the faded viridescent one-story building had been used as a headquarters by the Germans first, then the British, and now the Americans.

One of the officers handing over his papers was Colonel Jack Wood, the thirty-six-year-old commander of the 389th. A firm but fair leader, Colonel Wood was tall, trim, and already graying at the temples. He resembled a Norman Rockwell father figure who read his newspapers and smoked a pipe at the kitchen table each evening after supper.

Colonel Wood

His rookie group had redeemed themselves after their rocky start. In the eleven days since their disastrous raid on Crete, the 389th had flown five more break-in missions, alongside the other more experienced groups at Benghazi. Now, with six missions total under their belts, the youthful aviators were newly serious. The break-in raids had produced the intended effect: "We felt this experience [was] enough of the real thing to let us know we were now a combat organization, fighting a rough, mean war," noted one pilot. Having earned a spot at the table, the 389th's men were no longer the new kids on the block. They were ready and willing to face any mission head-on.

COLONEL WOOD AND HIS entourage entered the dim interior of the room, where cigarette smoke hung in the air. It was time to discover why every B-24 this side of the Atlantic was gathered in one place.

Lying on the table was a most unusual map, which allowed them to view their target in a way they'd never seen any target presented before: in three dimensions.

A general from the 9th Air Force addressed the high-ranking assembly. He informed them that all five bomb groups at Benghazi were being stood down from combat to prepare for and carry out a daring attack "against a military objective deep in enemy territory."

"This raid," the general said, "is considered of the greatest strategic import to the future conduct of the war."

The Great Raid was no longer just a rumor.

The general clarified that the intel boys hadn't pinned down a specific date for the raid yet, but he could tell those present this much: They had less than two weeks to prepare. Before revealing their target, he made this point clear: The commanders were forbidden from disclosing the location to their men until the 9th Air Force gave the go-ahead—the destination was still a closely guarded secret. Around the room, the statement was met with solemn nods.

That was when the general told them their target and described the 9th Air Force's strategy to tackle it.

They'd be flying against the single most strategically important installation for the German war machine: a network of sixteen interconnected oil refineries supplying the oil, gasoline, and lubricants—the "lifeblood of war"—that powered "Hitler's clanking panzers, roaring planes, and stalking submarines."

Their target wouldn't be in occupied France or Germany, as the combat crews would probably expect, but deep in central Romania, at a place called

Ploesti, a modern, affluent city of a hundred thousand people, nestled at the foot of the Transylvanian Alps.

And they'd be going in at low level—treetop height.

The revelation shocked some of the commanders. "Several expressed doubt about the feasibility of the plan," wrote one historian. "This thing can't work," declared the operations officer of the Liberandos at one point. "I'll have nothing to do with it. I figure we'll lose [all] thirty-two planes." But any dissent was promptly squelched. The operations officer who expressed his doubts would be sent packing within days.

The general noted that the directive for this mission came straight from on high. How high? As high as it went. What the bomb group commanders heard next would send a chill coursing through them. The world leaders who ordered the raid hadn't asked anyone at the 9th Air Force whether such a mission was possible in the first place.

They told them *it must be done.*

CHAPTER 7

SOMETHING IS UP

THE NEXT MORNING

ERNIE, BOB, AND SEVERAL OF THE CREW EYED *PISTOL PACKIN' MAMA* with concern but kept their distance. A small team of technicians had converged on their bomber and two of the men were inside the nose fiddling with a drill around the Norden bombsight.

"Security around the base seems to be tightening," an airman noted in his diary. "Something is up."

Just when the damage to *Pistol Packin' Mama* from the mission over Crete had finally been repaired, these strangers had unexpectedly shown up at Berka 4 and were taking their plane—or at least an important piece of it—apart. The technicians were from the Army's Proving Ground Command. They had traveled all the way from Eglin Field, Florida, to North Africa, where they promptly began removing the Norden bombsight from every bomber on the flight line. Adding to the intrigue were firm instructions from HQ to every man on base: "Don't get in their way."

A mission of some consequence, maybe "the one," was brewing. The technicians certainly weren't taking out the Nordens in preparation for sending the bomb group home.

Ernie and Bob already had enough reasons for concern. Aside from any latecomers to the group, theirs was the most unprepared crew in the 389th. During the eleven days while the other crews were flying break-in raids, Ernie and the crew of *Pistol Packin' Mama* had been stuck kicking sand around Berka 4. Their bomber had been grounded, under repair for the engine that had been damaged in the Crete raid. In Ernie's opinion, it was "just as well," because they lacked a complete crew anyway. Britt and their right waist gunner, Sgt. Donald MacLachlan, had both contracted amoebic dysentery—common in the desert, where standing water contained bacteria unfamiliar to American stomachs. A substantial number of men from the 389th had been sickened along with Britt and MacLachlan. Nobody seemed sure of the culprit. Some suggested that the pathogen had arrived with a bad batch of watermelons bought from local traders, but whatever its source, it caused violent diarrhea, which the guys called the Desert Quickstep, and Britt's case was so bad he was hospitalized in the 9th Air Force's medical unit in Benghazi.

Watching the technicians work on the planes was like watching a surgeon operate on a patient. Ernie and his friends looked on as the specialists unbolted *Pistol Packin' Mama*'s Norden and then shuttled the delicate instrument back to the bomb bay, where their comrades were waiting on the ground with open arms. Those men then brought the bombsight to a truck, while the men inside the bomber mounted a vertical two-foot-long aluminum stick with a small compass on top where the Norden had been.

Ernie and Bob were confused by this latest plot twist. The Norden was the most sophisticated bombsight of its day, capable of determining a bomb's drift by factoring in a plane's speed, height, and other conditions. The stick that went in its place looked like a navigation device, something Britt would use to plot their course.

The longer they thought about it, the more questions it invited in the minds of Ernie, Bob, and the other young fliers who'd been trained in the doctrine of high-altitude daylight precision bombing. If they weren't using bombsights to calculate their aim points, then *what*?

To get to the bottom of the matter, Bob pulled aside one of the technicians and asked for the lowdown. The technician revealed that the two-foot stick was, in fact, a bombsight for use at low altitude. Teams like his were going from base to base and swapping out the bombsights in every B-24 in Benghazi.

Well, I'll be damned!

Bob and Ernie exchanged knowing looks. There was no doubt in the pilots' minds anymore. Even if the 9th Air Force was keeping mum on the group's purpose in the desert, the lowly technician had just tipped its hand.

CHAPTER 8

BOMBS CAN FLY

SOON AFTER
Berka 4

THE OFFICERS RESEMBLED AN OIL DRILLING CREW ON THEIR COFFEE break. They kicked about in the shadeless dust on the empty side of the runway at Berka 4. Most were shirtless or wore T-shirts and khaki pants. Sunglasses lined their faces; some had topped off with sun helmets. Although the men of the 389th had been issued hot-weather khaki uniforms, which they called suntans, their new clothes weren't helping much. The searing brightness of the early afternoon sun defeated any attempt to stay cool.

About a hundred officers total were present. Together, they faced the great expanse of desert south of the base. Pilots, navigators, and bombardiers glanced at one another and shrugged. The gathering was shrouded in mystery. All they'd been told was to assemble for a demonstration and to bring their notepads.

In front of them, several specialists from Eglin Field fiddled with a radio on a table, trying to dial in a particular frequency, while their officer looked on. They alone were protected by a sunshade. The radio glowed while static hissed and crackled from a speaker. A short distance away, the 389th's ground echelon had set up in the sand something that looked like a wooden billboard. Roughly twenty by twenty feet, the billboard had fabric sheets draped from the top, rather than an ad for shaving cream plastered on it. Between the legs of the billboard sat empty olive-colored 55-gallon drums. Adding to the intrigue, a lone B-24 orbited in the distant sky.

"Well, this should be interesting," Ernie said as he took his place in the lineup with his fellow officers. At his side, Bob echoed the sentiment. The air thrummed with generator noise from the Eglin boys' setup.

"Something new is in the air," wrote one pilot in his diary. "We assumed the Air Force wouldn't be running experiments that far out in the desert for nothing."

Clues were dangling. First, it was the technicians yanking the Nordens from their ships. Then, Colonel Wood had gotten up on stage before the nightly movie in the base theater. Ernie and his friends were in the crowd. Their fatherly commander announced that the 389th had been given a "special job," a raid deep behind enemy lines, and that a rapid period of preparation was about to commence. That was all he could reveal for now. "This mission is the reason for our trip to Africa," he added cryptically.

The statement spread through the base like wildfire. On one hand, the colonel's declaration ended any speculation about their purpose in the desert. The rumors were true. Their next mission was the Great Raid itself, and the low-level nature of their task was no longer a matter of conjecture. It was happening.

On the other hand, the Colonel's cryptic statements only prompted more questions. Where were they going? When? And just how bad would it be? "We're all getting a few gray hairs over this big one," a crewman wrote in his diary.

As for the target, which the men had christened Target X, every man had a theory. Some figured the 389th had been tapped to assassinate Mussolini at his villa in Rome. But others shot that down—Italy was too close. Target X had to be somewhere farther, a destination worthy of the B-24's range. That meant Germany.

Those officers predicted they'd be busting more hydroelectric dams in the Ruhr, just as the British had done during Operation Chastise that spring. Still others speculated that Target X was Hitler himself, via a low-level strike into the heart of Berlin or straight to his alpine doorstep in Berchtesgaden.

Ernie had stayed out of the fray. What was the point in guessing? The B-24's long legs made anything possible. Even if they knew, what would it change? They were still going there.

Whatever the destination, there was one thing the young fliers of the 389th agreed upon: the Great Raid was going to be a "suicide run." It was one thing to buzz a beach full of friends, but heavy bombers, American ones at least, never flew low in actual combat. Not if they wanted to come back.

"At least we won't have to bring parachutes!" became the running joke on base.

Now, standing in the sun with the raid looming large, Ernie and Bob felt the unease settling in. Berlin? Berchtesgaden? The Ruhr?

Even if *Pistol Packin' Mama* was finally repaired, it was too late for their crew to pick up any additional combat experience. The last time they'd flown together, their gunners nearly melted their guns, they'd been almost shot down, and they'd bombed the sea instead of their target. When—or if—they got into the air for the Great Raid, they'd be the least experienced crew in the formation.

AN OFFICER CHECKED THE staticky radio on the table, stepped out from under the protection of the sunshade, and greeted the men. He introduced himself as Major Wagner, the officer in charge of the team from Eglin Field. Major Blank, also with the Eglin crew, was flying the bomber that was mysteriously circling their position in the distance.

"I understand there have been plenty of questions about the new bomb sights," Major Wagner began. "I promise, we didn't come here just to redecorate your ships."

That drew a chuckle from Ernie and the other officers. Wagner explained that he and his men were there to demonstrate how heavy bombers, armed with these tools and the right technique, could be employed to carry out a low-level daylight raid.

It was confirmation, plain and simple.

Ernie glanced around. Judging by the faces of the other officers, no one seemed surprised by the words "low-level raid." The cat was already out of the bag.

Instead, the men in the crowd were rubbing their chins at the feasibility of dropping bombs at minimal altitude. With or without new bombsights, it was difficult enough to "effectively maneuver" a thirty-six-ton bomber down on the carpet. How could you do that *and* deliver a payload *and* not blow yourself to smithereens?

Before his audience could object, Major Wagner reassured the men that his compatriots at the Proving Ground had crafted special delayed-action bombs that would detonate only after a plane had flown over and past its target. In fact, they'd be issuing the bombardiers new computation charts.

"Now we knew they weren't kidding!" one pilot remembered thinking.

Major Wagner explained the physics that made low-level bombing feasible. More than one branch of the American military had experimented with it already. Army flyboys in the Aleutians called it buzz-bombing, whereas naval aviators in the Pacific referred to the technique as masthead bombing, implying that attack runs would be lower than the mast of a ship. But the term that resonated across both branches was "skip bombing," although it wasn't technically accurate: Low-level bombs don't skip in every instance.

"We're going to show you that bombs don't just *fall,*" Major Wagner said. "They can *fly.*" Now he had everybody's attention.

Major Wagner gave a nod, and the technician at the radio issued a command to Major Blank, the pilot orbiting in the distance. The loudspeaker had been rigged so that Major Blank could address the men while flying the aircraft. Ernie, Bob, and the other officers opened their notepads.

The distant B-24 broke from its orbit and approached the runway as if coming in to land. Heads turned toward the bomber. Ernie, Bob, and the others moved closer to the speaker to catch every word.

"I'll put one right through the middle," Major Blank announced over the airwaves. The billboard on the sand was his target.

Major Blank leveled the bomber's wings and flew parallel to the runway, gradually descending toward the target. It looked like he was putting on an airshow just for the officers on the ground as he descended from a hundred feet, to seventy-five, to fifty.

The bombardiers suddenly understood why their new bombsight was just a two-foot stick. They didn't need anything more complex if they'd be dropping bombs at such a low altitude.

Major Blank stopped at twenty-five feet and leveled out. The top of the target stood at twenty feet, leaving only a five-foot margin of error.

Bob eyed the other pilot's approach with skepticism. He was cutting it awfully close.

When the aircraft was just about the length of a football field away, its bombardier dropped an inert hundred-pound practice bomb painted blue. Ernie and the others watched as the strangest phenomenon unfolded. For the first hundred feet of its journey, the bomb remained directly underneath the bomber, bucking gravity and wind resistance while flying at the same speed as the aircraft. Then it slowly began sinking, all the while still rushing forward. As the bomber roared over the target, clearing it by mere feet, the blue blur of the bomb punched a hole directly through the fabric in the middle of the billboard. The bomb didn't even touch the row of empty drums underneath.

The audience's jaws dropped. Ernie was surprised—it had actually worked!

With the plane now in the distance, Major Wagner said that skip-bombing was only possible because of the way the bombs were racked in American planes: horizontally, with their fuses forward, ready to fly.

The B-24's left wing dipped as it curved around for another pass. The radio crackled as the pilot announced he'd drop a bomb short this time.

The bomber leveled its wings and came in low again. This time the pilot released his bomb well ahead of the target. The bomb descended, struck the sand, and skipped forward like a stone on a pond—then flew "right through the center of the frame." The men of the 389th were impressed.

Major Wagner explained the versatility of the technique: Even if your aim was off, the bomb could still find its target.

Everything he described made perfect sense to Ernie.

The pilot circled the field, setting up for a third and final pass. For anyone still on the fence after everything they'd seen, Major Wagner drove the point home: "When you drop bombs from 25,000 feet, we measure the drift in *miles*. But with this technique, you can put your payload right through the front door."

Major Blank leveled his wings for his final pass. As he came in low, skimming the earth, the radio squawked again with his voice. "This time I'll knock out the cans in the middle," he said, referring to the empty drums between the legs of the billboard.

Ernie and the others exchanged uneasy looks. It seemed like the Eglin team were pushing their luck after a flawless demonstration thus far.

Major Blank came barreling in at twenty-five feet. At just the right moment, he let loose with another blue blur and the barrels went tumbling across the sand like bowling pins.

Ernie, Bob, and their fellow officers were converts. The display was astonishing. Bombing at treetop height in four-engine bombers? "The blueprint boys would have screamed 'impossible' had they known," concluded an intel officer.

As Major Blank touched down on the runway behind the audience, Major Wagner closed with an important caveat. He confessed his team's demonstration had a shortcoming.

That raised some eyebrows.

There was a substantial difference between what the 389th had just seen and what they'd be asked to do, he admitted, and he wasn't talking about the live bombs they'd be carrying.

"You'll have to do this while flying in formation."

Smiles dropped. Heads turned. Eyes went wide.

What?

CHAPTER 9

RAMPING UP

THE NEXT MORNING

THE 389TH HIT THE GROUND RUNNING.

All across Berka 4, engines roared to life. Flights of bombers taxied to the runway, nose to tail. One after another, B-24s clawed into the skies. The lumbering ships began grouping in tight three-ship formations. After doing final checks, each formation thundered by the airfield on their way out to the desert range.

Their training for the Great Raid was under way. Their first order? Get comfortable flying at extremely low levels. For all five bomb groups at Benghazi, buzzing had been "legalized."

"How low?" one nervous pilot in the Pyramiders asked his briefing officer when discussing the flying ahead.

"As low as you want," the officer said. "Just don't hit any camels because we don't know where to get more of them."

AFTER A TRAINING FLIGHT, Ernie and Bob exited from *Pistol Packin' Mama* at Berka 4. They'd flown that morning with only a skeleton crew. All gunners got the day off—but not because anyone felt generous. Rather, if a plane crashed there'd be fewer fatalities.

Ernie ran his fingers through his sweat-soaked hair. It was "hard, hot work," he later wrote in his diary. One slipup and you would get "a snoot full of sand."

Immediately the two pilots made a walk-around inspection of the plane, something they always did before takeoff but never after landing. They were checking for damage.

Pistol Packin' Mama was fine, but by the looks of things on the flight line, the order to get comfortable flying low was meeting unexpected results.

Several B-24s' bomb bay doors would be found jammed with scrub brush, while two ships had flown so low they'd scraped the ground, then miraculously bounced back into the air and kept flying.

It was the same across the other bomber bases at Benghazi. One ship from the England-based Traveling Circus famously limped back home with all the gray paint scraped off its belly. Its pilot had dived to avoid a collision with another flight of B-24s, skidding his bomber "along the desert for quite a distance, kicking up a huge cloud of sand and dust."

But it was a 389th plane that topped them all when it taxied back to the flight line with its lower fuselage splattered with blood. It turned out the crew had violated the only direct commandment they'd been given. They buzzed so low they'd hit a camel.

EACH DAY, ALL MORNING long, the 389th practiced, the endless maneuvers fueling a growing, brash self-assurance.

What began as low passes over the sands soon gave way to something bolder. Out on the range, the Eglin Field boys stood by with their two-way radio at the ready, waiting to coach the pilots' runs as the young aviators learned the art of skip bombing.

As their proficiency increased, their formations grew. Three-ship flights

B-24 formation, Benghazi

fell in line behind each other and bombers paraded past Berka 4 in flights of six, then nine, then twelve.

It was a marvel to witness from the camp: so many big, heavy machines plowing through the air in delicate unison. Trucks and jeeps screeched to a halt, their drivers gawking. Cooks ducked out from the mess tent and looked up. Mechanics leaned from their scaffolds and gazed to the skies. The ground seemed to quake and the snarl of so many engines "almost burst your eardrums" before the ships became quiet and small as they flew away.

The bombers of the 389th weren't alone in their unceasing operations. Anytime a man on the airfield looked north toward Benghazi, he saw formations of B-24s from the other groups heading out to train. The scope of all five bomb groups apparently preparing for the same mission staggered the mind.

"Something big is in the making," observed one airman. "Just to say you've been here will be some story to tell."

CHAPTER 10

THE TEST

A DAY OR TWO LATER, JULY 24, 1943

A SHORT CONVOY OF JEEPS AND TRUCKS PULLED UP TO THE DESERT bombing range several miles south of Berka 4. The 389th's commander, Colonel Wood, and his headquarters staff climbed out of their vehicles under the brassy midafternoon sun. A small army of GIs from the ground echelon joined them. It was around 3:30 P.M. Far in the distance, late-day clouds rose from the sea.

A huge, unusual, man-made structure awaited them on the sand. It looked like someone had built the foundation of a castle. Hundreds of empty fuel drums were stacked three high on the desert floor. Flags fluttered from poles spaced at equal distances along the drums. The whole structure stretched for more than the length of a football field. The colonel and his staff eyed it, marveling.

It was the handiwork of the ground echelon. For days in advance they had toiled in the sun, splashing hundreds of gallons of whitewash on the ground, then stacking the drums to follow a particular pattern. What looked like a wall from ground level appeared different from the air. The structure was a silhouette, arranged in an imperfect square. This was not by accident. The colonel and his staff were looking at the front of a replica of the 389th's mystery target. The ground echelon had built this mock target to match the dimensions of the real one.

Colonel Wood scanned the horizon over the sea and checked his watch. Earlier that afternoon, he had sent his group aloft in their biggest formation yet—thirty planes—to fly a four-hour course into the desert, then out over the sea using uninhabited islands as checkpoints. The training exercise would culminate with a skip-bombing mission on the mock target behind him. Wood had set up the exercise so a seemingly unconnected series of turns over the sea followed a deliberate pattern. What the crews didn't know was that the pattern mimicked the actual route to the place they called Target X.

The bombers were due to arrive soon at the structure in the desert. But the colonel had a few tricks up his sleeve. For these to work, a few tasks still needed completing. Colonel Wood directed his staff and the enlisted men into action. Some began digging holes along the face of the structure, while others unloaded buckets from trucks and placed the buckets into the holes the other men were digging. It was all part of the colonel's plan.

To make the rehearsal more challenging, Wood had instructed his operations officer, Major John Brooks, who was leading the aerial contingent, to make intentional wrong turns to try to confound the navigators. And if they still managed to locate the mock target, Wood had another twist. The buckets the men were planting were smoke pots. Once lit, they created a thick white smoke that would obscure the mock target. It was the exact trick the Germans might play if they knew the Americans were coming.

Wood's tricks were motivated by the best of intentions. He wanted to be prepared for everything. After the briefing about the mission in the Green Hut, Wood and his staff and squadron leaders knew many of the details, but not all, about what awaited them at Target X.

They understood it was clearly no small assignment. The orders had come straight from President Franklin Delano Roosevelt and Prime Minister Winston Churchill. In January 1943, Roosevelt and Churchill had met in Casablanca, Morocco, to plot the main warfare strategies for the European Theater. Soviet Premier Joseph Stalin had been invited to the meeting, but he had his hands full with the Germans at Stalingrad.

At Casablanca, the secret mission had been a top subject of discussion. Roosevelt and Churchill knew that the Axis powers in Europe needed to be met head-on. But before any invasion of northern Europe could take place across the English Channel, the continent's "soft underbelly" needed to be weakened. This meant first turning the Western Allies' attention on Sicily, Italy, and the raid on Target X. The raid's significance to the war effort could not be overstated; the operation had "a priority second only to the invasion of Sicily from a materials procurement standpoint."

As soon as the order was given, Colonel Wood was under the gun. By that point in the war, the average crew member in the other B-24 groups at

Benghazi had flown as many as fifteen missions. His crews of the 389th had, at the most, flown six. Not only did he feel the need to ensure their readiness, but his life was on the line, too. He'd be flying with them in the lead plane.

THE HOLES WERE DUG. The smoke pots were almost all in place. Colonel Wood and his men wiped their brows as they admired their work. The colonel, in fatherly fashion, had worked right alongside his men at the structure.

Wood checked his watch again, glancing to the horizon over the sea. Before takeoff, Major Brooks had calculated their time over target right down to the minute: 1603 hours, or 4:03 P.M. in standard time.

An officer on Wood's staff checked his watch. "Colonel, it's 1600."

"Don't worry," Wood said, "they'll never make it on time." He was certain the intentional mistakes would trip up the navigators.

Still, the officers and GIs with Wood didn't want to take any chances. The bombers were packed with blue practice bombs filled with flour to mark where each landed. Each bomb weighed a hundred pounds. If one of those fell on your head, it would kill you.

Quietly it was heard, a low metallic hum over the flags flapping in the offshore breeze. Wood glanced again in the direction of the ocean. A series of little green birds came into view, heading toward the structure from the Benghazi coastline. The colonel's eyes narrowed.

"Light the pots!" he shouted.

Wood's men raced between the smoke pots, struggling to ignite them all at once. Wood joined in, his lighter ablaze. The source of the metallic humming sound quickly took shape. A mile-long line of B-24s was scudding across the desert in formation. Most of the smoke pots puffed to life, but the men were out of time. The maelstrom of bombers, each with a shimmering glass face and four powerful propellers, barreled toward them. Already the bombers at the forefront were past Berka 4. End to end, the combined wingspans of just the first three ships was wider than a football field. The men on the ground had maybe sixty seconds to clear the area. Perhaps less. But where would they go? Wood looked to his left and right. There was nowhere to run.

"To the vehicles!" he shouted.

Enlisted men sprinted to their trucks. Officers dashed to their jeeps. Wood and a group of officers piled into his vehicle. The colonel slapped the side. *Go!* The driver pulled the starter lever. But the engine remained silent. Other jeeps around Wood's carved U-turns in the sand and sped away, while trucks tires spun wildly as the drivers floored it.

Wood's driver kept trying to start the engine. It wouldn't catch. A loud rumble above caught their attention. The colonel and his fellow passengers looked to the skies with horror. The bombers were here. And they were on target, on time. Bomb bay doors yawned open beneath each B-24. Among the lead flights flew *Pistol Packin' Mama,* with Ernie and Bob at the controls.

As the other jeeps and trucks fled the scene, the officers and enlisted men looked back helplessly at their commander stuck in his jeep like a car stalled on railroad tracks. Every man knew there was no way the pilots would see the colonel in time. When a plane was roaring along at 220 miles per hour at low altitude, a jeep would be just a blip on the sand.

As the B-24s reached the mock target, the lead three ships broke from low-level flight and began to rise from the ground. The ships behind them did the same, all the way back through the formation. Orders called for a power climb to two hundred feet. When the planes made the attack for real, they would need to clear the target. Whatever it was going to be, Target X would be something tall.

The first wave of B-24s were still climbing when they released their bombs, four from each ship, all flying momentarily underneath their parent planes. Then the bombs broke from the planes and dove from the sky like falcons.

Wood and the others covered their heads and made themselves as small as possible, preparing for impact. The sunlight turned to shade.

The first three bombers soared over Wood's jeep wingtip to wingtip with a deafening roar. A spout of dust surged up from the sands, blinding the men on the ground. The blue blur of practice bombs cut through the air. Some whistled straight over the men's heads. Others hit short and skipped before smashing against the wall of fuel drums, sending barrels flying.

Wave after wave of bombs fell as the long train of B-24s roared over the drop zone. Wood and the men in his jeep could hear the bombs whistling, feel them cutting the air overhead, see them splashing along the red terrain, hear them pounding against the barrels when they hit. Flour filled the air like fog.

Then it was calm. Wood and the others lifted their heads and looked around. Fine white powder coated everything in the drop zone. The jeep hadn't taken a direct hit. The men could see the twin tails of the lead formation shrinking into desert.

It felt like the worst was over, but they knew better. The 389th had been broken into two divisions for the rehearsal. Twelve planes flew in the first division. Eighteen more planes brought up the rear. The men on the ground were in the eye of a hurricane.

Again, Wood's driver tried to fire up the jeep. This time the motor coughed to life. The driver didn't need any orders. He threw the jeep into gear and floored the accelerator, leaving a trail of dust just as the next division of B-24s hit the zone and started dropping their bombs. The jeep wasn't in the clear yet. More blue blurs flew at them. The driver made a series of quick hard turns behind the wheel, "dodging the skipping bombs." Heavy projectiles punched the sand in front of the jeep and behind. The men held tight.

ONCE OUT OF THE zone, Wood's driver slowed to a safer speed. The officers started to breathe again. Most had lost their hats. The colonel looked back at the target, which resembled a medieval castle after a siege. Drums were scattered everywhere, the wall gaped with holes, and a man could see straight into the center of the silhouette. In short, the mock target was obliterated. The rehearsal was a smashing success.

Driving back to Berka 4, Wood felt breathless but relieved. At least no one got killed. Never again would he underestimate his own group. Not that his staff would let him.

"Well, Colonel, you knew our ETA," Major Brooks would remind his commanding officer that evening at dinner, the amusement palpable in his voice.

If Wood had any doubts about his men's effectiveness, the crews had answered them today.

They were ready.

CHAPTER 11

THE EXPEDITION

TWO DAYS LATER, JULY 26, 1943

ONE DIDN'T HAVE TO BE AN INTELLIGENCE OFFICER TO KNOW THAT something sizeable was unfolding at Berka 4.

Around dawn, several men from the 389th spied British soldiers unloading a large object from a truck parked behind the base's open-air theater. RAF officers supervised the process, while American MPs with Tommy guns provided security.

The mysterious cargo was cloth-shrouded and huge: eight by fourteen feet, equivalent to several household doors laid side by side. The soldiers carried the object to the theater like pallbearers at a funeral. The improvised theater's seats were made from the small, white, empty German fuel drums that had been cut in half.

The soldiers placed their delivery on a table in front of the stage, then departed. The MPs stayed behind to guard it.

LATER THAT MORNING, ERNIE and Bob filtered into the base theater with nearly 120 of their fellow officers and sat on the fuel drums. The theater's movie screen—a bedsheet—had been removed. The eyes of the audience were drawn to the mysterious object in front of the stage.

A mix of excitement and trepidation coursed through the ranks. The officers had been summoned for a highly classified briefing. The ramshackle nature of their surroundings made the gathering feel like an expedition to a lost city. Ernie, Bob, and the other young men talked in low voices, as if the enemy could hear them.

Maybe this was the briefing they'd been waiting for—the one where they would finally learn their purpose in this remote corner of the North African desert.

All the officers sprang to their feet as Colonel Wood and his staff entered the theater.

Wood took the stage. The men sat. "The 389th Bomb Group has been assigned to attack a very important target," Wood said. "The mission will be extremely dangerous."

The audience was rapt. This *was* the one they'd been waiting for. The biggie. The Great Raid.

Because of the high risk, Wood explained, their next assignment would be a voluntary mission. The decision to bow out would not be mentioned in any officer's fitness file.

Ernie glanced around the theater to see if anyone stood to leave. No one took to his feet. Instead, the young men began shifting to the edges of their seats.

Looking across the sea of eager faces, Wood continued. "Target X has a name—Ploesti. We're going to conduct a low-level attack on the Romanian oil refineries."

No one on Wood's staff, not even the colonel, could have anticipated the response.

The crowd collectively exhaled. *Romania?* That was it? The subject of all their furious speculation was a seemingly low-value target. Most of the officers didn't even know where Romania was on a map. Men grinned and elbowed each other, and "plenty of money changed hands" between friends who had placed wagers on their destination. Ernie and Bob exchanged looks of relief.

Romania? Are they even in the war?

THROUGH A TRAGIC TWIST of circumstances, the small nation with only half the population of Italy had landed in the fliers' cross hairs.

At the outbreak of the war, Romania and its king watched helplessly as Nazi Germany and the Soviet Union—who were allies before they were enemies—joined forces to conquer and partition neighboring Poland in 1939. Romania tried to stay neutral, but the USSR was insatiable, and the following summer Stalin demanded that Romania hand over its eastern provinces of Bessarabia and Bukovina (located in and around today's Moldova)—or face war.

Romania's King Carol II was desperate. His military was too weak to defend their own land, and far-right factions of his government demanded a response. The king looked to Romania's allies from World War I for help. Regrettably, France had already fallen to the Nazi Blitzkrieg, and Britain was under siege, while America broadcast no interest in crossing the ocean for another European war.

Isolated and "wishing to avoid the fate of Poland," in summer 1940, King Carol surrendered the lands to the USSR without a fight.

Then came a turn no one had foreseen. The Nazi-Soviet alliance began to crumble and from the dust emerged a suitor who hinted he could help Romania reclaim its lost lands: Adolf Hitler. But King Carol wanted no part of an alliance with Nazi Germany. His loyalty still lay with the Western Powers. He rejected Hitler's offer of help.

His refusal set off a firestorm. A homegrown fascist movement, the Iron Guard, staged a coup and sent the king running into exile, leaving behind his teenage son, Michael, as heir to a "powerless throne."

King Carol II (center) and his son, Michael

The Iron Guard wasted no time. They installed a dictator, the former general Ion Antonescu, to supersede the crown "as both head of state and supreme commander of the army." Germany had their Führer. Italy had

Il Duce, Mussolini. So Antonescu proclaimed himself the "Conducător" (Conductor) before brokering an alliance with Hitler.

The decision was one that even the Romanians who initially supported the coup would come to regret.

Under the guise of protecting the Romanian refineries, their new ally marched in troops and took over Ploesti, placing German technicians at the helm. Then they "helped themselves" to Romania's resources, pledging to pay in war matériel. Hitler and Antonescu labeled their arrangement a protectorate, but to the average Romanian, their country was under foreign occupation, just not in name.

The Conducător—
Marshal Ion Antonescu

That was how Romania came to be dubbed "Hitler's Gas Station." And by the time Ernie and his countrymen showed up in the desert, the small nation, slightly larger than Ohio, had become Germany's single largest source of oil, supplying one third of their petroleum products—4.8 million metric tons annually.

As *Life* magazine described it, Romania was trapped in "the horrible position of owning the oil that may win or lose the war for Germany"—a grim twist of fate that landed the country squarely in Uncle Sam's sights.

The American flyboys who were about to attack Romania knew little to nothing about how the country came to be enmeshed in the conflict. Not that the knowledge would change anything, anyway.

Their job was to bomb the hell out of them.

Ernie, Bob, and the other officers sat back in their seats and relaxed. For men who had envisioned themselves skimming the apartment blocks of Berlin or the alpine rooftops of Berchtesgaden, it felt like they'd been spared a death sentence. The mission to Romania sounded like a challenge, but it was a far cry from the suicide run they'd envisioned.

Now that one mystery had been solved, they turned their attention to the large covered object on the table.

Wood and his staff were pleasantly surprised by the reaction—the briefing was going better than anticipated. They expected more outcry about the group's target. Then again, the men didn't know the full facts yet.

The colonel continued. The Ploesti raid, code-named Operation Tidal Wave, would be an all-out effort involving all five B-24 groups in the theater. In other words, "Any plane that's flyable will go." The mission plan called for a simultaneous attack on Ploesti's seven largest refineries to overwhelm the enemy's defenses and deliver a single, decisive blow to the targets.

And the bombing had to be done at low level. The planners at the 9th Air Force had initially calculated that a high-altitude raid on Ploesti would require almost 1400 Liberators. The problem was, Uncle Sam didn't have that many. But a low-altitude attack, they calculated, could achieve the same result with the 180 bombers they did possess.

A low-level attack was simply more efficient. It improved the bombers' accuracy while inflicting maximum damage on the targets. In sum, the 9th Air Force could do more with less.

Churchill had offered to complement the attack force with two groups of RAF Lancasters from the Pathfinders, the best Bomber Command had. But the two types of aircraft were incompatible in terms of speed. So Tidal Wave—the "biggest low-level mass raid in aviation history," as the 9th Air Force called it—would be an all-American show.

Colonel Wood believed that a mission this daring and dangerous would be a tall order for any rookie group. And it was happening soon. How soon? The brass was keeping any inkling of the date of the raid under lock and key. Not even Wood knew.

The raid was, in fact, just five days away. The higher-ups at the 9th Air Force would set the date for August 1, a Sunday, a deliberate choice. It's when the brass expected the "pleasure loving" Romanian gunners to be at play, not at their stations.

In spite of the numerous obstacles ahead, Wood believed his group could pull off this job. In fact, he told the group, he planned to fly in the lead ship.

Ernie found the news reassuring. No group commander would risk leading a mission that could turn into a suicide run.

Now that Wood had revealed their destination, it was time to explain how they would get there. He turned the briefing over to his operations officer, Major Brooks. Tall, lean, and as earnest as a Boy Scout, Brooks had led the special mission rehearsal two days earlier—he'd been the one who'd informed Wood, after nearly dropping bombs on him, "Well, Colonel, you knew our ETA."

An orderly set a printed map on an easel. A red line traced their route: north across the Mediterranean, then northeast to Romania, before curling back to Berka 4.

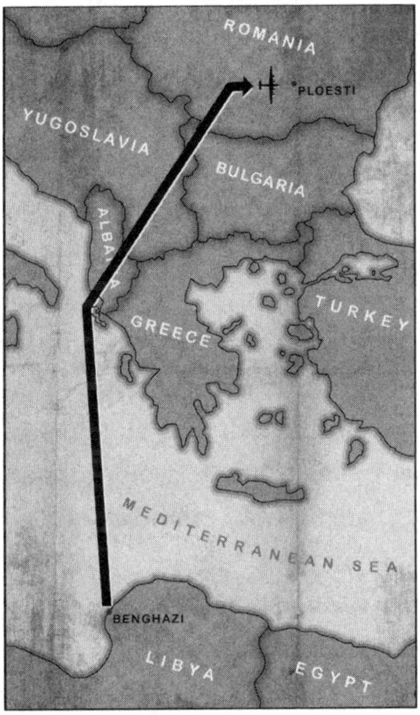

The distance drew whistles.

Brooks didn't sugarcoat matters. An attack on Ploesti entailed a grueling 2100-mile round trip—one of the longest missions ever attempted. Only the B-24 could even stand a chance of pulling it off: Its long, slender wings gave it a staggering range.

Ernie and Bob shifted in their seats. A flight that long meant they'd be in the cockpit for at least thirteen hours, longer than when they flew across the Atlantic, and even that flight was cutting it close on fuel. Ernie found himself wishing Britt was there to weigh in on the range of the mission, but Britt was still in the hospital. At least the Liberator was made for long hauls.*

Turning his attention to the target, Brooks briefed his fellow officers on Ploesti, the refinery city at the foot of the Transylvanian Alps, the beating heart that powered the German war machine and that therefore was arguably the highest-priority target in the entire war. But there remained an important detail: The 389th would not be attacking Ploesti itself.

That revelation raised eyebrows. *What?*

While the other four groups would swoop across the Romanian plain to attack the main Ploesti complex, the 389th had been assigned its own target, a northern offshoot of the Ploesti network called the Steaua Română refinery.

Brooks tapped the map to show the location of Steaua Română, eighteen miles north of Ploesti at Câmpina, a town of eight thousand people in the foothills of the Alps. Each of the nine largest refinery targets was assigned a color code. Theirs was "Red Target."

A few of the officers began to grumble. It didn't seem fair. Why did other groups get to attack the main complex, while they were stuck bombing Ploesti's ugly stepchild?

Brooks quickly quelled any dissent by explaining that the 389th had been given the most distant target because they had the latest D-model Liberators, with an extra fuel tank in each wing and thus greater range than the older planes in the other groups. On a mission where every drop of fuel was precious, this made the 389th the ideal candidates to travel the extra distance to Câmpina.

"Don't let the fact that Steaua Română is not situated in the main Ploesti complex fool you," Brooks said. "Our target is the most modern refinery of them all, and it specializes in producing high-quality aviation fuel." By one intel estimate, Red Target cranked out 400,000 tons of fuel annually.

* Of the bombers in the American arsenal, the B-24 was the best fit for the mission requirements of Tidal Wave. The Liberator could fly farther and faster than its rival, the B-17, while carrying a heavier payload. When making the transatlantic crossing to England, for example, the crew of a B-17 would need to stop for fuel in Greenland or Iceland, whereas a Liberator crew could make the trek from Canada nonstop. The B-24 was said to be five years ahead of the other bomber's technology. However, when it came to combat survivability, the B-17 won hands down.

Ernie and the others could read between the lines. At a time when Germany was so desperate for fuel that it had turned to making synthetic gas out of coal in order to keep the Luftwaffe flying, Steaua Română was producing the good stuff. This was the chance to hit Goering's boys where it hurt.

Brooks yielded the floor to the group's stately-looking intelligence officer for the next phase of the briefing. With thick swaths of white hair at the temples, Major Marshall Exnicios appeared older than forty-three. A former Washington, D.C., socialite and avid foxhunter, he'd traded his ascot for a suntan uniform these days.

Exnicios described Ploesti as "the number one air target in Hitler's Europe," which meant it had defenses to match its strategic value. On the basis of information from Allied agents in Romania and captured enemy documents, the 9th Air Force placed the number of anti-aircraft guns across the Ploesti network at 80 heavy and 160 light guns.

Ernie and the others had a kneejerk reaction: That was *a lot* of guns. But Exnicios explained that Ploesti's defenses were not quite what they appeared. There were few fighter aircraft in the area, and those that were present, he said, "are flown primarily by Romanian pilots—and they aren't very good to begin with."

That gave the audience a measure of comfort, considering they'd be going to Ploesti without fighter escort: The extreme distance was outside any fighter's range.

As for the anti-aircraft guns, Exnicios said, they, too, were crewed by Romanians, "who are tired of the war and will probably beat the civilians to the air raid shelters."

That drew a round of chuckles.

Even if the Romanians were at the top of their game, Exnicios predicted the element of surprise from the ships' low-level approach to the target would neutralize any defenses that were ready for them.

In later briefing materials disseminated to all the groups, the 9th Air Force reminded the forthcoming raiders: "Though the defenses at Ploesti may look formidable on paper, remember they are manned by Romanians." Curiously, there was little to no mention of Germans, as if the intel boys assumed there were too few of the Romanians' "protectors" left in the area to mount a serious threat.

In any other briefing, this was the part where Exnicios would have shown his audience some aerial photos of the target they were being sent to bomb.

But, he explained, he had nothing to show the men. The 9th Air Force had decided against sending reconnaissance planes to Ploesti rather than risk tipping their hand to the enemy.

The news drew uneasy looks. No one liked the idea of flying blind to Ploesti. But Exnicios had an ace up his sleeve. Orderlies lifted the shroud from the object on the table. Underneath was a perfectly crafted model of Steaua Română and the city of Câmpina, at 1/5,000 scale. The model, which allowed them to view their target in three dimensions, was a contribution from the Royal Air Force.

The British were supplying most of the intelligence for Tidal Wave, Exnicios said, offering a nod to several British intelligence officers in the back of the theater. They had built models like these for every American group in Benghazi. In fact, one of the officers had lived in Câmpina before being recruited for intelligence work. He could personally attest to the quality of the model.

"He'll show you where his house was," Exnicios said.

This bold claim was met with a murmur of approval.

Colonel Wood returned to the stage. As he concluded the briefing, he informed his men that the model would be on hand in the Quonset hut that served as the group war room, and he encouraged them to study it as much as they could.

Specific briefings would follow for the various crew specialties—pilots, navigators, and bombardiers—and the British intel boys would teach them the ins and outs of oil refineries.

"By the time we're done with you," the colonel said, "you'll be able to get a job at an oil refinery after the war—except there might be one problem with your résumé. You're going to be experts at *wrecking* them."

Ernie, Bob, and their fellow officers grinned from ear to ear.

The colonel and his staff left the premises. The men were dismissed. A mad rush to the model ensued.

Ernie and Bob had to stand on their tiptoes to see anything. Their fellow officers pointed at the model like kids at a toy train display in a department store at Christmas.

When at last they worked their way closer to the table, Ernie and Bob were impressed. The model, made primarily of plaster, was better than the grainy aerial photos bomber crews usually received before missions. The RAF had flown English craftsmen to Cairo, armed with every prewar postcard and photo of the Ploesti region and its network of refineries that could be found in the Cambridge University Library. Then they set the craftsmen to work building models. The extensive preparation led one airman to conclude: "This will be a history making mission."

Ernie squatted beside the table to get a closer look. He could visualize their approach to the target in minute detail: the valley they'd have to fly through, the river flowing from the Alps, and the road leading to Câmpina, before they reached Steaua Română, which was separated from the town by a single street. The refinery consisted of three large buildings surrounded by a blast wall that resembled the fortifications of a castle.

The detail was staggering, down to individual bushes and trees. Câmpina, even in miniature, looked idyllic, a place where you wouldn't mind living.

While admiring the artistry of the model, Ernie noticed the English craftsmen had overlooked one detail. He drew Bob's attention to the landscape around the refinery and asked, "Where's all the ack-ack?" No enemy anti-aircraft positions were represented anywhere around the refinery.

Bob shrugged. "It's just a model."

The omission unsettled Ernie. Colonel Wood and his staff had just delivered an extensive briefing that described the most important raid of the war to date, but they didn't know anything about where the opposition might be placed?

Ernie looked around him, but none of the other officers appeared to be alarmed.

Maybe it was nothing.

CHAPTER 12

FINAL PREPARATIONS

THE FOLLOWING DAYS

As the days ticked down to the raid, the airfields around Benghazi became a flurry of activity. All airmen were confined to their stations. Trucks and jeeps darted about. MPs patrolled the grounds. Security was so tight, "you'd think it was a prisoner-of-war camp," one gunner wrote in his diary.

For five straight days, the men of the 389th went in and out of the group's briefing huts as if they'd been built with revolving doors. They studied the target model and every scrap of intel about Ploesti, trying to absorb it all. The mission became the only subject of conversation. "The strain of waiting for The Day was terrific," noted the unit history.

In the base's outdoor theater, crews knelt on the sand for religious services. "There was little else to do," wrote one officer, but "to get down on one's knees and ask God's help for the ordeal to come." Seeing the turnout, one gunner noted: "There are no nonbelievers going on this mission."

Meanwhile, on the flight line, ground crewmen with rags in their back pockets readied bombers for the trial by fire. Tow tractors delivered stacks of bombs to each B-24. Extra fuel tanks were mounted in the planes' bomb bays, while out came any superfluous weight. Gone were the aluminum toilets. Gone were the ball turrets underneath the planes. The gunners who operated them would be armed on this raid with cameras to record the results of skip bombing. No one was worried about enemy fighters attacking a bomber from beneath when it was flying at twenty feet. Instead, some enterprising ground crewmen motored out into the desert and returned with armored plates they'd scavenged from wrecked German aircraft. They welded the steel onto the floors of the B-24s to protect the crews against small-arms fire from the ground.

The Eglin Field boys had brought one more trick to the desert. Their technicians installed a forward-firing .50 caliber machine gun into the nose of each of the three B-24s slated to lead the attack on Red Target. If it came to it, those first ships could strafe the enemy gunners—something no heavy bomber had ever attempted in combat.

FINALLY, IT WAS HERE: July 31, 1943. Tomorrow was The Day. And there was one last thing Ernie needed to do. He threw on his officer's cap and sunglasses, then slipped away to the base's ramshackle front gate for a delivery from Benghazi.

Ernie returned to the encampment carrying several small metal objects wrapped in cloth. He rounded up Bob and the crew's bombardier. They might have been confined to the base, but that wasn't going to stop Ernie from making some special preparations of his own. Together, the men began searching for a shady spot where Ernie could carry out his plan. He had said something about not wanting to mess up the floor of their tent. They found the ideal place, under the wing of a B-24 being repaired in the base depot.

The men rolled a fuel drum into the shade to use as a seat. Ernie opened his bundle on the sand, eyed the items closely, and debated where to begin. Inside were a pair of straight scissors, another pair of thin metal scissors with teeth, and hand-operated clippers, all barber tools. The only thing missing was the apron.

How hard could it be?

Ernie had seen a need among his crew, one the Army had overlooked. Nobody's hair had been clipped in at least a month. There had been no time for haircuts in England before the 8th Air Force had sent them to the most remote field on the planet, with no barber for miles. It felt like torture for someone like Ernie, who prided himself on being neatly groomed. And now they had a date with destiny tomorrow, the most important day of their lives, and Ernie had decided: He and his crew were going to look their best.

So he was taking matters into own hands. The tools? They might have been looted from an abandoned barbershop in Benghazi. Ernie wasn't about to question the source.

Bob protested. A haircut! That was what his friend had dragged him out here for? Bob, never one to fuss over appearances, wore his rumpled look like a badge of honor.

Second Lieutenant Albert "Al" Romano, twenty-two, the bombardier of *Pistol Packin' Mama,* hopped straight up onto the empty fuel drum without a fuss. The fourth and final officer of the crew, he wasn't about to pass up a free haircut.

Al's feet dangled above the sand. At just five foot three, he was the smallest of the bunch. His uniform pants always rode high on his waist. With thick black hair, hazel eyes, and a prominent nose that spoke to his Italian roots, Al was young in spirit and "happy-go-lucky."

Al Romano

Back home in Revere, Massachusetts, he was "well known about the city" for riding through the neighborhood on his bike, making deliveries for his parents' grocery store, Romano's Market. He'd shout greetings to neighbors, wave to old ladies on the porch, shoot a wink to the kids playing in the streets. And when he wasn't out on deliveries, he was behind the counter, cutting meat and chatting up customers.

Now, thousands of miles from Revere, home was never far from his mind. Al once closed a letter to his folks with the line "Give my regards to the whole neighborhood."

As Al sat on the drum, feet swinging, while Ernie warmed up his scissors, Bob looked on with a skeptical, almost protective eye. Bob and Al had a special bond—Bob had taken the little bombardier under his wing as a kid brother, even christening him Bambino. "You've done this before?" Bob asked.

"Oh, sure," Ernie said, with a smile in his voice. "On sheep."

Al's eyes widened as Ernie started snipping. Bob burst out laughing.

AS ERNIE CUT AL'S hair, a small crowd of gunners, pilots, and other crewmen drifted over. The curious onlookers eyed Ernie's impromptu barbershop with growing interest.

Ernie dusted off Al's shoulders and helped him to his feet. Al ran his fingers through his hair and thanked Ernie for the trim—he was a happy customer, even if he couldn't see the outcome. No one had thought to bring a mirror. Ernie stepped back and admired his work, pleasantly surprised: It wasn't half bad. Bob eyed Al's neatly trimmed locks and had to admit—he was impressed.

With his first client behind him, Ernie ushered Bob to the seat. Bob surrendered and sat down on the drum. Ernie paused to mop his brow and glanced at the growing crowd of onlookers.

Oh, brother.

Ernie didn't know most of them. His circle of friends was relatively small, because he'd joined the group late. But they were all as shaggy haired and disheveled as everyone else at Berka 4. It was pretty clear what the men were thinking as they eyed his barbershop on the sand, even if they were trying not to impose: *Is he taking walk-ins?*

Ernie faced a decision. Even in the shade of the derelict bomber, it was hotter than the hinges of hell's gates. Who wanted to work a minute longer than necessary? The raid was tomorrow. After this, Ernie needed to get back to his tent and give himself a trim using the small mirror he used to shave.

Ernie pondered his options. Cutting hair was probably the last job an officer should be doing. Undoubtedly there was some sort of Army regulation against it. It was probably deemed beneath the dignity of the uniform. After all, officers weren't supposed to fraternize with enlisted men, let alone groom them.

But Ernie was never a stickler for any societal hierarchy. The prestige of becoming a bomber pilot hadn't changed his view that even the lowliest private was worthy of respect. Besides, these guys would be heading to Romania tomorrow, and there was a chance some of them weren't coming home.

When Ernie finished trimming Bob's hair, he wiped his sweaty hands on his trousers and turned to the crowd.

"Okay fellas, who's next?"

CHAPTER 13

IF ONLY ONE COMES BACK

SEVERAL HOURS LATER, AROUND 4 P.M.

LATE IN THE AFTERNOON, WHEN THE SUN FELT DIALED DOWN, ERNIE and his friends joined an audience of three hundred men gathered outside the HQ area at Berka 4. They faced a small, hastily erected stage. The combat crews wouldn't fit in the base theater.

Major General Lewis Brereton, commander of the 9th Air Force, was going from base to base, giving each group a final pep talk before their mission. "The days of gloom and doubt were done," wrote historians James Dugan and Carroll Stewart. "Tomorrow there would go against fascism the poised strength of the finest aerial taskforce the world had ever seen."

Ernie, Bob, and Al were joined by a familiar face. Britt was back. He hadn't fully recuperated from his dysentery, but the navigator who had missed only two days of high school in four years wasn't going to skip out on his friends now. He was filled with the same fervor that had led him to drop out of college and enlist the week after Pearl Harbor because he felt America had been "stabbed in the back." When he heard about the removal of the aluminum toilets, however, his face fell.

There was even more worrisome news awaiting Britt upon his return. Each plane's position in the group formation had been announced, and *Pistol Packin' Mama* had been assigned to fly in the vanguard of the attack on Red Target. Colonel Wood had elected to ride in the first three-ship, and the crew of *Pistol Packin' Mama* would be in the three-ship flight behind him, second in a line of nine flights. It might be a dubious honor, depending on one's perspective: They could be among the first to lay bombs on Red Target, or the first to be shot out of the sky.

Bob tapped his foot, waiting for the pep talk to start. "Let's get on with it" was his attitude, and it wasn't mere impatience. The impromptu assembly had taken the men from their preparations, including personal ones. Each man had been encouraged to write a last letter home, referred to as a "just in case." The intelligence officer would mail it should a man fail to return. Only one letter per man was permitted, and the intel boys promised it wouldn't be opened or censored.

"You write yours yet?" Bob asked Ernie.

"Nah, I'll do it when we get back," Ernie said.

Bob gave him a funny look. "But that defeats the purpose."

Ernie grinned. *Exactly.*

He had no intention of writing such a letter. Any jitters or second thoughts he might have had from the initial briefing were gone. Besides, he'd been too busy trimming hair, incidentally cementing his status as the most popular man in the 389th. Still, the general's visit struck him as curious. They'd had numerous briefings. What could possibly be said that hadn't been said already?

GENERAL BRERETON STRODE ONTO the stage in the waning sun. The crowd edged closer to hear. Men stood on engine crates to catch a glimpse of the man.

At fifty-three, Brereton was short, with eager brown eyes hidden behind round glasses on a "dead-pan" face. He wore an unpretentious tent-shaped overseas cap that hid his receding black hair. He'd been the leader of the U.S. Army Air Forces in the Philippines until they were overrun by Imperial Japan.

General Brereton

Brereton began by saying he wished he could go to Ploesti with them. He had lined himself up to fly on the lead plane before General Hap Arnold in Washington grounded him because Brereton knew too much about the Allies' future plans. His deputy, General Uzal Ent, who'd been the one to brief the group commanders in the Green Hut, would ride along in the lead bomber in his place.

Brereton sounded genuinely disappointed to be handing over the reins. During his previous command, he had made American history when he led a bombing mission against the Japanese. It was the first time a general had ever led a raid.

Brereton was at Berka 4 to speak about Ploesti and the importance of their mission within the scope of the wider war. After the Axis failure at Stalingrad put the Russian oil fields out of the Germans' reach, he explained, Ploesti had become even more vital to the enemy. Hitler was now "almost entirely dependent upon Romanian oil."

Destroying Ploesti wouldn't just be a setback to the enemy. It would force Hitler to recast his entire plans for the war.

Without oil, the Germans would not be able to mount a defense of mainland Italy or start any new offensives on the Eastern Front. "It would take three complete army corps many months to accomplish what less than 1,800 of you men can do in one afternoon," Brereton explained. "The sudden, complete, and permanent denial of Romanian oil will inevitably result in the collapse of German hope."

Some of the men around Ernie were already patting themselves on the back for shortening the war, but no one was expecting what came next.

Brereton delivered his bombshell.

"If not one bomber returns tomorrow," Brereton said, "but that target is wiped out, the mission will still be a success."

Men caught on to what he was saying: *The importance of this mission justified its cost. Any cost.* A ripple of dismay ran through the audience.

Ernie and Bob looked at each other in disbelief. What had Brereton just said?

A gunner, Sergeant Russell Hayes, also questioned his ears. "Now that makes a lump in your throat right there," he thought.

One bombardier clued in to something missing from the general's speech all along: "He talked about getting to the target, not getting back. This scared the daylights out of me."

It was a chilling eleventh-hour realization: Brereton was forecasting a potential suicide mission for every man headed to Ploesti.

Ernie was still trying to fathom the disconnect. The message from Colonel Wood's earlier briefing still rang in his ears: "Remember, they're just Romanians."

What had changed?

Ernie wondered whether the general knew something the intel boys hadn't when they briefed him and the other officers about the raid. In fact, he did. Four days earlier, a shockwave had "hit the planners and the mission brass" in Benghazi. Word came from the British that a Romanian pilot had defected, flying his Ju-88 bomber all the way to RAF Nicosia, their airfield on Cyprus. The story sounded farfetched, and the British couldn't corroborate it, but the Romanian pilot swore that Ploesti was the most heavily defended airspace in Europe.

According to him, the Germans had built what they called Festung Ploesti—Fortress Ploesti—a 360-degree belt of anti-aircraft batteries bristling with nearly four hundred guns, almost twice the American estimate. And fifty thousand Luftwaffe troops had poured in to bolster the garrison, including a regiment of elite flak gunners from the Ruhr Valley.

Now Ploesti reportedly stood as a rival to the aerial defenses of Berlin, the most fearsome flak zone outside Germany itself.

Brereton wasn't about to tell the men any of that. There was no time to call off the raid, even if the Romanian pilot's intel was true. In Brereton's defense, the news wasn't easy on him either. As the general looked out at the concerned faces of the young men he was sending into battle, it wasn't lost on him that President Roosevelt and Prime Minister Churchill had ordered, not asked, him to carry out this mission.

He had seen this look before, when he was ordered to evacuate the Philippines with MacArthur and leave behind countless young airmen and pilots. Their fate was the Bataan Death March and the subsequent imprisonment of as many as 75,000 Allied troops.

Those men were still there. Still POWs. And he was in Libya.

Whenever Brereton talked about the men left behind, a reporter noted, "the tough, hard-boiled general suddenly finds he has to blow his nose so hard he must leave the room."

When the speech was finished, the men departed in silence. Britt looked pale, and not from the dysentery. Al was more fidgety than usual. Normally calm and good-natured young men, Ernie's friends were in the same state of semi-panic as the rest. Any hint of overconfidence they might have felt now lay shattered on the desert floor. The general "intended to be inspirational and reassuring," a pilot would remember, "but his speech fell flat. I went back to my tent, smoked half a pack of cigarettes."

Sergeant Hayes rushed off to visit the 389th's chaplain, Father Gerald Beck. Suddenly no precaution was too much.

One pilot wandered over to the cheerful "Limey Gunners," who manned the airfield defenses, and nervously asked, "Which plane would you aim at during a low-level attack?"

"We'd always go for the highest," a British gunner said, "since it's the easiest to hit."

The pilot made a "mental note" to fly as low as possible.

As Ernie filtered out of the crowd with his friends, he felt nerves in the pit of his stomach, as if he had forgotten something or should have done more to prepare. "We were now very serious and nervous about Ploesti," he would later confide in his diary.

Ernie realized he'd bought into the soft-pedaling about their target because *he wanted it to be so.* Now, in light of the shockwave Brereton had just delivered, Ernie came to his own unsettling realization about tomorrow's raid: Colonel Wood had not undersold the danger his men would face at the initial briefing, nor was General Brereton now trying to backpedal from earlier statements. The truth was more troubling than that.

They didn't actually know what the men were flying into.

Before they made it far, Bob looked to Ernie with atypical seriousness.

"You sure you're not writing that letter?"

THAT NIGHT, AFTER RUNNING a last pre-mission errand, Ernie and Britt walked back toward their tent. Neither expected to sleep much. It was moonless and cold, the dark sky was full of stars, and the men wore leather jackets to ward off the chill. Ernie and Britt could see every step in the starlight.

Neither spoke much. Ernie was focused on what he needed to do to get to bed as early as possible. They had a 5:30 A.M. wake-up call. All Britt had left to do was his nightly reading of his Bible.

As the men walked, the stillness of the night was shattered by a sudden "thunderous roar of B-24 engines being tuned up for the morrow's raid."

Ernie felt a chill down his spine. The sudden sound of engines only spiked his tension. On the flight line, "red-eyed" ground crews were working around the clock to tune up or swap out any potentially problematic engines. The dust and grit of the desert were brutal on aircraft. A bomber's Pratt & Whitney engine could run for three hundred hours in England. In the desert, an engine lasted for sixty before it needed an overhaul.

When Ernie and Britt reached the encampment, the sea of tents looked like glowing lanterns, each lit from within by oil lamps made from square cans that once held bomb fuses. The noise of the engine tests had died down again and among the crews "there was a quietness, quite unlike the usual buzz," wrote a pilot in his diary. Brereton's words lingered in the men's minds. "A great morale builder for all the combat crews," Sergeant Richard Byers, a gunner, scribbled sarcastically in his diary.

Inside the tents, men settled old gambling debts, and "some crews were quietly giving away their belongings," noted a copilot.

Earlier that day they had made a joke of it.

"Well, don't take your fancy shoes with you," one officer quipped to a friend with a wink.

"Don't take your camera with *you,*" replied the friend.

It was commonly understood that any survivors of the raid had advance permission to take items from the belongings of any man who didn't return. If something could help make desert life a little more bearable, it was fair game. All the men held to this rule.

But now, the young men were looking at their friends in different ways. They were giving away their souvenir camel whips, their fezzes, and, especially, any pinups they didn't want sent home to their folks.

The pre-combat jitters weren't limited to the enlisted men and junior officers. Before Captain Philip Ardery, a squadron leader in the 389th, turned in for the night, he hid a small hacksaw blade in the bottom of his boot, just in case he found himself in an enemy jail the next day. "I had a feeling that there was a more than fifty-fifty chance I would be shot down," he later wrote.

One gunner characterized the uneasy feeling that had settled over the aircrews by writing simply: "Time is running out."

Britt broke the silence between him and Ernie. He said he was at peace with whatever awaited them tomorrow. In his mind, even if they died trying to destroy Ploesti, their sacrifices would be "justified" by all the lives they saved.

"Think about it, Ernie." Britt stood a little taller. "We'll have achieved more in our young lives than most men will do in a lifetime."

Ernie took pause. Studying his friend closely, he couldn't help but admire Britt's conviction. This wasn't bravado. He knew that his navigator meant every word.

For Ernie, though, the thought of dying the next day carried a different weight.

In his early teens, Ernie had decided he had to escape the Sanpete Valley "to pursue my destiny—whatever it was." Following in his father's footsteps, hunting animals for a living, never appealed to him. It felt fruitless. He saw his family trapped in "a cycle of hard work and poverty," especially during the Depression, and knew that path didn't lead anywhere.

What he longed for was a mentor—someone to offer "wisdom, guidance, a philosophy for life." But his father couldn't serve that role, and his mother, Ada, a former librarian, was already consumed with raising Ernie's three younger sisters.

So, Ernie came to a hard truth: the only person who could change his circumstances was himself.

His mother had always encouraged learning, and Ernie refused to let his family's poverty stop him. Each morning, he arrived at school early to pore over newspapers before the bell rang, to expand his knowledge of the world. He bartered bottles of milk to the music teacher in exchange for lessons on the snare drum and Hawaiian guitar.

In high school, he joined the competitive debate squad and served as a class officer; after school, he swept floors and shoveled coal as a janitor, to save for college.

But the question loomed: How would he ever afford the full tuition?

The answer came in the form of the Utah National Guard. They paid $2 for every drill. And Ernie was a natural fit—his local unit happened to be the 115th Engineer Band.

By the time Pearl Harbor was attacked, Ernie was already in uniform. Determined not to spend the war "beating on a snare drum," he applied for aviation training and became a bomber pilot.

Ernie didn't have all the answers, but he knew this much: Whatever happened tomorrow, he wasn't ready to trade his life for a barrel of Romanian oil. He still wanted to go out in the world and make his mark. He was twenty-two and only getting started.

He couldn't reveal any reluctance or fear, not when Britt and the crew were counting on him and Bob to fly them safely to Romania and back. The silver wings on his uniform would not allow any hint of doubt. He had heard, "The confidence of the crew lies on the shoulders of the pilot," and he took the saying to heart.

This would not be a one-way trip. Turning to his friend, Ernie summoned a confident tone. "If only one plane comes back, we'll be on it."

Britt gave an appreciative nod. They walked the rest of the way in silence.

CHAPTER 14

OFF WE GO

THE NEXT DAY, AUGUST 1, 1943

IN THE DARK, COLD HOURS BEFORE DAWN, A CHORUS OF ALARM CLOCKS all suddenly blared in tents across Berka 4. Ernie and the other officers of *Pistol Packin' Mama* were jolted awake at 5:30 A.M. The synchronized clanging sounded like a hundred time bombs on the verge of exploding. Adding to the noise, "men in jeeps tore around from tent to tent blowing horns," remembered one pilot. Others yelled, "Get up, get up, you guys! This is the day. Get up! Roll out of those sacks!" The suddenness of all the bells, horns, and shouting produced a jarring, unsettling effect.

Whose idea was this? Ernie thought. *Couldn't they have just knocked?*

The squadron orderly ducked into the tent shared by Ernie and Bob and the others. "You fellas up?" he shouted. If a man wasn't up, he was pulled out of bed.

Ernie put on a tough face and began dressing.

The base was springing to life. Men puttered around in jeeps. Mechanics test-ran engines. Cooks rolled up the flaps of the mess tent.

As the crew of *Pistol Packin' Mama* left their tent, Bob, Britt, and Al placed their "just in case" letters on their cots, as the guidelines instructed. The envelopes were addressed to their parents, but Bob and Al had included letters to their sisters; Britt had written to his younger brother, Teddy.

Ernie's bunk stayed empty.

AFTER AN EARLY BREAKFAST of "rubber pancakes" and rehydrated eggs "with a good deal of dust scrambled in them," Ernie and the officers of *Pistol*

Packin' Mama headed to the weather briefing. The headquarters area was lit by cracks in the blackout curtains, and the men walked to the briefing room in silence. "One might have thought we were very calm because we were so quiet," wrote one navigator.

The truth was, no one said anything because no one wanted to show fear. "Most of us have already determined we will lose at least 50% of the striking force," noted one gunner.

The bomb group's assistant operations officer tracked down the officers of *Pistol Packin' Mama* and beckoned to Bob. "Lieutenant O'Reilly? We need you at Operations. There's a problem with your ship."

Bob flashed the others a "This is not good" look and went with the man.

"Gloom" settled over Ernie, Britt, and Al as they lingered in the shadows.

Bob returned from Operations with narrowed eyes. "Well, we got a new plane." He explained that when the ground crew started test-running *Pistol Packin' Mama,* her number one engine had malfunctioned. This was the same engine that had been damaged over Crete and repaired. There wasn't enough time to troubleshoot the problem, so the crew was given the standby ship from the 567th Squadron. It had belonged to a crew sent over to fly the raid with the Africa-based Pyramiders, who were running short on crews due to combat attrition. The fresher 389th, with manpower to spare, had loaned the Pyramiders six full crews—sixty men.

Ernie felt relieved. He didn't like the thought of flying in an unfamiliar aircraft, but even more, he didn't want to sit out the raid. Besides, the group needed them in formation. No pilot wanted to trade "a damn good wingman for a blank space of enemy sky."

BY 6 A.M., A warm glow appeared in the eastern sky. A truck carried Ernie and the crew along the flight line, where the headlights showed a string of B-24s parked wingtip to wingtip facing the taxiway.

Ernie and his fellow crew members were dressed for the low-level flying ahead. The officers wore their lightweight suntans, the sergeants their one-piece flight suits. Some had on their leather jackets.

Ernie was the only officer who'd brought a gun. In a holster on his hip, he carried a .45 automatic. Pistols were optional on bomber missions, needed only in case a mission went south and the men found themselves down behind enemy lines.

The men rode in silence. On this morning, as takeoff time drew close, their minds felt heavy. "One cannot help but wonder," wrote one gunner. "Who will get killed? Who will survive?"

Any loss would be deeply felt. Theirs was a tight-knit crew, from top to bottom. There was not a bad apple in the bunch.

"It was a good crew," wrote Britt. "The engineer, Frank Kees, held a degree in Mechanical Engineering. Clell Riffle was an experienced radio operator who was a little nervous about combat. Tail turret gunner, Louis Medeiros, was a good-looking fellow of Portuguese descent. Troy McCrary, ball turret gunner, was shy, quiet, and sported freckles to go with his red hair. Rurak and Bowker were the brawny waist gunners."

The crew of *Pistol Packin' Mama*. Back, left to right: Bob, Ernie, Britt, Al, Kees, Riffle. Front, left to right: Bowker, Medeiros, McCrary, MacLachlan.

Near the end of the long lineup, the truck stopped and Ernie and the crew climbed out. The driver kept his lights focused so the men could find their way around. The crew chief and his assistants were removing sun covers from the Plexiglas turrets.

The men congregated on the copilot's side and shined flashlights at the nose art. Their new plane featured a painting of a smiling winged boxcar and the name *Chattanooga Choo Choo.*

It was cute. A little too cute.

But that wasn't the real problem. Their roving flashlights spotted patches placed over flak damage from the break-in raids. A lot of patches. "Our first look at the plane was discouraging," recalled one of the crew.

"Are you kidding?" Bob said. "This ship should be named 'Borrowed Time.'"

Ernie tried to reassure his friend. "It's just another B-24, Bob. We have no reason to doubt it."

Bob shook his head in skepticism. He wasn't convinced.

B-24 *Chattanooga Choo Choo* and its original crew

AFTER CLIPPING ON THEIR parachute harnesses and gathering their bags, Britt, Al, and the sergeants boarded the plane while Ernie and Bob lingered to confer with the crew chief. The tired mechanic reported any potential mechanical quirks to watch for during the long flight ahead, although even at that late moment the ground crews didn't know where the aircrews were going, and Ernie and Bob couldn't tell them. The destination was such a closely guarded secret that ground crews and British AA gunners wouldn't be told until the bombers were over the target.

Ernie and Bob began their walk-around inspection. Bob kicked the tires, literally, to make sure they were properly inflated, then lingered at landing gear and shined his flashlight on the strut underneath the wing.

"You gotta see this." Bob wasn't smiling.

Normally a red line ran across the strut, indicating the maximum weight that could be loaded onto the bomber, similar to a Plimsoll mark on a freighter's hull. The line on this plane couldn't be seen. The bomber had been loaded so heavily the strut housing covered it.

What was she clocking in at? Bob asked the crew chief.

The man did a quick tally in his head. "Well, including bombs, extra fuel, and ammo, I'd say around 64,000 pounds."

Ernie remembered what he had been taught in flight school. "Do not attempt to taxi if over the redline." And that was merely taxiing. Could a B-24 even take off at 64,000 pounds?

Ernie and Bob shook the chief's hand, thanking him for the care he'd given their new ship. The fact that the plane was overloaded wasn't his fault.

While Bob, who smoked, stepped away from the plane for one last cigarette, Ernie ducked into the bomb bay and climbed aboard.

Immediately inside the plane, Ernie was hit by the sharp smell of aviation fuel. Their plane was essentially a gas station with wings, filled to the brim with 3200 gallons of 100-octane fuel. Most of the fumes were seeping from her two spare tanks, rubberized fabric bladders.

Al was already at work in the bomb bay, checking the four large yellow M44 bombs in their shackles. He threaded his way down the narrow metal catwalk with two bombs on either side of him, giving each bomb a shake to ensure it was secure in its rack.

At the nose of each bomb lay a fuse with a metal propeller that spun as the bomb fell to earth. Normally, it took 150 revolutions to arm a bomb. But since the group was dropping at such low altitudes, each fuse needed a head start. Al pulled the steel arming pins and wound each propeller 75 times, being careful to count each turn. He returned the arming pins for takeoff. After they were airborne, over Romania, he would return to the bomb bay and remove the pins for good.

Meanwhile the gunners were settling into their positions. Medeiros tested the hydraulics of his turret in the tail, while McCrary, the ball turret gunner, checked the camera he'd be shooting from the hatch in the floor instead of his usual guns. The crew's two waist gunners, Rurak and Bowker, removed the covers from their .50 caliber Browning machine guns. They opened the breeches, wiped off any dust stuck to the grease, then cleaned the links between the large bullets.

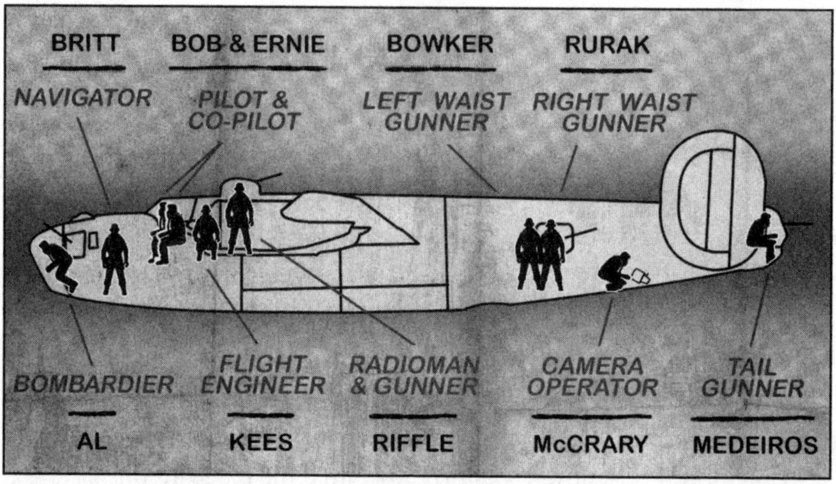

Ernie passed through the small radio room behind the cockpit, where Riffle was already perched in the seat of his top turret, testing the electric motors that moved his twin fifties. On the other end of the compartment, Kees, the flight engineer, was checking fuel gauges.

Ernie slid into the right seat of the cockpit. The air carried the familiar scent of "raw metal and zinc-oxide paint."

He tossed his straps over his shoulders, while from the outside one of the ground crew members gave the windscreen a final polish. The light from the eastern horizon hinted at a beautiful day, revealing what would become a cloudless blue sky. The fair weather prompted one man to think it would be "a good day for a picnic or a day at the beach."

Ernie did not let the pleasant desert morning deceive him. He knew the mission to Ploesti would be tough, perhaps the worst second mission a pilot could ask for. But Ernie had come to terms with his role in the greater scheme. Of course, their mission was formidable. Any target as vital as Ploesti would be heavily defended. That didn't change a thing. Tidal Wave was a job that needed doing. Nothing more. Nothing less. Ernie had resolved himself to the task ahead. *Roll up your sleeves, get the job done.*

Al finally joined Britt in the glass-plated nose of the bomber.

"Look at this," Britt said.

Al glanced at where Britt pointed, and his eyes went wide.

The crew from the 567th had left a message in chalk on the metal sidewall of the compartment. "The Flying Coffin," they'd scrawled. "You'll never get back in this crate." They were obviously mad to give up their plane and go over to the Pyramiders.

Nice cheerful sentiments, Britt thought. He looked for something to wipe away the graffiti.

IN THE COCKPIT, AFTER Bob had caught up, he and Ernie finished their preflight checklist, then threw on their helmets. Neither man wore the flak jacket they'd been issued: They were too uncomfortable. Ernie checked his watch. It was nearly 7:00 A.M., the designated start time.

The sun cracked the horizon. All around the base, British anti-aircraft gunners donned their gas masks. Next to the runway, non-participating officers hurried to a small viewing platform with a windsock.

When the clock struck 7:00, the long line of twenty-eight bombers began to start their engines. "Starters whined as the props rotated then disappeared into blurs as the engines caught, coughing and belching blue grey oil smoke," wrote one historian. What began as a "nervous bark of engines" soon became "a sustained roar."

"Let's crank her up," Bob said.

Ernie flipped the ignition switches, one by one. Soon all four propellers were spinning.

Waves of red dust slapped the windscreen of *Chattanooga Choo Choo.* Out his side window Ernie saw scrub brush flying past, blown backward by the force of the engines, as if they were trying to wipe clean the desert.

There was no time to idle on the ground. Every drop of fuel was precious. A green flare cut the sky, the command to proceed to the runway. The flight line of bombers began a near-synchronized right turn onto the taxiway, each falling in line with the plane ahead as they queued for the runway. Brakes squealed. The planes lumbered toward their takeoff positions. The plan called for a rapid-fire takeoff with Colonel Wood's plane, a B-24 named *The Scorpion,* leading the group. The runway was wide enough so three planes, staggered, could take off at a time.

Dust engulfed Ernie and Bob. They leaned in their seats to see where they were going. Their heavy plane rolled reluctantly. Once Wood's flight launched, they were due to take off next. There was no time to run the engines up to see if everything was registering. They were either firing on all cylinders or not.

Several ships behind *Chattanooga Choo Choo* crept a bomber named *Ole Kickapoo.* In the copilot's seat sat Second Lieutenant Ron Helder, twenty-six, who had been a pharmacist before the war. He'd written to his parents in South Dakota the night before. Without revealing the group's specific destination, he told his parents simply that the next day would be "a full day for us," then added, "The big shots around here say they are going to make us work on the Sabbath and really do humanity a good turn." Helder was ultimately proud of what they were about to do, and if something should happen to him, he instructed his folks: "Turn back your calendar and take a look at August 1st."

At 7:15, Wood's flight of three revved hard, then began their takeoff roll. From behind, Ernie and Bob watched the bombers race down the dirt runway, throwing back a cloud of fine red dust in their wake. Halfway down the runway, the heavily loaded planes were obscured by dust. There was no waiting to find out if they had made it aloft. The orders called for flights to take off every thirty seconds.

Bob made a turn onto the runway and lined up to the right of their flight leader, First Lieutenant Elmer Rodenberg, in *Yours Truly;* First Lieutenant Ken Matson, piloting *Wolf Wagon,* fell into position on the left. The copilot's side of *Wolf Wagon* was adorned with clever nose art: a cartoon wolf in a dinner jacket lobbing a bomb. Both Rodenberg and Matson were from the 565th Bomb Squadron, same as Ernie and Bob, but Ernie didn't know either man well. They would race down the runway already in wedge formation, as usual.

Ernie tugged at his straps, struggling for a view forward. From his seat he couldn't see if Wood's formation had lifted off—the runway was enveloped in red haze kicked up in the wake of the lead planes. The dust of Berka 4 was back with a vengeance. The ground crews had hosed the runway the night before, but the watering had no effect. The cloud of sand was expanding

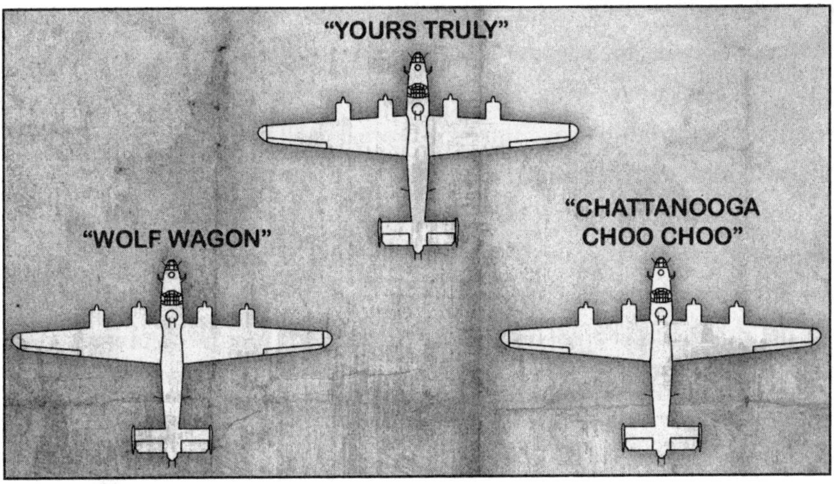

upward and outward by the second, and the remaining bombers would have to fly through that, each flight keeping formation during takeoff in almost zero visibility.

Ernie turned up the turbo boost selector to give the engines more power to help with the additional weight. Apprehensively, he set a hand on the throttles. Rodenberg's ship belched dust, revved hard, and began rolling. Ernie advanced all four throttles. The engines roared in unison and the instrument panel and seats vibrated with power. Bob released the brakes. The overloaded plane dipped forward, then began the takeoff roll.

Chattanooga Choo Choo rolled slowly at first as the engines, each making 2700 revolutions per minute, strained to build momentum. The bomber accelerated along the runway. Ernie and Bob were pushed back into their seats. They plunged into the red haze, racing through it. The bomber shook and rattled as if it was going to break apart. Ernie kept his eyes glued to the engines' temperature and pressure gauges, while Bob kept his eyes fixed on *Yours Truly* to his front left. Plumes of dust shot back from her engines, leaving a "rooster tail" of red dust in their wake. All Ernie and Bob could see was the lead bomber's twin tails sticking above the cloud, in and out of visibility. Bob focused hard to make sure he didn't overrun his leader. Fortunately, each B-24 rolled straight as an arrow. Where other planes would fishtail and require rudder corrections, a B-24's twin tails kept it going straight.

Chattanooga Choo Choo's airspeed indicator ticked up. Ernie called out their airspeed so Bob didn't have to look away: 90. 95. 100. Normally at 100 miles per hour, they could feel lift from the wings, and at 125, a bomber would fly itself off the ground. But as they raced forward at 115, 120, and 125, the plane stayed glued to the earth. *Chattanooga Choo Choo* shook like a wooden roller coaster. The dust fully engulfed the lead ship as it lifted off. Ernie and Bob couldn't see a thing anymore. For all they knew, the end of the runway could be right in front of them.

Gingerly, Bob pulled back on the yoke, hoping for the best. Sure enough, the nose gear of the bomber lifted off the ground. Slowly, ever so warily, one, two, three tires broke from the dirt. The 64,000-pound machine "groaned into the air" as it took flight under that wing-sagging weight, climbing blindly through the murk.

Their climb rate was low and slow for a Liberator. They needed to reach 200 feet or higher to clear the dust cloud. Ernie reached over to Bob's side and shoved the lever to bring the landing gear up—anything to make the plane slicker and produce more airspeed—then raised the flaps on his side of the console. Hearing a reassuring whine, Ernie checked outside to see the gear folding outward and into the wing. Bob found *Yours Truly* in the gloom and held formation as well as he could, but the flying boxcars shimmied and pitched through the dense air. *Wolf Wagon* pulled parallel to them but barely stayed visible. Normally, a B-24 could reach two hundred feet in about thirty seconds; this slow climb was feeling like an eternity.

Dazzling rays of sunrise reached into the cockpit. The three ships emerged together from the murk into the dawn.

"That's 200," Ernie said, his relief palpable.

Bob uttered a nervous laugh. "Well, that was fun."

Ernie rechecked all the gauges. He slid open the side window. A cool gust chased out the stale, dusty air. Bob tightened up his position on *Yours Truly*. *Wolf Wagon* did the same. "We looked to our engines, but they gave no indication of weakening under the heavy load we carried," recalled one pilot.

So far, so good.

LOOKING NORTH TOWARD BENGHAZI, Ernie could see the B-24s from the four other groups assembling in the distance, circling over their airfields as they waited for other bombers to take off. Beyond them lay the Mediterranean, warm with color as it soaked up the dawn's early light.

Seeing the bombers from the other groups somehow felt like a reunion, even if Ernie hadn't flown with them before. Soon the skies around Benghazi would be filled with 178 bombers from five bomb groups.

When Ernie looked ahead, he caught a glimpse of Colonel Wood's flight banking above them, slowly corkscrewing upward toward their assembly point at two thousand feet. Once all twenty-eight planes from the 389th reached the ceiling, they would head for the coast and fall in line with the rest of the force.

One sergeant flying with the Liberandos felt the weight of the task ahead: "The target must be destroyed to win the war, period," he remembered thinking. "Coming back is secondary today." Colonel John Kane, the group leader of the Pyramiders, put it more bluntly when he proclaimed: "Either we hit Ploesti or we'll die trying."

The Axis powers still controlled a third of the globe. It was time to start taking it back.

Ernie braced as Bob followed *Yours Truly* in a synchronized climbing turn to join up with the colonel's flight.

They were on their way.

CHAPTER 15

THE WRATH OF OLYMPUS

ABOUT FOUR HOURS LATER, 11:15 A.M.

IN THE CRISP LIGHT OF A MEDITERRANEAN MORNING, THE LONG LINE of B-24s skimmed the sea at wavetop height, bound for the European mainland.

The massive sky train stretched for nearly five miles, more than 170 bombers motoring in deadly unison, as if each three-ship flight was invisibly lashed to the one ahead. History was being made. A force from the New World was over the sea once sailed by the ancient Greeks. It was the biggest fleet of bombers America had ever mustered in the Mediterranean.

At the head of the procession—which the men would dub the Ploesti Express—flew the African-based Liberandos, their planes sun-bleached and tinged pink from wear. Behind them came the faded green ships of the Traveling Circus, the most seasoned England-based group, with the Pyramiders and Eight Balls following close behind. Bringing up the rear were the rookies, the brand-new dark green B-24s of the 389th.

The Ploesti Express was running radio silent and flying at low altitude to hide from German radar as long as possible as they raced across "the bluest Mediterranean you can imagine."

In the 389th, flying second in the lineup of nine flights, was *Chattanooga Choo Choo.* The roar of four 1300-horsepower engines filled the cockpit as Bob motored in formation with Rodenberg and Maston, making a steady 160 miles per hour. Bob had his side window cracked open and sunglasses on. An endless blur of cobalt blue slipped beneath the wings.

Ernie was missing it all. He had his nose in a book, relaxing before his turn to fly. Ernie's favorite books were educational: How to understand economics. How to take better photographs.

In other planes, officers passed the time by reading or napping on the floor of the radio room behind the cockpit. A man felt safe in the powerful aerial armada.

One pilot in the Liberandos decided to "play Combat Correspondent." He handed the controls to his copilot and snapped some photos of the formation around him. "A nice souvenir for my grandchildren," he mused.

It was almost possible to forget their destination, and that it was a Sunday, "a morning when one would rather go to church and then leaf through the Sunday papers than be winging his way into the heart of Hitler's 'Fortress Europe.'"

Ernie felt a nudge in his ribs. He set down his book. What had he missed?

Bob nodded at a faint line on the horizon. "Land ho."

Ahead, they could see Colonel Wood's flight of three bombers and then the massive line of B-24s. Far beyond the lead planes, a jagged line of arid mountains took shape in the coastal haze. It was the Pindus Range, also known as the Spine of Greece. Its ridges ran up the length of the Greek peninsula, rising to 8,600 feet.

Ernie smiled. The mountains were a sight for sore eyes. They signaled that the overwater leg of the journey, which made any pilot nervous, was almost completed.

But something stood out as strange to him. It was hard to tell from this distance, but the tops of the mountains looked blanketed in snow. In August?

Across the formation, pilots and copilots set down their cameras and books. Others stirred from slumber and returned to the cockpits.

To reach Romania, they needed to cross the mountains.

Starting at the front of the Task Force, the overladen planes lifted their noses, "painfully, sluggishly," and began to climb.

FORTY-FIVE MINUTES LATER, ERNIE slid back into his seat after putting on his leather jacket and taking a swig of coffee from his thermos. He buckled his straps. Now at ten thousand feet, the temperature inside the bomber had fallen to forty degrees. Bob had rolled down the sleeves of his suntans. Already it was cold enough for Ernie to see his breath.

After climbing to altitude, the pilots had wheeled northeast to face the mountains. The Pindus Range loomed closer, now just twenty miles away. In less than ten minutes they would make landfall over the portion of the mountains that crossed into Albania, just north of Greece. When they reached land, it would be Ernie's turn to fly.

Ernie reached for his binoculars to scan the path ahead. Binoculars were a copilot's best friend when it came to spotting landmarks from high altitude or for joining up with other formations. Ernie squinted into the distance, then lowered the binoculars. "We've got a problem."

Behind the coastal range, a mass of dense clouds was boiling up, moody with moisture, stretching endlessly across the sky. The mountains were not blanketed with snow after all. What they'd seen from a distance was a wall of clouds.

Bob glanced up from his duties and looked more closely. His face fell. The intel boys hadn't accounted for the sky train slamming into a wall of hazardous weather. It was as if the gods on Olympus had unleashed a barrier, daring the young men from the New World to enter.

Ernie stowed his binoculars and took the controls. "Okay, Bob, put on your jacket before you freeze to death." For the next three hours, almost to the target, the bomber would be Ernie's responsibility.

Ernie sat tall in his seat for a better view ahead and clutched the control yoke in a firm grip. Bob hesitated—he felt bad handing over the plane just when they faced a new predicament—then lifted his hands. "All yours."

Ernie took control of the ship and immediately began working the controls, moving the yoke slightly forward and back, as if there was slack in it. The Flying Boxcar was "not a pilot's airplane." The same long wings that gave the B-24 its tremendous range came at the expense of flight stability. At the slightest change in balance or aerodynamics, the bomber would pitch up or down. Ernie could even detect when one of the crew got up and started walking around.

Closer the clouds came. Closer still. There was no way around them.

When the Ploesti Express reached the mainland, the air grew rougher as the moody cloudbank towered seven thousand feet above the formations of bombers, a silvery slab of weather. The lead groups of the Task Force kept powering straight toward it.

While Ernie focused on flying, Bob kept his eyes on the Liberandos in the vanguard four miles ahead, waiting to see whether they would try to circumvent the foul weather or push through it.

That decision would fall to the mission commander, General Uzal Ent, who was perched on a stool behind the pilots on the flagship, *Teggie Ann.* Stocky, with a deep cleft in his square jaw and "a fiery temper when provoked," Ent hailed from Pennsylvania's Amish country, and had been nicknamed P.D. during his West Point days—short for "Pennsylvania Dutch."

He was an old-school aviator, a man who'd flown blimps during the 1920s. And like his boss, General Brereton, Ent had reservations about sending heavy bombers into Ploesti at low level—but "like it or not," wrote one historian, "he was trapped into doing something he believed would produce more casualties than acceptable."

Bob was becoming impatient. Ent and the groups ahead were still holding their course, flying straight at the weather like men with a death wish. Had they forgotten that clouds were full of bad news—turbulence, icing, and the risk of smashing into another ship?

Finally, *Teggie Ann* rocked its wings, a signal that meant both "Attention!" and "Follow!" One by one, each plane passed the message back through the formation. Behind the first group, a green flare arced from the lead bomber of the Traveling Circus—"Affirmative."

At once, the two lead groups began climbing. The sky train was headed up and over the clouds. The detour up to fifteen thousand feet would burn precious fuel, but it was safer than barreling through dangerous weather. Inside the lead B-24s ahead, crews began putting on oxygen masks.

But the third group in line, the Pyramiders, remained frozen in level flight.

"What are they waiting for?" Bob muttered.

What he and Ernie didn't know was that the other veteran Africa-based group wasn't following Ent's orders, because they *couldn't.* They had been assured the mountains were the highest altitude they'd face that day, so they hadn't filled their oxygen tanks back in Benghazi.

In truth, Ent was violating his own mission orders by leading anyone up to fifteen thousand feet.

Instead of climbing, the lead Pyramider ship wagged its tail, the signal to the two trailing groups to "loosen formation." The message was unmistakable. They would attempt a maneuver known as frontal penetration. They were going through the weather.

Ernie and Bob exchanged a look of disbelief. The Ploesti Express was coming uncoupled right before their eyes. The 389th had brought oxygen and could have gone over the clouds with Ent, but their standing orders were to follow the group in front of them, the Eight Balls, no matter what. The Eight Balls followed the Pyramiders, and now the Pyramiders were calling the shots for the two England-based groups behind them. There was no debate.

Instead of climbing, the Pyramiders entered a steep leftward bank, putting space between the groups. The Eight Balls followed, banking left but not as sharply, while Colonel Wood's flight kept the 389th going straight. Now the three groups were flying abreast, with about a mile of sky between each of them. Nothing stood between them and the cloud bank, looming like a pillowy wall.

Bob grew quiet for once.

Ernie addressed the crew over the intercom: "Copilot to crew—put your chutes on if you haven't already."

The air grew choppier. Jagged mountain peaks began slipping beneath the planes. Ahead, Ernie watched the silhouettes of Wood's flight blur, then vanish into the onrushing clouds.

Here we go.

The mountains below disappeared, misty tentacles slipped around their flight, and the bombers plunged into semi-darkness. Ernie could just see the fuzzy blue formation lights glowing on the tails and wings of Wood's flight. He snapped his attention back to Rodenberg's plane ahead and to his left. Out of the corner of his eye, he tracked *Wolf Wagon* flying parallel to him on the other side of Rodenberg. But that was where visibility ended. The other two groups had disappeared. Hopefully they would meet up on the other side.

Turbulence tossed the three planes around. Ernie gripped the yoke with one hand while jockeying the throttles with the other, fighting to stay in position and maintain visual contact with Rodenberg. The flight bobbed in the mountain gales, rising and falling with the currents. The other B-24s flickered in and out of sight. They were playing follow-the-leader in low visibility, all clinging to the same invisible rope.

Ernie remembered the planes behind and called to his tail gunner: "Louie! Make sure the guys behind us know we're here."

In the back, the dapper, cool-headed Sergeant Louis Medeiros triggered his Aldis signal lamp. His job was crucial: Keep other ships from plowing into them. Flying directly behind was *Ole Kickapoo,* helmed by Lieutenants

Louis Medeiros

Lloyd Hughes and Ron Helder. If *Ole Kickapoo* flew too close, Medeiros flashed his light to tell the pilots to back off.

Normally in desperate weather, an aircraft commander like Bob wouldn't relinquish control to his copilot. But Bob trusted his friend. And Ernie wasn't *just* any copilot.

One morning back in April, during his B-24 pilot training in Arizona, Ernie had been called before the base adjutant. A bomb group in Denver was about to deploy overseas, but one of their pilots had fallen ill. They needed to fill the crew vacancy—fast. The catch? The ailing man was a copilot.

"Sorry," the adjutant said, as he handed Ernie his orders. "But you're taking his place. Be on the 3 P.M. train to Denver."

Ernie felt dismayed. He was on the verge of becoming an aircraft commander, not the copilot on someone else's crew. "Why me?" he asked, the slightest note of protest in his voice.

"Well, why not you?" the adjutant replied.

The next morning, after an overnight train ride to Denver, Ernie dropped his bags in the massive prewar hangar at Lowry Field. He was assigned to the 389th Bomb Group. Becoming the tenth man on a crew that had been flying together for months made him anxious, and the pilot of the newly christened *Pistol Packin' Mama* didn't like the deal any more than Ernie did. Bob arrived in the hangar with his guard up. As far as he knew, the Army had just saddled him with a disgruntled copilot who would question every decision he made.

But Ernie didn't give him any grief. What would that accomplish? Instead, Ernie introduced himself, stuck out his hand, and said, "I'll do the best I can for you."

Bob was immediately disarmed. He shook hands and confided that if their roles were reversed he'd have reported to the 389th kicking and screaming. "They gave you a raw deal, Ernie."

But Bob would make things right. He proposed an arrangement: They would operate as partners, sharing flying duties and trading legs. This way, each of them would always stay sharp. "You tell me when I'm doing something wrong," Bob said, "and I'll do the same for you."

Ernie knew he was exactly where he belonged.

Flying in formation over the mountains, in low visibility, Ernie now drew on every ounce of skill he could muster. He kept his eyes glued on Rodenberg's ship, wrestling with the uneasiness of not seeing what lay ahead. At any moment, a mountain peak could leap up right in front of them. Rodenberg was the only pilot in their flight with any eyes forward—and he was following Colonel Wood. The entire bomb group could be flying to their doom, but they wouldn't know it until they pancaked into the side of a mountain. The blind were leading the blind.

MIDWAY ACROSS THE MOUNTAINS, Britt was huddled over his tiny backward-facing desk in the corner of the nose of the plane when he felt a fiery burble in his gut. He wasn't fully mended. In an airplane where the toilet had been removed to save weight, his dysentery—the dreaded Desert Quickstep—was back.

Seriously? Britt was dismayed. That toilet was aluminum. How many pounds could removing it have saved?

Britt didn't have time to think. Normally, a man would have used an empty ammo can. But all were full of bullets. He grabbed his helmet off the floor. It would have to do. He called over his shoulder to Al, who faced forward in the nose in the bombardier's position, "Bambino! Don't turn around!"

Al glanced behind, then quickly faced forward again.

Britt was awkwardly tall and tethered to the intercom. He braced himself against the sidewalls and ceiling as the bomber rattled through the murk. His embarrassing predicament almost went unnoticed. But the nose compartment wasn't fully enclosed by bulkheads. From Britt's desk, he could glance upward and see the pilots' feet on the rudder pedals.

In the cockpit, Bob smelled something funny. An electrical fire? He switched the intercom to the plane-wide setting.

"Pilot to bombardier," Bob said, urgent. "What's burning up there, Al?"

An awkward static filled the silence. Finally Al said, "Britt took a crap!"

"In what?"

"His hat!"

The plane erupted with laughter.

Britt still needed to flush. In the noisy rear section of the bomber, two waist gunners and the ball turret gunner–turned–cameraman huddled on the floor for warmth. Their flight suits were zipped, but cold wind curled in through the waist windows, turning the compartment into an icebox. Their feet felt frozen. It could have been worse: Some crews in other bomb groups had worn sandals and shorts.

The gunners fought back grins as Britt, holding his helmet, ducked through the small doorway and stepped up to one of the waist gun windows. By Britt's last calculation, they were over Yugoslavia. The Balkan nation was mostly occupied by Germans, although some Communist partisans were friendly to the Allies.

"Bomb's away!" Britt shouted, and pitched his helmet out the window.

TWO HOURS LATER, WITH Ernie still at the controls, he and Bob noticed the clouds growing more luminous. Sunlight peeked through. Wood's flight came into view and stayed visible. Below, the Balkan Mountains in Bulgaria gave way to foothills, signaling their arrival into Romania.

Ernie thumbed the intercom switch. "Copilot to crew, hold tight."

Ahead, Wood's flight pitched forward, settling into a fast descent to "duck in" beneath enemy radar. Rodenberg followed. Ernie pushed over after them, the Liberator nosing into a steady, obedient dive.

The air grew warmer, turning thick and steamy. Ernie felt a wash of relief to be leaving the rough weather behind. The clouds in front thinned, then dissipated entirely, and the flights motored into the glare of a hot and hazy summer afternoon. It was just after 1:00 P.M. locally. Ahead, a lazy brown river snaked through the countryside. Beyond that lay a patchwork of rich green farmland venting in the summer heat. This was the Danube Basin, fed by the mighty Danube River. The land beyond the river was Romania.

Ernie and Bob exchanged grins. They felt like explorers who'd found the last undiscovered place on earth. Romania looked peaceful, pastoral, as if war had never touched this land. Far in the distance, the fields turned golden on the Wallachian Plain; beyond lay another mountain range, the Transylvanian Alps, where summer squalls were drifting through. Where the plain met the foothills of the Alps lay Ploesti. A straight shot on this same heading would take them there.

But first, they needed to re-form the Task Force. Bob looked to his left and saw a group of green B-24s quickly descending. Desert-pink bombers descended beyond them. The Eight Balls and the Pyramiders were through the clouds. In all, about a hundred bombers became visible, flying side by side over the foothills. But something was wrong. Bob chewed his lip as he scanned the skies ahead.

"Where's the 376th and 93rd?" Bob said.

Ernie looked for himself. In front of Wood's flight was nothing but the summer haze over the fields. The Liberandos, the Traveling Circus: They were gone.

The two lead groups had vanished into thin air.

CHAPTER 16

THE HAND OF FATE

FORTY-FIVE MINUTES

Over Romania

IN THE COCKPIT OF *CHATTANOOGA CHOO CHOO*, ERNIE FLEW WITH A furrowed brow, his ears filled with the anxious chatter of his gunners, his eyes locked on the plane next to him.

The sky train was dramatically shorter now. Every so often, Ernie glanced forward, straining to see the tails of the lead two groups materialize from the haze ahead, but there'd been no trace of them since the Pindus Range, where they'd flown up and over the clouds.

Ernie's spirits sank. Still nothing. He tightened his grip on the yoke. This wasn't good at all.

It was hotter and hazier at two hundred feet as the remnants of the Ploesti Express pressed east, following the foothills of the Transylvanian Alps. Visibility was down to five miles. After the flight had crossed the Wallachian Plain, the alpine peaks rose off their left wing. Ploesti lay just eighty miles away.

The occasional turbulence only served to tighten the knot in Ernie's chest. Minute after minute passed. The three trailing groups were flying faster, running at higher power settings, engines straining, trying to pick up the trail of the missing lead groups, wherever they were.

But time was running out.

While Ernie flew, Bob peered through the bubble-like blister window at his side, watching the scenery slip by below. It was as if the bombers were flying through a steamy valley in Northern California. He could see farmers checking their crops, keeping a close eye on fields of leafy green plants venting moisture in the heat.

The bombers flew over Mediterranean-style homes, their faded red terra-cotta roofs and whitewashed walls reflecting the afternoon sunlight. Romania felt ancient and unchanged, a lost Roman colony that had somehow survived the fall of the empire.

Some farmers impassively looked to the sky as the three groups motored past. "Others ignored us completely," remembered a pilot.

When the sky train powered over three young women driving a horse-drawn haycart, they leapt from their cart and hit the dirt initially. The girls might not have been sure what side the airplanes were on, but "nevertheless, they smiled and waved."*

Surprised, Bob leaned further into the blister. No one had expected this sort of reaction from the civilians. Romanians were supposed to be the enemy. "Think they know what we're here to do?" he asked, a nervous edge to his voice.

"They will soon enough," Ernie replied, doing his best to hide his trepidation.

It was bravado. Ernie's stomach churned with unease over the missing groups. Tidal Wave hinged on surprise. All five outfits needed to hit their targets simultaneously to catch the enemy napping and overwhelm any defenses. Surprise was their one real advantage. If they could keep it, they just might prove General Brereton wrong when he'd grimly told them, "If not one bomber returns tomorrow . . ." But what if the lead groups got there first? They might have a shot at taking Ploesti by surprise, but the groups behind them, including the 389th, wouldn't be so lucky.

Ernie checked his watch. Time was slipping away. The Liberandos and the Traveling Circus had to be somewhere ahead—but where? Surely they would throttle back so the three remaining groups could catch up. Surely the general wouldn't leave them behind.

BUT HE HAD. TWENTY minutes of flying time ahead, the two lead groups were running radio silent through Romanian airspace, closing in on Ploesti.

* Some crews caught a glimpse of a young woman bathing in a river that flowed from the Alps. It had been a long time alone in the desert for the men of the Ploesti Express, and the bathing beauty almost pulled "the entire outfit off course," a pilot recalled. Other pilots edged their planes closer for a better view. "This is where I bail out!" one crewman was heard to shout. "We thought this was going to be heaven," recalled another.

When the lead groups had gone up and over the cloudbank, a sudden, howling tailwind had hurled them far ahead. Dropping down on the far side of the mountains, the tail gunner of General Ent's flagship, *Teggie Ann,* looked back—and blinked. Then blinked again. No one was behind his group except the Traveling Circus. The sky was empty.

General Ent faced a difficult decision. His splintered force could linger in hostile airspace, waiting for the trailing groups to catch up. But what if enemy fighters intercepted them? They could be shot out of the sky before the remaining groups caught up. Or should he break radio silence to re-form the task force and risk broadcasting their position? If the Germans didn't know the Ploesti Express was in Romania, they would then.

Really, there were no good options. Ent was not about to put the entire mission at risk even if it meant arriving at their target out of order. Besides, the intel boys figured the defenses of Ploesti were questionable. *Remember, they're just Romanians.* These were the guys who would beat the civilians to the air raid shelters.

What the general did next would shape the future for every man in the air. Ent gave the command to his pilot: Press on to the target without them.

ERNIE, BOB, AND THE men in the three trailing groups had yet to realize it, but there would be no catching the missing lead groups, no last-minute reunion in the skies. Thanks to a cloudbank, the whims of nature, "there was now no hope of all five groups striking Ploesti simultaneously."

And fate had more cards to play.

Sergeant Frank Kees, the crew's flight engineer, steadied himself by the seatbacks behind Ernie and Bob and plugged into the intercom. Hailing from Alexandria, Kentucky, Kees was short and strong, with a bulbous nose and the look of a man used to hard work. A trained aircraft mechanic, he was responsible for monitoring the aircraft's vitals and for tackling minor issues in midair. Kees served a big-brotherly role in the eyes of the enlisted men. He was twenty-six, "older and wiser," and kept them "in line." He looked concerned.

"Bad news, Lieutenants," Kees said. "We've already gone through half our fuel."

He had been monitoring the fuel gauges in the radio room. The outer wing tanks were dry. They had also gone through one of the spare tanks in

Frank Kees

the bomb bay. Even if *Chattanooga Choo Choo* turned around now, they wouldn't have enough to make it back to Benghazi.

Ernie, still flying the bomber, was in disbelief.

Bob turned in his seat. "How the hell is that possible, Frank?" Their new B-24D had the extra fuel tanks built into the wings. Range should have been their least concern.

Kees reckoned it was all the jockeying they'd been doing. Flying at the end of the task force meant regularly adjusting the throttles and revving the engines to adjust their spacing in response to the movements of every plane in front of them. But he saw a glimmer of hope: Once they dropped their bombs and burned off some more fuel, they'd be lighter. "Maybe we can pick up some miles?"

It would have to work. Tomorrow was Bob's birthday. He was due to turn twenty-five, and he had every intention of celebrating with a cold beer in Benghazi.

Kees left and returned to his duties.

Bob switched the intercom so only he and Ernie could hear.

"Bet you wish you wrote that 'Just in case'?" Bob said. Neither man smiled. It was gallows humor.

IN THE REAR FUSELAGE of *Chattanooga Choo Choo,* the waist gunners were getting itchy at their windows. Back to back with the other burly crewman, the right waist gunner, Staff Sergeant Phil Rurak, twenty-four, shielded his eyes as he scanned the skies for enemy fighters with his .50 caliber machine gun. Standing five eleven, with the build of a heavyweight fighter, Rurak had a prominent narrow nose, a thin black mustache, and cheerful brown eyes. He hailed from the Polish community in the factory town of Chicopee, Massachusetts, where he worked as a skilled tradesman at the Uniroyal Tire Company and played football in the "industrial leagues," where each factory put up a team. By now, Rurak had been sure Romanian airspace would be swarming with German and Romanian fighters hungry to intercept them. But there was nothing.

"Has the Luftwaffe taken the day off?" one crewman wondered aloud.

"Navigator to crew." Britt's voice crackled on the intercom in Rurak's earphones. "We're coming up on the IP." The IP was the "Initial Point," the aerial staging marker for the attacks. This was where the 389th would leave the Ploesti-bound groups and head farther north to the city of Câmpina, in the valley above Ploesti, while the others continued to the main refinery complex. The gunners and camera operator in the rear of the plane knew what that meant: *fifteen minutes to target.*

Rurak and the others peeled themselves from their windows to prepare for battle. Hurriedly, Rurak picked up his M1 flak vest from the floor. Nobody liked the vests. Newly issued for the raid, they were heavy—twenty-three pounds—and cumbersome. The front and back were filled with steel plates sewn inside nylon, and the apron extended down to the groin. The gunners joked that it made them look like umpires. But the vests were necessary, because the men would soon be flying within range of small-arms fire from the ground.

Rurak slipped his vest over his head and onto his shoulders as if it were a toy. Nearby, the other waist gunner, Sergeant Jack Bowker—twenty-three, burly, thick-chinned, always cracking jokes and peppering his speech with comic-book idioms—and the camera operator, Troy McCrary, were suiting up, too.

Phil Rurak and Jack Bowker

Rurak wasn't a usual member of their crew. He had arrived in Benghazi five days earlier with a few other spare crews of the 389th. His regular crew was too green to fly the mission, but he'd heard that *Pistol Packin' Mama* needed to replace their right waist gunner, who was still battling dysentery. Rurak spoke with Bob and volunteered. Tidal Wave would be his first mission of the war.

Rurak donned his helmet and goggles, then moved to help the camera operator with the fitting of his vest. He was eager to pull his weight in any way he could with the tight-knit crew, even if their duty together would only last one long mission.

BACK IN THE COCKPIT, Bob took his helmet from beneath his seat, put it on, and set his hands on the yoke. Earlier, he and Ernie had decided that Bob would fly the attack run. "It was your ship before it was mine," Ernie said.

Ernie gave a nod and Bob took control of the plane. Ernie shook out his tired arms and put on his helmet. By then the atmosphere inside the bombers had turned serious. The intercom had once been full of men "talking and joking nervously." But as the planes drew closer to Ploesti, one pilot recalled, "the idle chatter died away."

Ernie tightened his chin strap.

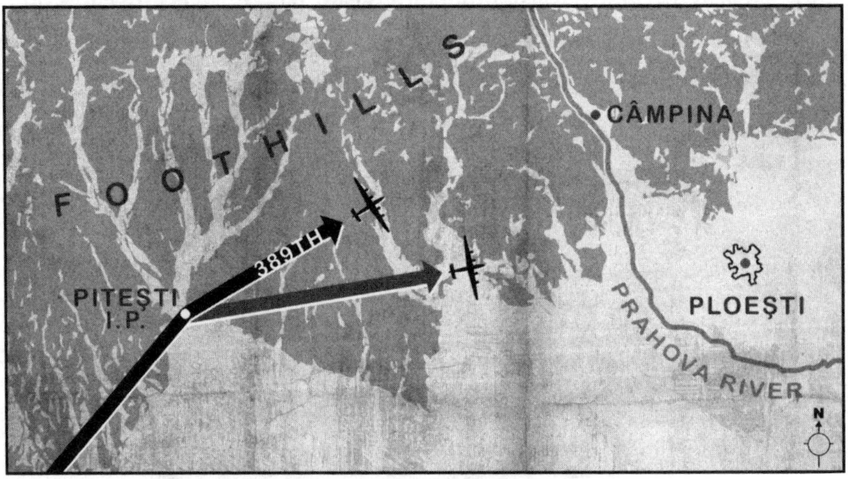

THE 389TH HAD TRAVELED as far as they could with the other groups. From here, the rookie outfit would complete the rest of their mission alone. At 1:55 P.M., Ernie and Bob knew they'd reached the IP when Wood's flight veered slightly left toward the Alps, like a train deviating onto a siding at a station. Bob stuck close to Rodenberg and Matson as they followed their leader. It was time to go find Câmpina. In unison, the 389th split off from the bomber stream while the Pyramiders and Eight Balls pressed straight ahead toward Ploesti.

The fading drone of formations diverging filled the sky. Through his side window, Ernie watched the Ploesti-bound groups become smaller as they followed in the wake of the missing lead groups. After flying east a little longer, they would swing south to make their attack.

Ernie didn't envy them. They were hurrying to get to Ploesti before Tidal Wave kicked off without them. This was never the plan. But the raiders faced their lot with "grim determination."

For many young Americans, including one man from Ernie's own crew, these were the last fifteen minutes of their lives. No one could know it yet—certainly not Ernie, as he watched the Ploesti-bound groups dissolving into the haze. Still, a sense of unease tugged at him, a hint of trouble ahead.

Good luck, Ernie thought. *Godspeed.*

They were going to need it.

All of them.

CHAPTER 17

BENDING THE POPLARS

SOON AFTER

Ten miles northwest of Ploesti

THE CONVERSATION UNFOLDING IN THE ROMANIAN HOMESTEAD WAS anything but ordinary. In the enclosed veranda of a stately hilltop estate, an elegant middle-aged Romanian woman shared lunch with a shy, eleven-year-old blond girl who might easily have been her granddaughter. They were speaking English.

With kind dark-blue eyes and neatly arranged gray hair, the woman carried herself with the quiet poise common to English high society—a refinement she'd cultivated during her childhood in England.

Princess Ecaterina Caradja—"Catherine"

She was Princess Ecaterina Caradja, "a handsome, robust, blue-eyed woman of fifty with a managerial ability equal to that of any man in the kingdom." But to her American and British friends, who had operated the Ploesti refineries before the war, she was simply Catherine.

The princess belonged to one of Romania's oldest and most storied families, whose land holdings stretched across the Ploesti region. In fact, she owned more than a thousand acres of her surroundings, fields rich in oil. It was around 2 P.M. on that leisurely Sunday, and Catherine was teaching the girl English. From the sunlit veranda, they enjoyed a view of the estate's gardens, framed by poplar trees, tall, hedge-like, and narrow against the hazy backdrop of the Alps to the north. The white manor house perched atop a fortress-like fieldstone foundation at the edge of the village of Nedelea.

Their peaceful day of study didn't last. The voices of Catherine and the girl were gradually drowned out by "the most awful roaring noise from outside." The noise grew louder and louder. The princess swore the walls and earth beneath them were shaking. The sound came from the northwest, as if "a dozen trains were bearing down on us," she would later recount.

But they weren't trains. Her cousin was a military pilot for Romania. She knew the sound of aircraft.

Those are low-flying planes.

Just as the thought struck her, three heavy bombers burst into view, skimming the treetops. In a flash of green, they thundered across the estate's grounds in tight formation. Wide wingspans filled the sky, whirling propellers beating the moisture-rich air.

Catherine barely had time to react before another flight of three bombers screamed overhead, chasing the previous flight. They were massive machines with faded green bodies and gray bellies and unusual twin tails. It felt like an invasion.

Her chauffeur burst into the room, pale and trembling. "They're touching the tops of the poplars in the garden!" he cried.

Catherine knew she should have stayed inside, but she was feisty-natured and determined to see this for herself. With the little girl clutching her and her chauffeur trailing behind, she led the way from the enclosed veranda out onto the terrace.

No sooner had they stepped outside when they "were nearly bowled over by air blasts" from another flight of bombers powering past. The ear-shattering snarl of the engines was even louder outdoors. These were the "lowest-flying planes" she'd ever witnessed. Her chauffeur was hardly exaggerating: "The planes were so low that the backwash of their propellers were bending the slender trees," Catherine would recall.

The green bombers kept coming. Wave after wave soared over her estate. The noise of so many engines blended into a singular, unremitting roar. It was terrifying. The little girl was "clinging" to her skirt. The chauffeur wanted to run.

The invasion from above was greater in scope than Catherine could ever have imagined.

When she looked north, she could see a long line of pink-colored bombers a few miles away, skimming the countryside in unnerving, perfect formation. Even an untrained eye could discern that the two strings of bombers were from different outfits. The direction of their flight made it clear. Both formations were cutting a path straight to Ploesti with frightening determination.

But who were they?

When Catherine spotted white stars on their fuselages, her fear surged. They were Russians! she concluded—Romania's archenemies.

The massive machines tearing past her were the planes that had crossed the mountains with the 389th. Ripping over her estate were B-24s from the Eight Balls, and the ones in the distance belonged to the Pyramiders.

Suddenly, the staccato of gunfire erupted from the planes above. The American gunners were testing their machine guns, firing in sporadic bursts, warming them up for the impending battle. Catherine watched in horror as glowing tracer bullets slanted down from the sky and chopped through the tops of her poplars.

"Run!" she cried, seizing the girl by the hand and fleeing in one direction as her chauffeur fled in another. Running from the hail of bullets, Catherine and the girl reached the icehouse behind the estate. They took shelter beneath its concrete roof as bullets continued to rain down.

Then, almost as quickly as it began, the crackle of gunfire ceased. The thunderous drone of engines faded away.

Holding the girl close, Catherine cautiously stepped outside and scanned the skies over her garden. They were empty. She could hear the faint sound of engines receding.

Whoever they were, they were gone.

Surveying the damage to her garden, she realized that not a single shot had touched the manor house. The gunners hadn't been aiming to kill: The trees had been their target. But she was shaken nonetheless. Even a stray bullet could be lethal.

That's what you get for being a nosy spectator!

An ominous, distant booming note struck her ear, like the start of a fireworks show. The princess, with the girl in tow, followed the sounds to the other side of the manor, where they had an unobstructed view toward the plain where Ploesti and its refineries stood. Catherine's brow furrowed with worry. Ten miles away, the Romanian refineries were under attack and some were burning. "We stood and watched the huge columns of black smoke climb into the cloudless sky," she recalled.

Flak shells furiously exploded as bombers, tiny in the distance, flew seemingly every which way around Ploesti, assaulting the ring of refineries. Roaring toward their targets, coming off their targets, the bombers were meeting stiff resistance, being chased by weaving tracers that "looked like a fishing net woven of fiery cords." The fearsome flak zone that the Germans had built—Festung Ploesti—was no rumor. It was real. It had sprung to life. And already, damaged bombers were going down in fireballs.

Set against a backdrop of burning refineries, the scene was a hellscape, "the closest thing to Dante's Inferno anybody has ever seen," a reporter would write.

Princess Catherine lingered, transfixed by the symphony of violence, "the loud explosion of bombs, the duller thud of exploding oil tanks and the hoarse coughing of anti-aircraft cannon."

A human tragedy was unfolding before her eyes, and she had the sinking feeling that the worst was yet to come. The planes that had overflown her estate had yet to join the fray. They were still racing across the sunlit plain toward the distant fighting, desperate to catch up to an attack that had begun without them.

The chaos of August 1, 1943, was just beginning.

CHAPTER 18

RED TARGET

AT THAT SAME TIME
Twenty-two miles north

THE LEAD FLIGHT OF THREE B-24S TURNED HARD IN WEDGE FORMATION and burst into the steamy Prahova Valley, eyes sharp for Câmpina. Another flight of three chased close behind, while the rest of the 389th Bomb Group followed, descending like shadows from the skies above. Every plane remained cloaked in radio silence. One by one, the flights straightened out their wings and began a quick, steady descent toward the valley floor.

The thick valley air clung to the planes. Mist curled around the wings of the B-24s, wisps dissolving in the weak light that filtered through the haze. Everything shimmered with a fuzzy, ethereal glow.

At the bottom of their descent, a hundred feet above the leafy trees, the bombers leveled off. Below them, the Prahova River ran down the center of the valley, guiding them to their target. The navigators had successfully found the valley above Ploesti. Next came the most daring flying of the entire raid. The rookie group set course for a low-level run from the north, where the valley was narrowest: an audacious gamble meant to catch the enemy by surprise.

Inside the cockpit of *Chattanooga Choo Choo,* Bob steadied his grip, holding formation on Rodenberg in *Yours Truly,* while Matson in *Wolf Wagon* flew parallel off their left wing. Ernie braced himself while Bob fought the controls. In the narrow valley the ride grew bumpy. The bombers shook and shimmied in the sky, hitting wake turbulence caused by propwash from the lead planes in the confines of the valley. It wasn't easy to hold a tight formation in the rough air.

Ahead in the lead, Colonel Wood was riding aboard in *The Scorpion,* his flagship, its nose emblazoned with a yellow scorpion clutching a bomb in its tail. Wood's tail gunner must have alerted the colonel that the ships behind them were getting slapped around by propwash. If one plane lost control and caused a midair collision the group's attack could be ruined before it even began. Wood had to do something, quick.

From behind, Ernie and Bob saw *The Scorpion* suddenly surge forward, accelerating away from the pack. Bob swore under his breath, cursing their luck. This wasn't part of the plan. Wood's two wingmen, *Sack-Time Sally* and *Golden Sandstorm,* took the cue and slipped in behind him, assuming a trail formation. Flying single file gave them room to breathe, exactly what they needed as they threaded through the narrow valley.

But there was another problem. The first three ships held their higher power settings, quickly pulling away from everyone else.

Ernie glanced at Bob, who kept a steely focus on Rodenberg's twin tail. What now? Finally, Rodenberg's ship revved harder and gave chase. Bob gunned the throttles and used his rudder to slip in behind the leader. Matson fell in behind Bob.

The wake turbulence dropped off, but a new problem surfaced. A sizeable gap had opened, a mile at least, between them and the colonel, and another mile stretched between their flight and the bulk of the 389th behind them. And Wood showed no sign of slowing down. That wasn't good, Ernie thought.

The first six planes would be hitting Red Target ahead of the pack.

INSIDE THE NOSE OF *Chattanooga Choo Choo,* Britt and Al had donned their flak vests. Al fastened his helmet and crouched behind his bombsight, the two-foot aluminum stick with a small compass set on top. Britt looked around for his helmet, then remembered he'd tossed it over Yugoslavia. *Dang it!*

Britt clutched his .50 caliber machine gun, its barrel protruding from the left side window.

Outside, small settlements clung to terraced hillsides, blurring past at eye level. Mediterranean-style homes snapped into view, their red terra-cotta roofs lending a "typically romantic" charm to the landscape, in Britt's opinion. With about twelve miles to go, there was no more navigating to do.

In the cockpit above, Ernie and Bob strained to see ahead, but the haze limited their visibility to about five miles. The air became hotter, thicker. Condensation formed and ran down over the windscreen.

Mercifully, as they neared the target, the haze thinned. The valley opened up around them, allowing shafts of sunlight to sneak through. Lush farmland began to slip beneath their wings, revealing fields of corn and sunflowers. No two fields were shaped alike. Ernie and Bob could see a small city and industrial zone taking shape ahead. It looked just like the model they'd viewed back in the theater in the desert. Near the mouth of the valley, left of the Prahova River, stood Romania's most modern refinery, Steaua Română.

"Target in sight!" Al called, giving the bearing—one-seven-zero degrees.

Ahead lay a tangled mass of pipelines, vertical fractioning towers, and storage tanks—an industrial beast cranked up to high velocity for Hitler's war machine. Day and night, the refinery boiled raw crude, distilled it into fuel, and concocted the 100-octane "good stuff" that powered the Luftwaffe's reign of terror over Europe. At the heart of the complex, four brick smokestacks stood like sentinels, each nearly two hundred feet tall and emitting a steady spurt of white smoke. Encircling the refinery like a parapet, strong concrete firewalls stood as barriers, and Steaua Română's upper surfaces were painted in camouflage.

In contrast, the cheerful red roofs of Câmpina stretched between the bombers and the refinery. The 389th needed to be highly precise in their bombing run to avoid the town.

It was time to get down on the carpet.

Colonel Wood led them lower. Almost in unison, the six planes dipped down to a height just above the crops. At two hundred miles per hour, the racket inside *Chattanooga Choo Choo* made communication impossible without the intercom. The speed felt dizzying. The bomber raced past haystacks that "reflected the bright sunlight." Outside Ernie's window, the propellers whirled like buzzsaws. It was the lowest they'd ever flown. A waist gunner recalled, "We were so low you could pick an ear of corn off the stalk." Bob stayed tight on Rodenberg, whose whirling props kicked up a storm of vegetation from the fields.

Ahead of them, Wood made small corrections, lining up their attack run like a torpedo aimed at a battleship.

Ernie glanced at his watch. It was nearly 2:15 P.M. Some twenty miles to the south, the lead groups were surely attacking Ploesti by now. Yet here, no flak marred the sky. No enemy fighters were waiting to pounce. The Americans were almost on the doorstep of Câmpina, and not a single shot had been fired. *So far, so good,* Ernie thought.

One pilot recalled, "Maybe we were actually going to get away with a surprise?" But Ernie knew better than to get his hopes up like that. If the men of the 389th could see the target, the enemy could see them.

IT WAS MARKET DAY in Câmpina, an opulent Victorian-era-looking town of wrought-iron lampposts, stately cafés, and eight thousand residents. Beneath colorful awnings, people shopped at stalls and carts, "attended by women in embroidered skirts and old men in white tunics." Voices mingled with the scent of fresh produce and bread, cured meat, and cheese.

Suddenly the bleat of an air raid siren knifed through the air. Bewildered, unfamiliar with air raids and unsure what to do, the city's residents looked at one another. There had never been an air raid on Câmpina, or even a practice test.

Between the bleats of the siren, a deep bass note caught their ears, something heavy and ominous, a sound that didn't belong in the air, "an unnatural noise," remembered one man, "growing in a frightening proportion."

Motors were approaching from the sky.

Run!

The civilians began scattering.

IN THE DRY RIVERBED next to Steaua Română, German flak gunners picked up the sounds. Stationed at batteries of 20mm and 37mm guns, one by one the soldiers in pale blue shirts and tropical shorts turned and looked north.

Each spring, the Prahova River would be swollen with runoff from the Alps, but at the height of summer, the river was reduced to a trickle. Vast stretches of its gravelly riverbed revealed themselves, pebbles, sand, and stone creating a protected sunken alleyway. The Germans had concentrated most of their fifteen fast-firing guns in the dry riverbed. Contrary to Allied intelligence, which had barely noted their presence, 80 percent of the antiaircraft crews at Ploesti were, in fact, German.

No strangers to combat, these were seasoned Luftwaffe flak crews from the Ruhr Valley. But even Germany's best weren't expecting what they saw next.

Eyes went wide.

Six American bombers were "hurtling down the valley," racing so low over the fields their "propellers threw up chopped leaves like lawn mowers." And more bombers were emerging from the haze behind them. The planes were barreling straight toward Câmpina, to the refinery they were tasked to defend.

As if on cue, the Germans realized that their guns were pointing the wrong way—south, toward Ploesti, where they had assumed any attack would come from.

At once they sprang into action, scrambling to swivel their fast-firing guns to face north. They had planned for every contingency in their defense of Steaua Română. At least, so they thought. But a low-level attack in broad daylight? This was something they'd never imagined.

Each gunner settled into his seat behind an armor shield. Two loaders took their places on either side of him, ready with their box magazines full of shells. Another member of each crew peered through a rangefinder scope, screaming out the attackers' elevation.

The word from the battery sergeant was brief and sharp, edged with the slang for bombers: "Möbeltransporter, kommen schnell!"

Furniture vans, coming fast!

But these guns had limited range. The Romanians on the hillside east of the refinery had the big guns and were supposed to form the core of the refinery's defense.

The Germans turned toward their Romanian counterparts in disbelief.

Why aren't they firing!?

UP ON THE HILLSIDE pasture overlooking the refinery, the battery of Romanian flak gunners of the 5th Anti-Aircraft Artillery Brigade were struggling to catch up. They, too, were expecting an attack from Ploesti and had their six German-built 88mm guns pointed the wrong way.

Officers barked orders as the panicked crews swung the big unwieldy 88s around in the direction of the bombers. The soldiers in the pale blue uniforms and dark steel ducktail helmets of the Royal Romanian Air Force shot worried glances toward the incoming planes, but no one was running to beat the civilians to the air raid shelters. For once, they had a common interest with the Germans: Protect Romania from falling bombs.

Their 88s were, indeed, the refinery's strongest line of defense, a dreaded weapon capable of cutting through the skies with deadly precision. Each 88 could hurl a 20-pound shell more than six miles straight up. The warhead would explode with such force that even a near miss could toss a heavy bomber fifty feet off course. Already the bombers were well within range.

The gunners spun handwheels to depress their guns, while loaders formed a line to shuttle shells into the breech. But when they attempted to target the low-flying planes, the gunners were thwarted: The 88s' muzzles stopped at the level of the horizon, too high for the Romanians to get a shot. Before the fight had even begun, the Romanians were out of it.

Their only hope now was their German "protectors."

ON THE OUTSKIRTS OF Câmpina, the bombers in front of Ernie and Bob began rising to rooftop height for the attack run across the city. Bob inched *Chattanooga Choo Choo* higher. The roofs of Câmpina began slipping by below. Nerves taut, pilots prepared their crews. "Gunners, keep your eyes open for fighters and ack-ack batteries!" said one. "Don't shoot civilians unless they are throwing bottles at us!"

Without warning, bursts of sporadic "orange blips" flickered on both sides of the refinery, isolated at first, then multiplying like wildfire. The realization of what the blips were gave the pilots a cold chill: "That was us looking down the barrels of the guns as they fired at us." The German flak defenses were awakening.

Near the orange blips, glowing orbs began to stream upward, like water shooting from a hose. Tracers. Ernie and Bob watched, transfixed, as the glowing projectiles climbed in their direction, each stream full of 20mm antiaircraft shells designed to explode on contact. The orbs moved slowly at first, then faster, with deadly intent. At the last second they appeared to speed up. *Zip! Zip! Zip!* The orbs whizzed by the ships ahead before flashing past *Chattanooga Choo Choo*. Ernie and Bob both flinched. Hot damn!

Ernie grabbed the yoke, ready to take over in an instant if Bob was hit. Tracers kept whizzing past them. The heaviest fire came from the riverbed to their front-right. The bombers in front of *Chattanooga Choo Choo* began weaving with their rudders to dodge the shells without leaving formation. Bob mirrored their maneuvers. Flying single file, the B-24s were sleek, elusive, harder to hit. But the flak gunners were learning.

Ernie found himself instinctively leaning side to side as shells sliced past the windows. The bulk of the ground fire was aimed at Wood's lead ship, but any random shot could be lethal. "Lead, they're shooting at us!" one wingman was famously said to have called. His leader's reply was darkly reassuring: "That's okay, they're allowed to do that."

The most frustrating part? The Americans were under strict orders not to fire anywhere near Steaua Română until Wood's flight had dropped their bombs. It was strategic. A stray bullet from a B-24 gunner might hit an oil storage tank or a railcar full of fuel and start a fire whose smoke could blind the colonel's plane on approach and throw off the whole attack. But tactical soundness didn't make the order well liked.

"You can't fight back," wrote one blunt gunner in his diary. "Drives you crazy."

All Ernie could do was tense his shoulders and take the abuse.

AHEAD IN THE LEAD, Wood's ship, *The Scorpion,* roared over the market square of Câmpina. His wingmen, *Sack-Time Sally* and *Golden Sandstorm,* followed closely. With their wide wings and snarling engines, the bombers seemed less like machines and more like predators making a ravenous dash across the city. They lunged toward their target, as if daring anyone to try to stop them.

Standing behind the pilots, Colonel Wood gripped the seatbacks, bracing himself against the storm of flak ahead. At the controls sat Captain Kenneth Caldwell, twenty-eight, who'd already logged a decade in uniform. With his square-jawed resolve, steady dark eyes, and slim mustache, the Kansas native might have stepped straight out of the Old West, the gunslinger Doc Holliday reborn.

Pandemonium ensued in the market square below as Wood's ship soared over the civilians. Romanian parents searched frantically for their children, their voices swallowed by the roar of engines. Civilians sprinted for their lives, "running in all directions desperately seeking shelter, bewildered, not knowing from whom." One American pilot observed, "Farm couples down in the streets fall on their knees to pray. Kids toss rocks at us. Horses bolt, overturning wagons full of families."

To the future Romanian journalist Valeriu Râpeanu, who was twelve at the time of the attack, seeing American bombers overhead, flying "so low that I could discern the faces of those inside," was like experiencing "moments of apocalypse."

At the end of the city lay the refinery. Wood's flight was almost upon their target. But as they prepared to unleash their bombs, a spray of small green glowing bolts suddenly spat from the refinery toward their B-24s. Ahead on a rooftop in the complex, German machine-gun crews were crouched behind sandbags, firing their MG-42s. Known as "Hitler's buzz saw," the MG-42 fired at a ferocious rate of twenty shells per second. Their sights were set on Wood's ship.

Inside *The Scorpion,* the colonel clutched the seatbacks behind his pilots, "helplessly looking" at the rooftop guns as the green bolts sliced the air around them. He could only watch, powerless, until something clicked in his memory.

The nose gun!

The Scorpion—alone—could fight back. They had the Eglin boys' special modification: the forward-fixed .50 caliber machine gun set in the nose to suppress flak positions.

Only the colonel could give the order to shoot in the direction of the refinery, and only if he deemed the action urgently necessary. This was urgently necessary.

Wood voiced the command. His pilot, Caldwell, lifted the bomber's nose slightly. The copilot flicked a toggle switch on the yoke in front, triggering the gun.

Two could play at this game.

The machine gun came to life, sending a fiery stream of bullets back at the enemy gunners. Caldwell kicked the rudders, rocking the bomber's tail to rake the rooftops. Sandbags shredded. Bodies folded. The firestorm carved through them in an instant. This section of the enemy was decimated, out of the fight, like the Romanian 88s.

The lead ships bore down on their target. It was too late for the German gunners. Nothing could stop what came next.

At the last instant, Wood's wingmen fanned out to attack their designated portions of the six-hundred-yard-wide refinery. One swung left, the other right, while Wood ran straight up the gut.

From a mile behind, Ernie watched as Wood's flight released their bomb, the payload tumbling swiftly to the refinery below. The three lead B-24s soared up and over the refinery complex, drawing the enemy fire away with them. Wood's flight had made it—barely scratched.

While Bob kept his eyes fixed on the twin tails of Rodenberg's ship, Ernie squinted, looking beyond, in the direction of the refinery, searching for a sign of impact. From their distance, it was hard to tell whether the lead ships had hit the target or missed it altogether. The bombs' delayed-action fuses were set so the last planes over the target wouldn't get caught in the blasts. They weren't supposed to detonate for a whopping forty minutes. But the planners hadn't accounted for one crucial fact about oil—its volatility. One spark was all it took.

Kaboom!

A building inside the refinery complex erupted in a blinding flash. Windows shattered. Brick walls buckled and blew apart. Fire leapt skyward, flickering an evil eye.

Ernie and Bob reeled back in their seats. They hadn't been expecting this. Even the enemy gunners in the dry riverbed stopped firing momentarily. Then—

Kaboom! Kaboom! Kaboom! Kaboom! Explosions began erupting wherever bombs had landed. A roof ruptured, "flinging up a fountain of debris." Flames launched from smokestacks. Fires were spreading across the complex, and still, not a single bomb had detonated.

Only later would Ernie and Bob learn that the 9th Air Force planners had overlooked the crucial fact that in an oil refinery, everything is combustible. If you send five tons of cast-iron bombs skidding through the inner workings of a complex full of petroleum products, they'll shatter pipes and holding tanks and release vaporized aviation fuel. Add friction, sparks, and ruptured furnaces. The bombs didn't even need to detonate.

Steaua Română did the job for them.

As the debris slowly began to settle, vast oil fires raged across the complex, fed by thousands of gallons of burning fuel. Rolls of black smoke boiled upward, obscuring smokestacks and the heights of the buildings. One pilot behind them recalled, "Explosive flames were leaping high above the level of their formation."

Ernie was horrorstruck. Were they supposed to fly through that?

As if on cue, the enemy ground fire resumed. Bullets whizzed past *Chattanooga Choo Choo.* This time, the tracers streaked horizontally across their view, coming from their right as the bombers paralleled the riverbed. The German gunners were still in the fight.

From his top turret, Riffle had his twin guns trained on the enemy. He shouted over the intercom, "Can we shoot?"

"Of course!" Bob barked. The lead planes were already well past the target.

"All gunners, you are clear to fire!" Ernie called. "Suppress that flak." Then, the awareness hit him. Ernie glanced up at the glass ceiling directly above and cursed. Riffle's muzzles were over his head—again. He'd forgotten the earplugs.

Riffle cut loose with his twin .50s. Flashes hammered the cockpit with sound and light. Ernie clenched his jaw. What else could he do? As they ran the gauntlet, every available gun on *Chattanooga Choo Choo* fired back at the riverbed. Rodenberg's gunners were doing the same in front. Matson's lit them up from behind. It was chaos. The bomber's frame shook around Ernie from the recoil of the guns. The sharp smell of cordite choked the air. Dust from Benghazi, loosened by the pounding, filtered down from the ceiling, making it harder for Ernie and Bob to see.

Caged in the nose clutching his machine gun, Britt had never felt more vulnerable. Tracers ripped toward him from a "small wooded area" east of the refinery, but he couldn't pinpoint the source. The glowing shells appeared to be coming straight at him. But at the last second they arced and buzzed over and under the plane.

One 389th gunner remembered his reaction when a "ball of fire" came at him: "I jumped back, thinking I was going to get it in the nose!"

Anything was better than being a "sitting duck," so Britt squeezed his trigger lever and fired back, sending his own glowing rounds into the clump of forest.

Looking down into Romanian backyards, one waist gunner saw a man dart onto his lawn, shotgun at his shoulder, ready to fire. To the gunner it looked as if they'd just "interrupted his Sunday dinner." What happened next "resembled a guy shooting skeet," recalled the gunner. "He just kind of looked for one of the targets to take a shot at and did shoot at it." The American gunner didn't have the heart to shoot back.

RODENBERG, MATSON, AND ERNIE and Bob still had a job to do, to ensure that the Germans, for all their industrial might, could never revive Romania's most modern refinery. Fires could be quelled, machinery replaced. They needed Red Target struck beyond all repair.

More than halfway across Câmpina, Rodenberg signaled with a wag of his tails: *Spread out!* Matson, behind Ernie and Bob, swept out 150 yards to the left, while Rodenberg held his course straight ahead. Bob was supposed to head right to attack their designated portion of the refinery, but he hesitated. Spreading out into the preplanned attack formation would put his crew directly in the line of fire. That was where all the enemy guns were!

"Go right, Bob!" Al demanded. It was his job to direct the bomb run. "Right! Right!"

Bob snapped out of his hesitation and edged the plane to the right.

"More!" Bambino commanded.

Bob slipped the B-24 hard to the right before leveling out, still over the city. The bomber raced along the river, flying parallel to the enemy gunners, unwillingly presenting the plane as their nearest prime target.

In the riverbed, the German battery sergeants screamed and pointed. Flustered gunners swung their guns, firing as they tracked the low-flying bomber. Loaders shoved fresh magazines into the breeches. Every gunner was desperately trying to set his ring sights on the B-24 with the smiling boxcar on its nose. A dozen explosive shells per second blasted from each 20mm gun's four barrels, sending a waterfall of empty casings down a central spout.

Noise in the riverbed reached a terrible, cacophonic climax. Every gun blazed. Gunners stood hard on their foot-activated triggers. If the Germans could just land a shot in the cockpit of the American bomber, they could deliver the death blow.

Chattanooga Choo Choo immediately began taking hits.

Thunk! Thunk! Thunk!

In his turret, Riffle was returning fire when he heard it—a sudden jarring banging sound behind him. He glanced back toward the tail section, and nearly fell out of his seat. Jagged holes were appearing on the plane's roof. The bomber was being punctured—but not from the outside. The punctures came from the inside, like someone trapped in the plane was trying to hack their way out with an ice pick. Multiple 20mm shells were exploding inside the bomb bay. What Riffle saw was their shrapnel exiting the ceiling.

On the roof behind the bomb bay was a teardrop-shaped dome that housed the antenna for their radio compass. A shell blasted off a chunk of it, right in front of Riffle's eyes. He triggered the intercom in a panic. "We're getting clobbered here!"

Ernie didn't need to be told they were drawing all the 20mm fire from the riverbed. He could tell by the sound and feel of the thuds of the shells. *Chattanooga Choo Choo* was being pummeled. As a fellow pilot described it, first you'd hear "chunk!" as the shell entered, "then the explosion with a big 'blam!' and the rattle of the pieces of the 20mm shell as they flew."

Ernie ducked his neck into his shoulders, trying to become as small as possible. The bomber was a flying gas can. One tracer in the right place and—poof!

"Chunk! Blam!"

Where are we hit? he thought. *How bad?*

"Chunk! Blam!"

When will I get it?

"Chunk! Blam!" A 20mm shell exploded at the edge of the radio room behind Ernie, throwing sparks and flinging shrapnel. He felt a punch under his left armpit and a kick in his right ankle. He'd been hit by shrapnel.

Ernie probed under his armpit for the wound and felt a sting like a jab from a needle. The smell of burnt gunpowder hung in the air. A small piece of shrapnel had passed through the soft muscle under his arm. Fortunately, his armored seatback had shielded him from most of the spraying metal fragments. It only winged him.

"You okay?" Bob shouted.

"I'm fine!" Ernie fired back. He glanced out his side window, his gaze dropping to the guns that had wounded him—only to be met by a terrifying sight.

He could see into the eyes of the men firing at them.

IN THE REAR OF the plane, Rurak, the heavyweight gunner with a small mustache, stood tall at his window, firing down at the flak positions.

Behind the wing a man could barely hear himself think with the noise of the engines "grinding in your ears." Yet, Rurak could see and "plainly hear" the flak guns shooting back at them. Suddenly, a string of blazing tracers punched through the fuselage to his left, slicing through the waist of the bomber before ripping out the other side, fortunately without exploding.

Rurak recovered from the close call and returned to his window in time to see a 20mm gun emplacement sliding past the plane, perhaps the same that had just shot them. The gun was "really pouring it out," belching flame and smoke from its four barrels. Most of the German gun crew were concealed behind armored shields, but two loaders were exposed. Rurak swung his gun in their direction and fired hard. His gun bucked. The enemy gun fell silent.

When Rurak let off the trigger, and the steam cleared his muzzle, he observed the results. The two German loaders? His .50 caliber had torn them apart. It was as if they'd evaporated.

NOTHING SEPARATED *CHATTANOOGA CHOO CHOO* from the inferno now. A blazing mass of mangled pipelines, towers, and smokestacks was filling their windscreen. And they were on course to run right into it.

"Move to climb power setting!" Bob called.

Ernie fought through the pain under his arm, adjusting fuel mixtures and prop pitches. Then he shoved all four throttles forward. Everything was happening so fast he was operating on instinct. The 1300-horsepower engines surged. Ernie felt the change in power through his metal seat and rudder pedals. The bomber roared forward.

Over the intercom, Al reported that he had opened the bomb bay. Outside, the two roller-style bomb bay doors opened outward and slid flush with the plane. Ernie tensed. They were on the bomb run now. Just one mile to go. Amid the blaze ahead, he could see their target building: the cracking plant, a narrow four-story brick building with cylindrical metal towers behind it. Inside, crude oil was broken down—cracked—to extract gasoline. They were at eye level with the cracking plant. There was only one problem.

It was already on fire.

Black smoke billowed from gaping holes in the roof. Flames leapt higher than the bomber flew, twisting and curling into the sky. And Bob was still steering straight at the target. Both his hands stayed put, white knuckled, on the yoke.

Every instinct screamed at Ernie: *Pull up!* As tempting as it was to take the controls, he held himself back.

In his headset, Ernie could hear Al's disembodied voice directing Bob on the bomb run. Ernie gritted his teeth and tucked his chin. They were playing chicken with a brick building. This was going to be close.

When the blazing refinery had almost filled the windscreen, the flight leader made his move. It was as if he had heard Ernie's desperate thoughts. Rodenberg lifted his plane's nose—barely—and started to climb.

Ernie felt the plane rise as Bob finally eased back on the yoke, guiding the bomber into an upward climb, just enough to clear the leaping flames. B-24s didn't like sudden moves; if you yanked too hard, the force would rip your wings off.

Britt steadied himself in the nose, bracing against his gun with one hand. The cityscape below was coming to an end. He was too close to the target to have any more chances at the flak gunners. To his right, Al crouched behind his bombsight, holding a photo of their target building as he directed the bomb run.

Britt locked eyes on Rodenberg's plane, flying ahead and to the left. Rodenberg was climbing higher than them; he had farther to go to clear the smokestacks over his target, the powerhouse for the complex. *Yours Truly*'s bomb bay was open, four yellow bombs poised and waiting. Britt flicked his gaze back to the ground, gauging the distance. The city blocks came to an end below Rodenberg's ship. Only a stretch of railroad track stood between them and the blazing refinery. Rodenberg released his payload. Britt's eyes tracked one bomb as it glided down toward the refinery's powerhouse, falling in slow motion as if "gently lowered by some invisible arms."

At the last second, Rodenberg's B-24 pulled sharply up and out of sight. Below, the bomb tore through a set of powerlines, snapping them like threads before punching into the powerhouse and disappearing inside. The torn lines thrashed and threw "blue-white" sparks onto the ground.

All around Ernie, the bomber began quaking. The air became choppy. A wave of heat from the nearby fires hit the approaching planes. *Chattanooga Choo Choo* pitched and rocked, but Bob quickly regained control.

It was time.

About a football field's length from the complex, Al feverishly pressed a clicker to release *Chattanooga Choo Choo*'s payload. *Click, click, click.* The bomber leapt for joy as it released its heavy payload. "Bombs away!" Al shouted over the intercom.

Through the windscreen, Ernie and Bob stared ahead at a blood-curdling sight. An inferno was reaching up from the cracking plant, jaws wide open for the bomber with the smiling boxcar on its nose.

One thought gripped them both: *Climb!*

Bob pulled back on the yoke. In one swift motion, the bomber threw back its head, and the cracking plant dropped from view. G-forces pushed Ernie back in his seat as *Chattanooga Choo Choo* rocketed upward, freed of the weight of its bombs. Ahead, a wall of black smoke stretched across the immediate horizon. Bob couldn't veer to avoid it, not with smokestacks on the left and enemy gunners on the right. There was only one way forward: straight through.

Ernie drew a sharp breath before the sooty black cloud swallowed them. The cockpit plunged into darkness. Bob held his course. The plane became an oven as they flew over the heart of the refinery. Heat poured from the burning complex below, lifting and jostling the bomber. Through the yoke, Ernie could feel Bob fighting the currents, straining to keep the wings level. Ernie's nostrils stung from burning oil.

Somewhere to the left of them stood a two-hundred-foot stack that towered higher than they were flying. Ernie had lost sight of it in the smoke. He shot a glance out Bob's window. *Where was it?* Clip it with a wingtip, and the last thing they'd feel would be the bomber wheeling violently before it cartwheeled into the flaming refinery. Would they clear it?

For a split-second longer they flew blind. Ernie held his breath. *Chattanooga Choo Choo* punched free of the smoke and emerged into the sunlight on the other side. Two hundred and fifty feet below them was a series of narrow, low warehouses. They had made it. They had survived the bomb run.

Behind the three-ship of B-24s, their bombs came crashing down. The firewalls around the refinery didn't stand a chance. Yellow thousand-pounders crashed like wrecking balls through the concrete and kept going, plowing through brick walls and disappearing into the core of the refinery like "rats, gnawing through building after building to find a better place to rest." Cavernous fifteen-foot holes appeared in the brickwork.

One of Matson's bombs drilled a hole through the highest smokestack. Another bomb that fell short would be seen careening "down a narrow city street from side to side" during its commute to the target. Some bombs hurtled through the complex and out the other side, missing a point of impact altogether. Each bomb that landed stoked the fires raging in the complex. "It was like stirring up a bee's nest."

A rearward-facing view of Steaua Română during the attack

COMING OFF THE TARGET, Ernie, Bob, and the crew were not out of danger yet. Flak guns were still firing, and even if the ground fire didn't feel as threatening on the other side of the target, *Chattanooga Choo Choo* was still vulnerable. Everyone felt the overwhelming desire to get as far from Steaua Română as possible.

Bob shoved the nose forward. The plane plunged. The crew felt the floor fall out beneath them. Ernie's stomach floated. Then, with a smooth pull on the yoke, Bob brought them level, skimming just above the warehouses.

As they made their furious escape from the target, Ernie could see Rodenberg's ship a good distance ahead. Medeiros reported that Maston's ship was back behind their left wing, also flying down on the deck. The news came as a relief for Ernie and Bob. Everyone had survived.

Quickly the refinery grounds were behind them, and neighborhoods began passing beneath the bombers. All signs pointed to a successful attack, judging by the smoke billowing from the refinery behind them.

But just when *Chattanooga Choo Choo* seemed safely beyond the enemy's reach, a burst of green tracers zipped toward the bomber from their left and cut past the nose. A German gun crew at the foot of the hills was still tracking them. Ernie looked left, straining to see them through Bob's side window. *Of all times, not now!*

More shells ripped through the air, first from the side, then from slightly behind the wing. The persistent gun crew was chasing them. Nipping at them. *Bam! Bam!* Ernie felt the bomber take hits in the fuselage somewhere below his feet and on the left wing. The enemy wasn't giving up.

Bob spotted the perpetrators. "Port side—eight o'clock! Bowker, Medeiros, get him!"

In the tail, Medeiros swung his backward-facing turret to his right just in time to spot the gun "drift away" from him. His twin .50s had been silent the entire attack, but not anymore. Medeiros fired a good burst of "45–50 rounds" at the emplacement.

The enemy fire instantly stopped. The gun crew was either dead or scared senseless. No further shells came at the bomber.

Soon the noise of the imploding refinery fell away. Ernie turned his attention forward again. Ahead lay Romanian farmland, calm and serene. But Ernie's thoughts weren't on the landscape.

Let's get the heck out of here.

CHAPTER 19

EVERY TRICK IN THE BOOK

MOMENTS LATER
South of Câmpina

THEY RAN FROM RED TARGET LIKE MEN WHO'D CHEATED DEATH.

Below, the blur of sunlit farmland raced past, just a hundred feet beneath the wings of *Chattanooga Choo Choo* as Bob followed the Prahova River out of the valley with the rest of their flight. With every passing mile, Ernie felt relief. Each second carried them farther away from Steaua Română.

Wolf Wagon pulled up off their left wing, a welcome companion for the ride home. All that remained was for the wingmen to re-form on Rodenberg, who was a couple of hundred yards ahead. Ernie was amazed that everyone in their flight had made it. In the cockpit of *Wolf Wagon,* Matson's copilot glanced over at *Chattanooga Choo Choo* and grinned. It felt as if they were making their getaway from a heist.

As they raced from the valley, the pair of bombers soared past wooden oil derricks scattered across the fields, each drawing black gold from the ground. Whatever was left of their precious oil industry, the Romanians could have it. Ernie felt a surge of elation. They'd done it. The 389th's daring attack had paid off, and he'd managed to keep his vow from Benghazi: *If only one plane comes back, we'll be on it.*

Medeiros cut in on the intercom from the tail. "Airplane going in, starboard, five o'clock!"

Ernie twisted in his seat, looking back from the blister in his side window. Behind, a B-24 peeled off from Red Target, flames engulfing its left wing. The pilots fought to put the bomber down in a field on the other side of the Prahova River, but the burning wing suddenly folded. The plane hit the ground and cartwheeled in a rolling ball of smoke and flame.

Ernie reeled back, the shock hitting him like a physical blow. The sight was jarring. He was still in disbelief, unable to accept that he had likely just watched ten men die.

IN THE TOP TURRET of *Chattanooga Choo Choo,* Riffle kept his guns trained backward, eyes fixed on the fiery crash. But something felt off. He was the first to sense something was wrong with their bomber. *Chattanooga Choo Choo* "was acting funny." Riffle looked to Bob's side of the plane. Smoke drifted from the outboard engine. It must have been from the hits they took from that last persistent gun. With his left shin covered in dried blood, Riffle hurriedly limped forward into the cockpit and steadied himself by the pilots' seatbacks. He'd been hit by shrapnel during the attack, maybe from the same 20mm shell that winged Ernie, and his leg was riddled with small holes.

Ernie lifted his earphone. "You okay?" Almost simultaneously, Ernie felt vibrations in the controls. Something was wrong.

Riffle had bigger worries than his own wounds. Leaning in, he shouted in Ernie's ear: "There's a fire in the number one engine!"

Ernie shot a glance out Bob's side window. Sure enough, the outboard engine was burning. His eyes snapped back to the controls. The needles in the instruments for the number 1 engine flickered.

Bob wasted no time in ordering that the engine be shut down.

Ernie cut the fuel flow and throttle, then feathered the propellers, rotating the blades forward like a knife edge to create less drag. The men felt a noticeable deceleration when the burning engine coughed to a stop. Bob shoved the other throttles further forward, determined to keep pace with *Wolf Wagon.* But engine number 1 was still burning, fueled by air rushing through it.

A flurry of thoughts raced through Ernie's mind. *Can we stay with our formation on three engines? How bad are we crippled?* There was always the possibility that the fire might go out on its own. Ernie hoped for the best, but the options were thinning. Ploesti lay about fifteen miles away, too far for Ernie to see the planes of the other American groups, but near enough to see the smoke rising from the destroyed refinery. They couldn't go there.

Britt came on the intercom. "We're coming up on the waypoint, Bob."

It was time to turn. After striking their targets, the plan was for all the ships of the 389th to make a 20-degree turn west to avoid overflying Ploesti.

Then the flights would reform and fly home together. Rodenberg's *Yours Truly* began banking right. *Chattanooga Choo Choo* and *Wolf Wagon* were to follow. Bob turned his control yoke, but the bomber didn't respond.

"Try yours," he barked at Ernie.

Ernie tried. "Ailerons inoperative!" The controls hung slack.

Bob glanced out his side window and cursed. Matson's plane was about to turn in their direction, but they were stuck flying straight ahead.

A cold weight settled in Ernie's gut. The controls were damaged, either partially severed or entirely destroyed, probably by any number of earlier flak hits. *Chattanooga Choo Choo* wouldn't turn.

Through Bob's side window, Ernie and Bob watched in horror as the big green bomber next to them dipped its right wing and began sliding in their direction. Ernie and Bob couldn't look away. No one would be walking away from a midair collision at an altitude of a hundred feet. Ernie could see the crewman in the top turret of Matson's plane and the pilots in the cockpit. The bomber slipped closer. When the whirling propellers of *Wolf Wagon* were about to come through Bob's window, Ernie ducked his neck into his shoulders, clenched his eyes, and braced for impact.

But instead of a furious crash, he heard the drone of Matson's engines beneath them and felt a sudden lift from the displacement of air caused by another large object passing dangerously close. Ernie pried his eyes open and glanced out his side window just as *Wolf Wagon* slid out from underneath them and appeared off their right wing. Ernie stared, astonished. Matson's copilot must have seen the impending catastrophe and forced their bomber lower at the last moment. *Wolf Wagon* rose to eye level with their cockpit. Matson, visibly shaken, looked over at the other plane for explanation.

Ernie gestured frantically to say: "Our controls are out."

Matson nodded and glanced to the right where Rodenberg was pulling away. *Wolf Wagon* couldn't stay with *Chattanooga Choo Choo.* Matson's crew needed to get back in formation if they had any hope of making it home. The decision had already been made for them. Matson gave a somber salute, then banked away to catch up with Rodenberg.

THERE WAS NO TIME for self-pity. They were flying for themselves now. Ernie and Bob assessed their situation. They had a smoldering engine. Their

B-24 wouldn't turn. And they were heading straight for Ploesti, to a refinery complex the other groups had just bombed.

Both men forced themselves to stay calm. As a 389th pilot once said, "Panic may be the equivalent of suicide." There was only one choice. Bob spoke the fated words first.

"We have to put her down."

Ernie felt sick. No pilot wanted to hear those words. *Chattanooga Choo Choo* was flying about ten stories above the terrain. But the crew was lucky. They were still over the dry riverbed of the Prahova, several football fields wide and covered in gravel. It was as good a place as any to go down.

"Crash procedures?" Ernie asked.

Bob nodded somberly.

"Prepare for forced landing!" Ernie called to the crew. "Navigator, bombardier, clear the nose!"

In the rear of the bomber, the waist gunners and camera operator scrambled into crash positions. But as Rurak sprawled out on the wooden floor, he caught sight of a yellow object wedged in the bomb bay. Oh, no! One of the thousand-pound bombs was still in its racks, hanging by its tail. Shrapnel must have jammed the release mechanism. If the plane crashed with the bomb aboard, it would explode and kill them all.

Rurak had already unplugged from the plane's intercom, so he drew the attention of the other waist gunner, Bowker, who was still connected. Bowker, in turn, alerted the one man whose job it was to fix a problem such as this. "Lieutenant Romano! We've got a hung up bomb still in the racks!"

In the nose, Al and Britt were tearing off their flak jackets when Bowker's message crackled through. Al flew into action. He flipped a switch to open the bomb bay, yanked a lever to salvo the bomb, then braced himself, waiting for the plane to lurch if the bomb came loose. But nothing fell. Dang it! Al tore off his headphones, pulse hammering, and grabbed his tools.

In the cockpit, Ernie was frantic to reach the bombardier, but couldn't raise him despite repeated attempts over the intercom. He was probably unplugged already, Ernie thought. Someone would need to go get Bambino. Riffle was still hovering behind the pilots' seats. Bob turned to shout instructions at him, and for a split second, only Ernie was looking ahead. He saw it all in a flash. They were heading straight for two towering structures on opposite sides of the riverbed. Oil derricks, or so it seemed. But as they flew closer, Ernie spotted silver wires draped between the derricks.

High-voltage towers.

The power lines were dead even with their windscreen, an electricity-filled clothesline in the sky. *Chattanooga Choo Choo* was about to fly straight into them.

Reverting to his aircraft commander training, Ernie grabbed the controls, shot a quick glance at the instrument panel to make sure they had enough airspeed, and hauled back on the yoke. *Chattanooga Choo Choo* couldn't turn, but the plane's elevators might still be operational. These were the control surfaces on the tail that allowed the bomber to go up and down. There was no time to warn the crew.

The smoking bomber pitched skyward. Bob whirled around with alarm. Riffle grabbed the seatbacks to keep from falling backward. In the rear of the plane, the gunners in their crash positions clutched at their gun mounts. Brass casings tumbled toward the tail. The guns and ammo belts above them floated and danced like snakes.

Ernie glanced out his side window just as the powerlines zipped past. *Chattanooga Choo Choo* sliced through the air above them. He pushed the yoke and leveled the bomber.

Bob was still catching his breath from the close call. "Thanks," he said, relief in his voice, as he rejoined Ernie on the controls. He knew Ernie had just saved their lives.

It was a momentary reprieve. The drastic maneuver had brought them up to maybe 150 feet, half a football field above the ground. But time was not on their side. Smoke was still seeping from the disabled engine.

"We've got to put her down while we're over the riverbed," Bob called. The riverbed below was still straight and wide like a beach, but at any moment it could narrow or turn in a different direction.

As Ernie and Bob resumed looking for the safest spot to put the plane down, the left wingtip suddenly dipped. The bomber listed like a sailboat in a heavy wind. Gravity pulled Ernie and Bob leftward in their seats. Bob instinctively turned the yoke to the right, hoping to level the plane, but nothing happened. The wing sank even further, pulling the pilots harder against their straps. The plane began to roll to the left uncontrollably. The burning engine was the culprit. Drag from it was pulling them out of the sky. *Chattanooga Choo Choo* flew at a 45-degree angle. Then a 50-degree angle. The wingtip sank farther and farther. If the bomber rolled any more, they would wing over into the ground.

Bob blinked with recognition. Once. Twice. As if he was waking from slumber. He had a plan: "On my call, you close throttles on three and four. I'll advance number two full!"

"Roger!" Ernie snapped. It could work. Still holding the side rail, he used his free left hand to reach for the throttle controls on the console between them, while Bob reached over with his right.

"Now!" Bob shouted.

Ernie hauled back on two throttles, cutting power to both engines on the right wing, while Bob poured on the power to the sole functioning engine on the left wing. As the engines on Ernie's wing revved down, the Pratt & Whitney outside Bob's window roared louder and the propeller spun faster, surging with torque.

As if compelled by magic, the sunken wingtip slowly rose. The sole functioning engine was counteracting the roll.

When Bob had the plane as level as possible, he nursed back the throttle and settled the bomber onto a somewhat steady flight path.

"That was a wonderful bit of thinking!" Ernie said.

Bob wiped his brow. There was no time for backslapping. The momentary loss of control had cost them half their precious altitude. They were at seventy-five feet—twenty-five yards—and sinking steadily. It was *Chattanooga Choo Choo* against physics now. The designers of the B-24 would be the first to say it: You can't keep a heavy bomber flying on one engine.

Both men held back pressure on the yokes, begging the machine to keep flying. They needed to give Bambino time to kick out that bomb.

Near the center of the fuselage, Al crawled on hands and knees through the tunnel under the cockpit floor. Emerging into the bomb bay, he spotted Kees, the flight engineer, on the other side, already working feverishly to free the bomb. The bomb bay doors were open beneath him. The compartment was deafening, filled with wind and engine noise.

Al crept forward onto the eight-inch-wide catwalk, placing one foot in front of the other as if walking a metal tightrope. The view downward was like looking off the top of a three-story building, with the riverbed below rapidly rising toward them in a beige blur of gravel. Back home, Al loved roller coasters—he lived for them. But after this ride, maybe not anymore. Al reached Kees and offered his screwdriver.

"I can't get it loose!" Kees shouted over the noise. "You take over! I'll go help the pilots."

Al nodded, but the two men couldn't move around each other. The catwalk was too narrow. Kees stepped back, so Al could work on the bomb. Bambino balanced on his tiptoes, prying at the bomb with his screwdriver. One slip meant a fall. Death would be quick.

Click!

The latches snapped open. The dislodged bomb fell. It hit the riverbed in a splash of dust and stones. Al spun around and moved toward the cockpit to alert the pilots, making way for Kees to follow.

The bomber was still going down. "120, 115, 110 . . ." Ernie called out their airspeed for Bob as the bomber descended. The pilots were not flying the plane as much as they were guiding it to a crash.

Al entered the cockpit, breathless. "It's out!"

"Okay," Ernie shouted. "Get to your crash position!" Bambino had done it—he'd given them a fighting chance at survival.

Al exited the cockpit, while Ernie toggled the flaps to slow their speed of descent. The flaps lowered from the wings with a clunk, and the bomber felt suddenly lighter. But Ernie and Bob knew the reprieve was momentary. When it came to keeping their flying boxcar in the air, they'd exhausted every trick in the book. Now the bomber felt like a sinking submarine with no ballast left to shed. They were bleeding speed and coming down fast.

In the radio room, Al dropped to the floor and joined Britt and Riffle, sitting against a bulkhead with their backs to the pilots. Riffle's top turret was above them. Al leaned forward for a view into the bomb bay but was met by a terrible sight. Kees was still there! The flight engineer was frozen onto the catwalk, staring down through the open doors. The riverbed was thirty feet away. Twenty-five. Twenty. Kees was paralyzed with fear.

"Come on, Frank!" Al screamed. But the man wouldn't move.

In the cockpit, Bob and Ernie strained to hold back the controls in a desperate attempt to keep the plane flying. Ideally, they would surf the B-24 into the riverbed on a cushion of air. *Hold it up,* Ernie told himself. *Mush it in.*

On Bob's side of the plane, an embankment with a road on top ran along the riverbed, a scary blur at a hundred miles per hour. They flew even with the embankment. Then below it. The riverbed disappeared below the instrument panel. Ernie braced himself, waiting to hear the wrenching scrape of the plane's belly against the rocks. He wondered whether they should try to force the plane down.

The bomber decided for them. *Chattanooga Choo Choo* was still flying ten feet above the earth when the speed dropped below 95 miles per hour. The bomber stalled. Losing all forward momentum, the B-24 dropped like a rock. Ernie felt the floor vanish beneath him like an elevator cut loose.

The riverbed rushed up to meet them.

Bam!

The bomber slammed down and skidded across the gravel. Ernie and the crew could "feel the earth" through the airframe. It was bedlam. Ernie's ears filled with the "horrible sound of metal scraping, screeching" against stone. The bomber was "tearing apart."

Abruptly, the nose plunged forward, like a horse whose front legs had collapsed. *Crunch!* The sidewalls of the cockpit blew out. The world around Ernie spun. One moment he was sitting upright; the next, he was hurled sideways as the entire cockpit twisted to the right like a wrung-out dishrag. His left wrist slammed against the throttles. His shoulder and helmet struck the sidewall of the cockpit, once, twice, three times, four. The bomber plowed a jarring path through the gravel. Ernie closed his eyes tightly, "wondering when consciousness would leave, almost hoping it would."

Then, all at once, the bomber stopped in a spray of gravel.

There was nothing but dust.

CHAPTER 20

THE HUNTED

MOMENTS LATER
The Prahova riverbed

IT WAS ALMOST HEAVENLY.

Dust settled into the cockpit, drifting down in slow, weightless filaments, catching the sunbeams as Ernie opened his eyes. For a moment he wondered if he had awakened in some angelic realm. But the ache in his banged-up wrist reminded him he was still alive, sitting partially upright, still strapped in his seat.

The entire cockpit—windshield, instrument panel, and his seat—had rotated about 40 degrees to the right. The cockpit ceiling had peeled back like a door on a hinge. Above him was blue sky. To his left sat Bob, groggy, still secured to his seat.

Ernie smelled fuel. A spare 450-gallon tank had ruptured, producing a swell of gasoline that had sloshed forward from the bomb bay. He could see smoke rising on Bob's side of the plane. The engine was still burning! It wouldn't be long before the seep of fuel connected with fire.

Ernie yanked at his seatbelt, but before the metal restraint gave way, Bob stepped on his thigh, using him as a human springboard to push himself up and out through the hole in the ceiling. "C'mon!" Bob said. "We gotta get out!"

Ernie tried his seatbelt again. This time Al jumped on his lap and pushed himself out. Riffle followed. The men had all smelled the fuel and were rushing to exit the plane before it exploded.

Ernie yanked at his buckle again. It released, and he scrambled out. "Clear the plane!" he shouted to anyone remaining. His first steps felt like being born again. "It seemed incredible that I could still walk around," he later recalled.

Chattanooga Choo Choo seen crashed in the Prahova riverbed.

From a safe distance, Ernie surveyed the damage, trying simultaneously to determine a headcount. The bomber's wing had driven itself forward into the bomb bay, crushing everything in front of it. Behind the wing, the crew was still emerging. The nose of the bomber was flattened, and the floor in that section had compressed into the ceiling. He caught sight of Bob and Al scaling the embankment and gave chase but could only manage a half stumble. His ankle still stung from shrapnel.

At the top of the embankment, Ernie dropped to the grass. A familiar drone filled the air. He looked north. The last planes of the bomb group flew past, heading for home. A sinking feeling settled in. That vow of his—*If only one plane comes back*—wasn't going to be fulfilled now.

The crew gathered around the pilots, taking stock of their surroundings. Rurak carried Riffle over and carefully lowered him to the ground. In addition to his flak wounds, Riffle had broken ribs from the crash, though he didn't know it yet. Bowker lugged Medeiros up the final steps of the hill, the gunner's flight suit soaked through. The hydraulics in Medeiros's turret had ruptured, spilling fluid all over him. His legs were banged up and bruised. Each man wore his helmet and life preserver. Each was trying to come to grips with what they had just survived. Uphill from the wreckage lay a fancy garden and a manor house. Evidently, they had crash-landed on the edge of some Romanian's estate. They were about ten miles from Câmpina.

"Where's Dick?" Ernie said, looking around for Britt. A quick count revealed eight men on the hilltop. Two were missing.

"Who's not here yet?" Bob barked.

"Britt and Kees," Al said. "Britt was smashed on the flight deck. And Kees—Kees is in there." He pointed to the tangle of wrecked metal "that had been our powerful warbird." When the wing had crashed through the fuselage, it tore loose the top turret, sending it flying downward. Kees had been completely crushed. Riffle murmured his concurrence. He'd seen it too.

They were both dead? Ernie struggled to comprehend the news. Before he could get far, Bob cut in. "Look sharp. We've got company."

A half mile down the embankment, a group of Romanians had gathered. Some were civilians. Others wore brown uniforms, guns drawn. They moved toward the Americans, walking a few steps, then breaking into a run.

All thoughts turned to survival. Across the roadway lay a cornfield. "Best we conceal ourselves in there," Ernie said.

The gunners lifted the wounded men, and the crew moved across the road. Riffle would recall later: "I found I could walk by dragging my leg a little." They pushed into the field about two hundred yards; then everyone took a knee. Bob and the other city boys looked to Ernie, the outdoorsman. He quickly assessed their options. They needed to make their way to the Alps, where their chances of escape would be better. But for now, they simply needed to get as far away from the wreckage as possible.

"Split up and make a run for it," Ernie said. The wounded men would slow them down, but they couldn't leave them behind. "Bob, you take Riffle. I'll take Louie"—Louis Medeiros. Al volunteered to help with Medeiros. "Everybody, work your way toward the foothills," Ernie said. "Head west over the mountains to Yugoslavia." Bob and the others hesitated, grasping for details. But Ernie shook his head. "No time. They saw us head into the field. We gotta go."

Ernie hoisted Medeiros up and slung the wounded man's arm over his shoulder. Bob headed in the other direction with the rest of the group. With Al's help, Ernie pressed deeper into the cornfield. Cornstalks slapped them in the face. Ernie winced with every step.

We can still get away, he told himself.

As Ernie's group moved through the corn, the scream of airplane engines overhead drew their attention upward. The men peered through the stalks at the pale blue sky. One after another, four Messerschmitt 109s streaked overhead at one thousand feet, chasing the fleeing American bombers. Overall, the Romanian and German fighters had been duped. They'd been at high altitude over Ploesti searching for the Americans, thinking they would attack at 25,000 feet. But they'd figured it out by now.

Ernie set aside his concerns for his fellow fliers and led his men forward.

The high cornstalks bristled against them, slowing their progress. On the fly, Ernie stripped off his helmet and life preserver. The others did the same. They'd be faster now. He pulled out his small survival compass, pausing to orient himself. He let go of Medeiros to read his compass. The tail gunner sank to his knees.

"We gotta keep going, Louie. Can you crawl? We'll be with you."

Medeiros nodded.

Ernie and Al dropped to their hands and knees with Medeiros, and Ernie led them deeper into the field, the cornstalks bending and snapping as they crawled forward. A low rumble swelled to the north. The bombs that had been on acid-fuse timers were now exploding in the distant refinery.

Shouts rang out behind them. The Romanians were homing in, voices sharp. They were at the edge of the cornfield. A chill shot through Ernie. All those times he'd gone hunting with his dad, he never imagined himself being at the other end of a rifle barrel. More shouts were heard, this time farther up the field. *They're surrounding us. Just like quail.*

A pursuer let rip with a handheld machine gun. Bullets snapped and whizzed through the cornstalks. Al and Medeiros hit the dirt. Ernie drew his .45 pistol and whirled around, ready for the enemy to come charging through the corn. But no further shots rang out. It had been a warning, Ernie concluded. If the Romanians wanted to kill them, they would have strafed the entire field.

Instead, the Americans heard more "excited voices," in a foreign tongue, "talking and jabbering." To Al's ears, the language sounded like Italian. The Romanians had found their tracks. Slowly the pursuers advanced.

Ernie sensed there was still time to escape. All he needed to do was get up and run like hell. But he couldn't leave a wounded man. Ernie concealed his compass in the small watch pocket on the front hip of his pants. He took a twenty-dollar bill from his wallet and slid it into his sock. The thrashing noise came nearer. Ernie holstered his pistol and turned to Al. "Got a handkerchief?"

Ernie was the tallest. He stood and hoisted the small patch of white above the cornstalks. Al stood alongside Ernie and raised his hands in surrender. Medeiros "crawled about 5–7 paces away" and buried his face in the dirt.

What will they do to us? Ernie wondered. *Will they beat us? Shoot us?*

Ernie spotted their rifles first, aimed from the hip. The Romanians—middle-aged soldiers from a Home Guard unit, wearing brown uniforms and caps with soft points at the front—rushed at Ernie and Al. One grabbed Ernie's pistol and tied his hands. Tagging along behind the Home Guard men were a few teenage peasant boys. One boy snatched Ernie's knife, while soldiers searched Al. Ernie stood stock still. Playing possum proved futile for Medeiros. Two hands grabbed him by the legs and swiftly dragged him toward the others.

The Romanians prodded Ernie and his party back to their wrecked bomber. Bob's group had not been caught yet. The captors set armed guards on the Americans and forced them to lie face down near the remains of their aircraft. The smell of burnt wires and rubber filled the air. Fortunately, a few teenaged boys wielding fire extinguishers arrived to dowse the smoldering engine.

"Scores of pistols and rifles were cocked and pointed at us," Ernie later recalled. "Their shaky hands on their cocked pistols gave me a good deal of worry. Although their speech was foreign to us, we could tell they were arguing about what to do with us."

Ernie lay with his cheek on the ground, eyes locked on *Chattanooga Choo Choo* in the near distance. The bomber lay dead, like a great beast brought down on safari. The crash had almost completely broken up the airplane.* Only the wing and the twin tails were reasonably intact. The rest was a tangle of metal.

Medeiros eyed the twisted nose of the plane and whispered, "How in the hell did you get out of that cockpit alive, Lieutenant?" The smiling boxcar's face was flattened into the stones.

"A puzzled sigh was all I could offer," Ernie would later write. "My mind was occupied with the unpleasant thought that Dick's and Frank's bodies were twisted and smashed in that mess."

WITHIN A FEW MOMENTS, a crowd of civilians formed, drawn to the wrecked bomber "the way people always do when there's a crash." Fifty people? A hundred? They came from fields and farms, some armed with pitchforks and double-bladed axes, the wheels of their wagons painted with bright, col-

* The B-24 had a reputation for breaking apart in a crash, and it tended to live up to expectations. The issue lay in its design. The fuselage was built beneath a high-set wing, not over it as on the B-17. During a crash, all that dead weight would come crashing forward, compounding any destruction.

orful patterns. Other spectators looked to be middle-aged couples in their Sunday clothes. Teenaged boys strolled in with their girlfriends, as if on a date. The Romanians were raven-haired like the Italians, but sharp featured and not as tan. Everyone seemed to be pointing at the white star on the wing of *Chattanooga Choo Choo* and talking fast. Ernie noted that "their hands trembled, and their voices were shaky"; they murmured the same word over and over. But what did it mean?

Romanian locals explore *Chattanooga Choo Choo*

As the crowd pressed closer around the Americans, Ernie and his crew would learn a harsh truth. A downed airman needed to worry about the civilians the most. "The military personnel have at least some semblance of order and discipline," explained another captured B-24 pilot. "But you never know what to expect out of the civilian population, especially if they have been bombed."

Civilians began shouting and screaming. The crowd whipped itself into a frenzy, singling out the tallest of the three captured invaders: Ernie. Someone kicked him in the ribs as he lay on the ground. Medeiros saw a peasant woman come "from nowhere" and fling herself on Ernie, pounding away at his body with her fists and shouting, "Ruski!" A guardsman "pointed his gun at her," but she didn't stop.

When at last the woman tired, the teenage boy who'd taken Ernie's knife stepped forward. He held the blade poised over Ernie's chest, then ripped the silver wings from the breast of his suntans. Beside him, Ernie heard Al "furiously" reciting the Hail Mary and Our Father prayers.

The mob was getting out of control, shouting insults, spitting, their screams rising to a fever pitch. Finally, one of the Home Guard snapped. He "cut loose" with his machine pistol, firing a burst of gunfire into the ground so close to Medeiros's face that he felt the spray of dirt. The crowd recoiled, retreating for the moment, but they kept murmuring, "Ruski. Ruski."

Ernie connected the dots. To a Romanian civilian, any star on a plane, red or white, signified the same thing: Russia. The Russians were Romania's enemy, "for whom they have a real mortal fear, and loathe to no end." The Soviets had dragged the Romanians into war by invading their territory. The Soviets had killed or captured 150,000 of their boys at Stalingrad and 70,000 more at Odessa. The Soviets were the reason all the young farmers were gone from their fields and fighting for Hitler. Ernie thought fast.

"Yo sunt aviator American!"

A hush began to spread.

"Yo sunt aviator American!" Ernie called again, this time louder.

The crowd calmed a bit more.

Ernie had studied the Romanian phrase book issued by the intel boys. Slowly, two new words began to form on the crowd's lips. "Sunt Americani!"

"I think they understood," Ernie would later recall, "but were nevertheless fearful of us."

One civilian stepped forward and tried to communicate with the Americans in fractured English. But the Home Guard ushered him back to the crowd with their rifles. Their superiors would handle the interrogation.

The guards loaded Ernie, Al, and Medeiros into a horse-drawn cart and cracked the whip, leading them back up the embankment toward the hilltop village of Nedelea. Ernie stole a last fleeting glance at their plane and the distant Alps.

Minutes later, the three Americans were unloaded at a derelict farm on the edge of the village. The Home Guard used this as a makeshift defense post. The guards freed the airmen's hands and searched them again, this time taking their watches and leather jackets and Ernie's wallet and ring. They opened a trapdoor to an abandoned cistern and shoved a ladder down the hole.

Ernie and Al inched their way down the rungs. Medeiros labored the entire way. The room below was about twelve feet high and twenty feet across, with a dirt floor. The guardsmen slammed the trapdoor, plunging the chamber into darkness.

A million thoughts raced through Ernie's mind. A few minutes passed before he broke the silence.

"Well, this is a pretty bad way to spend the summer."

Al and Medeiros wanted to laugh, they truly did, but any sense of humor had gone out the window when they crashed. The joke fell flat.

Ernie couldn't blame them.

It wasn't supposed to go like this. But it had. They had no idea who else had lived or died from the 389th and there was no telling whether the overall operation was a success. The other four groups could have been wiped out for all he knew.

They were prisoners of war. And the hardest part for Ernie was accepting that one of his closest friends was dead.

It was almost impossible to believe. Britt was gone?

CHAPTER 21

BACK TO LIFE

SOON AFTER
The riverbed

INSIDE THE WRECKAGE OF *CHATTANOOGA CHOO CHOO*, THE RADIO ROOM lay in ruins. On its floor, wedged against the bulkhead, one of the dead men opened his eyes.

Britt began "coughing and gasping for air," looking around, trying to get his bearings. Crumpled aluminum encaged him. The radio room, coated in neon-green zinc chromate paint, had become his tomb. Britt tried to recall the crash, but everything was a blur. He remembered a grinding noise, seeing Kees thrown forward by the momentum. After that, darkness.

Light spilled through the Plexiglas dome of the top turret in the ceiling above. Normally the turret sat high atop the bomber, but the ceiling lay much closer now. It had collapsed, bringing the turret down on Britt. Normally, two .50 caliber machine guns bracketed a gunsight, and below the turret lay a gunner's seat. Beneath the gunner's seat were two yellow bottles filled with compressed oxygen that Riffle used to breathe at high altitude. When the turret had ripped out of the ceiling, the dome stayed, but the gunner's seat and the oxygen bottles came crashing down on Britt, pinning him in place.

Another man had it worse. To Britt's right lay Frank Kees, his back toward Britt. Kees had taken the full brunt of the falling turret. The heavy guns and boxes of ammo had crushed him.

With his fingers, Britt felt something wet. He recognized the smell. A steady trickle of gasoline was leaking in from the bomb bay. The rubberized fabric tank that held 450 gallons for the trip home had ruptured and Britt's lower body was already soaking in a bath of 100-octane aviation fuel. One spark and he'd face a hideous death. He could move his arms a little, but they were useless against the constriction of the metal. He tried to free his legs, but the weight "was so great that the turret might just as well have been a mountain."

"Ernie?" Britt's voice bounced off the steel walls. "Bob?

He could hear a crowd chattering outside. What if someone came close with a lighted cigarette?

Britt thought of his father, who ran the electrical grid for Chicago. From him, Britt had picked up his habit of reliability. The family had already suffered great losses. Britt's mother had died when Britt was ten, his sister when he was eleven. *What will happen to Dad if he loses his son?* Britt needed to survive. If nothing else, for him.

The metal pressed in around Britt. The aviation fuel inched toward his torso. He heard a strange brushing sound near the ceiling and froze. A shadow flickered above. Through the Plexiglas dome, a young man's face peered down. Then another face, a boy's. Britt held his breath. Before he could speak, they vanished.

INSIDE HER HILLTOP ESTATE in Nedelea, Princess Catherine was trying to reach Bucharest on the phone, but all lines were down. One of the young men who worked on her estate burst into the room with news. The loud noise they'd heard was a "flaming" bomber as it crashed in the riverbed. Two dead men were inside. The rest of the crew had run away.

Before the young man could finish, a boy rushed to Catherine's side. "The dead man is moving!"

The princess gathered her chauffeur and helpers and hurried to her car, a sporty 1939 Chevrolet business coupe with big, arched fenders and whitewall tires. Turning to the little girl she'd been teaching English, Catherine said, "Now, my dear, you must go inside and not come out until I return."

The chauffeur drove the princess, the young man, and the boy down the embankment to the crash site. "The crumpled plane was almost hidden by the crowd that had gathered," Catherine would recall. People pointed to the plane and touched its fuselage. Fear and suspicion had been replaced with wonder. Most had never been up close to an airplane, let alone one this size.*

* In the opinion of Valeriu Râpeanu, "the terror exerted on people's morale" from the low-level nature of Tidal Wave was unprecedented: "A psychological shock of such proportions had never been experienced by anyone before."

An older peasant greeted her with a salute. "Your Honor, the Russians have come."

Catherine studied the white star near the tip of the bomber's right wing. She knew the Russian star was red. But a white star? She moved closer to the wreck, peered through a crack in the fuselage, and saw Britt "making feeble movements and heard his moans of pain." Turning to the young man and boy, she told them to fetch hacksaws.

BRITT HEARD UNFAMILIAR VOICES on the side of the plane where Ernie usually sat. The rasp of a handsaw cut into the flank of the plane, and he winced, hoping it wouldn't create a spark. A hole appeared in the fuselage. Daylight streamed inside.

Much to his surprise, a woman peered into the plane. She studied him for a moment, puzzlement written across her face.

"You're not a Russian, are you?" Her voice carried a strong British accent.

"I'm an American, ma'am," Britt managed, his voice weak.

"Good! We'll have you out in a jiffy!"

They widened the hole until it was large enough to step inside. The young man, chauffeur, and several bystanders carefully pulled Britt from the plane. It wasn't easy. The tall American was heavy. "My legs were quite useless," Britt would recall. "I had to move them with my hands."

Romanian civilians watched the rescue effort with bated breath. When the rescuers lowered Britt to the ground, the crowd uttered a "loud sigh" of relief.

"I was surprised to see they were more curious than angry," Britt would remember. "This was not the kind of reception I expected."

Shock set in quickly. Britt began "shaking violently." The aviation fuel had dried, leaving his uniform spotless, as if it had been "freshly drycleaned," but a look underneath revealed he'd been badly burned by the high-octane gasoline. Beneath Britt's suntans, his skin was a mass of angry, red blisters. Catherine examined his skin and knew he needed medical attention, fast. The princess instructed her helpers to carry Britt toward her car, but "an angry murmur swept the crowd." She whirled to see a pair of "cold-faced" German officers forcing their way through the mass of civilians, accompanied by several armed soldiers.

"We will take that man, your highness," snapped one of the Germans.

The other officer indicated they had a medical facility at their station where the American would be looked after.

"I had an idea of what would happen to the wounded airman if the Nazis got their hands on him," Catherine later wrote, "and the knowledge angered me."

Catherine whispered to her helpers to get Britt to her car. They backpedaled, carrying the injured American, but "the Nazis followed, demanding that we give them the prisoner." She told her chauffeur to run ahead and start her car. As the engine sputtered to life, Catherine and her helpers moved fast, easing Britt into the backseat on the passenger's side. Before the door could shut, an enemy officer lunged forward, gripping Britt's ankles with both hands.

"We will take him," the officer said.

"He is a prisoner of the Kingdom of Romania!" the princess retorted.

A scuffle broke out. The supposed allies found themselves in a "tug of war" over the limp American. The princess pretended to slip, jabbing the nearest enemy officer with her elbow, knocking him off balance. He righted himself with a snort, unwilling to strike a woman. Seizing upon the disarray, the princess darted around the car, jumped into the backseat, and pulled Britt in by his shoulders.

"Go!" she shouted.

Her chauffeur floored it. With a kick of dust, the car pulled a U-turn and raced up the embankment with the open door flapping wildly, leaving the Germans behind, cursing. In the backseat, the princess steadied Britt on her lap.

One American was safe. But this day was far from over.

CHAPTER 22

HELLO, BOYS

ABOUT HALF AN HOUR LATER
Near Nedelea

WHEN THE CHAUFFEUR STEERED THE CHEVROLET COUPE FOR HOME, the backseat next to Princess Catherine was empty.

She'd delivered Britt to a local clinic, where the staff moved swiftly to tend to the injured American. The princess left instructions to care for him, although she knew what she hoped for was already assured. Lieutenant Richard Britt was going to be okay.

Passing through Nedelea, the princess and her driver were "halted by the sight" of a throng of Romanian villagers of all ages running across the road. They were flocking to a commotion in a backyard, moving like children up to mischief, equal parts enthralled and frightened.

The princess shook her head. What now? Her curiosity sometimes got the best of her. She asked her chauffeur to pull over, then got out and found one of the elders in the crowd of stirred-up villagers.

"We captured more men from the crashed plane," the elder reported, lifting his chin in pride. "For safety's sake we hid the Americans in a cellar!"

Catherine wanted to slap her forehead.

"Idiots!"

AT THE BOTTOM OF the cistern, Ernie, Al, and Medeiros huddled for warmth, their bodies aching from every bruise and cut sustained in the crash. The air was cold and clammy, as if they'd been trapped at the bottom of a well. And they weren't alone down there. Toads croaked in the darkness. Rats scampered across their legs, their claws pricking through the men's uniforms. The three men wriggled to shake off the vermin.

Above them, they could hear voices—enemy voices—and the scrape of boots. Their captors were debating what to do with them. "It all seemed almost like a dream, or more correctly termed, a nightmare," Ernie would write. Their bomber would soon be categorized "FTR"—Failed to Return.

The worst part was the waiting. They stared toward the trapdoor, wondering what would happen when it opened—if it opened. Would they be dragged out and shot? Would they vanish in the Romanian countryside, never to be heard from again?

The thought struck Ernie with a chill. If something happened to him, would his parents even know? Would Helen?

Ernie had a girlfriend, sort of. Her name was Helen Lillywhite. Despite Ernie's movie-star looks, it had taken a fellow cadet to fix him up on a blind date during flight training at Thunderbird Field in Arizona.

Ernie with Helen Lillywhite

Helen was nineteen, blond, confident. A "widely-known" Phoenix girl, as the newspaper called her, she worked as an executive assistant in the defense industry and ran a sorority for young women trying to break into business. Her father, H. F. Lillywhite, and his family were "old time residents" who owned a sprawling dairy operation in neighboring New Mexico.

When graduation came—the day when cadets would be given silver wings, lieutenant's bars, and a sharp new officer's uniform—Ernie faced a choice. Each cadet could invite one woman to pin his wings.

Who would it be—Helen, or his mother?

Helen was sweet, but still new to his life. His mother, Ada, had been there all along. The former librarian, she'd never learned to drive, and hadn't left the valley since she was a teen.

Ernie chose his mom. He bought her a bus ticket to Arizona and when the day came, she stood proudly in front of him and pinned on his wings.

Afterward, Ernie only made things harder with Helen. He'd been too busy hosting his mom, too caught up in the moment, and "regrettably did not include Helen in the graduation scene."

Then came the next assignment. He shipped out.

Now, as he sat in the damp darkness of that pit, it struck him: He and Helen had shared only about nine dates before he left, and since then had exchanged a few letters. Would she ever know that his plane had gone down half a world away?

Maybe she'd already moved on.

From above, Ernie and his friends heard a sudden rush of muffled voices. They braced for trouble. Instead of angry captors, the trapdoor opened, "and a lady of about 50 years greeted us," Ernie recalled.

"Hello, boys," she said simply.

"What welcome words they were!" Ernie would write.

"Boys, there are only friends here," she continued. "Now come up and let us help you."

A ladder was lowered, a guard came down to untie the prisoners, and they all climbed up the rungs. At the top, Ernie and his friends were greeted by Princess Catherine, who steadied each grateful man by the arm as he stepped to the surface. But the Romanian guards and villagers drew back like children who had trapped bugs in a jar, only to find that the bugs had gotten out. The woman reassured her countrymen that the prisoners were friends—"They're Americans." Soon, the guards and villagers were shaking their hands apologetically. Watches and rings were returned, although someone made off with Ernie's jacket.

The princess asked the Americans if they were hungry. That was an understatement. Their last meal had been ten hours earlier in Benghazi.

"Bring food!" she called. The princess had a motherly way of ushering around the locals. She turned back to the men and apologized for the imprisonment, explaining that the villagers thought they were Russians. "Everyone has lost family fighting against them," she added.*

She introduced herself as Catherine Caradja and explained that their bomber crashed just down the hill from her "country home." (She was being modest: She didn't mention the thousand acres she owned around Nedelea.)

"I have good news," she added. "Your friend Britt will be okay. We got him out of the plane and to my clinic."

"That can't be," Al said. "He's dead. I saw him myself."

Catherine weighed Al's words, her puzzlement giving way to certainty. "Richard Britt, a big fellow, from Chicago? No, he's very much alive." Her face fell. "The other man, however, is dead."

Ernie, Al, and Medeiros exchanged wide-eyed looks. Britt was alive?

Catherine recounted how they had extracted Britt from the wreckage, almost losing him to the clutches of the Germans. "The chief harm to him has been the burns he received from the gas. But he's not in a real serious state and is getting on all right."

The men hung on every word. Hearing of Britt's rescue was "one of the most joyful bits of news" Ernie had ever heard. He was both elated and disappointed in himself for writing off Britt too soon.

THE FOOD ARRIVED, CARRIED by cheerful young women with flowing white dresses. They brought platters piled high with cheese, bread, tomatoes, and fresh fruit. A villager poured Ernie a tall glass of milk, and the three Americans settled in and ate "ravenously."

Friendly locals crowded each other for "a peep" at the fliers, watching intently and with approval as they ate with gusto. Some attempted conversation, despite the language barrier.

Ernie came to see the Romanians as passionate people, "gay and vivacious," owing to their Latin roots. They were quick to fall in love or take

* Romania's human suffering had, in fact, begun a year before the war. When Romania was forced to relinquish its eastern territories, Bessarabia and Northern Bukovina, in the summer of 1940, the Stalinist reign of terror began immediately: "The Romanian army was looted by the Soviet forces tasked with overseeing the agreement. Simultaneously, they began seizing automobiles and capturing prisoners of all ranks, shooting some members of the Romanian authorities who were waiting to hand over their respective institutions." Within a year, the Soviets had deported 53,356 ethnic Romanians to slave labor camps in Siberia and across the USSR.

offense, and just as quick to make amends. Above all, they prided themselves on their hospitality, and their display of generosity and forgiveness "astounded the Americans," Catherine would write, who "had thought they would be hated."

"We like Americans very much," she told the men. As she later recalled, "I explained to them that Romanians, on the whole, did not consider themselves at war with America, but only with the Russians." The princess would go further: "We're on the wrong side of this war only because we joined Hitler to chase the Russians out of a province they had taken away from us. It was later that he turned on France and England, and then on us, too."

Romania's affinity for Americans ran deeper than their population's hunger to see movies such as *Gone with the Wind,* which had been banned by Antonescu. Their two nations had been allies in World War I, fighting on the same side against the German-led Central Powers. Even now, with the military dictatorship in power, the Romanian populace still leaned toward the Allies. "While officially Romania is an Axis partner," wrote a director of the YMCA charity in 1943, "we should never consider the mass of the people as Nazis."

Catherine told the men she'd spent her youth in England, where she'd learned the language. She spoke it better than Romanian. And something caught the ears of the American fliers. The guards and villagers addressed her as "Prințesa."

Prințesa? Was she a princess? A real one?

"Yes," she said, and shrugged. "The perks of being born to the right mother!"

The Americans were dumbstruck.

In no time, the princess was playfully pinching Bambino's cheeks, as if he was a beloved pet. She tested out her American slang on them, expressions she'd picked up from reading *Reader's Digest* and *Good Housekeeping* before the war.

The men were all taken with her, the energetic glimmer in her blue eyes, her feisty determination, her international charm. She, in turn, was impressed by the airmen, their youth, politeness, and obvious courage. She vowed to do all in her power to help them survive their ordeal and get them home to their mothers. Until then, she would refer to them as "her boys." Being enemies is a choice.

"We began to see that maybe we had a future after all," Ernie recalled.

THE HOME GUARD MEN showed the American fliers to two idling cars. One was the princess's 1939 Chevrolet with whitewall tires. The other was her black 1938 Ford Tudor sedan, quick-looking with a sloping fastback. It was around 4 P.M., and the raid had been over for nearly two hours.

"Sorry, but I have to turn you over to proper military authorities," she said.

"The Germans?" asked one of the men. After the damage they'd done, Ernie knew Hitler's boys had to be "clamoring for our custody."

"No, never in my life," added the princess. She explained she wanted to keep the Americans in Romanian hands, as far away from the Germans as possible. She'd been instructed to bring them to a Romanian military outpost in the outskirts of Ploesti.

Ernie and his friends were uneasy. They felt safe with Catherine. In a short time, she'd assumed the role of their mother and protector. Ernie would have hung on to the hemline of her dress for the remainder of his captivity if he could.

"Now, we'd best get going," the princess said, "before the Germans find out you're here." She didn't have to repeat herself. The Americans were already moving for the cars.

She would personally drive them to the outpost. Her chauffeur would take the Ford while she drove the Chevrolet. The princess sent their guards to ride in the Ford behind them; the Americans would ride with her.

This was not by accident.

ON THE ROAD TOWARD Ploesti, the two-car convoy moved cautiously through the Romanian farmland.

From the front seat, next to Catherine, Ernie peered through the windscreen, already wishing they could turn around. Beyond the tall hedges and trees that leaned across the road, big, angry columns of black smoke—a telltale sign of burning oil—rose in the distance. The refineries around Ploesti were burning in the aftermath of the raid, darkening the late afternoon sky. "It was scary and awe-inspiring seeing what the other groups accomplished," recalled Ernie. And the bombs weren't through yet. They would be going off for hours.

At sporadic intervals, trucks loaded with German troops roared and rumbled past the convoy, bound for Câmpina. The princess was unfazed. She had lived amid the German occupation of Ploesti since fall 1940. But for the downed American fliers, the only German soldiers they'd seen before were in newsreels. Seeing them now, in the flesh, and armed, was unnerving.

Princess Catherine fished a small black notepad from her purse and passed it to Ernie. "If you want," she said, "write down the names and addresses of your parents." She didn't turn her gaze from the road. "I'll get a message to them through the Swiss Legation so they know you're alive."

She was taking a great risk, and Ernie was immediately grateful. In the back of his mind, he was worried about his mother getting a War Department telegram with the "cold declaration" that her son was "Missing in Action." And maybe Helen would now find out, too. Ernie scribbled his address, then passed the pad back to the others.

THE TWO CARS SOON arrived at their destination, a Romanian military outpost on the outskirts of Ploesti. The outpost buzzed with activity as Romanian soldiers, clad in puttees and dovetail helmets, came and went.

The princess gathered the fliers near her car before letting the soldiers claim them.

"You can try to escape, but please don't," she said. "You're only safe if you *stay put.*" She met their eyes briefly in a subtle signal. Her message was *Trust me.*

Taking one look at the armed soldiers around them, Ernie readily agreed.

"I promise I'll keep in touch," she added. She said she'd even visit them.

"No, we will never see you again," said one of the fliers, despondent.

Ernie, however, wasn't betting against the princess. He'd only met her an hour ago, but he already recognized that she was unlike anyone he'd ever known in his twenty-two years.

"Ma'am, can I give you something to hold on to for me?" Ernie said.

"Sure, Ernie."

When the Romanian soldiers weren't looking, he slipped her the $20 bill he'd hidden in his sock.

The princess took it and shot him a wink.

It was time to part ways.

"Goodbye!" she said. "I'll look after Lieutenant Britt for you."

With those words, she returned to her car.

The soldiers claimed their prisoners.

AROUND MIDNIGHT THAT NIGHT, when Ernie looked out from the window of his cell in the outpost, the sky to the southeast glowed. Fires illuminated the darkness for miles, throwing ghastly orange radiance on the clouds. Ernie felt a primal urge to run. The conditions in the Romanian outpost weren't like being in a German stockade, but they were a far cry from their backyard mixer with the princess.

The Ploesti refineries were still ablaze, their oil fires nowhere near burning out. Al and Medeiros sat on makeshift beds, heads in their hands. Had the five American groups truly smashed Hitler's Gas Station? Had they pulled off a win? It was still too soon to gauge the effectiveness of their mission.

And it was still too early to know the cost in American lives when the Germans were still rousting downed airmen from the fields and foothills, and collecting soot-covered fliers in a schoolhouse turned field hospital on the edge of Ploesti where, "in the main hall, upon a straw-littered floor, lay thirty Americans, burned and broken, naked and dying."

To Ernie, it felt like ages ago that he and his friends had been roused from their slumber in Benghazi by honking horns. How fate can turn on a dime.

Now, as the longest day of Ernie's life ended, one question loomed large in his mind: Whose prisoners were they? He knew their lives would hinge on the answer, and one outcome was scarier than the others.

The Germans want us.

CHAPTER 23

THE AFRICAN KNIGHTS

THE NEXT DAY, AUGUST 2, 1943

Romania

THERE WAS WORK TO BE DONE.

Dust and smoke from the raid still lingered in the air as Catherine raced in her Chevrolet to Bucharest, the capital of Romania, located thirty-five miles south of Ploesti and still in sight of the Transylvanian Alps.

In its streets, the city of 600,000 shimmered with a new hollow grandeur. Its modern Art Deco buildings and lavish turn-of-the-century Parisian-inspired architecture stood in stark contrast to the foreign banners and marching jackboots that now staked their claim to the city once called "Le Petit Paris." German soldiers rumbled through the streets in motorcycles with sidecars. The city's largest roundabout had been renamed Piața Adolf Hitler—Adolf Hitler Square. And Kriegsmarine sailors from the German Black Sea fleet could be seen on sidewalks walking arm-in-arm with local girls, the girls' laughter tinged with unease.*

The princess had a house in Bucharest, along with charitable ventures, but she was not in the capital on a social call. She was here to keep her boys out of German hands. "A plan had been forming in my mind," she recalled

* There was strong Francophilia among Romania's upper crust. They admired France's democratic values, culture, and fashion, and looked to France as a "sister nation." Ties between the nations were strengthened during World War I, when France came to Romania's aid, sending a military mission all the way up through Norway, to Sweden, and down through Russia to reach the Romanians. There, France set about overhauling Romania's military—which was why a Romanian squadron was called an Escadrilă in World War II and their planes sported tricolor bars on their tails, just like French aircraft.

years later, "and I decided to pursue it." With that brisk, determined stride of hers, she made a beeline for a café.

INSIDE THE CAFÉ, PRINCESS Catherine convened a meeting of her friends—women from Bucharest's high society, among them "several wives of cabinet ministers"—to talk about their American "visitors." Today wasn't a typical coffee date. Catherine had a plan, but to execute it she needed to mobilize her social circle. She needed their help and their connections.

By early counts, more than a hundred American POWs were being held between German and Romanian forces. The princess was determined to keep them in Romania. She was certain that not only would the Americans experience more humane treatment in Romania, but also they "would have a better chance of being liberated" than in a stalag, a German POW camp, deep in the Reich.

The clock was ticking. What happened in the next few hours would seal the prisoners' fate.

"The Americans are trying to help us fight the Germans," she told the women. "They were shot down in Romania and should be our prisoners." She chose her next words carefully. "What falls in our country is *ours*. What falls in Germany is *theirs*."

"I used every argument," the princess later recalled.

The women had every reason not to help her. Reports from Ploesti had just come in: The damage from the raid was extensive. The princess's "boys" and their friends had hit hard, striking seven out of the nine largest Romanian refineries and sending almost 38,000 barrels of oil and petroleum products, their nation's chief economic asset, up in flames. And that wasn't even counting the toll on Romanian railcars, storage tanks, and pipelines.

All that was of little concern to Princess Catherine. For nearly two years, she and her countrymen had endured the Germans' "pillaging" of their national resources. In truth, she would rather see the refineries destroyed than let another drop of oil reach Hitler. What troubled her were the graver implications of the raid: Romania was at war with the wrong people—with America.

Now she was asking her friends to protect the very men who'd just crippled their oil industry. Their answer took her by surprise.

"I don't blame the Americans," said one.

"They are not mad at us, just trying to stop Hitler," said another. "*He* is taking all our oil!"

To them, the attack was "an understandable military necessity."

There was another factor in the fliers' favor. The raid was the talk of the town, and word on the street had it that the American flyboys had attacked at low level—at greater risk to life and limb—to avoid injuring Romanian civilians on the ground.

Even if that wasn't the mission's original intent, the precision of the low-level attacks *had* spared Romanian lives. The high-altitude raids over Germany would produce civilian casualties in the thousands; by contrast, eighty-one Romanian civilians died during Tidal Wave. And sixty-one of the victims were inmates of Ploesti's women's prison—"shoplifters, political opponents of Antonescu, and farm girls serving short terms for watering milk"—killed by accident when a B-24 shot down by a Romanian fighter crashed into the facility.

And the worst part? The death, the destruction—they never had to happen.

When Hitler launched his surprise invasion of the Soviet Union in June 1941, he kept his promise of helping Romania reclaim its lost territories from the USSR. By August, it seemed to the average Romanian that the war was over. Hitler could have their oil; at least their prewar borders were restored.

But Hitler had his eye on another of Romania's resources: its soldiers. The Führer cabled Antonescu requesting that Romanian troops follow his forces east and fight alongside them in the Soviet Union.

The Romanian populace was vehemently opposed to further action. When Romania had gone to war to free their two lost territories, Antonescu "had at that time the support of the whole country, including the King." Invading the USSR and joining Hitler's war with the world was never part of the plan. Besides, following Hitler further would pit them against England, "Romania's natural ally." It would mean entering World War II.

"We do not have one Romanian soldier to sacrifice for foreign purposes," declared the leader of the National Agrarian Party. "We have to spare our army for our Romanian goals." Romania's young king, the nobility, and commoners alike urged Antonescu to "declare Romania's war goals complete." Even the chief of Antonescu's general staff sided with the people, warning that "Romania had no place in Hitler's war." It was their last chance to pull the country back from the slippery slope that Antonescu and his fascist allies had set it upon.

To Princess Catherine's eternal regret, "They failed to stop him."

In the mind of the Conductor, Hitler's crusade in the east was a "holy war" against "Judeo-Bolshevism" that had to be fought here, and now. So, Antonescu sent word to Hitler: Romania would "continue their advance" east into Soviet Union. With that, Antonescu and a small cohort set the entire nation on a path to ruin.

Now, here they were, nearly three years later, Germany's most prominent ally after the Italians, pitted against England and America. It was hard to believe. "What a reversal of concepts, what paradoxes of the times," wrote one popular Romanian author in his journal. As Catherine looked around the café at her friends, she knew the fight had come to their own backyard—and it would only get worse.

Who should take the blame for the loss of life on August 1? Who killed the prison inmates? And the nineteen other civilians who died? And the more than 200,000 Romanian servicemen who'd perished in the war so far? Catherine's friends were unanimous in whom they blamed.

Antonescu. The fascists. And ultimately, Hitler.

In the mind of the average Romanian, the Americans were heroes. Already, the populace had taken to calling the men from Benghazi "Cavaleri Africani," African Knights.

The women would help. *Being enemies is a choice.*

"It wasn't difficult to get their support," the princess later recalled. "Many had been involved socially with Americans through the years of oil production activities." They liked Americans just as she did.

The princess instructed her friends to urge their husbands to go to Antonescu and the fascists and insist that the Americans were "*Romanian* prisoners." The princess lowered her voice and added that if the women needed "extra incentive" to sway their husbands, she had a suggestion. "Threaten to lock your bedroom door until he agrees!"

The quip brought a round of laughter. "Sometimes women have to use a little persuasion when they feel the cause is just," the princess would later write.

The plan was in motion. Her friends were mobilized. Could they make a difference? Time would tell.

CHAPTER 24

ORPHANS

A DAY LATER

Near Nedelea

MIDMORNING LIGHT STREAMED THROUGH THE WINDOWS AS BRITT sat up in bed, in the small medical clinic in Felipestii de Targ, the village across the Prahova River from Nedelea. The walls were clean and white, and the ceiling was anchored by "heavy brown wooden beams." Flowers grew outside the windows. For the better part of two days, Britt had been given morphine for his pain. His mind was only now beginning to catch up.

The crash was all still a blur. He could picture the face of a young Romanian man, then a boy, then a middle-aged woman, saying, "We'll have you out in a jiffy."

He'd been so out of it, he still didn't know who his rescuer was. But he remembered a tussle. People were tugging at him, shouting in German. The woman elbowed a soldier, a car was speeding off. Now here he was.

Could it have been a dream?

Britt looked down. His legs were so heavily bandaged he looked "like an Egyptian mummy."

It was real.

Britt noticed that the hospital staff seemed to be hurrying more than required as they went about their morning tasks. Maria Novleanu, a middle-aged doctor with dark hair, raced in with a thermometer, measured his temperature, then raced out. A nurse ran in and just as quickly swapped Britt's bedlinens for fresh sheets.

"Why the hurry?" Britt later wrote. "I could sense something or someone was expected. Out in the hall, the scrub lady was polishing the floors."

In the room, standing watch, was a Romanian Home Guard man. He was straightening his uniform and combing his hair with his hand, as if preparing for inspection.

"What's going on?" Britt asked.

The soldier ran off a string of phrases, none of which Britt understood, then went back to his grooming. He didn't speak a lick of English.

But one word caught Britt's ear—faintly familiar, almost English.

"Prințesa."

Britt blinked, trying to clear the fog of painkillers from his mind. A princess? He wasn't sure what he expected next, but the word set his thoughts in motion.

Moments later, Britt heard tires crunching over gravel and looked to the window, where tall trees shaded the clinic's front yard. A fleet of expensive cars rolled up outside, their polished exteriors gleaming in the sun. Through the open door in his room, he saw his doctor and nurses flock to the hallway and line up like soldiers on review.

In the corner of the room, Britt's guard straightened and stood a little taller. An entourage of local dignitaries and Romanian military officials greeted the doctors and nurses, then funneled into Britt's room. Everyone was respectfully abuzz, leaning in for a view of the patient, although no one spoke English.

Britt spotted the familiar face of the woman who'd rescued him. She pressed through the crowd, and he quickly connected the dots. His "English-speaking friend"? Her? She was the princess? Catherine walked straight up to Britt and greeted him. She explained that her entourage wanted their turn to meet a real American in person, while she was here for an update on his health.

"How are you feeling?" she asked.

Britt said he was getting better by the day and asked if his crew was all right.

Catherine told him that "one Ernie Poulson was quite concerned about you," and that Ernie, Al, and Medeiros were in captivity but safe. She'd seen to that personally, but she didn't know about the rest of the crew.

Britt felt a wave of relief to hear the news of Ernie, Al, and Medeiros, but his worry for Bob and the others still gnawed at him.

Turning to her entourage, the princess formally introduced Britt to the dignitaries and officers. The visitors were all smiles, apparently honored to be in his presence. While her entourage chatted among themselves, Catherine sat in the chair next to Britt's bed and gave him her full attention.

"Are you really a princess?" he said, and would later write, "I needed to know who my benefactor was."

Princess Catherine laughed off the question, but nodded it was true. Her name was Princess Ecaterina Caradja, and just as she'd told Ernie, he could call her Catherine. She explained that Caradja was her married name, and she was now separated from her husband, a scoundrel. Her mother's maiden name was the one she was proud of: Cantacuzino. They were the oldest oil family in the world. Her grandfather Cantacuzino had been Romania's prime minister, and the first oil well in history had been sunk on his estate.

Her family lineage carried a more recent claim to fame: Her younger cousin was an aviator, just like Britt, although he piloted a Romanian fighter, not a bomber. Princess Catherine wasn't sure where he was stationed these days. Maybe in the skies defending Ploesti?

Wherever he was, she hoped he was okay.

Ever since the rescue, Britt had been meaning to ask Princess Catherine something. Who were the teenagers who had cut him out of the aircraft? They had saved him from becoming "a human torch." Were they her relatives? Servants?

The princess chuckled; as Britt later recalled, "She looked at the others who were talking together on the other side of the room." It was okay, she had time to talk.

The princess explained that the teens who had freed Britt from the bomber, just like the little girl she was having lunch with at the start of the raid, were orphans who lived or worked on her estate.

Britt was intrigued. How many orphans did she look after?

"Three thousand." She beamed with pride.

Her answer threw Britt for a loop. He would learn that the Cantacuzino family used their wealth and status in a way few would expect. They operated a charitable foundation called Saint Catherine's Crib, an orphanage founded by Catherine's mother in Bucharest at the turn of the century.

The foundation was Catherine's true passion. She had personally administered the family charity since she was twenty-five, and the thousands of children in her care ranged in age "from infancy to young adulthood."

Most were not even Romanian, she explained. They were primarily refugees from Poland, war orphans whose parents had been killed during Hitler's invasion. Back in 1939, so many orphans were sent to her by train that the national railway put her name on the side of the reserved carriages—"Saint Catherine's Orphanage, Prahova"—so she could find them before the kids came pouring off.

"How do you support three thousand children?" Britt asked.

The logistics were staggering. It turned out that the Princess had built an intricate foster system, spreading out "1,000 of the older boys and girls" among twelve villages around Ploesti. Each set of Romanian parents was paid to care for the children. She'd built schools for the orphans, and even medical clinics like the one Britt was staying in.

The princess explained that the German takeover of the Ploesti region hadn't made her work any easier. She needed to walk a fine line to keep her foster system operating in an active air defense zone.

"I managed to provide for my children by maintaining a front of politeness toward the Nazi 'protectors' and humbling myself to the Fascists," she would later say. "I hated to do so, but pride has never clothed, fed, or sheltered a hungry child. I swallowed my pride so often, I considered it part of my diet."

She admitted her life "centered" around her orphans. It was why she kept a home near the orphanage in Bucharest and was always commuting back and forth. But to her, the work was worth every mile. She called them "my kids," and in a way, she had personally adopted each one. Even if they went through life without parents, they would always have a family with her.

"There aren't enough hours in the day for all I want to do," she told Britt.

Britt was stunned and humbled. Later he wrote, "My admiration for this woman was increasing every day."

AT LAST, "THE OFFICER stepped out of the group and indicated it was time to go," Britt recalled.

The princess told him to get some rest and reassured him she would see him again.

"With a wave, she was gone," Britt later recalled. "For a few minutes, I had forgotten about my pain and being a prisoner. Her story left me with a lot to think about."

He still had so many questions. How long could he stay at the clinic?

Could the Germans walk in at any moment and nab him? Why was the princess helping them?

He tried to think it all through.

Romania was supposed to be allied with the Nazis. Catherine was obviously a proud Romanian. The Americans were bombing her country—she should have been angry at him and Ernie and the others. Technically, she was their enemy.

Yet, somehow, he felt safe with her.

And something else made the princess's help even more puzzling. *Her cousin is fighting against us?*

CHAPTER 25

THE ENEMY OF YOUR ENEMY

TWO DAYS LATER, AUGUST 5, 1943

Kirovograd, Ukraine—the Eastern Front

IN THE HUBBUB OF THE MESS HALL, THE ROMANIAN PILOTS OF THE 7TH Fighter Group were drinking champagne. Some celebrated hard-fought victories, others toasted to another day of survival on the Eastern Front. Some, perhaps, drank to forget.

Buzz, newly promoted to captain, stared into his drink, lost in thought. He was Princess Catherine's cousin, thirteen years her junior. As a boy, he had raced with her through the halls of their grandfather's castle, laughter echoing between the stone walls. But that had been another life, years before they were both embroiled in a global conflict.

Most of the pilots gathered around Buzz were at least a decade younger, lean and deeply tan, but all carried the weight of old souls. There was a world-weariness about them, a look in their eyes that said they'd been at war too long. Yet they carried themselves with obvious pride, wearing sharply pressed blue uniforms with black ties and fancy jodhpurs tucked into their boots. Buzz preferred simpler attire, often wearing straight-legged trousers and leaving them untucked.

These days, Buzz couldn't relax. That morning, "waves" of Soviet Il-2 ground-attack planes and Yak escort fighters had hit the front lines, but Romanian pilots had beaten them back. Buzz knocked down two Il-2s and a Yak, bringing his count to nineteen enemy aircraft destroyed. His score in this single morning marked a monumental feat for any fighter pilot. Yet instead of reveling in the achievement, he sat in silence, his thoughts miles away. He had just learned of the American raid and was "worrying about the suffering of those at home and fearing for his family, who were not far from the Ploesti area." The fact that he was a massive shareholder in one of the oil companies didn't matter now.

His heaviness was compounded by what the attack signified. America had fully entered the fight, which promised to "amplify the sufferings of the Romanian people."

On top of everything, August 1 marked a personal loss for Buzz. His former flight instructor, Captain Marin Ghica, thirty-four, who'd taught him aerial gunnery, had just been killed. Flying a twin-engine Bf-110 fighter provided by the Germans, Ghica was one of the pilots who chased down the 389th as they fled Câmpina. He'd caught up with an American bomber at low level and attacked it from behind. The tail gunner fired, hitting the radio gear behind Ghica's cockpit. His rear gunner, seated backward, smelled smoke and felt heat from a fire below his seat. They had to bail out, something Ghica had done at least once before. Ghica pulled his fighter up, so he could bleed speed and gain altitude. His gunner jumped successfully, but it was too late for the pilot.

Villagers found Ghica near the smoldering wreckage of his Bf-110. He was lying face down with his hands in the soil, his parachute only partially unfurled behind him.

BUZZ COULD HAVE BLAMED the Americans for the loss of his mentor. But the truth was more complicated. In many ways, he felt a deeper kinship with his enemies than with Romania's so-called German allies.

He liked the Americans, even if they had just bombed his country. He liked the British, too. As early as 1941, Antonescu's secret police—the feared Special Intelligence Service—had begun to surveil him. His file branded him a "fervent" Anglophile whose "close friendship ties" with Jews, journalists, and Westerners were "enough to draw conclusions" about his loyalties.

Buzz was an Allied sympathizer. And the regime was on to him.

These days, he was more careful. But not even the bombing at Ploesti had changed his feelings toward the Americans.

Nor had it softened his distrust of the Germans.

He'd been fighting alongside them for three years now, but he knew that they were allies only on paper. They saw themselves as the Herrenrasse, the master race, and had always regarded Romanians as inferior.

Buzz first witnessed this attitude while on leave from the front line in

1941. He was having dinner with his pilots in the fancy Cireșica Hotel on the Black Sea when two German officers burst through the front door and looked around. They were new to Romania and amazed see "a wealth on the table, both of drink and food," while in the background "the grills were smoking," preparing the next course.

One of the Germans turned to his comrade and quipped: "Schau wie die Rumänen fressen!"

Fressen. The other officer laughed. To an untrained ear, it sounded like *essen,* the German word "to eat," as if the German officer was expressing admiration for his new allies by saying, "See how well the Romanians eat!" But Buzz spoke fluent German, learned during his school days in Switzerland, and he detected a subtle difference. *Fressen* was the word Germans used to describe when *an animal* eats.

"Look how these animals eat!"

Buzz translated what the man said to his fellow pilots.

"That was really insulting!" remembered Lieutenant Ion Dobran. It was no secret the Germans looked down on them. They mocked the Romanian pilots as "Gypsies," snickering when they had their new Me-109s blessed by an Orthodox Christian priest. It was one thing to use a slur behind someone's back, quite another to besmirch the Romanians to their faces.

The German officers weren't expecting what happened next.

"Bâzu stood up," Dobran recalled. The prince addressed the officer, speaking in perfect German. "Why would you say that?"

The officers' faces dropped in shock. *Who was this man?*

The tall, sturdy Romanian fighter pilot waited for them to correct themselves, but the Germans didn't know where to begin. They muttered excuses about how back home in Germany they were still using ration cards, it wasn't easy to come by butter, meat, and coffee, "let alone chocolate," and they hadn't realized before now that Romania was without food shortages.

Having exhausted all excuses, the officers left with their tails between their legs to find somewhere else to eat.

THE STING FROM THAT evening had faded, but Buzz and the other pilots no longer saw themselves as allies with Germany. They were co-belligerents, two parties fighting a common enemy—the Soviets.

From time to time, he flew with a German wingman, Feldwebel (sergeant)

Ernst Stengl, a liaison pilot attached to his squadron. Buzz accepted German medals. When he was awarded the Iron Cross for his heroics, he wore it. And he could overlook their ethnic disdain for him, personally.

Most people wouldn't understand how familiarity, even camaraderie, could exist between men who didn't like one another. But when fighting with your back to your homeland, losing ground, and with Romania teetering on the edge of annihilation at the Soviet Union's hands, there was no room for choice.

No, you don't have to like the man fighting alongside you.

The enemy of your enemy is your friend.

BUZZ FINISHED HIS CHAMPAGNE. Another friend lost to an unnecessary war.

The damage to his people was only beginning.

More bombs would fall, maybe next time on Romanian cities. The next time the bombers came, he would need to fight the Americans directly. The inevitability didn't escape him, and it was an uncomfortable thought for an Allied sympathizer. But what could he do? Buzz knew he was stuck fighting for the wrong team.

The less he thought about it, the better.

Forced to compromise his morality, maybe even beyond redemption, Buzz adopted a particular mindset that justified his powerlessness and reflected his growing weariness with the war.

Russians? Americans? Just point him in the direction of the enemy.

I fight who's in front of me.

CHAPTER 26

EMPLOYEE NO. 158

FOUR DAYS LATER, AUGUST 9, 1943

Nedelea

IT WAS MIDMORNING WHEN CATHERINE OPENED HER FRONT DOOR. UNDER the covered entryway stood a broad-shouldered young man with deep-set blue eyes. He stood six foot two and wore a sandy-colored suit and dark tie. He was no traveling salesman, that much was clear. Behind him stood an entourage of military officers in riding pants that flared at the thigh, more men in suits, and a Rolls-Royce limousine.

"Your majesty." Princess Catherine bowed.

King Michael I—Mihai I, in the Romanian form of his name—twenty-one, was the namesake of the yellow Michael's Cross on Romania's fighter planes. Michael carried himself with quiet dignity. He was "shy in the presence of strangers," wrote *Life* magazine before the war, "with a tendency to blush." Observed another journalist: "There was a certain gentleness in his expression, a lazy good-heartedness in his smile."

Although he was descended from German royalty, the king's heart belonged to Romania.* His reign was already different from his father's and grandfather's. Antonescu and the fascists had reduced him to a figurehead, dismissively calling him the Boy King, but Michael had something the fascists did not: the fealty of the Romanian people. Observed *Life:* "Romanians, who all love him as their own child, enjoy telling of his exploits."

* Romania's German king was no accident; it was a decision born of pragmatism. When Romania's ancient families united for mutual defense against the Ottoman Empire in 1866, rather than select a king from amongst themselves, which might favor one house over others, they decided to "import a king" from elsewhere in Europe. The council voted, choosing the German Hohenzollern line beginning with Michael's grandfather, Carol I.

Mihai I—
King Michael

Catherine's family and the king's shared a friendship that went back decades.

Had Michael heard the good news out of Bucharest? Of course he had—he was the king.

Word was sweeping the capital, splashed across headlines, and Catherine's telephone hadn't stopped ringing: The American prisoners were staying in Romania.

Her friends had made it happen. Their husbands had "bucked up" Antonescu, urging him to appeal to the Luftwaffe general who oversaw Romania for Hitler and to claim the Americans as a matter of national honor. Their timing couldn't have been better. Even Antonescu had grown tired of the Germans' bullying. The Nazis were constantly demanding more oil, but refusing to pay. So the dictator gave in and went to his German partners.

The Luftwaffe general thought it over, then snapped his fingers. Done. "I shall hand over all those we have arrested," he said.

What the newspapers didn't report was that the Germans, staggered by the American raid, now faced a herculean task. Between fighting a war on two fronts and a network of Romanian refineries to repair, prisoners were, in fact, the last thing on their minds.

As always, Catherine took no credit for the result. It had taken a small army to convince Antonescu to do the right thing. She had simply set the wheels in motion. What mattered was that her boys were safe. For now.

Meanwhile, she could focus on another development. She had called Michael's mother, her close friend Queen Helen, who served as the honorary chair of her foundation, to discuss orphanage matters. To Catherine, the queen mother was simply "Helen." She and her son were quiet opponents of the Antonescu regime, although they were powerless to change anything.

Helen had a curious request. "Do you happen to know where we can find a crashed bomber?" She said Michael was on his way to their summer palace in the resort town of Sinaia at the foot of the Transylvanian Alps and he "wanted to see some of the downed American planes." Helen knew Catherine owned vast tracts of land around Ploesti.

"Oh yes," the princess said. "There's one just below my garden."

Now Michael was here, eager to take her up on her offer. A downed bomber was waiting. "Shall we see it?" the princess asked.

A smile creased Michael's face.

THE CONVOY OF CARS rolled to a stop next to the riverbed where *Chattanooga Choo Choo* lay face down, twisted in the rocks. The king stepped from his limousine and donned sunglasses, trying to hide his enthusiasm. Catherine led him over.

He was instantly taken with the green bomber with the yellow Xs on its tails. A lifelong grease monkey, he'd always been fascinated by machines and their engineering. His biographer noted that "he liked delving into the interior of car engines, and was as much mechanic as chauffeur."

During Michael's palace school days, he'd convinced his schoolmasters to let him become an understudy at Ford's Bucharest assembly plant. "Every Friday morning he went to the Ford garage, put on overalls and worked under the supervision of trained mechanics," wrote a biographer. He was simply employee "No. 158," working for the equivalent of twenty cents per hour. Although he never attended higher education, along the way "he became an excellent self-taught engineer."

Several Romanian troops were guarding the bomber's wreckage to prevent peasants from scavenging its metal. The guard contingent came proudly to attention. *Salută!* The king was the last person they were expecting. With

Michael (tan suit) visits *Chattanooga Choo Choo*

his arms casually tucked behind his back, Michael reviewed the troops while Princess Catherine snapped photos.

Chattanooga Choo Choo was one of thirty-four American bombers that had come down in Romania during the raid. More were shot down at sea on the return leg. Of the 178 bombers that took off from Benghazi, not counting those lost to accidents and aborts, 45 B-24s were lost to enemy fire. Nearly one out of every four planes failed to make it home, the equivalent of more than an entire bomb group.

The king began a slow walk around *Chattanooga Choo Choo,* studying the wreck intently, like a mechanic preparing an assessment, as if he had plans to rebuild it. "He was impressed with the size of the plane," recalled the princess.

Michael had flown the royal plane, a German Junkers Ju-52, as copilot when he went to the Eastern Front to visit the troops. But this B-24 offered a whole new level of aeronautical technology.

When he came to the shattered cockpit, he paused, removed his jacket, handed it aside, and surprised everyone by climbing inside. The king sat in the copilot's seat, Ernie's, and moved the yoke and throttles, taking in the setting, imagining what it once took to fly this intricate machine, his mind likely drifting to another matter.

Americans bombing Romania. It was never supposed to come to this.

The king had tried to steer his country away from war against the Allies. After Romania won back its two territories, and Hitler asked Romania to follow him into the USSR, Michael and his advisors implored Antonescu to resist—do not set Romania against the Allied cause.

Then the queen mother called Michael one morning with disturbing news: BBC radio reported that Romania had declared war on the Soviet Union. The king immediately called Antonescu's deputy, the foreign minister.

"What is this?" Michael asked. "Is it true?"

"Yes," the minister said. The invasion was already under way.

"But why did you tell me nothing about it?"

"Well, I thought you were going to see it in the newspapers."

The king later wrote, "My country declaring war against the Russians, and I'm not even told. You sort of remain speechless."

Michael had a hunch why his warnings fell on deaf ears. Antonescu gave no weight to the king's opinions because of his father, King Carol II, who'd surrendered Romania's territories to the Soviets without a fight. After the 1940 coup by the Iron Guard unseated Michael's father, the disgraced king fled with his mistress (and the majority of the national treasury) to Switzerland, leaving behind his wife, Queen Helen, and Michael.

Antonescu promptly relegated Michael to the status of a figurehead. The king could bestow decorations and titles, host foreign ambassadors, and issue pardons. But that was it. The dictator made it clear: Romania was his now.

Queen Helen was convinced that she and her son had been lucky: If the Romanian people weren't so attached to Michael, who knew what Antonescu would have done.

But even a figurehead could fight back. During the monarchy's traditional New Year's radio broadcast, the young king flipped the script. "He called for Romania to discontinue the war alongside Hitler. In effect he was sending a message to the Allies on behalf of himself, the political leaders, many in the army and a large part of the civilian population."

King Michael wanted Romania to divorce the Axis.

The German ambassador "protested violently" to Antonescu. And Hitler "blamed the Marshal for this unpardonable 'stab in the back.'" The German military was already reeling from crushing defeats. Now this?

Antonescu, "furious," accused the queen mother of inciting her son. Surely, the Boy King was not himself capable of a move like this.

KING MICHAEL TURNED IN the copilot's seat and studied the wreckage. He saw the fallen turret. The radio room was crushed like a tin can. His initial curiosity about the machine shifted to a deeper understanding.

Men had fought and died here. They were probably near his age, twenty-one.

The smashed machine was both a memorial and a testament to the bravery of the men from Benghazi. *The African Knights.* They were flying for their country and, in a way, for his. If they succeeded, Romania would move one step closer to freedom from its authoritarian yoke.

Michael wouldn't forget this.

He knew he needed to find a way to extract his country from the war. His people had suffered immensely. But first, he wanted to help these Americans. They were stranded in his nation, facing an uncertain future, and many were badly wounded.

An idea began to form.

Taking one last look around the bomber's interior, Michael knew what he needed to do.

CHAPTER 27

MEET THE NEIGHBORS

SEVERAL DAYS LATER

Sinaia

THE SEVENTY AMERICAN POWS WERE FULL OF QUESTIONS AS THEY gathered in the lobby of a stately hotel in the Transylvanian Alps, a half hour's drive north from Ploesti.

Sergeant Clell Riffle, the top turret gunner of *Chattanooga Choo Choo,* hobbled in on a crutch, his right shin bandaged where shrapnel had peppered it, doing his best not to aggravate his broken ribs.

He didn't know what to make of any of this.

Unease was written on his face and on the faces of the men around him, a stark contrast to the elegance of their surroundings. These were most of the wounded survivors of the raid, and they collectively wondered what they were doing here.

Men were bandaged, on crutches, or confined to wheelchairs. Burn injuries were the most common. Flying too low to bail out, some men had been forced to ride their planes down while engulfed in flames. When the bombers crash-landed, some couldn't get out.

The POWs' confusion was understandable. One day they were lying in military hospitals, many under German control; the next, they were collected by the Romanians and brought here, to the Hotel Palace, one of the "most comfortably furnished" hotels in the country, nestled against the mountainside in the resort town of Sinaia, gateway to the Transylvanian Alps.

Now the men milled about in clean pajamas on polished parquet floors beneath wrought-iron chandeliers. Nearby, a team of Romanian doctors and nurses moved among them, watchful and attentive.

The Hotel Palace

To Riffle, the events of August 1 felt like a dream—like he'd taken a spill and rung his bell. But every ache reminded him it was no dream. It had happened.

He, Bob O'Reilly, and Sergeant Bowker hadn't made it far after the crash. They were taken prisoner by the same Germans who had tried to grab Britt. Minutes after he was captured, Riffle "had a brief encounter with his own mortality." A German officer, unaware of his wounds, barked at him to get to his feet. When Riffle couldn't move, the officer casually reached for a hand grenade, and leveled it at the helpless airman. The message was unmistakable: Get moving—or else. Before the downed fliers could find out whether the German meant it, Bob and Bowker scooped up Riffle and hurried him along.

Since then, they'd been separated. Riffle knew that Bob and Bowker survived. As for the rest of the crew, he wasn't sure. But he'd found camaraderie among his new companions—the wounded men from the other four bomb groups. They were young, good-natured, and resilient, just like the fellows of the 389th. And despite everything, they considered themselves lucky. Of the 340 Americans who had come down over Romania, only 110 were still alive.

Riffle and his fellow fliers were on the mend and grateful for their surroundings, albeit confused. None could figure out why they were being treated so well. They were the only guests at a hotel with five floors, located next door to the Casino of Sinaia. The iron benches around the palatial grounds were engraved with the names of royalty who'd slept here. "It looked like a setting for a Hollywood movie," recalled one POW.

Now, the hospital staff had invited the Americans to the lobby to meet their Romanian neighbors, and they promised the injured fliers it would be worth their effort. And even if they were moving slower these days, the Americans hadn't lost their humor. Several men were chuckling among themselves at their latest predicament—living with Romanian neighbors.

Think they'll bring a casserole?

OUTSIDE, A CONVOY OF stately cars pulled up. Riffle and the others heard excitement and glimpsed dignitaries, even before the double glass doors were opened. An attendant announced: "His Majesty Mihai the first!"

In walked the king.

Queen Helen

Michael was accompanied by an elegant woman of forty-five, lithe with a narrow face, sharp features, and black hair curled neatly under. She was his mother, Queen Helen, the "pillar" of his life. Deeply religious, with a "luminous personality," she was the source of her son's Christian faith. From her, Michael had learned that "prayer is our most needed deed in relation with God." When someone once asked what his favorite book was, he didn't hesitate. "The Bible, undoubtedly," he said.

It had been a short commute for Michael and his mother. Peleș Castle, the royal family's alpine palace, lay just a quarter mile up the hill.*

They were the neighbors.

Curious murmurs rose within the ranks of the POWs. Riffle and others were surprised—the king of Romania was young, maybe their age. Most of these young Americans had never met the mayor of their own hometowns, let alone a king or queen. Back home in West Virginia, Riffle had managed a small retail shop. How did one act around royalty? On the surface, they had nothing in common.

"The kid looks like good college football material," one airman observed.

Another agreed, "He might make a good tackle."

Facing a lobby full of wounded POWs, the king approached with trepidation. His countrymen had shot down many of the men in this room and were responsible for their wounds. He was the face of an enemy nation.

This was his attempt to make amends. On his orders, the Hotel Palace had been re-designated Military Hospital No. 415, and quickly converted into a full hospital, staffed with some of Romania's best doctors and nurses to care for the wounded raiders.

Riffle and the other Americans were under his direct patronage. Antonescu wasn't footing the bill. The Germans certainly weren't.

Michael was. He and his mother had chosen to house the wounded men in Sinaia, close to their home, so the queen mother could personally check in on them. *Being enemies is a choice.*

Silence fell on the lobby as the young king strode forward alone. Even the way he walked was deliberate. An observer once noted that Michael "made his way across the room in that quiet, measured step of his. There was thought and method in the boy. One could see he thought things out for himself."

King Michael stopped and stood in a semicircle of seventy POWs. Up close, he could see that their wounds were worse than they'd seemed from a distance. He looked with sympathy at the "men with the lobes of their ears burned off, eyebrows gone, skin a hard congested weal."

* Connected to Bucharest by the only paved road in Romania, Sinaia had been King Michael's stamping ground since boyhood. The drive there was a thrill ride for any motor enthusiast. At a banquet one evening, his father, King Carol II, boasted of having made a record run from the capital in his automobile. Michael leaned toward a friend. "Don't tell him," he whispered, "but I did it in fifteen minutes less."

At first, he stuttered and shot a nervous glance around the room. He asked if they were being well cared for. The wounded men were silent, their expressions unreadable. Michael promised they would be "well-treated" during their time in Romania and revealed that they were neighbors now, adding that he expected the fresh air would be good for them and help their recovery.

Still, the men said nothing. The silence hung heavy; it was hard to read the room.

The king offered a slight smile. "If you'd like, I'll write to your parents, saying you are safe."

That got Riffle's attention—and everyone else's. Every downed flier had the same fear: their families at that very moment might be thinking they're dead. A postcard would be nice, but one airman had an even better idea. Every minute mattered.

From "the rear ranks of the crowd," the airman shouted: "How about cabling?"

Riffle and the POWs erupted in laughter, and the king couldn't help but laugh with them.

That broke the ice.

The POWs and their new neighbor would get along just fine.

LIEUTENANT JOHN PALM, TWENTY-SEVEN, woke to sounds of "a lot of excitement" outside his newly appointed hospital room. A hefty, dark-haired Texan, he lay with his leg in traction—what was left of it, anyway.

A pilot with the Liberandos, Palm had crash-landed his B-24, *Brewery Wagon,* after a direct hit from Ploesti's flak knocked out one engine, damaged two, and nearly tore his lower leg clean off. "It was hanging by a few strands," he recalled. Palm had ripped out the Plexiglas side window with one hand, grabbed his mangled leg with the other, and dived through the opening, holding his right leg like a quarterback clutching a football. Then he forgot himself and tried to run through a Romanian field. He didn't get far.

Romanian doctors had finished the job, amputating below the knee.

Still "doped up" on painkillers, Palm looked up and saw "a tall young fellow" standing at the foot of his bed, "a distinguished-looking lady" at his side.

The young man seemed familiar. Palm had seen his face before—in a 1940 issue of *Life* magazine, which his father's shoe store subscribed to. The wounded American blinked, wiped his eyes. Was he seeing things? Then he recognized Queen Helen and made the connection.

It was the king!

Michael and his mother weren't about to neglect the seriously injured men who couldn't be moved.

When Palm reached out to shake the king's hand, the hospital staff cringed—Americans didn't know the rules. You were never supposed to touch royalty.

The king didn't care. He shook Palm's hand anyway.

Queen Helen struck up a conversation with the wounded pilot. She put Palm instantly at ease. There was something effortlessly regal about her, charming, gracious, empathetic. She was Greek, in fact. Her father had been the king of Greece.

She asked tenderly about his wounds.

"Hurts like hell, ma'am."

The staff winced again at the language, but the queen only smiled.

Palm told them he remembered seeing their story in *Life.*

"So they know us in America!" Queen Helen said, evidently "pleased all over."

"We certainly do," Palm replied. He noticed that the king was shy, a man of few words, while "the queen was a great talker."

After some time, the queen's tone changed; she glanced over her shoulder, lowered her voice, and leaned closer. Behind her, a small army of Romanian generals and advisors had drifted in—they were never more than a few feet away.

Palm connected the dots. "I don't think the queen wanted them to hear what she was saying," he later wrote. He was right. Even a king and queen had to watch their words in Antonescu's Romania. There were "people with big ears" everywhere, Michael recalled. One general in their entourage even reported to the dictatorship, writing up the young king's every move. Michael had figured it out when Antonescu knew exactly "about something I talked about."

The queen asked in a near whisper, "Do you think the Americans understand our sympathies are all with you?"

"I didn't know," Palm later admitted. "But I decided this was the time to be diplomatic, so I said, 'Oh, yes—sure!' And there were a lot more smiles. They fraternized with me, all right. They were good and sick of the Germans and glad of anybody's help to get rid of them."

At some point, Palm began to grasp just how perilous the Americans' situation really was. Watching the king and queen cast wary glances at their own entourage, it hit him. The POWs did have something in common with royalty—and it wasn't good.

These folks are prisoners, too.

CHAPTER 28

SCENE OF THE CRIME

SIX WEEKS LATER, SEPTEMBER 23, 1943
North of Ploesti

ON A CRISP AUTUMN MORNING, TWO SMALL ROMANIAN BUSES ROLLED north through the Prahova Valley toward the Transylvanian Alps. Both carried American airmen under guard—prisoners from all five bomb groups.

Inside the lead bus, the officers of *Chattanooga Choo Choo* sat together. Ernie sat across from Bob and Al, relieved simply to be among his friends again. From their bomber, Britt was absent, still recuperating in the hospital. And Frank Kees, the crew's big-brotherly flight engineer, had been laid to rest by Princess Catherine in the most unlikely of places: her family's own cemetery on her estate. In time, she would write to Kees's mother, "inviting her to visit the grave."

The morning sun slanted through the windows. From his seat on the left side of the bus, Ernie gazed outside. It was almost harvest time. Bales of wheat and pumpkins stood in the fields.

"Looks like we're home," one man said, longingly. Romania looked like an "American harvest scene."

Ernie's bus was only half full, carrying nineteen officers. The enlisted men rode in the second bus, about twenty sergeants in all, including the gunners of *Chattanooga Choo Choo.* Mixed into the two buses were four British POWs who'd escaped German camps only to be recaptured in Romania.

The emptiness of the buses haunted Ernie. Of the 110 downed fliers who had lived to be made prisoners of war, only forty escaped serious wounds. Not even enough to fill two small buses.

The skill with which they'd crash-landed—plus a heaping dose of luck—

had spared most of their crew from the worst. Many of the other crews hadn't been as fortunate.

The first time Ernie saw Bob after the raid, he had a question for his friend. "Think they mailed your 'just in case'?"

"Shut up," Bob muttered, half smiling.*

No one from their crew—or perhaps anyone on the buses, for that matter—was more uncomfortable being a prisoner than Bob. He'd already tried to escape once from the schoolhouse in Bucharest where they'd been held since the raid. Even now, he was cagey and restless, periodically glancing around as if searching for a way out. Fifty-three days had passed since they were shot down, and now the Romanians were moving them again. Word was, they were bound for a permanent POW camp deep in the Transylvanian Alps.

And they had a high-ranking Romanian escort. At the front of Ernie's bus, Colonel Gheorghe Săulescu of the Romanian general staff sat with his guards. A short, middle-aged man, "he was of great girth, and wore a cap as wide proportionately as he was." He oversaw all the POW camps in Romania. Săulescu had come along to personally see the Allies to their new billeting, and he took great pride in his job. Earlier in Bucharest, when loading the POWs aboard buses, he had "strutted about importantly, rubbing his hands with a bring-'em-back-alive air."

Ernie pondered the situation. A colonel for an escort? A new camp in Transylvania? He figured a Romanian camp would be like a German one, with barbed wire and guard towers, someplace cold and dismal. He wondered what kind of tough treatment awaited them, especially after the damage they'd done.

Ever since the POWs from the five bomb groups had been brought together, they'd compared notes, and a fuller picture of the raid had come into focus.

It was just short of a disaster.

Instead of the four groups arriving at Ploesti together and surging down like a wave to overwhelm the defenses, the lead two groups had arrived ahead of schedule. And the repercussions from General Ent's questionable decisions didn't stop there. Not only did he leave half the task force behind, but

* Fortunately, the POWs knew the Army wouldn't mail a man's goodbye letter if there was any doubt about whether he was missing or killed in action.

on his call or his pilot's (this was hotly debated), the Liberandos had turned too soon, following roads that would lead south to Bucharest, not Ploesti.

Behind them, Lieutenant Colonel Addison Baker of the Traveling Circus spotted the general's error. "If we didn't bomb Ploesti on that day, we'd have to return to do it another day," he had warned before the raid. "And the Germans would be even more prepared for us the next time."

So the Traveling Circus broke off from the Liberandos, and Baker led his group in a daring solo attack on Ploesti. Before the mission, he'd told his deputy lead, Captain Walt Stewart: "I intend to go over that target. If I go over it in flames, I'm going over it!"

Tragically, that's what happened. Baker and his copilot, Major John Jerstad, went to their deaths leading the initial headlong charge.

Soon enough, the Liberandos, which had once been the lead group, found themselves flying alone. They corrected course, and although some brave elements launched attacks on Ploesti, it was too late for most of the veterans to lend their weight to the attack.

By the time the Eight Balls and Pyramiders—who'd flown through the clouds with the 389th—arrived, the outcome of the raid was hanging in the balance. The German trap was already sprung, and anti-aircraft defenses fired at full tempo.

The situation was nothing short of a hellscape, "a pitch-black inferno filled with bursting flak, barrage balloons, and towering smokestacks." Flames from ruptured oil tanks were reaching as high as the tallest buildings, while delayed-action bombs from earlier waves detonated. Thick smoke obscured the targets they were supposed to hit.

The groups flew into the maelstrom anyway. "Either we hit Ploesti or we'll die trying," Colonel John Kane, commander of the Pyramiders, had vowed. Tragically, his group and the Eight Balls also paid a steep price: thirty of their seventy-six bombers were lost during the raid.*

The only good news was this: The attack on Ploesti had paid off. That morning, as they'd driven past the main complex, the men had seen the proof with their own eyes—vast refineries left "in desolate ruin," stacks

* Tidal Wave resulted in the most awards of the Medal of Honor for a single raid. One went to Lt. Lloyd Hughes of the 389th, and the rest to pilots who attacked the main complex. Medals went posthumously to Lt. Col. Addison Baker and Maj. John Jerstad, and were presented in person to Col. John Kane of the Pyramiders and Col. Leon Johnson of the Eight Balls, who arrived last and still pressed the attack in the face of seemingly insurmountable odds.

"no longer puffing smoke." From where they sat, there was plenty to be proud of. Together, the Traveling Circus, Pyramiders, and Eight Balls, with brave rogue elements of the Liberandos, had done it. They plastered their targets.

But what about the rookies, the 389th?

WITHOUT WARNING, THE ROMANIAN guards got up and went seat to seat, shutting each window blind. The buses suddenly accelerated to race past whatever the POWs were approaching. Ernie cocked his head. *What don't they want us to see?* The POWs at the front of the first bus saw it through the windscreen and shouted in excitement.

"Red Target! One o'clock!"

They were passing through Câmpina. The refinery lay just ahead. A brown-uniformed arm reached in front of Ernie's face and snapped shut his blind. Romanian pride was at stake. But Bob's rebelliousness flared. He snapped open his blind again and called, "They can't stop us all!"

The POWs roared with laughter. Up and down the bus, POWs began hiking up the blinds. Noted the historian Michael Hill, "The fun-loving Americans figured they had paid the price of admission to see their handiwork." Hesitating a moment, Ernie finally did, too. It became like a scene from Abbott and Costello. Guards ran back and forth, tugging down blinds all over the moving bus. The moment a guard moved on, a POW lifted his blind again. Finally, the guards gave up and returned to their seats.

Outside the windows, the massive refinery slid by, a stone's throw from the road. Ernie and the others rushed to the right side of the bus, where Bob and Al sat staring.

One by one, the men quieted as captor and captive alike stared at what was left of Steaua Română. The once-protective firewalls were in ruins. The grounds were upheaved and cratered. Ruptured oil tanks leaked their final remains. Twisted pipes and melted metal lay tangled in the destruction. Brick buildings stood hollow, gutted by fire. Burnt tank cars had been tossed from the railway tracks. Collapsed smokestacks lay shattered on the ground. By the looks of things, the fires in the refinery had raged for several days, resisting the exertions of German firemen. The entire site was charred, as if someone had painted the whole thing with a black brush.

Smiles began to twitch on the men's sobered faces. "There was an ap proving hum and elbows in neighboring ribs," recounted a historian. "Boy, that one is hammered but good!"

The rookies had wiped Steaua Română out.

Bob turned to Ernie, eyes wide with astonishment. "Are you seeing this? Look at that!" he said, his excitement barely contained.

Ernie stayed glued to the window, taking in the desolate wreckage. "My God," he murmured. "Look what we did."

The 389th's target was so demolished that when a British recon plane had flown over the area two days after the raid, it "could not locate or make out the refinery." The 9th Air Force's post-mission assessment would show "a near perfect strike at Câmpina." Other refineries had been hit by forty, fifty, and even fifty-nine bombs—and that seemed a lot. The 389th had placed 131 bombs on target. Historians would call it a "classically executed" performance, "the most accurate and successful attack of the Tidal Wave mission." And the 389th had suffered the fewest losses of groups that hit their targets. Just four bombers had been shot down. Ernie only wished theirs hadn't been one of them.

In a blink, the buses roared past the shattered refinery. The Romanians gazed out at the destruction, their expressions a mix of shock and disbelief. Among the POWs, emotions swung from awe to quiet jubilation as the scope of their accomplishment sank in. Despite the very real human cost, they had succeeded. It didn't matter which group they belonged to—American fliers turned to one another with grins. Red Target was the last remaining piece in the puzzle. *They had done it.* Hitler's Gas Station lay in shambles.

Bob grabbed Ernie by the shoulders. "We clobbered it."

Ernie cracked a smile. "Yes, we did."

Ernie headed back to his seat. After seeing the stricken refineries and reliving the memories of the attack, he needed a cigarette. Since becoming a POW, he'd taken to smoking to handle the hunger and stress. Ernie fished one from his pocket, lit it, and sat back in his seat with relief. Romania's most modern refinery was out of the war.

At least it had all been for something.

COLONEL SĂULESCU AND HIS guards seemed glad that leg of the journey was behind them. The buses followed the "rushing, cascading waters" of the Prahova River north into the foothills. As the POWs entered Sinaia, the road snaked through an explosion of fall foliage. Old-growth trees shimmered with red and yellow leaves. Inside the town, everywhere Ernie looked were winding lanes lined with half-timbered mansions. The homes of the Romanian upper class peeked through the trees with their sharply slanted roofs and tall windows, remnants of a grander past.

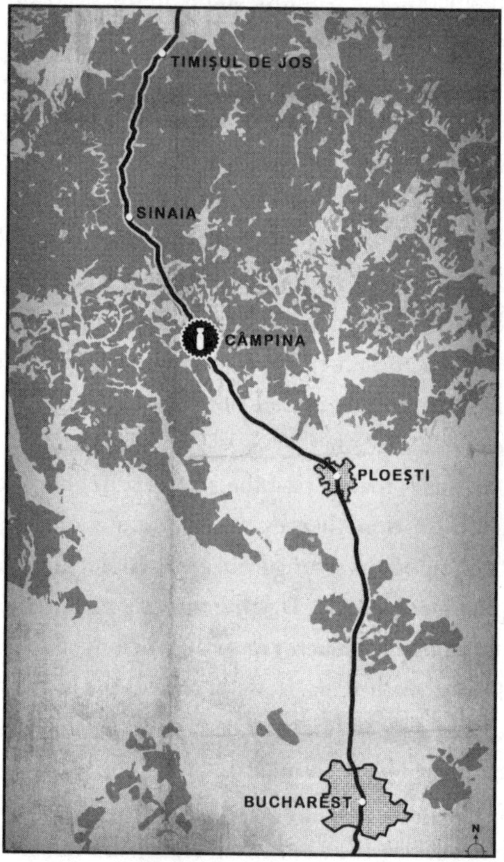

Colonel Săulescu stood and faced his passengers. The portly little man wore an impeccable uniform: riding breeches with a chest full of ribbons, each earned in the Great War. "For in Romania, one could not speak of officers and men in the same breath," observed a POW. "The officers were fashion plates—not a crease in their tunics, box shoulders, mirror-like boots tightly clasping their legs up to their knees."

Săulescu glanced down at a book in his hands, then looked up again. With the practiced diction of a tour guide, he began a simple narration for the POWs, relying on an English phrase book to communicate. "There's the

King's Palace." He pointed to Peleș Castle, the royal family's dreamy Neo-Renaissance palace, half-timbered, its numerous turrets rising sharp and pointy like weathervanes. "And there's the royal villa." He gestured to a chalet where King Michael and his mother stayed.

Ernie began to enjoy himself. He felt less like a prisoner and more like a man on a sightseeing tour. He and the others saw the Hotel Palace, where their wounded friends—now including Britt—were recuperating under the eye of King Michael. And a small, lavish train station where the Orient Express used to stop. On the way out of town, Săulescu pointed proudly across a long bridge to their right. There, perched on the hillside, rose a romantic

Peleș Castle

stone palace with sharply slanted roofs—Cantacuzino Castle, he said. Built at the turn of the century, it had once been the summer home of Princess Catherine's grandfather, though Ernie didn't know that then. Its arched windows glimmered in the sun.

The buses left the city and came to a pass in the mountains where the road narrowed. Dense forests of leafy yellow trees squeezed the vehicles from both sides, the canopy of foliage reaching overhead with an enchanted quality. On the other side of the pass lay Transylvania, the mysterious land Ernie had seen in the 1931 film *Dracula*. Ernie thought about what he knew about Transylvania. It was synonymous with horror, howling wolves, full moons, and Bela Lugosi rising from his coffin. Was Frankenstein's monster from there, too?

Cantacuzino Castle

The convoy emerged into a long, narrow, picturesque valley in the Alps. Ernie blinked. This was nothing like the horror flick. Immense, rugged mountains framed the valley with quiet majesty. Dark green fir trees swayed in the breeze. Grassy meadows stretched wide. Streams bubbled with milky blue water. "The scenery is beautiful, and even these characters fall quiet for a few moments," remembered one of the British POWs.

Săulescu consulted his phrase book and called out, as if delivering a wonderful surprise, "You are on your way to a hotel!"

Ernie and Bob looked at each other, eyes wide. Several minutes later, it all made sense. The buses slowed in the tiny hamlet of Timisul de Jos. Across the road and through pockets of trees, Ernie saw a three-story building on a layered fieldstone foundation. It was more of an alpine lodge than a hotel, like something from a Christmas movie. The building had a peaked tower, and a veranda with a view. Off to the side stood a small, picturesque lake, "and on all sides, boxing the location in, rose tier on tier of mountains."

It was called Lagărul Prizonieri Nr. 2 (Prison Camp No. 2), the successor to the schoolhouse in Bucharest, which was matter-of-factly referred to as Lagărul Prizonieri Nr. 1.

Romanian guards opened the gate, and the buses turned left across the railroad tracks, pulled in, and crunched to a stop on the gravel driveway. The

Lagărul Prizonieri Nr. 2—"the lodge"

POWs stepped out of the buses. Many carried their meager belongings in "little tied-up bundles, or small Red Cross boxes." In late September, the weather was only beginning to turn chilly. "Some had flying-coats on, but many no more than shirts and trousers," noted a British POW, "and, but for their caps, there was little to suggest they were in uniform at all."

This is our new POW camp? Ernie and Bob almost laughed.

It turned out that Lagărul No. 2 had been a resort before the war. All the Romanians did was put a barbed-wire fence around it and add a guard post at the gate.

While guards in brown uniforms with soft caps and puttees paced the fence line, Săulescu rubbed his hands in glee. The portly colonel smoothed his spotless uniform. It was time for the dramatic finale. He swept an outstretched arm toward the lodge.

Well? He grinned.

Even Bob was impressed. The Romanians had it all worked out. The Allied officers would dwell in the main lodge, while the enlisted men would stay two hundred yards away in the "sergeants' camp," a cozy alpine building with a slanted roof that had once been a private school for girls. The camp offices and guard barracks lay between the two compounds.

The POWs were dismissed to their new home. Ernie, Bob, and the wide-eyed officers craned their necks at their surroundings. Some men began walking fast, then faster, eager to claim the best rooms. The irony. They were going back into captivity, "but somehow it doesn't seem so bad," one man recalled.

INSIDE THE TILED ENTRYWAY, the lodge was cozy, with arched doorways and white plaster walls. There was no need to dash to claim a room, for the entire building was theirs. While some men chose rooms on the first floor, Ernie, Bob, and Al went to the second. Ernie secured a room for himself and Britt, when he was healed, while Bob and Al took the next room to the right. Ever since the crash, Bob had taken Bambino, who worshipped the ground he walked on, under his wing like an older brother.

Ernie was surprised by what he found waiting in his room: real beds, a beautiful porcelain heater, a private bathroom, and wide windowsills that offered a prime view where he could see trains go by. A push button on the wall by the door drew Ernie's curiosity: It was a bell for room service in the camp's past life as a fancy hotel. The only things missing were stationery on the desk and a chocolate on each pillow.

A guy could get used to this.

Bob and Al poked into Ernie's room, all smiles. Bob shot a look around. Was Ernie's room as nice as theirs?

Ernie cracked a grin. "They forgot the flowers."

DOWNSTAIRS, ERNIE AND HIS friends fell in with an orientation tour already under way. A Russian POW named Victor, speaking in broken English, beamed as he showed the new POWs around. The Americans were shocked to discover the lodge was already staffed by Russian POWs who served as orderlies. They would cook and clean for the Americans, serve them at mealtimes, and fix their beds every morning.

Ernie felt a little embarrassed. We have *servants*?

The perks of Lagărul No. 2 went beyond the housekeeping. The Americans were to be paid the same as their equivalent Romanian rank, minus deductions for food and drink and toiletries, and a barber would come by daily, who'd give them a shave and a haircut for just a few coins. When that news broke, every head turned toward Ernie, grinning. The men could even buy beer with their pay. The tour screeched to a stop.

Beer?

Bob, in particular, couldn't believe his ears. Except maybe for Scotch, there was nothing he loved more than beer. The guards would bring it over from the pub across the road that doubled as their canteen. A Red Cross observer explained: "A Romanian regulation has been specially issued for the American Officers to bring them from this inn all that they wish as additions to their diet: beer, mineral water, etc."

After moving through the coatroom toward the dining room, the men poked their heads into a spotless kitchen, where Russian orderlies were preparing a steak dinner for that evening. They obviously had American tastes in mind. "Someone had been priming Ivan, the cook, well," remembered one man. In the dining room, where sunlight poured in, Ernie and the others found tables "set with flowers, with cutlery—actual knives and forks for prisoners—white cloths and white paper serviettes."

The men nearly fell over. And the cherry on top: "Finally, on a large table against the wall stood a large wireless," recalled one of the Brits, "and even now a Romanian officer was tuning in—not to Bucharest or Berlin, but London."

Ernie and his friends stood and listened. They hadn't heard music or news in fifty-three days. Was this a dream?

A smile creased Ernie's face. He'd come a long way from the subterranean rat-infested hole that he, Al, and Medeiros first found themselves in.

We are pretty darn fortunate.

Ernie was almost afraid to blink for fear their plush new surroundings might disappear. Already, he was growing concerned. It seemed too good to be true. His biggest question . . .

How long could this possibly last?

CHAPTER 29

THE BRIBE

SIX WEEKS LATER, NOVEMBER 4, 1943
Timisul

IT WAS A GOOD MORNING TO LOUNGE AROUND.

Most of the POWs reclined in folding chairs on the front porch of the officers' lodge in Lagărul No. 2. It was the last day of fall. The sun shined warmly on the men, the crisp air carried the scent of the season, and leaves listed down in shades of amber, red, and brown. Music wafted from the radio—"our pride and joy." Sometimes "Vera Lynn singing in the rainbow club" could be heard from London, or Ernie's favorite, "good old American jazz" from the States.

Ernie spent much of his time reading and scribbling in his journal. Back when his guard unit was on active duty, he wrote a regular column for the tiny local newspaper about their band unit, recounting what the various local boys were up to. At least when he read or wrote, he felt like he was doing something.

It was easy duty in the camp. Any man at any time might be sipping a Bragadiru brand beer. Whenever the POWs ran out, they simply placed their order with the American mess officer, First Lieutenant Albert Aaronson, a navigator, who sent the guards to the pub opposite the lodge to get more.

When trains went by bound for Bucharest, the POWs audaciously flashed two fingers in a V for victory. The German and Romanian passengers looked stunned. Who were these men, and why were they here?

Despite the vacation-like atmosphere, a subtle crackle of anticipation could be felt throughout the compound. No matter what they were doing, Ernie and the POWs kept an eye fixed on the front gate. Every man knew.

Today was special. More of their countrymen, maybe even Britt, were coming to the lodge.

Meanwhile, the guards stayed busy walking the fence line. In and out they came from a small stone cabin by the front gate, faithfully doing their rounds. They watched the POWs but they never stared for long before their eyes darted away and they looked down.

Most of the guards were uneducated farm boys. About 75 percent of Romania's troops came from the peasantry, drafted from agricultural work. Most were stocky young men, muscled from days of hauling hay and digging fenceposts. But the Americans noticed something unusual in the guards' behavior: fear.

Nazi propaganda had indoctrinated them. One flier recalled how the guards believed that "American bomber crews had been recruited from the gangsters of New York, Los Angeles, Chicago and every other large city—and that we were paid five thousand in gold for every raid we ran." The guards might have been afraid, but even so, "they had no intention of letting us go. We were like specially rare animals at the zoo; to be pandered [to], but all the more carefully to be watched."

Only one guard showed no fear. First Sergeant Copil was as finely cut as a bodybuilder. Or perhaps a bully. He had muscles on top of muscles and a chiseled jaw that one American described as "box-like, the jawbones seemed to be at right angles."

The Americans made him a pet project. Whenever the men saw Copil coming, they shouted in English, with a good-natured wave, "Good morning, Hog Jaw!"

Sgt. Copil had no clue. He stuck out his chest with pride.

All fun and games aside, Săulescu had laid out one rule for their new "guests": Do not try to escape. Any attempt would be a grave insult to Romania's hospitality, and worse, the guards would be forced to shoot. The kicker? Săulescu added, "Anyone thinking of escape should know the fence is mined."

Escape? Who even thought about escape? For all practical purposes, they were left to govern themselves. Their camp mysterious commandant, Major Cavaropol, had only been glimpsed in passing. Their steak dinner on the first night might have been an exception, yet no one was complaining about their day-to-day meal plan. A typical breakfast included "one fried egg per man, coffee, stewed pears, and bread." Lunch consisted of "potato pancakes, salad, marmalade, watermelon," and more bread. Dinner was "bell peppers stuffed with rice," and cheese, coffee, and yet more bread. The POWs were fed better than most Romanians.

Bob, ever suspicious, called the treatment a bribe. He figured the good food and lax conditions were meant only to discourage them from escaping. But Ernie wasn't complaining. He'd concluded that if you'd survived the raid, you were lucky to be alive. As for Săulescu's warnings, escape was the last thing on Ernie's mind.

You'd have to be crazy to want to escape.

ABOUT 10 A.M., TWO buses pulled up in front of the officers' lodge. The men on the porch leapt to their feet. The first group of wounded men had arrived from King Michael's hospital. More were set to follow in the upcoming weeks.

About ten officers were dropped off; these were the guys who'd recovered fastest. The buses drove away to deliver about twenty enlisted men to the sergeants' camp, including Clell Riffle, whose leg had healed.

A few of the wounded men arriving at the officers' lodge were badly scarred. Some struggled with burned hands that wouldn't flex, and others with arms that wouldn't fully extend. They carried their belongings as well as they could; their khaki uniforms were worn and some were in tatters.

Among the new arrivals was Britt. Ernie, Bob, and Al dashed forward and reunited with their friend near the gate. A quick tear came to Britt's eye, and Ernie gave him a bear hug, but Britt winced—he was not yet fully healed. He hiked up his pant leg, showing the guys the large patches of purple-red discoloration where the aviation fuel had burned his skin.

Small knots of officers formed in the driveway. There was a lot of handshaking and backslapping, and for some it was the first real chance to talk since the ordeal. "In some planes, no more than one or two or three members of the crews came through. Some had scarcely any recollection of how they survived; some pulled their parachute cords and landed on the ground almost simultaneously," remembered one POW.

Ernie picked up Britt's parcel for him and led him to the lodge. He mentioned he'd saved his friend a bed.

"Sounds great," Britt replied. "But slow down. I still can't move too fast."

The officers of *Chattanooga Choo Choo* began to rattle off all the perks of the lodge: the daily barber, the monthly pay, the beer. They were really getting into it until another of the new arrivals overheard the conversation and cut in with a grin.

"We had nurses."

Britt nodded. It was true.

Bob cracked a jealous smile. Okay, you win.

A HALF MOON HUNG over the valley in the early evening as Ernie led Britt through the lodge toward the dining room. It felt like Halloween weather. Dinner was already finished, and the men were warm with food in their bellies. All that was missing was a crackling fireplace. The POWs had a clandestine activity planned for later that evening, and Ernie promised his friend that he didn't want to miss it.

The dining room buzzed with music and activity as the POWs played poker and roulette. At the center of it all was Bob, fiercely competitive, who thrived on any challenge. A Romanian corporal wandered through for his nightly head count and soon left, leaving the POWs to their own devices. "The lights were to stay on as long as we wished," recalled a POW, and the men sometimes played games and gambled all night. If a Romanian sentry on night duty gazed through the window, his eyes would go wide when at one gaming table, "he could see more money change hands in ten minutes than he would earn in his life." Most of the American officers were paid a Romanian lieutenant's wages of 9,400 lei per month (about $57). The sentry took home a monthly pay of two lei, about the price of a pack of cigarettes.

Ernie and Britt pulled up chairs near the radio. Bob and Al soon joined them. By the stroke of nine, everyone had folded their cards and gathered around the radio. It was time to introduce the new POWs to the men's clandestine routine.

A man opened the cabinet next to the radio, revealing a neat stack of plates. Tucked within the cabinet's inner panels was a map of Europe hand drawn by their navigators. Pushpins riddled its surface, connected by lines of red string.

Britt nodded silently, admiration in his eyes. This was a masterpiece of quiet defiance. The men were charting the opposing front lines.

Bob, Ernie, and Al beamed with pride. They kept the map hidden during the day, so the guards wouldn't think they were plotting an escape. The other officers eyed the map with knowing grins, anticipation rising as they drew their chairs closer to the radio. The wait for a show to begin reminded Ernie of home. "It was a great family event when we got a radio, and I loved to sit with my Dad and listen to the prizefights."

Someone tuned the dial to the BBC, and the room hushed in anticipation. "Good fiery stuff was what the airmen liked to hear," observed a British POW, "[commentary] which had the war won and neatly put away every day."

"The first clear sounds were the familiar tones of Big Ben, in London," recalled Britt. The men exhaled slowly, listening for what was to come. The war updates would begin soon. Just hearing the news made the officers feel connected to their mission again. As if they were following a goal line stand in the fourth quarter, every night the men "sweat out each foot of ground gained," Ernie wrote in his diary. "Each and all seemed to bring us steps closer to home and nearer to termination of the European conflict."

At last the war news came on. As the BBC broadcaster recounted the latest developments, several of the navigators scribbled down the fast-flying news in notepads, while others leaned over the map, carefully shifting the pushpins and string. They had been appointed "marshals," charged with documenting each hard-won advance or crushing setback. Every pushpin represented miles gained or lost, the cost counted in lives. "No one spoke during the broadcast," Britt later wrote. "But there were cheers or groans depending on the news."

The lack of progress in Italy elicited disappointment. Now two months into the invasion, the map of the boot was a grim sight. The Allied lines had completely bogged down north of Naples, and two thirds of the country was still in Axis hands. The liberation of Rome was nowhere in sight.

News from the Eastern Front felt far away. It was still anyone's guess who would get to Romania first, Stalin or Uncle Sam.

The most anticipated news was the European bombing campaign. The room fell silent as the marshals put pushpins on the 8th Air Force's latest target: the German port city of Wilhelmshaven, on the North Sea coast. The raid had barely crossed German soil, and for a reason. The 8th was still reeling from the bloodiest month of their entire daylight bombing campaign. Raids deep into the Reich were on hold for the rest of 1943, until the Americans found a fighter that could escort bombers to faraway targets and back.

The POWs in Lagărul No. 2 could read between the lines. The 8th had taken a beating. The newscaster prattled on, but Ernie's mind was far away—with the 389th, now back in England from Benghazi, flying under a new nickname: the Sky Scorpions. While the BBC recounted the broad strokes of the conflict, the bitter reality was that Ernie and his friends personally knew the men who were fighting and dying.

Their flight leader, Lieutenant Elmer Rodenberg? After getting back to England, he took off on a routine maintenance flight, lost an engine, crashed, and died at twenty-three, leaving behind his fiancée, Virginia, a stenographer.

Their other wingman, Lieutenant Ken Matson? He'd been shot down by flak over Austria, losing half his crew. Bleeding heavily, Matson managed to pull the ripcord of his parachute a split second before blacking out.

And Captain Kenneth Caldwell, who'd led the attack on Red Target? The twenty-nine-year-old, who'd earned the Distinguished Service Cross for Tidal Wave, would soon die over France, taking a direct hit in the cockpit from a rocket fired by a German fighter.

In time, half of the 389th pilots who flew from Benghazi on August 1, 1943, would be dead or captured.

The most painful part for Ernie and his fellow officers was that they knew their friends were trying to bring this war to an end to free people just like *them.*

Bob fidgeted in his chair, restless. Abruptly he stood and left the room. It wasn't like Bob to be the first to turn in for the night. Britt noticed that he was edgier than before he'd been shot down, like a cat crawling up the wall.

Al, too, had heard enough of the bad news. "We're spending the war sitting on our butts!" He felt the same as Bob.

They were ashamed to be POWs.

Ernie didn't disagree with his friends. They were highly trained fliers, but their crew had flown only two combat missions: Crete and Tidal Wave. That was it.

He knew one thing for certain: They'd had enough of lounging and drinking beer in the sun for one war. They couldn't simply ignore the news from the outside world. But Ernie was at a loss. He stared at the glowing dial of the radio. What could they possibly do for the war effort when they were stuck behind locked gates?

CHAPTER 30

THE COLONEL'S CALL

A FEW DAYS LATER
The lodge

"IS IT MAIL CALL?" A SLEEPY POW ASKED.

"This is no mail call! This is the colonel's call. Get your fat ass off that sack," another POW was heard to say.

Men filtered from their rooms, wiping sleep from their eyes, grumbling about the disturbance and shouting for their friends to get a move on. The call came at 9 A.M., far later than the men's usual reveille in the service of Uncle Sam, but they still griped.

Ernie was already showered, shaved, and ready to go. He worried that the prisoners were growing too comfortable in their new surroundings, lulled into complacency by the Romanian hospitality. But this was decidedly *not* a hotel. They were prisoners of war, at the mercy of their Romanian commandant, whoever that was.

At the main door, a friendly Romanian officer urged the men, "Out, out, out!" Skinny and narrow-faced, with a long nose and a ready grin, Lieutenant Sandescu was the only English-speaker among the five officers of the guard. There was something disarming about him—his relaxed, good-natured manner made him seem like the kind of man who could be anyone's best friend. Already, he and Ernie and Bob had grown especially close. They called him Sandy.

Sandy explained the situation in passing at least a dozen times as the men shuffled and sauntered through the door. Colonel Săulescu was back at the camp. He'd ordered an inspection, probably due to the arrival of the new POWs. He wanted everyone assembled outside on parade. But Sandy's explanation only elicited more groans.

Lieutenant Sandescu—
"Sandy"

"Parade? Parade? No one had ever heard of such a thing in Lagărul No. 2," wrote one POW. "Aw, brother, here we go!"

Any number of the men grumbled. Bob grumbled, so Bambino grumbled along with him. Sandy told them not to cause a fuss. He didn't make the rules.

"We know, we know."

Ernie kept his mouth shut. His primary interest was their survival, making it home alive. The Romanians were in charge. If survival meant following their rules, so be it.

Outside, a chill lay in the air. It was beginning to feel like time for American Thanksgiving. "The trees on either side of the road, the railway, and the camp had passed from yellow to red-brown and now stood bare, half lost in the somber mists of a drooping November day," wrote one of the British POWs.

Few of the prisoners recognized the man who stood on the gravel driveway. He tapped his foot.

Major Mihai Cavaropol was tall and fit with brooding eyes. Beneath his crisp, tent-shaped cap, his head was shaved. He retrieved a snuffbox from his coat, took a pinch, inhaled with a quick sharp sniff, then wiped his nose and tucked the box away. Every movement was calculated. It was the first time most of the POWs had seen their camp commandant, and some had already been here a month and a half.

Many Romanian officers of the day were known to treat their subordinates like "vassals," and Cavaropol was one of them. "Should a momentary swirl of dust mar their boots, a soldier was always on hand to run forward with a cloth. And should the soldier displease, as he knelt there, his officer might slap his face, as he often did." Observed a POW: "In their army, the louder you yell, the more rank you have."*

Cavaropol wasn't yelling just yet. But his displeasure was written plainly across his face. A proud officer, reduced to the role of jailer, he scanned the ranks of Americans before him. His eyes narrowed at what he saw.

The American officers assembled in "a slipshod way" in two ragged rows with the British POWs at the end. Many wore hospital attire or the same scorched and threadbare khakis they'd been shot down in, which even Ernie wore. Included in their outfits were "pajama pants, vests, shirt-sleeves, slippers, flying-jackets, air force pants [all] mixed up in a jumble of wayward informality."

The Americans' choice of clothes wasn't entirely accidental. Some men looked slovenly on purpose. The POWs had been issued Romanian uniforms, the same brown fatigues their soldiers wore, but most of the POWs refused to wear them. The Romanian uniforms were stiff and scratchy, and besides, a fellow looked the same as the guys who might have shot them down.

Cavaropol looked away in disgust. These men called themselves military officers?!

Tension was already brewing between the commandant and the prisoners. With winter coming, they had asked a representative from the Red Cross to find their commandant and secure a second woolen blanket for each man. Cavaropol's response? The Red Cross delivered the bad news in writing: "The Commandant informs [you] that, since only one blanket is issued to each Romanian soldier, it is impossible to issue two blankets to the prisoners."

With the POWs assembled and the commandant waiting, Săulescu strolled into the camp, short and portly in all his glory, ready for the inspection.

Back in World War I, he'd commanded a machine-gun section as a young lieutenant in the 1st Mountain Hunter Battalion. He and his outfit had done good work in holding off the Germans during a crucial battle in the Roma-

* Unlike American military officers, Romanian officers were permitted to slap their men as a disciplinary measure. "To have his face slapped was a normal part of the Romanian soldier's training," learned a POW, "and what more natural than that he in turn, when placed in a position of power over another, should hand out the same treatment, or worse?"

nian mountains. But Săulescu had been badly wounded and never regained his former agility. No longer able to fight as he once had, he made up for it in his spit and polish, working "with great conscientiousness, punctuality, and order."

Săulescu took one look at the sloppy, half-dressed men and stopped in his tracks, aghast. "I believe he was, or meant to be, a genuine friend of ours," wrote one POW. "But he had come on a disciplinary visit, and he looked for respect."

Where were the ranks of obedient prisoners? Where were the Romanian uniforms he had issued? These men looked like they'd washed up from a shipwreck!

"He looked distastefully at us and spoke in Romanian to the major," Britt recalled. A man didn't have to understand the language to know what he was saying. The colonel waved his riding crop in the direction of the Americans, turned on the heel of his polished boots, and strode back and forth in front of the men, crunching the gravel with every step.

Săulescu stopped, his eyes settling on two men who had dared come to the assembly in their slippers. "You, you! Inside!" he barked in Romanian and pointed to the lodge. Lieutenants Helin and Hubbard got the picture and skulked away, while "the rest of us tried to remain calm," Britt later wrote. It was a minor humiliation. A reprimand at worst. As the colonel continued to speak, Sandy translated his words, "I cannot come out in *my* slippers!"

Perhaps the man had a point.

Săulescu's glare swept past Ernie and fell on Bob, then inched down to the American's broken-down brown shoes. Bob's shoes had been falling apart before the crash.

"You! Inside!" He waved his crop.

Bob held Săulescu's gaze, sizing up the order and the man who'd given it. He didn't appreciate being singled out or disrespected at the best of times. But by this portly Romanian fashion plate, his jailer? Bob's expression hardened.

Sandy stepped forward and grabbed Bob by the arm, interrupting the stare-down.

The young Romanian lieutenant steered Bob to the lodge with mock forcefulness.

Bob's scowl softened and he went without a fight. Sandy was the only Romanian he liked right now.

A chance remained to salvage the morning, to restore respect between opponents and instill military discipline in the prisoners. Perhaps most important, it offered an opportunity to mend Săulescu's "wounded" honor. The Geneva Convention prescribed "that prisoners of war and their captors will exchange all the common military courtesies."

What could be better than a formation drill?

Săulescu spoke to Sandy, who had returned to his side. Sandy translated: "The colonel will now call the men to attention!" But something got lost in translation, and before Săulescu could issue his command, an American beat him to it.

"Atten-tion!"

Instinctively, some men stood with straight backs. But others like Ernie, who understood Sandy perfectly, waited for Săulescu. A few seconds ticked by. Some of the POWs leaned forward or stepped out of line to see what went wrong. Recalled one POW: "The fellows were laughing, and there was nothing one could do."

It was the final straw. Săulescu turned red and exploded. Recalled a witness, "The colonel bounced about, a demon of rage, shaking himself before the commandant and the prisoners." From his perspective, the Americans had insulted his country's hospitality. He threatened to bring military manuals and implement early-morning drills. "I know the American Army does have discipline!" he shouted. "Maybe this will get you to improve yourselves?!"

An immediate punishment was in store. "He barked an order at a trembling Romanian corporal, who ran into the dining-room," while Cavaropol, unperturbed, took another pull from his snuff box. A few minutes later, the Romanian soldier emerged from the lodge carrying the POWs' pride and joy—their radio.

Săulescu spun on his heels and "stamped off."

After a fleeting pause, the POWs were dismissed and headed "gloomily" back inside. An empty space lay on the table where the radio used to sit. More importantly, their maps were useless now.

"This was a pity," remembered one of the British POWs. "The Geneva Convention forbade collective punishment of prisoners, but then it did not stipulate either that prisoners should be allowed a radio. We were sorely bitten."

Ernie headed into the dining room and spotted Bob casually holding a

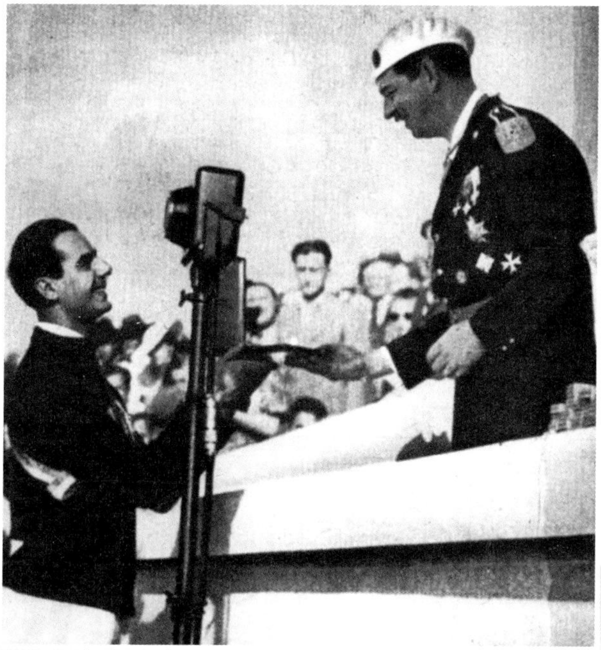

King Carol II awards Buzz the National Grand Prize of Sports, June 1936.

A B-24 of the Liberandos taxis to its desert roost.

Lieutenant Ernie Poulson, 1944.

Ernie, standing, third from left, in the Utah National Guard.

The crew, stateside, left to right: Riffle, Al, Bob (in blister), Ernie, Medeiros, Kees, MacLachlan, Bowker (standing), Britt. "Joel" references the copilot Ernie replaced.

Al suited up for high-altitude flight during training in Victorville, California.

Buzz on the ice in Davos, Switzerland, 1935.

A Romanian ground crewman helps Buzz with his straps before a mission.

Buzz with his 1934 Fleet F10G biplane before the war.

Buzz during his airline days as a pilot of the Lockheed Electra.

Buzz waits to be awarded the Order of Mihai the Brave medal while his superior, Capt. Alexandru Șerbănescu, is decorated, August 1943.

Romanian soldiers parade before banners of Antonescu, Hitler, and Mussolini.

Wongo Wongo of the Liberandos lifts off for Tidal Wave. In several hours this B-24 will be lost with all hands.

B-24 *The Sandman* of the 44th Bomb Group,
the Pyramiders, over Ploesti.

Câmpina as seen looking back from Col. Wood's ship.

A Romanian soldier guards the wreckage of *Chattanooga Choo Choo.*

The future King Michael, then thirteen, with his father at the Aeronautical Order banquet in the botanical gardens, 1935.

King Michael (second from right) visits the Eastern Front with Antonescu (center). Antonescu wears a German decoration, the Luftwaffe Pilot-Observer Badge with Diamonds, awarded for political friendliness to the Luftwaffe.

Officer POWs at the lodge in Timisul. Their tunnel was constructed beneath the barred window at ground level.

The officer POWs, wearing flannels from the Red Cross, with Romanian commandant Moruzi (center) and the photographers' daughter, 1944. Circled, front to back: Al, Ernie, Britt, Bob.

Buzz by the rudder of his Me-109, adorned with victory marks scored against the Soviets.

Buzz in the cockpit of his Me-109G-6 before a mission in 1944.

P-51s of the 325th Fighter Group escort B-17s, June 1944.

Bob (foreground) and Sandy (right) during a moment of relief in Pietroșița.

"Brothers-in-arms." Freed POWs with Sandy in Pietroșița, left to right: Lt. Wilmer Bassett, Al, Sandy, Lt. Lindley Hussey, Bob, Lt. Willard Beaumont.

The American Messerschmitt at San Giovanni. Traces of the original white German spiral show through the red spinner.

Streaked paint on Buzz's Me-109, a result of him taking off before it was dry.

Officers of the 15th Air Force explore how Gunn managed to fit in the fuselage of Buzz's Me-109.

At Popeşti, Buzz (left) shows a compatriot the Mustang after his flight from Italy.

B-17s of the 15th Air Force steer for Romania during Operation Reunion.

A B-17 taxis forward to pick up the next group of POWs at Popești.

A 15th Air Force airman greets POWs as they clamber aboard.

Other POWs await their turn to board at Popești.

Relieved ex-POWs arrive at Bari airfield, Italy. The POW at right wears a Romanian cap and insignia.

Repatriated POWs of the 389th Bomb Group back at their base, Hethel, in England, September 1944. Rurak, Riffle, and Medeiros are at the right end of the front row. In the middle row, Bowker is third from left and McCrary is third from right. In the back row, left to right: Wallace, Neef, Smith, Britt, Bob, Cavit, Ernie, Al.

conversation with a fellow officer. He expected his friend to be smarting from the humiliation, but Bob's behavior was calm, almost too calm.

Ernie quickly sized up the situation. This wasn't good.

His good friend was short-tempered at the best of times, used to getting his own way in St. Louis's high society, and one hell of a combat flier. The scrappy Irish-American was livid, holding all his anger inside like a powder keg. Already he'd been frustrated by being imprisoned and out of the fight. Now Săulescu had lit the fuse.

Săulescu had singled out the wrong guy.

Ernie pulled his friend aside as soon as he got a chance and whispered, "Bob, don't do anything rash."

Bob stared at Ernie a moment, then cracked an uneasy grin. Ernie knew him all too well. Without a word, Bob had already spoken volumes.

Oh, you can count on it.

CHAPTER 31

EVERY OUNCE OF BATTLE

THE NEXT MORNING
The lodge

THE GUARDS NOTICED NOTHING UNUSUAL AT LAGĂRUL PRIZONIERI NR. 2. The POWs milled around outside in the crisp mountain air, trying to soak up as much sunshine as possible before winter came. Some strolled the grounds, their boots crunching through fallen leaves the color of amber and rust.

Even the guards seemed happy to be outdoors. They kept up their constant pacing along the perimeter fence, looking for trouble. But trouble never came. Everything seemed quiet and routine. Duty at a prison camp full of Americans was boring.

Ernie spent the morning walking circles around a shallow acre-sized pond fed by a small mountain stream. Other POWs joined Ernie in the steady routine. The Red Cross dictated that prisoners could "remain in the open air all day long," and Ernie was taking full advantage of the dictate. He loved being outdoors.

In an open spot between the pond and the lodge, Bob, Al, and a dozen others stretched their legs for a footrace. It seemed like a fine pastime for a beautiful late-autumn day. Conditions around camp had tightened some since the blowup on the parade ground. Săulescu had immediately sent word demanding a full "apology" for the Americans' lack of military discipline. The highest-ranking American considered the options, then, on behalf of all captives, complied.

The apology rankled a few men, especially Bob, who still smarted from his humiliation. He loathed the idea of bowing his head to anyone, especially his captors. And for the Romanians to cause such a fuss for such a small infraction as soiled uniforms felt so petty.

Bob still lived and breathed the events of August 1. He was ever cognizant of what the men had just been through. They were all plane crash survivors. Every man had been shot out of the sky and hurled into chaos. The psychological and physical toll of such an ordeal would be immense for anyone, and "most of the officers had pretty bad nerves," recalled one of them. "I don't think anyone had [full] presence of mind." The least the Romanians could do was cut them some slack.

Bob thought of Second Lieutenant Charlie Wallace, a slim bombardier with a perpetual grin who couldn't get out of the nose before his plane crashed. Wallace's head had been pinned between a seat cushion and the metal ceiling like he was in "a giant vise" for four hours before they cut him out.

Or Second Lieutenant Jerome Savaria, a short, balding copilot whose pilot, First Lieutenant Clarence Gooden, held their flaming bomber up so Savaria could bail out. Savaria miraculously survived the jump from one hundred feet—only to watch his pilot crash in a fireball.

Or there was Captain Wallace Taylor, an easygoing pilot with a square, determined chin. He and his men had tried to bail out of their stricken B-24, *The Vulgar Virgin,* when it caught fire at low altitude. One by one, they leapt—but only Taylor walked away. The others struck the ground before their chutes could bloom. In an instant, his entire crew was gone.

Lectured? Punished for wearing the clothes they got shot down in? By *Romanians*? The guys who shot them down and put them here?

Bob felt like spitting.

He was the least athletic of any of his crew, but, driven by fury and defiance, Bob was ready to run. He jogged up to Ernie by the pond and motioned toward the starting line, inviting his friend over. "We're going to have a race."

"That's nice," Ernie said. "But I'm walking." Remembering that several weeks earlier Bob had tried to escape from the Bucharest schoolhouse, he sensed a catch. Bob had asked Ernie to join him then, and after Ernie refused he started spending quite a bit of time with two other downed pilots from the 389th, First Lieutenant Melvin Neef and his copilot, Second Lieutenant Carl Larson. One evening, at the schoolhouse's suppertime, Ernie looked around and saw Bob and his two accomplices missing. The prisoners heard whistles. Shouts. Several guards went running.

Someone spotted Bob, Neef, and Larson climbing out of a high window, all wearing dark clothes. The guards waited below with flashlights, guns drawn.

Bob and his accomplices quickly slipped back in the window, changed back into their suntans, then mixed back in with the other POWs. When the guards burst back into the dining room, they saw all their prisoners at their tables, looking as innocent as altar boys. The guards were fairly sure of who had tried to escape, but "no disciplinary action was taken." They'd been lucky that time.

Near the pond with Ernie, Bob shrugged and didn't press the matter. He headed back to the starting line and got on his mark with the other runners. Ernie stopped walking in circles and wandered closer.

"Go!"

The race went off without a hitch. Bob and the other POWs ran down to the other end of the yard. A few prisoners cheered them on. A few guards saw the races being run. And when the sprint was over, life at Lagărul No. 2 returned to normal.

That's not what Bob was after. He was thinking many moves ahead. He needed the Romanian guards' rapt attention.

So, Bob called for another lap, and more spectators were gathered. The racers sprinted down the field, stirring leaves, and as they ran, Bob glanced toward the guards. The second race had piqued the guards' interest, but not enough. So, when that race finished, Bob gathered even more spectators, including Britt, and encouraged the guys to cheer louder. You know, to really give it up for the runners.

The bulk of the Romanian guards now watched. Again, the runners ran their race. The gathered POWs clapped, hooted, and cheered with all their might. This time, the race had the guards' full attention.

In the quiet shadows of the lodge, another American officer, who was in cahoots with Bob and the racers, watched the competition from a distance. When the cheering was in full force, he strolled over to the fence on the north side of the camp and casually gazed beyond.

The fence was seven feet high, with barbed wire curled on the ground outside it, but the officer didn't care about the fence's height. They'd never get over it. Besides, the guards patrolled the wire. As the officer headed back to the lodge, he silently counted his paces a second time. Just to make sure. *Forty feet.*

At the finish line, Bob bent over, panting. The last race had ended. Even some of the guards were clapping. All the runners were winded. Bob grinned. He and the other sprinters headed back to the lodge for water.

"Gotta go," Bob said to Ernie in passing.

Ernie shook his head in mock disgust. "You S.O.B."

Bob grinned again. Al and Britt followed him closely inside.

So they were in on it, too.

But in on what?

A DAY OR SO LATER

WHEN ERNIE PEERED INTO the room shared by Bob and Al, his friends were gone. Britt was missing, too. Ernie made his way down the hall and spied other POWs at their windows, just sitting, smoking. None looked at him as he passed. The lingering seemed too intentional. Then it clicked for Ernie.

Lookouts.

From there, the bread-crumb trail was all too easy to connect. Ernie walked downstairs and spotted another American officer lingering by the door to the basement. The man gave Ernie a warm nod and stepped aside. Normally, the door was locked. Somehow, some enterprising POW had gotten hold of the key, probably from one of the Russian orderlies. Ernie crept down the steps into a cavernous unfinished room with a high ceiling. The only light came from cracks in the windows, now shuttered for winter. The outdoor furniture had been brought inside and piled high against a wall. Ernie paused and listened carefully. He heard hushed voices coming from an unused antechamber along the east wall.

Ernie peered behind the door. Through thin shafts of light, he spotted five POWs huddled like grave robbers in the northeastern corner of the antechamber, digging a four-by-four-foot hole in the earthen floor.

Bob, Britt, and Al had dirt on their knees. Neef and Larson used soup cans as shovels. All 389th men. Together they were filling a vegetable box with soil.

Ernie wanted to slap his forehead.

Oh, just great.

They were tunneling.

LATER, WHILE EVERYONE WAS getting cleaned up from their secretive foray, Ernie slid into Bob's room, shut the door, and said, "When were you going to tell me?"

"Once we got far enough that you couldn't talk us out of it," Bob replied with a grin.

Bob's plan was substantial as he explained it. They were going to attempt the first large-scale breakout of POWs in the European Theater. They would dig their way out from the lodge, surface on the other side of the fence after dark, and move west across the mountains to Yugoslavia, hoping to link up with either Chetnik guerrillas or Communist partisans.

Ernie stopped him. "Are you nuts?" Yugoslavia was two hundred miles away, on the other side of the Danube. If they somehow made it that far, they'd stand a fifty-fifty chance of finding friendly rebels. Yugoslavia was swarming with Germans.

Besides, the plan invited a bigger question: Why would they leave? "We have it good here," Ernie said. He reminded his friend of the perks—three meals a day, warm beds, no one trying to kill them. All the Romanians asked was that no one try to escape.

Bob's rebuttal was short. Ernie was forgetting one thing. The war wasn't over just because they'd been shot down. Romania was at war with America.

Ernie wasn't sold. He worried his friends would never reach Yugoslavia. They'd freeze, starve, or get gunned down first. "You'll never get there."

"What if it doesn't matter if we get there?"

He had Ernie's attention.

Bob had thought through the angles. Even if just a couple of men got out, they could tie up hundreds—maybe thousands—of Romanian troops in a search for the missing POWs. That would consume precious enemy resources. And if the whole Romanian army was in a tizzy, that would drive the Germans nuts. Just when they needed every soldier focused on the Eastern Front, the Romanians would be hunting for Americans headed west.

Ernie felt his resolve began to soften. "They will shoot, you know?" he said, thinking of their Romanian guards.

Bob brushed aside the question. Their fellow fliers were still up there flying and dying and getting shot at. Every single day. Săulescu had unintentionally reminded them of their duty. They were still soldiers first. Bob stated it plainly: "We owe it to the guys to try."

Ernie knew who Bob was talking about. He thought of his friends often—not only the guys still flying over Germany, but the guys from the 389th who had come to rest in Romanian soil.

The guys who had given everything.

Ernie had collected bits and pieces of information about the fate of the other 389th ships.

The B-24 named *Hitler's Hearse* had been seen wobbling in distress as it exited Red Target, preventing its wingmen from falling into formation. Something was clearly wrong.

At the controls had been Captain Robert Mooney, twenty-three. He and his older brother, William, had always been inseparable—two Nebraska boys who'd attended the same college and worked the same job at the Mid-Continent Supply Company. When the war came, both became fliers. Each named his bomber *Hitler's Hearse*—one flying a B-25 in India, the other a B-24 over Europe.

Now, one of them was gone.

A shell had punched through the windscreen, killing Robert instantly. His copilot, himself spattered with glass and blood, used one hand to prevent Robert's body from slumping over the controls. With the other, he fought to keep flying.

Robert Mooney and Robert Horton

The B-24 *Sand-Witch* also came off target in trouble. Flames poured from the bomb bay and spread across the lower fuselage. At the controls was Lieutenant Robert Horton, twenty, of Cincinnati, who'd been voted "the outstanding boy of his class," back at Western Hills High School in 1941.

From the waist window of the bomber next to it, Sergeant Russell Hayes watched the "horrible sight," powerless to help.

The gunners of *Sand-Witch* kept their eyes fixed on Hayes. They were going down, and they knew it.

Hayes offered the only gesture he could think of, "more or less a goodbye wave." The doomed men waved back at him. Moments later, the stricken bomber crashed and "crumpled into a fireball."

By the time *Ole Kickapoo* was barreling at Red Target, flames were leaping higher than the rooftops below. The B-24 was already damaged. A shell had hit the left wing, causing a massive fuel leak. Gas poured from the bomber in torrents, spewing so much fuel that the men in the plane next to it could barely see the waist gunners.

At the controls of *Ole Kickapoo* were First Lieutenant Lloyd "Pete" Hughes, a "fine, religious, conscientious boy with a young wife waiting for him back in Texas," and Second Lieutenant Ron Helder, the former pharmacist who'd written to his parents that they were going to "do humanity a good turn," and if something should happen to him, "Turn back your calendar and take a look at August 1st." Hughes and Helder knew their orders: Flatten Red Target and make sure it never springs back to life.

Hughes's fellow pilots alerted him on the radio, "You're streaming gas!"

"Okay," Hughes replied. "[But first] I gotta get the bombs on target."

"He stuck right in formation with us," his flight leader, Captain Philip Ardery, later wrote. "As we were going into the furnace, I said a quick prayer." On the other side, Ardery looked out his right window. Hughes was still holding formation, and his bombs had been "laid squarely on the target." But by then, *Ole Kickapoo*'s left wing was covered in flames. "I could feel tears come into my eyes and my throat clog up," recalled Ardery.

The fires of the refinery had climbed up the streaming gas.

Only with his orders complete did Hughes leave formation, banking right. Both pilots were seen fighting the controls, trying to steer for a flat spot along the river, anywhere without trees. But just before they could put the bomber down, the left wing burned off. They were still fifty feet above the riverbed. "The heavy ship cartwheeled, and a great flower of flame and smoke appeared just ahead of the point where last we had seen a bomber."*

Ernie had seen that crash when Medeiros called out: "Airplane going in, starboard, five o'clock!" Ernie witnessed Hughes's and Helder's last moments on earth.

Ernie wasn't fixated on escape the way his friends were. He had no prob-

* Hughes and his crew were posthumously recognized for their heroism. Hughes was awarded the Medal of Honor, and his deceased crewmen each received the Distinguished Service Cross, the nation's second highest award for valor. Together, they stand as one of the most decorated bomber crews in history.

The crew of *Ole Kickapoo*. Standing, left to right: Lt. Lloyd Hughes, Lt. Ron Helder, Lt. Sidney Pear, Lt. John McLoughlin. Kneeling, left to right: Sgt. Joseph Mix, Sgt. Louis Kase, Sgt. Malcolm Dalton, Sgt. Edmond Smith, Sgt. Thomas Hoff, Sgt. Avis Wilson.

lem apologizing for rumpled clothes, and he felt no vendetta against his captors. But when Ernie thought about the guys who gave their all, he knew Bob was right.

A tunnel.

They owed it to them.

The words of Hughes's eulogy applied now. His flight leader, Ardery, had given a solemn tribute after the mission was complete: "To the very end, he gave the battle every ounce he had."

"Okay, Bob," Ernie said. "When do I start?"

CHAPTER 32

THE PROJECT

SEVERAL DAYS LATER
Lagărul No. 2

FORTY FEET.

Just a bowling lane's length. A few seconds of flat-out running. That was all that separated them from the other side of the fence. But digging a tunnel? It was hard, measured going, and each day of clandestine work passed slowly. For secrecy's sake, the conspirators called it the Project.

Ernie faithfully joined the digging team, along with Al and Bob and a select number of other officers. The crew of *Chattanooga Choo Choo* always took their shifts together. Ernie's friends were happy he was with them, even if he wasn't overly optimistic about their odds of success. Whenever they finished, *if* they finished, he still wasn't sure whether he would join the escape. He figured he'd decide once the day came.

Still, they needed him, for many reasons. He was levelheaded and calculated and one of the few lightly wounded and therefore able-bodied POWs in the group. Many of the prisoners, like Britt, weren't fully healed yet. When it came time to go, Britt would have only a slim chance of being able to flee very far in his current condition. But Britt made sure he was part of the digging team. The boy who had missed only two days of high school wasn't about to start shirking now.

To preserve their suntans, the men wore their brown Romanian uniforms as work clothes. The first time they suited up, they just laughed. Wouldn't Săulescu have loved to see them now?

THEY DUG A SHAFT straight down at first and cobbled together a ladder so they could reach the bottom. Since the lodge was set higher than the land around it, they had to dig down a dozen feet "before beginning to go outwards."

Ernie and his friends stared down the ladder. Their creation was no longer just a hole in the ground. It was the entrance shaft to a tunnel, and it was dark at the bottom. One pilot had seen a work crew disappear into the dark hole and quipped, "No one on this crew has any intelligence."

You had to be half-crazy to go down there.

Ernie brushed off any jitters and climbed down the ladder. Britt climbed after him, a little more slowly, but just as determined. When they reached the bottom, they began to crawl forward. Already the tunnel was twelve feet long.

As Ernie crawled, he pushed a homemade oil lamp in front of him. At its broadest, the tunnel was four feet wide, squarish, and just high enough to crawl forward using both arms. It wasn't even possible to crouch. Hot oil from the lamp threatened to spill on his hand each time he moved it. Ahead lay total blackness. Ernie kept going until he met a wall of dirt and roots staring back at him.

There was no room to go forward, and with Britt behind him, no quick way to get out. Ernie couldn't sit up. He couldn't even scratch his back if a centipede crawled over him. He'd never been particularly claustrophobic, but the men had calculated that seven or eight feet of dirt lay above them. Without boards to brace the tunnel, the concern was real: A sudden cave-in could bury them alive. Ernie felt like he was already lying in his own grave.

Just breathe, he told himself, trying to steady his nerves. *You can handle more than you think you can.*

He'd learned that lesson long ago. When he was eight, he and his father had spent three weeks up in the mountains. One day, Ernie just wasn't himself anymore. "I gradually lost my desire to eat; I felt sick and I couldn't sleep," he later recalled. "Dad correctly diagnosed it as a severe case of homesickness."

"Want to go home?" his father asked.

Ernie nodded.

His dad pointed west. "It's about eighteen miles that-a-way." Lester wasn't about to stop work just because his boy missed his mother.

Ernie hesitated. Eighteen miles, alone, through dark country full of mountain lions and bears?

His father's answer was simple. "You're big enough." Without saying it outright, Lester was teaching him something.

So, Ernie saddled up his old blue mare—a black face, dark legs, and shimmery roan coat—and set out. It was "pretty scary" for an eight-year-old, but he made it home "wet, tired, and very hungry."

Now, years later, lying flat in a tunnel partway to freedom, Ernie called that lesson back to mind. *You can handle more than you think you can.*

There was only one way to make this harrowing duty go away. They needed to dig past the fence.

Only about twenty-eight more feet to go.

Ernie flashed a thumbs-up to Britt, and Britt passed forward an empty gallon soup can. Ernie began scraping and scooping the black soil. The dirt was crumbly, easy for tunneling but dangerous for cave-ins. Ernie collected a canful and passed it back to Britt, who relayed it back to Bob, who brought the dirt to the surface and dumped it into a vegetable box. Al would take the filled box and scatter the dirt behind the stacks of lawn furniture in the main room of the basement. It was the one place in the lodge the Romanian guards never checked: The cellar door was always supposed to be locked, so why bother?

As Ernie scraped and dug, he thought about Săulescu's one warning: *Do not try to escape.* He wondered what would happen if they were caught. He didn't want to be the first to find out.

The dimness and muffled silence of the tunnel gave the work a strange sense of timelessness. An hour could pass—perhaps two—and no one would know. In the tight space, the heat from the lamp grew unbearable. Sweat ran down the men's faces, soaking their shirts, mixing with the soil. Each new foot of progress brought fresh tension. Would this section of the shaft hold?

More than once, Ernie feared a cave-in was imminent. One moment he would be scraping at the black earth; in the next, a shower of dirt would come cascading down. His lamp would flicker and be snuffed out. Total darkness. Ernie would lie still a long moment, each gritty breath belabored, the blackness squeezing him, the sidewalls seemingly inching closer. *Don't panic,* he would order himself.

Behind him, Britt would see the tunnel go dark—then, after a few agonizing seconds, a flicker of light would return when Ernie had struck his Zippo, reigniting his lamp. He would clear the fallen dirt and go back to digging, this time more gingerly.

DAYS PASSED IN THE tunnel, one blending into the next. The farther the men dug, the more a problem took shape. Oxygen levels in the tunnel were dropping. After a stint underground, "a man would emerge black in the face and coughing and gasping," recalled one POW. The lamps were sucking up what little air there was.

One day, while digging at the far end, Ernie began to feel light-headed, as if hands were clamped around his throat. He flicked his Zippo. The flame sputtered weakly, starved for air. They were probably near the halfway point, he guessed—but the full forty feet? That was beginning to look impossible.

After his shift below, Ernie found Bob and pulled him aside. He didn't sugarcoat the news: "The project is in trouble," he said quietly. They weren't going to make the fence.

CHAPTER 33

THE AMBASSADOR OF GOODWILL

A DAY OR TWO LATER, NOVEMBER 15, 1943
Lagărul No. 2

ALL THE OFFICERS IN THE LODGE GATHERED IN THE DINING ROOM around 10 A.M., waiting for someone important to arrive.

A smaller group broke off to form a tight knot, speaking among themselves in hushed tones about the Project. The showers of earth that threatened a cave-in were occurring more frequently, and the rising heat and dwindling oxygen made conditions more dire. The men talked about their tunnel as if it were a "living friend." And now that friend was on its last legs.

As quietly as possible, Ernie and the officers of *Chattanooga Choo Choo* generated a mental list of items they desperately needed if they were to finish the tunnel and make it out the other side. They tried to keep their voices down, hiding their frustration from anyone but themselves. They knew what they needed and what was required to pull off an escape. But actually getting these things?

Impossible.

AT THE SAME TIME the officers waited inside, the Romanian commandant, Cavaropol, paced outside at the gate, along with a small honor guard. The grass in the alpine meadows lay dormant now. The trees swayed leafless and cold in the November wind. Cavaropol was brooding as usual, as he sniffed from his snuffbox and wiped his nose. He was required to be present when *she* arrived, this woman who was quickly becoming a thorn in his side.

Princess Catherine was coming to check on the POWs. And Cavaropol didn't like it one bit.

"WHAT'S THE DEAL WITH this lady?" a POW asked Ernie and his friends. Not everybody knew who she was.

Ernie had long hoped for this day, their reunion. He explained how Princess Catherine had rescued him and the others. Britt cut in. "She likes Americans. She enjoys fighting for the underdog"—in this case, them. Britt said he personally owed her his life.

It was no exaggeration. Without her intervention, he wouldn't be here, and they all might be deep inside Germany instead. Back when he was in King Michael's hospital, Britt heard about First Lieutenant William Little, twenty-seven, a handsome square-chinned bombardier from the Traveling Circus. After Little's bomber crashed, he wound up in the same predicament as Britt, pinned in the wreckage, inhaling gasoline fumes, soaking in the toxic fuel. By the time rescuers were finally able to free him, eight hours later, all the gasoline fumes he'd inhaled had weakened his lungs. They rushed him to King Michael's hospital when it opened, but it was too late. Pneumonia set in, and Little died. The Romanians buried him with honors in the hotel grounds, among the benches etched with the names of royalty.

Britt knew the only difference between Little's fate and his was the princess's speedy intervention. He assured his fellow officers that Princess Catherine was on their side.

But "would she be of help with escape plans?" they wanted to know.

"I answered that she was a loyal Romanian and would do nothing to aid us if it were in conflict to her primary loyalty," Britt recalled. "She was a woman of high principle," he explained to his friends.

That didn't do much to cheer his fellow officers. She sounded like any other gladhanding Romanian dignitary.

A STRING OF FANCY cars pulled to a stop in the camp driveway, and when the princess entered the lodge with a Romanian general from Bucharest, all the Americans snapped to attention. You could have heard a pin drop.

"We had learned our lesson from the little colonel," Britt recalled. "We understood it was expected."

The princess smiled to see her boys, Ernie, Britt, and Al—she hadn't met Bob yet—but she couldn't display her affection with a hug or even a formal handshake, not with a stern Romanian general watching. These were *prisoners,* after all. And she was royalty.

But after making introductions, the princess sat on the windowsill while the general stood at her side.

"Welcome to Romania," she said to the men.

A few of the officers groaned at the sound of their foreign home, but Ernie, Britt, and Al shot them sidelong glances, telling them to knock it off.

"Just a moment," she said, with a smile. "We were your ally in World War I. It was by a fluke we wound up on the wrong side this time. We like Americans. Your oil people have been here for years. You boys are now under the protection of the Romanian government." Britt recalled the reaction: "This statement brought some laughter with the jeers."

The princess knew she had her work cut out for her. "Don't laugh," she scolded gently. "It could have been a lot worse. We could have turned you over to the Nazis. But we fought them to keep you here."

The princess explained that she'd convinced the Romanians and Germans to let her be a civilian "Ambassador of Goodwill." She was adopting the prisoners just as she had her orphans. It hadn't been hard for her to win over the Romanian side, but the Germans took more convincing. They still wielded the ultimate power over the American captives; a German officer could overrule almost any Romanian and "cut him down with a few sharp phrases."

She had gone to the German authorities in Bucharest and formally asked to visit the Americans. The princess later recounted the interaction:

"I know English very well," she told the German general. "I have also been a constant reader of American magazines for years, and I know the American mentality and customs. I can be of help to you. Let me go among them, and I shall tell them why we don't like the Russians."

She showed the general a written description of the numerous Russian invasions of Romania since Napoleon and added, "I want to tell the Americans that, *why* it happened that we fight the Russians."

"Ja, ja, that's not bad. You want to go two, three times?"

She asked to visit regularly, once a month.

The general stamped a note. Permission granted.

Back at the lodge, some of the men shot questioning glances at the princess. She "made no bones about her opinion," one POW recalled, "that the end would see Romania and our countries fighting on the same side against the Germans. She had forceful opinions, this visitor, and expressed them forcibly."

And as she spoke, her sprinkling of American idioms began to make the Yanks feel at home. She was proficient in colloquialisms such as "wet my whistle," "in a jiffy," "scoot," "something the cat dragged in," and "devil of a time."

And she knew her audience. Rather than delivering a full-fledged anti-Russian diatribe, she cut her talk short and put their brief time together to good use. "What would you like to make your lives a little easier here?" she asked. "What can I bring?"

"There was a stunned silence at first," Britt recalled. "Then all spoke at once."

The men crowded around. Requests flew at the princess. Prisoners had great hopes for "ping pong tournaments, bridge tournaments, chess, checkers, [and a] Glee club." The men longed for reading materials, particularly "American books." Some wanted to read about "Greek philosophy. Metaphysics. Stocks and Bonds. Animal Husbandry." The princess took notes.

Beside her, the general looked confused and asked what exactly the men were requesting. She handled him effortlessly, speaking in Romanian for him, English for the POWs. Ernie could never be sure exactly what she translated, but the general didn't bat an eye.

As the requests thinned out, the officers of *Chattanooga Choo Choo* exchanged glances. Each man knew it—this was their big chance. Britt would need to do the talking for them. He was her favorite, and he had a sense of how cautiously to tread without overstepping.

Britt gave a small nod to his friends, then raised his hand.

The princess's eyes found him at once. She listened, intrigued, as Britt made his polite requests. Yet something in his tone caught her ear—an undercurrent, a subtle hint that there was more to his requests than he was letting on. Still, she smiled, jotted her notes, and gave a knowing nod.

THE VISIT WASN'T OVER yet. Princess Catherine had brought small gifts from her charitable foundation for the officers and their enlisted comrades in the nearby camp. Nothing terribly exciting, she explained, but they would find the items useful with the bitter cold Romanian winter ahead.

She brought sewing kits, so they could mend the holes in their khakis.

And she brought more than a hundred pairs of "union suits," long woolen underwear that buttoned up the front. The men all knew them as long johns. Getting one hundred pairs hadn't been easy, she added, but she had marshalled the wealthy women on her charitable board to help clean out all the stores in Bucharest.

Britt and the others were amused by the idea of all those high-society women combing the stores in search of warm skivvies.

The Romanian guards went to her car, secured the packages, and dumped heaping boxes of long johns onto the table in the lodge.

"Now," she said. "You select your underwear, and the general and I will inspect your camp."

The Americans swarmed the pile. To Britt, "it looked like a department store bargain basement with everyone grabbing, trying to find the right size."

With the men busy at the table, Britt helped the princess off the windowsill where she sat. Ernie and Al came over to say hello. Princess Catherine was glad to see they were safe and being well cared for. In closer conversation, she referred to Bambino as "my Al."

"Well," she said, smiling, "I made it, didn't I?"

The men introduced her to the stranger in their midst. Bob. He was instantly smitten.

"Oh, Ernie," the princess said, remembering something. "Here you go." She handed him the $20 he'd given her the day of the crash. Ernie was grateful and a bit astounded.

Overall, all the prisoners were charmed by the princess. She was everything that Britt had said about her and more. In time, the men would come "to know and love this motherly woman, who had an uncanny understanding of Americans and who spoke their language with a British accent."

Later that evening, Ernie would pen in his journal: "A more well-versed and interesting person I've never met."

IT FELT LIKE AN early Christmas. After the princess departed, the lodge buzzed with laughter and mischief. Officers paraded around the first floor in their new long underwear, some "doing graceful ballet steps," others "posing like statues."

From a distance, the men of *Chattanooga Choo Choo* watched quietly. None of their fellow officers—certainly not those laughing the hardest—

caught the meaning woven into Britt's words, or the message the princess now carried away.

Thanks to Britt, that "living friend" beneath their feet might have just been given a second chance at life. But now, it was out of their hands. The fate of the Project rested entirely with the princess.

CHAPTER 34

SEPARATION

SOON AFTER
The lodge

WORD OF THE PROJECT SPREAD AMONG THE OFFICER POWS OF LAGĂ-rul No. 2, and nearly every man found a way to contribute. They had arrived as strangers, separate crews from five bomb groups with a sprinkling of Commonwealth men among them. Now, working together, they became a team.

Some prisoners helped below with the digging. Others worked on lookout duty, their steps particularly light over the tunnel area. Constantly, they listened for any sounds that could betray the work going on below, all while watching for any unexpected visit from the Romanians.

One of the British POWs described the feeling of excitement: "To stand in the compound, knowing what was going on down below, was to experience the thrill of secrecy and conspiracy. It was all we could do to stop ourselves nudging and winking as we looked at the guards."

On a crisp November morning, less than two weeks before Thanksgiving, the men spotted Sandy entering the front gate of the compound, headed for the lodge. A lookout in the yard nodded to several lookouts on the lodge's second floor, who promptly disappeared inside and ran to the room service buttons on the walls of their rooms. The men pressed the buttons and didn't let up.

In the kitchen of the lodge, several bells rang all at once. The Russians heard the din as they prepared lunch. In the lodge's former life as a hotel, a single bulb would illuminate on a wall panel to tell a bellhop which room requested service. Today, bulbs were lit up across the board. The Russians laughed it off as the usual American hijinks. In Lagărul No. 2, room service didn't come with the meal plan.

At the same moment, Ernie crouched at the entrance shaft of the tunnel down in the basement, head cocked, ears sharp. He heard the bells above. His job was to be the lookout for Britt and First Lieutenant Bud Smith, a copilot, working at the far end of the tunnel underground.

Inside the hole, Britt and Smith were problem-solving a new and gut-wrenching hurdle. All work had ground to a halt when crews hit a massive boulder that blocked their progress. By their estimates, they were well past the halfway mark to the fence. Britt, who'd studied architecture, and Smith, armed with engineering experience, were weighing their options. Dig left or right? Try to chisel through? Every choice carried risk, and time was slipping away.

Ernie hurried down the ladder and shouted into the shaft as loudly as he dared: "Get out, guys! Evacuate! Evacuate!" Ernie retreated upstairs.

When Britt and Smith ran up from the basement, Ernie was waiting.

"She's back!" Ernie said, quick and breathless. The princess. Sandy had come to say she was at the commandant's office. She would be at the lodge at any moment.

Britt lit up—had she brought the stuff for the Project? Ernie didn't know. But if Britt wasn't around to greet her, the princess would know something was afoot. Britt darted upstairs to change out of his dirty fatigues.

By the time Britt returned in clean khakis, almost all the officers were swarming the big Chevrolet outside. It was almost lunchtime. The POWs cheerfully greeted the princess as others unloaded boxes from her car.

She'd brought everything they'd asked for. A volleyball. Cards. Board games. Books from her personal library. Even a harmonica for a glee club—although the princess, a devout Orthodox Christian, handed it over on one condition: "On Sundays, you're only to play hymns!"

When the princess spotted Ernie, Bob, Britt, and Al, she called them closer and announced she'd secured everything they needed for their "theatrical."

A stage play—that was Britt's cover story.

Thinking fast during her first visit, he'd told the princess they were putting on a play for the men. Skits. Comedy. Drama. The sort of thing to keep the spirits up. Britt ran through their wish list: planks to make a stage, a string of footlights, and costumes, everyday Romanian clothes, peasant attire if possible.

His ruse wasn't much of a stretch. The officers really had planned to stage "a few theatricals."

"The costumes are in the back seat," the princess told her boys from *Chattanooga Choo Choo*. "The electrical wiring and other things are in the trunk." The officers tried to hide their eagerness as they crowded around her Chevy.

Every item she'd brought would serve a purpose for the Project. The lights would allow them to ditch the oil lamps. The wood would brace the tunnel walls against collapse. And the peasant costumes—those were for the final act. After making their escape, the men planned to vanish into the Romanian countryside disguised as common villagers.

Ernie carried a box of costumes from the back seat. Britt reached in and lifted out the first piece of clothing.

A tuxedo.

The men exchanged worried glances. This wasn't peasant clothing! Rummaging deeper, Britt found flapper dresses and more tuxedos. The princess had brought them Romanian attire—high-society Romanian attire.

"Hope that will do?" she said.

Ernie saw her fighting back a smile. Almost a knowing wink. She didn't want them to escape, and she'd seen straight through their request. *Well, she isn't wrong*, he thought.

Britt hung his head. He later wrote, "She outfoxed us."

But all hope wasn't lost. She'd only pieced together part of their scheme. In the trunk, the men found planks and a string of floor lights for a stage. The largest boards she could get were two-by-fours. Those items were still innocuous in her mind.

At most, she figured, the men were planning to slip into the countryside after snipping the wire. Never could she imagine that all these supplies were meant for a tunnel.*

A tunnel? *Her* boys? Unthinkable.

SEVERAL PRISONERS ASKED THE princess to stay for lunch; she accepted, and after eating she asked Ernie and Britt if they could talk in private. They showed her to their room, and without a chair to offer, she took a seat on the edge of the opposite bed.

* It would be four more months before the British staged their "Great Escape" through the earth of a Luftwaffe camp a hundred miles from Berlin. POW tunnels had yet to enter the Axis public's imagination.

Her brow was furrowed. "I'm asking you again—do not try to escape."

Ernie and Britt stared down at their boots, feeling like schoolboys caught cheating—Ernie especially. She had warned him to "stay put" when she delivered him into Romanian custody after the August 1 crash.

"Here you are safe," she continued. "We will take care of you, and when the shooting is over, you will be returned home. Should you escape, you cannot trust anyone. People will betray [you] for a little money."

Britt later wrote, "We could not disagree with her. She was thinking of our safety."

But Ernie felt a flicker of frustration. The princess spoke of captivity under the Romanians as though it were a stroke of luck. How could he make her understand their duty to their fellow fliers? And now she was trying, no matter how good her intentions, to foil their only chance at freedom so they could get back in the fight. Besides, when the time came to slip beyond the wire, it would be they, not she, who faced the danger.

It was an indelicate question to raise, but Ernie had to know. "Why are you doing all this?"

The princess looked as if she had been waiting to be asked. She said she had more in common with the POWs than they realized. She knew the hopelessness of captivity and loneliness. The longing for escape. She had been a prisoner once, too.

Ernie almost fell out of his seat. *What?*

The princess gathered herself to share a portion of her life that most people never knew of.

Her parents' marriage had been turbulent. Her father, Prince Radu, was a "flamboyant playboy," and when her mother, Princess Irene, asked for a divorce, the prospect of her leaving him landed like a punch to the "imprudent" man. But not for romantic reasons.

It was all about the cash. His wife, Irene, was a Cantacuzino. If he stayed married to her, it meant a lifetime of wealth. But if they broke up, his access to her dowry was finished.

Catherine was just three years old when her mother took her to an exposition in Paris. Aware of a momentary lapse in security, Prince Radu seized his fiendish opportunity. He physically overpowered his daughter's nanny and abducted Catherine, taking her to England, and stowing her in an orphanage under an alias.

Prince Radu told the Cantacuzinos he would reveal her location for a price. But they were sure he'd take the money and run. Catherine's uncle wanted to settle matter with a duel, but what good would that do? If he killed Radu, they would never learn their little girl's whereabouts.

The Cantacuzinos searched far and wide. Catherine's poster was displayed all over Europe. The little girl could not be found.

Catherine grew up thinking her name was Jeanne Bardin and that she was a French girl whose parents had died in a trainwreck. She had no visitors. No friends. The years passed, lonely and unremarkable, until her childhood slowly faded in the orphanage. Back in Bucharest, her mother, still longing for her daughter, never recovered from her grief. She died of a broken heart.

After twelve long years, the Cantacuzinos finally found and rescued the girl. At age fifteen, she learned her real name. She was informed she was wealthy beyond comprehension. She was no orphan.

She was a princess.

They brought her back home to Romania. At first, she didn't even speak her native tongue. But she had family, and the Cantacuzinos were overjoyed to have her back. Her grandparents formally adopted her. Her cousin, Buzz, was just a boy who loved to run around their castle pretending he was a pilot.

Her main home, in Bucharest, was called the Palace with Lions. It looked like the Casino de Monte-Carlo. They had twenty-four servants, and the family was so wealthy they even shipped their laundry to their summer palace near Ploesti to have it washed. Most weekends were spent in Sinaia at Cantacuzino Castle, the romantic stone palace that the POWs had driven past.

A bigshot Hollywood director came to Romania, wanting to make a film about Catherine's life. But her grandfather felt it was in "bad taste." The little girl had been through enough.

It turned out that Catherine's mother had left her a legacy of a different sort. One day, the grandmother led Catherine to Bucharest, where a beautiful two-story building lay behind a marble gate. Inside, children played in the sunshine and fresh air. It was an orphanage, but not the kind Catherine had known. The name on the gate read "Saint Catherine's Crib," and a marble plaque bore an engraving of a little girl and her mother. Above the doorway, a simple but profound dedication was etched into stone: "A mother who lost her child, for children who lost their mothers."

The orphanage was named after her.

It was a heavy thought for a teenager. Her grandmother explained that Catherine's mother had started the orphanage to cope with the pain of losing her. But "not many people have a monument erected to them while they are still alive," the grandmother added. "Now, you must live up to it."

Catherine knew she'd found her life's calling. After her education was finished and she married Prince Constantin Caradja, she took over the formal management of the orphanage. She was twenty-five. Saint Catherine's Crib had thirty children then. Now it provided for three thousand.

That was why Catherine was doing all she could for Ernie, Britt, and their comrades. She knew what it was like to be in their shoes, to feel isolated, even abandoned.

Sobered, Ernie told her she meant a great deal to them. But he wouldn't lie and promise they wouldn't try to escape. They had to. They owed it to their fellow fliers.

An unspoken understanding passed between the unlikely friends. The princess had shared her warning with their best interest at heart. And the POWs could not—and would not—stop the Project.

Looking a little forlorn, the princess rose and said softly, "I wish you all the luck with your theatrical."

She couldn't mother them forever.

Ernie and Britt followed her down the stairs. But when she closed the car door behind her, Ernie felt a sudden pang of trepidation.

The princess's deep concern weighed on him, and her plea lingered in his mind. He knew where the downed fliers' duty lay, with their country. But he also sensed that the princess understood her country in far deeper ways than they ever could. She was a woman of deep wisdom and impeccable instincts. And she was deeply unsettled by the thought of what they were about to do next.

Should they be worried, too?

CHAPTER 35

THE BIG BREAK

THE NEXT MORNING
Lagărul No. 2

THE OFFICERS HIT THE GROUND RUNNING. BACK IN THE TUNNEL, ERNIE and his friends braced the ceiling with wooden planks. Others strung lights throughout the shaft. The men felt safer now, and the diggers could breathe more easily without oil lamps.

The POWs powered around the boulder more quickly than they'd expected, and went another three feet, four, five. By their estimates, they had just a few more days of tunneling and they'd clear the perimeter and bust out. "Each scoop of dirt meant we were a little closer to freedom," Britt wrote.

Ernie found himself warming to the possibility of success. He'd come to see the Project as a challenge, and he was beginning to entertain the idea that the plan might actually work. A few days earlier, he'd thought they were done for. But now one thought lodged securely in his mind: *We just might make it out of here.*

Then, about a week before Thanksgiving, the enlisted men came calling.

The Romanians permitted the men a weekly visit between camps. This time, the sergeants whispered serious news of their own. The enlisted men, too, had dug a tunnel, and it was ready to go. They'd declared war on Săulescu and the Romanians, too. Led by two British sergeants, both seasoned escape artists, they'd toiled around the clock. Now, everything "was ready for the big break."

The officers' jaws dropped.

Bob was mortified when he heard the news. We just got the lights up in ours! He tried to convince the sergeants to delay their breakout, but winter was fast approaching and they didn't want to wait.

"When?"

"We're going out tonight."

AFTER DINNER IN THE lodge, Ernie and his fellow officers were a bundle of nerves. Bob had taught everyone how to play bridge, but not even he could focus. Britt recalled: "It was difficult to play that evening as we waited anxiously for some sign of their activity."

The sergeants had every right to try their luck. They'd beaten their superiors to it, fair and square. Besides, there was no stopping them even if the officers had pulled rank, not when the men spearheading the sergeants' tunnel wore British uniforms.

Ernie kept glancing at his watch. By 6 P.M., it was already dark outside the dining hall. At any moment, the attempt would take place. Lives hung in the balance, not to mention the fate of the officers' tunnel. Whether the enlisted men got away or not, the Project would be at risk. A question hung over Ernie like a weight.

What will happen to our way out of here?

OUTSIDE THE FENCE LINE of the sergeants' camp, on the south side of the yard, the earth stirred, the dirt fell in on itself, and a hole formed, as if something was rising from the grave. A threadbare British cap perched on a stick rose from the hole, "the way the cowboys do it in the movies." The cap hovered above the ground, tempting any Romanians to take a shot. But the coast was clear.

Sergeant Doug Collins, a British sergeant with a blackened face, pushed himself and a small bundle of belongings out from the tunnel. He lay flat and motionless in the shadows.

It was good and dark, the moon choked by clouds. Empty branches rattled in the nearby forest, and pale, dead leaves rustled in the wind. It was the kind of night that made the Romanian sentries walk faster and stick to the light.

Plucky, with a square, tight-lipped face and blazing blue eyes, Collins was part of a pair of British escape artists. Legend had it that he'd made ten attempts since being captured at Dunkirk in 1940. None had gone the distance—yet.

Collins oriented himself. The wire fence ten feet to his right sparkled as if dusted in frost. From his "worm's eye view," he could see back into the camp. Collins squinted. It looked "like prewar Piccadilly [Square]"—worryingly bright. Inside the fence line, farthest from the camp, two armed Romanian sentries paced back and forth, at times drifting within thirty yards of him. The sergeants hadn't dug far enough. The tunnel exit sat barely outside the glow of the compound's lights.

About fifty yards west of Collins lay the quickest route to freedom: the forest at the foot of the mountain. The trunks of the old-growth trees looked gaunt and ghoulish in the camp lights. Aiming for the tree line, Collins began crawling parallel to the fence. Slowly. He was a dark form, but a form that hadn't been there a moment ago, a form any guard might spot if he moved too quickly.

Glancing under his arm, Collins spotted Sergeant Ted Lancaster, the other seasoned British escape man, slipping out from the exit. Six Americans were behind him, still in the hole.

Next emerged Sergeant Phil Rurak, the heavyweight gunner from the crew of *Chattanooga Choo Choo.* During their four months in captivity, Rurak had grown a thick black beard. With his darkened face, scowl, and soiled gunner's flightsuit, he looked like a demon from the underworld. When their bomber crashed, he'd carried two men from the wreckage before he and the cameraman, McCrary, set out to evade the enemy. They made it three days on the run, "wading streams and crossing wheat fields," subsisting on turnips. Hiking into mountains, they came across a trusty Romanian woodcutter, who gave them food, then had them arrested.

This time would be different.

Rurak began crawling for freedom.

COLLINS, THE LEAD MAN, was halfway to the woods. Four snaking forms followed. More emerged from the tunnel. Then, sharp, sudden, a dog in the neighboring compound barked. The POWs froze. The dog could smell them.

Two guards exchanged words. One swept his flashlight across the fence line. Collins lay motionless, hesitant even to breathe.

The beam fell short of him by a few feet. After a pause, Collins resumed moving. He flattened himself again. A sentry paced fifteen feet away from him, so close the POWs heard him cough. Then the Romanian pivoted on his heel and headed the other direction.

At last, the fence next to Collins dropped off. Nothing stood between him and the woods. He felt tempted to rise to a crouch and run, but he fought the urge, stayed flat, and slithered to the tree line. "The bushes, thank Christ!"

A moment later, Sergeant Lancaster joined him. Collins nabbed him by the arm and moved forward. The two Brits began scaling the forested mountain behind the camp. Glancing back, Collins observed: "Below us the camp is an oasis of light." How had they made it out of there alive? They weren't sticking around to figure it out.

Rurak reached the tree line next and crouched in the darkness. Four more Americans joined him at the bottom of the hill, tense, waiting. One more man, and they'd set out together, keeping safety in numbers. But looking to the sky, the men saw that "the clouds have cleared and the moon is up." By the time the eighth and final airman, Sergeant Joseph Brown, set out from the tunnel, the camp was bathed in moonlight. His friends could see him crawling.

Brown sensed the danger. Older than the others at forty-three, Brown was a round-faced former Chicago policeman. He'd been in tight spots before, but nothing like this. He tried to time his movements, slowing each to the barest of minimums, but the escape was taking too long.

One of the sentries stopped pacing. He turned to his comrade across the yard and shouted. Maybe just asking him the time. Maybe if he wanted coffee.

But Brown heard the shout and panicked. He jumped to his feet and bolted for the woods.

He made an easy target to spot. One of the guards fired his rifle into the air. A warning shot. When Brown didn't stop, the guard leveled his rifle and shot again. Higher up the mountainside, the Brits knew something had gone wrong. "Only one thing for it now. Run like hell."

At ground level, with bullets cutting through the darkness, Sergeant Brown hit the dirt. This was not worth dying over.

Romanian sentries quickly swarmed him, holding him down. More guards came running, shouting, pointing. *The woods! The woods!* One guard with a machine gun fired blindly into the tree line. Then came a shout to hold their fire. Troops with flashlights and rifles darted toward the forest. Rurak and his three friends didn't make it far. As soon as they'd heard the bullets, they'd pressed to the wet leaves. In moments, they felt the tips of bayonets in their backs.

Nearby, Sergeant Harry Baughn, a tail gunner, lay still "in a patch of deep shadow. Showing remarkable nerve, [he] huddled there in the wild confusion that followed the alarm." Baughn saw a fury of ankle-wrapped Romanian boots stomp past his face; then he silently slipped away.

Furious, the guards prodded Rurak and the others with the sharp points of their bayonets, driving the recaptured prisoners along the fence line back to camp.

Okay, you got us! Ease up, pal!

But the big Romanian farm boys were deadly serious. They knew the score. Antonescu's men had made it clear: If any American POWs escaped, particularly after they'd claimed them from the Germans, it meant a national disgrace. And pity the poor commandant and his men who allowed this: They'd be reassigned to "permanent duty" on the Eastern Front. It was a death sentence.

But the Americans weren't aware of this. They figured they were dealing with the same affable fellows who'd been guarding them for the past seven weeks.

In a flash, the big Romanian guard in front of Rurak tossed his rifle up in the air and vanished from sight. One moment he was there, the next he was gone. Captive and captor alike looked and found him. He'd fallen "into the gaping tunnel exit." The Americans couldn't help themselves. They burst out laughing. The scene was straight out of Abbott and Costello—pure slapstick. But "this sent their captors into a rage."

Didn't the Americans realize what an escape would do to the guard staff?

Fists and boots started flying. The POWs took their first beating.

ERNIE AND THE OFFICERS heard the shots fired in the sergeants' compound. Their eyes darted fearfully around the dining room. A swift reaction was a bad sign.

A Romanian lieutenant clattered up the steps and flew through the front door, pistol in hand. He wasn't their friend, Sandy. Sandy and Sergeant

Copil, Hog Jaw, were likely searching the woods. This lieutenant, one of six in the camp, was spindly, with a prominent Adam's apple, like Ichabod Crane. His pistol shook. The officers looked down its barrel.

"Merge la sus!" he cried, pointing to the second floor. "Merge la sus!"

He wanted everyone upstairs. The compound was in lockdown mode. The guards didn't want any escapees, if the officers were in the mix, to try and get in through the windows.

"His forehead was wet with sweat," Britt remembered. "We were afraid he might pull the trigger accidentally in this nervous condition."

The Americans hustled for the hallway, but the men in the front ran smack into a cluster of Romanian guards charging the other direction, who leveled bayonets in their faces. From the other side, Ichabod had his gun trained on them, his hand still shaking. "Merge la sus!" he repeated, his voice reaching a fever pitch.

"Get a move on it!" the POWs behind yelled to their friends in the front. Lieutenant Aaronson was the first to sort out the situation. Turning to the shaking Romanian officer, he snapped: "If you want us to 'merge la sus,' get these bastards out of the way!"

Ichabod barked at his guards—disperse!

Ernie, seeing the terror and anger written on the Romanian faces, feared for the enlisted men.

He was right to worry.

IF IT HAD BEEN a fair fight, the five American sergeants would have stood a good chance. But the big Romanians were armed, and they were clearly in charge. Enraged, panicked, the farm boys pounded and kicked the Americans all the way to the guardhouse in the middle of the compound. Inside, every guard took a swipe.

Rurak, the biggest American, took the most abuse. For reasons unknown, the guards vented the bulk of their frustration on him. The heavyweight gave them his back to protect his face, but a guard still managed to jab him in the head with a rifle butt. "Sergeant Rurak's skull was cut open. [It] bled badly."

A Romanian officer, Lieutenant Ayir, burst into the guardhouse, pistol drawn, and demanded to know how many escapees were still on the run. He was of medium height and build, "with very black hair slicked back."

Three—two Englishmen, one American.

With his pistol, Ayir clubbed first Rurak, then each of the other Americans. One man went to the ground. Ayir kicked him in the face. He would have gone further, but just then the commandant strode in with a stumble. Major Cavaropol had had his "evening's drinking interrupted."

The guards and Ayir stiffened at the sight of their commander. Coldly, Cavaropol demanded a report. Three prisoners lost on his watch? His death sentence was as good as inked. With nothing left to lose, he turned on the POWs. "Drunk on both anger and liquor, he took wild swings at each but connected properly only with Brown, who quickly grew an enormous black eye." Hollow-eyed, sadistic, and unsteady, Cavaropol lunged for Rurak, grabbed him by the beard, and yanked. The two men spun violently, while the Romanian major yelled something in a garble about "Stalin!? Stalin!" He pulled Rurak out the front door, barked a command to his guards, and pointed Rurak toward the seven-foot fence.

It was clear what the commandant wanted. Rurak was to climb the fence so the guards could shoot him. Cavaropol wouldn't stoop to outright murder. But if an American was killed in the act of escape, his hands would be clean.

Rurak refused. Not a chance.

Cavaropol shouted at a guard to stick the big American with his bayonet to make him climb. The big farm boy trembled, lunged, and hesitated, his blade an inch away from the prisoner. He couldn't do it.

Cavaropol, still drunk, roared back to the guardhouse and grabbed Sergeant James Brittain, a young blond gunner from the Eight Balls, along with two of his guards. This time, the commandant devised a more careful plan. He and his guards led Brittain to the hill behind the camp, where the trees stood ghoulish in the light. Cavaropol calmed himself, gave the prisoner a cigarette, then pointed to the dark hillside in front.

The message was clear: Go. Up the hill.

Cavaropol gave orders to his guards too. You. Go with him. When he's at the top, shoot him.

The guards were afraid to incur their commandant's wrath. But Brittain's reaction was the same as Rurak's: No damn way.

Cavaropol shouted at his guards again. They hauled Brittain back to the guardhouse.

THE ROMANIANS WERE IN a quandary. Some sort of punishment was needed. But they didn't have a solitary confinement cell in their guardhouse. They hadn't expected to need it.

At Cavaropol's command, they stuffed Rurak, Brittain, and the three other POWs in a closet to double as a sweatbox. The commandant snorted, then stumbled out the door to sleep off his drunk.

Five men were crammed into a space meant for a few coats, a space "so narrow that a man's shoulders touch the sides," remembered Rurak. There wasn't room to sit. Rurak was bleeding, and a patchwork of "about 40" welts and bruises were forming on his back.

What had angered the Romanians so strongly? Quietly, the men compared notes, shocked by the reaction. The Romanians had never behaved like this before.

"At least we ain't been shot," Brittain said with a sigh. "Things coulda been worse."

But all their effort, stress, and suffering would be for nothing.

In a few days, Sergeant Baughn, the lone American escapee, would take a chance by asking some peasants for food. They called the gendarmes. A day later, the two British evaders, Collins and Lancaster, would try to pose as German civilians. They were recaptured.

To his superiors, Cavarapol came off spotless. No one got away. Why go through the headache of replacing him?

But the Romanians were now on high alert. And they began to ask a critical question:

If there was one tunnel, could there be two?

CHAPTER 36

THE TIPPING POINT

THE FOLLOWING MORNING
Lagărul No. 2

FROM HIS ROOM ERNIE HEARD THE BOOTS CHARGING UP THE FRONT steps. A moment later, Romanian guards, led by Hog Jaw, burst through the lodge door. Ernie set down his book without saving the page. He swung his feet to the floor and eyed the door, tense. He heard shouts, the hard crash of bookcases being knocked over and beds being overturned. The guards were turning rooms upside down, trying to ferret out another escape attempt.

Everyone in the officers' camp had been waiting for the other shoe to drop—and now came the reckoning.

Without a knock, Ernie's door flew open. The brawny farm-boy guards shoved their way into Ernie's room and shouted in their tongue, "Out of the way."

Ernie tried to look surprised, but his expression didn't convince them of innocence. He jumped to his feet and backed to a wall. The guards tossed the straw mattresses. Bed boards clattered to the polished wood floor.

A guard held his hand over the ceramic heater and noticed Ernie's stove wasn't running. No heat, on a cold day like this? The guard reached inside, felt around, and yanked out Ernie's diary. He shook it in Ernie's face and cursed. Ernie had hidden it there, hoping the Romanians wouldn't gain anything they could use against him. So much for that.

No matter where a man was in the lodge, a whistle's shrill blast reached every ear, slicing through the air like a blade. A Romanian guard, "yelling at the top of his voice," bolted up from the basement and out the front door. Ernie glimpsed him through the window. The guard ran straight for the commandant.

They'd found the tunnel.

—

STUCK DOWNSTAIRS DURING THE shakedown, Britt and several others had moved to the dining room when Cavaropol entered the lodge with his reinforcements. The commandant gnashed his teeth. Another tunnel? The guard who'd found it led the way to the door to the basement, wiping sweat from his brow. He reported with relief that the tunnel was unfinished. No one had gotten out.

Cavaropol pounded down the stairs to inspect the transgression for himself, then came back up in a cold rage. Glaring at the Americans, a conflicted look overtook his face. He didn't know who to target, because no one was working on the tunnel when it was discovered. The commandant ordered everyone to their room.

The Americans hesitated: The guards were tossing their rooms.

The commandant barked another order. No one needed the threat translated: You'll be shot! The men scattered toward their rooms.

Cavaropol wasn't finished. While the POWs were still filing out of the dining room, he swung his gaze around the room, looking for someone to hurt. He ordered his guards to attention on the terrazzo tiles near the entryway, then singled out Hog Jaw, and bawled him out like a drill sergeant tearing into a raw recruit. Again, his meaning was clear: Another tunnel! Right under your nose! Because you were too busy playing nice with the Americans. The guards shook in their boots.

Britt was one of the last up the stairs. "His anger increased as he [Cavaropol] yelled louder," Britt recalled. "Getting out of control, he started slapping the guards." Again and again. He moved from man to man, smacking their faces hard, admonishing them for their stupidity. For a few moments Britt watched the scene, horrified. The Romanian guards winced, but none resisted "against this barrage of anger." They were too afraid to defend themselves.

Britt and the last of the Americans disappeared up the stairs before Cavaropol could turn on them.

FINALLY, THANKFULLY, THE SHOUTING and hitting stopped. Ernie and his friends waited until they heard the guards exit the lodge before creeping wearily down the stairs to survey the damage.

In the guards' quest to find the tunnel, the lodge had been ransacked.

The POWs' battle maps were confiscated. Tables and chairs were overturned. Cavaropol had left one humiliated guard standing watch in the entryway. His face was stinging red from being hit.

A chilling thought ran through Ernie. If the commandant had disciplined his own men this severely, what had he done to the sergeants who tried to escape?

They were in the hands of a maniac.

SEVERAL DAYS LATER, ON Saturday, November 20, 1943, frost clung to the grass when Princess Catherine pulled up to the front gate of the camp behind the wheel of her Chevrolet. The gate was closed and locked.

It was puzzling. "There was no one to let me enter," she recalled. She'd brought more books for the boys and a treat: watermelon marmalade from her estate. But no POWs were on the porch or in the yard.

"After a few honks on the horn, the camp commandant appeared," she later wrote.

"Go away!" he snapped. "You aren't welcome anymore!"

They argued until Cavaropol put his foot down and declared she could no longer visit the men. The princess was officially banned. Catherine held her own and demanded he send out the American interpreter, Medeiros. By then, the dapper tail gunner of *Chattanooga Choo Choo,* who already spoke Portuguese, had picked up Romanian, becoming both translator and spokesman for the POWs. Catherine knew Medeiros. He was one of her boys, one of the first she'd rescued.

Medeiros walked out but stopped a short distance from the fence. Cavaropol stood near him, trying to intimidate the American. Princess Catherine stepped from her car, leaving it idling, puffing exhaust in the cold.

"What has happened?" she asked.

They'd been caught making tunnels, Medeiros explained. Two of them. One by the sergeants, and one by the officers.

The princess shook her head. She'd known the boys were up to something, but not a tunnel. Wondering why the commandant was so mad at *her,* she asked Medeiros for more details.

"We used your wire [lighting]," Medeiros said. "They got pretty upset when they found it."*

* Years after the war she would admit, "I innocently played a part in the plot."

Oh, brother.

There was more to the story, she was sure. The princess could see Medeiros was afraid to speak freely with Cavaropol behind him, but she could sense "an undercurrent of dislike for the man."

"Not wanting to make any more trouble," she would write, "I gave him [Medeiros] the boxes of books and marmalade, turned the car around, and headed down the road. But not before I heard the major shout, '. . . and don't come back!'"

IN THE FOLLOWING DAYS, one POW ventured outside the lodge on a regular basis. Ernie thrust his hands into his pockets and walked circles around the cold black pond in the pale winter sunlight. No one had told him he couldn't go outside, and Ernie had willed himself to exercise every day with no exceptions. He wanted to keep fit, and he knew he needed to combat depression. It was easy to lose heart in a situation like this.

It was nearly December. Gray clouds papered the sky, and the biting wind held a warning of impending snow. The Romanian sentries plodded from one checkpoint to another, chins lowered. One man walking around a pond wasn't much to guard.

Already they'd sealed the door to the basement and filled in the officers' entrance shaft, leaving the rest of the dirt where it lay. Ernie keenly felt the loss of the tunnel. Even if he didn't want to admit it, he'd become attached to the Project.

Now it was gone, and Ernie was left with regret. *We never got a chance to try.*

Britt felt the same. "A feeling of gloom descended on us," he recalled. "All that work for nothing."

The men's fears eased, but lethargy set in. The doldrums were widespread at Lagărul No. 2. Bob threw a small log out the window at a guard, just for the hell of it. Some men slept around the clock.

When Ernie wasn't walking, loneliness crept in. He felt homesick and worried. He'd had no contact with home since he went MIA. Per protocol, the prisoners had sent Red Cross postcards, but no mail ever came back.

Al had written his parents asking for small comforts from home. Back in Revere, his mother worked the register and his father stocked the shelves at Romano's Market. They were a tight-knit family. Al's parents had come from Italy and built their little store from the ground up.

"We are all lucky to be alive after being shot down," Al had written home that August. "Send me gum and the *Revere Journal* if you can."

No reply.

In September, he tried again: "Let me know who is the winner of the World Series—[and] put some chocolate in the packages?"

Again, nothing.

With their radio confiscated, there was no news from the outside world. Ernie and his friends didn't know how the war was going—whether Hitler was winning, or whether Japan had taken back the Pacific. The POWs were lost in Transylvania, isolated and forgotten.

To top it all off, the princess was gone, out of their lives, perhaps for good. Her Chevrolet had once carved its path through the valley in the Alps, each trip a lifeline. The distance was fifty miles each way, and she "broke speeding laws" in her "rush to get to the mountains." But what she brought meant so much more than the small gifts and necessities packed in her car. She brought hope.

She lifted their spirits, offered guidance, and provided a parental presence, wise and unwavering. Without her, they'd have been in the hands of the Germans. And the crew of *Chattanooga Choo Choo,* especially, could never forget how she had championed them.

Britt had once praised her "stubbornness" because she never took no for an answer. "Oh, no, my dear," she corrected him, "I am not stubborn—just determined, and that is a lot different."

She didn't owe the men anything. Yet she had stayed in the picture when anyone else would have left long ago. Already she had three thousand orphans to care for. Yet she'd taken on 110 more by adopting these POWs.

Now she was gone, and it was their fault.

IN EARLY DECEMBER, THE pond froze. Snow fell, like "white fur on the hills." Guards stomped about in the cold, shaking the snow from their boots and clapping their hands to keep warm.

The official start of winter was drawing near, and change lay in the air.

"One morning, several military vehicles came down the mountain road," wrote Britt. They stopped at the sergeants' camp, first. "About a half hour later, they came to us. It was obvious that our new commandant was here."

This time, the gate to the lodge opened. The official story, at least according to the Red Cross, was that Cavaropol was gone, "relieved of his command because of the escapees."

But there was more to the story.

One of the arriving military cars passed through the gate unimpeded, its tires crunching on the snow. The car stopped and a moon-faced Romanian major in his thirties stepped out. He offered his hand to the person inside.

Princess Catherine was back.

INSIDE THE WARM DINING room, the officers gathered around the princess like a sports team searching for direction before a big game. She offered no grand explanations and few details, only introducing their new commandant as Major Moruzi and adding, "Be nice to him."

One by one, smiles began to twitch at the corners of the prisoners' mouths. It was too good to be true. Somehow the "Ambassador of Goodwill" had gotten Cavaropol booted from his post. Had she gone to King Michael? Had she twisted Săulescu's arm? Was the brooding major on a train to the Eastern Front at that very moment?

The princess offered only a polite smile.

Pieces of the story would emerge slowly, and some the men could only guess at. No one had even told Catherine that Cavaropol had nearly killed a member of her boys' crew. But the princess knew that Cavaropol had violated an unwritten code between the Romanians and the Americans. They were supposed to be opponents, not enemies.

There was no question that things would be different under the command of Major Moruzi, "who was openly an Allied sympathizer." Apologies had already been rendered to Rurak and the other abused men, and the prisoners' comforts and privileges were restored. Ernie's diary was put back in his hands. And Colonel Săulescu must have felt bad, because the POWs' radio was sent back, with specific encouragement to listen to Christmas music.*

* On Christmas Eve, when Ernie and his fellow officers sat down to dinner, President Roosevelt's Christmas address crackled through the radio. Voices fell silent. The president spoke to America's fighting men across the globe—especially POWs. Wrote Ernie: "At the close of his speech, without a word, every man stood at rigid attention while the Star-Spangled Banner was being played. We were indeed proud to be Americans!" In his diary, Captain Clay Ferguson noted: "I felt like crying when the national anthem was played. It's fine to know that there is still a place like America. I had nearly forgotten what it was like."

WHILE THE OFFICERS MARVELED among themselves at the turn of events, the princess took aside her "original boys," the officers of *Chattanooga Choo Choo,* so she could talk with them privately. By the look on her face, she was just as glad to see them as they were to see her. Sure, she had the foundation and her orphans, but these were her adopted sons.

Catherine's blood family was small. She hadn't seen her husband for years. He'd married her for her family's wealth more than love. She had a twenty-three-year-old daughter, who "was tall, beautiful, and knew it"—but the daughter was absorbed in her social life in Bucharest. Growing up, she had come to resent the amount of time her mother devoted to the orphans. When she came of age, she chose not to participate in the foundation's work.

For Princess Catherine, the officers reminded her of real family. Even when they were "bad boys," as she put it, she still cared about them, and they for her. The mutual affection was obvious.

Things would be better going forward, she assured them. *Trust us.* At the same time, without saying it, she was getting at something deeper: *Forgive us.* Not just for Cavaropol and the actions within the wire of this camp. For *everything.* Both sides were going to have to put the bombing raid of August 1 behind them to make it out of this war alive.

Before Princess Catherine left, there was something she thought they'd like to know. The tunnel was "the talk of Bucharest." A thirty-foot tunnel, fully illuminated? Romanians were praising the Americans' ingenuity. The princess chuckled as she walked away.

Ernie and his friends fought to contain their smiles. They might have been stranded in Transylvania, but they were far from alone.

They found themselves reinvigorated, full of hope, and conscious of a renewed vow.

Come hell or high water, they were going to find a way home.

CHAPTER 37

SPRING

FOUR MONTHS LATER, APRIL 4, 1944

Bucharest

THE SHARP WAIL OF AIR RAID SIRENS CUT THROUGH THE CALM OF A spring afternoon. It was about 1:30 P.M.

King Michael hurried out from a small white villa in the gardens behind the royal palace. Queen Helen and General Constantin Sănătescu, the Marshal of the Palace, followed close behind. Everyone still wore long coats against the early April chill.

Sănătescu was fifty-nine, gray at the temples yet "still as slim as a young cavalry officer. With his soft Moldavian voice, which he never raised, he always seemed to calm any disagreements within the Palace." In Nazi-aligned Romania, he was one of the good guys, quietly loyal to his king despite Antonescu's shadow stretching over the country.

General Sănătescu

The king, queen, and general had been having lunch in the royal family's garden retreat, the Casa Nouă—the "New House." The first sunshine of the season had arrived only three days earlier, and the Alps in the distance still wore their white caps of snow. With spring came a fragile sense of hope among the Romanian people that the long, unpopular war might finally be drawing to a close—even if that meant defeat and whatever consequences would follow.

And then, *bombers.*

Everyone looked up. High above, the first of 350 heavy bombers were arriving over the northern fringe of Bucharest. From the palace grounds, they looked like small white crosses in the pastel sky. Flying at 22,000 feet from west to east, the long line of planes seemed endless, their vapor trails "marking their passage like the breath of the gods."

Queen Helen gasped. These were Americans—they were the only ones capable of sending so many planes. But to her, another bombing raid didn't seem possible after Tidal Wave. She still visited the few American POWs who remained in the hospital. She listened to their stories, laughed at their jokes, and even confided her uncertainty about the times they were living in. Her friendships with the men had made it easy to forget that their two nations were still at war. How could the Americans be bombing Romania again? Romania was protecting American airmen from the Germans!

Above, the bombers droned on, indifferent, part of a grander plan.

This was the opening act in a new American campaign designed to aid the Red Army's spring offensive, launching about three hundred miles to the northeast. As Soviet tanks advanced through the spring mud, driving toward Romania proper, American flyboys would play their part from above. Their mission: to smash transport hubs, choke off supply lines, and obliterate the railways and depots "used by Nazi Germany to transport troops, large quantities of fuel, and other supplies."

If it worked, the campaign would cripple the German and Romanian armies' ability to hold the front—and maybe take Hitler's "lesser partner" out of the war altogether.

Antonescu couldn't say he hadn't been warned. Two weeks earlier, on March 23, the BBC had broadcast a grim message: "At this eleventh hour, unless Romania breaks with the Axis immediately, she will be bombed to destruction." Still, Antonescu refused to yield—not if doing so meant bending the knee to Stalin.

The writing was on the wall for Romania. Even her "protectors" could read it. "For the first time German soldiers were now being seen drunk on the streets."

Glancing to the sky, General Sănătescu, a cool-headed veteran of Stalingrad, knew trouble when he saw it. The airmen up there weren't thinking about friendships—they were following orders. This time, the bombers belonged to the U.S. 15th Air Force, flying from their newly established bases in Italy. Sănătescu barked an order to the royal guards: Get the queen to safety.

Men in stone-colored tunics hurried forward, their boots crunching the gravel as they escorted Queen Helen toward the palace bomb shelter. Sănătescu turned to the king. He needed to take shelter as well.

But the young monarch lingered, his gaze locked on the bombers. Now twenty-two, he had heard of the Americans' famed daylight raids over Germany but never witnessed one. These bombers weren't on a course toward the palace. Anyone could see that. And besides, everyone knew the Americans' reputation. Their high-altitude precision bombing, it was said, "could hit a barrel from 25,000 feet." Whatever their target was, it wasn't as if they'd miss.

Dark specks began falling from the bombers high above. The Americans had released their payloads. From the looks of it, they were targeting the city's northern rail yards, two miles away.

Sanatescu urged the king to get moving. The king snapped out of his trance. With one eye still to the sky, he followed Sănătescu inside.

But on the steps down to the shelter, he could hear the deep concussion of exploding bombs. For the curious young monarch, the missed opportunity to witness such a moment was unbearable. He slowed, spun on his heel, and sprinted back up the stairs.

Your Highness! No! The king's secretary, a middle-aged man, and others saw the king's reversal and protested—guards, aides, even his own mother called after him. But Michael didn't stop.

The secretary gave chase and caught up with the king on the rooftop, where Michael stood beneath a cloud of planes, smack in the middle of an air raid. Michael brushed aside the man's concern. Didn't they understand? This was precision bombing. There was nothing to worry about.

Outside the city, German and Romanian anti-aircraft guns were firing back against the bombers. Gray puffs of flak burst all around the planes.

The secretary begged the king to retreat to the palace shelter. What might happen if the bombardiers dropped their payloads while being bounced by flak? How might wind change a bomb's trajectory? Any number of factors could throw a bomb off course.

The secretary was on the verge of breaking decorum, grabbing Michael by the arm and pulling him to the shelter when all at once, a shrill, whistle-like noise sounded above them. For a split second, the two men froze. It took a moment to process it.

A stray bomb screamed toward them.

They had to get down!

A thunderous crack split the air as a bomb punched through the roof of the Splendide Park Hotel next door.

A fiery explosion hurled a geyser of debris and bomb fragments skyward. The ground beneath them quaked. Shards of glass showered down on the men, while bomb fragments plinked across the palace rooftop. The shock-wave threw dust in their faces.

The young king and his secretary lay prone, hearts racing, the pungent scent of smoke and plaster filling their nostrils.

A Romanian journalist caught in the attack recalled, "You hear the terrible explosions all around you. The dust of destruction, and the smoke of fires blind you for a moment. And in your consciousness, light suddenly emerges; you have escaped, the wave is receding. The roar of the wave diminishes, and now the explosions, softer, perform their melodic opera on other streets."

When the dust settled, the king stood wearily. The sirens still blared but the bombers were in the distance now, their formation wheeling for home. The Americans' famed daylight precision bombing apparently wasn't always that precise. He'd come within fifty yards of being blown up. Investigating the bomb fragments that littered the rooftop, Michael picked up a jagged piece of shrapnel and almost dropped it. Hot!

A wail of fire engines drew the king's attention. Michael spotted smoke rising over the rooftops to the north, and his face fell. Two miles away, the largest train yard in Romania was burning.

Without a word, he turned and sprinted for the stairwell.

THE ROYAL PALACE—CLEAN, WHITE, and colonnaded—stood like a smaller cousin of the Louvre, its grilled black gates reminiscent of Buckingham Palace. Only after the all clear had sounded would General Sănătescu allow the guards to open the palace gates.

The Royal Palace of Bucharest

As soon as the gates opened, King Michael roared out of the grounds in his fastest sports car. The guards jumped out of the way as the sleek machine tore past, and black staff cars carrying the king's bodyguards gave chase. But the king wouldn't be deterred. Serious with concern, Michael steered north toward the rail yard where the bombs had fallen.

He knew he was nearing his destination when the street in front of him glowed red. The pavement was on fire.

He hadn't been expecting that. American incendiary bombs—meant to burn German boxcars—had spilled into the city and set the road ablaze. Flames were literally flaring up and "leaping from the asphalt."

The king worked the wheel—left, right—zigzagging around the burning patches. Still, he kept going. Still, his bodyguards gave chase.

At the Bucharest North rail yard, the king's headlights cast ghoulish beams through the smoke-filled air. Michael screeched to a stop and stepped out to a sight he'd never imagined. Romania's largest train yard looked like a wildfire had torn through it. German firefighters rushed toward the smoke, red-banded helmets glinting, axes and crowbars clutched tight. Flames licked from buildings. Oil-spattered locomotives lay tipped over, their giant metal bodies charred. Boxcars burned behind them, feeding the inferno. Wounded people lay on the ground. Survivors stood amid the ruins, shaking their fists at the sky.

And dead travelers lay everywhere among the twisted rails.

"There was nowhere to step without encountering the dead, wounded, and pools of blood," a Romanian historian wrote. "Calls for help, the screams of the wounded, couldn't be heard due to the different noises coming from all directions. The wooden walls of the burning train cars could be heard crackling."

People were suffering. Dying. The king had to do something. He began to move forward into the swirling panic, fear, and confusion. His bodyguard pulled him back. What if there were unexploded bombs? The king indicated it was a risk he was willing to take, but his guards were not: They had a duty to protect him. They stood in his way and wouldn't let him go forward. The nation needed him alive.

Michael relented. The quiet young king stood at the edge of the disaster, tight-lipped, eyeing the destruction, his blue eyes stunned and saddened, "his spirit heavy with the knowledge that this was only the beginning."

Yet his presence did not go unnoticed.

Was that the king? Survivors and rescuers couldn't believe their eyes. "That he was there at this ghastly moment was not lost on his stricken people." Dictators might call him the "Boy King," a "Paper Monarch," and a "mere spokesman," but the everyday people saw that he was there, suffering with them.

They had to wonder: Would Antonescu have done this?

That day, even the king's own men—from his bodyguards to the Marshal of the Palace—began to see him in a different light. He might have been young and driven by what some called "heedless curiosity," but he'd also raced to the scene of a disaster and stood with his people in shared grief. That took a kind of courage not seen in most heads of state, an undefinable quality that makes other men follow.

As the king lingered on the fringe of the burning train yard, the men loyal to him began to collectively think a dangerous thought. They saw new and powerful potential in him, potential that perhaps the king had yet to see in himself. He might be the only one daring enough to try what desperately needed to be done.

This young man could stand up to Antonescu.

CHAPTER 38

EVERYTHING THAT EVER MATTERED

ELEVEN DAYS LATER, APRIL 15, 1944
Bucharest

THE LIGHT OF DAWN CREPT THROUGH THE WINDOW ABOVE THE CURTAINS as Romania's second-highest-scoring ace opened his eyes in bed. Buzz, with twenty-four victories now to his name, rolled over, taking in his surroundings. If a man had to fight a war, this was the way to do it.

His third-story corner apartment in the historic city center exuded luxury, with high ceilings, half-paneled walls, and polished wooden floors. He had slept on crisp sheets instead of lying under a rough wool blanket. His head rested on a real pillow instead of tossing and turning on a sack filled with straw. In the evenings, lamplight warmed the room, music drifted through the air, and the rich aroma of dinner rose from the kitchen. There weren't even any mice! His unit, the 7th Fighter Group, had been reassigned to defend the capital, and consequently its pilots lived among the civilians. Compared to the front lines, this was heaven.

Beside him, Buzz's girlfriend, Nadia Herascu, twenty-four, slept softly, her auburn hair curling across her face. She was the only thing on earth he loved more than flying. During the day, she glided around his apartment, ever keeping a low profile. Her every movement carried "the grace of a ballet dancer."

Theirs was a "genuine love story," though war had done its best to make it anything but easy. It had begun, in fact, with a twist of fate.

Before the war in 1939, when Buzz flew commercial planes for the state airlines, he took off from Bucharest one day in a twin-engine transport, ferrying passengers on a domestic route. Almost immediately an engine caught on fire, and Buzz quickly and skillfully landed the plane on just one

Nadia Herascu

engine. Once the flames were doused, Buzz positioned himself at the foot of the stairs behind the wing where he "personally assured each exiting passenger that the incident was nothing."

Midway through the line came a slim young woman with a striking face and bright blue eyes—Nadia. Buzz reached up and led her to the ground, then offered a hand to her mother. The two women, from a wealthy Bucharest family, had been traveling together.

When Buzz first spoke with Nadia, he was taken by her beauty and personality. She was captivating, possessing "natural poise." In turn, she was highly intrigued by the dashing airline pilot in a navy-blue suit with the gold flourishes around the cuffs. When he asked to see her again, she said yes. Only then did she learn his last name—Cantacuzino. A prince flying an airliner? Buzz explained that he flew flights now and then to avoid being stuck behind a desk.

On their first official date, he took her flying. Nadia sat in the front seat of an open-cockpit biplane, with Buzz manning the controls from the backseat. When they "looped the loop," she handled it like a champ.

Back on the ground they talked for hours. During quiet pauses, Buzz found himself studying her more closely. She was sharp, articulate, fluent in four languages, and already pursuing a degree in theater. Something deeper was taking root. A storybook romance was unfolding.

But when the Antonescu regime found out, they set their sights on destroying it.

PEERING INTO THE BATHROOM mirror, Buzz combed his hair back from a sharp widow's peak and straightened the tie of his uniform. Nearly three years ago, when he'd first reported to his wartime fighter group in 1941, they'd been wearing different uniforms. In those days, he and the other Romanian pilots wore white, one-piece British flying suits and flew Hawker Hurricane fighters from England. Romania was at war with the USSR then, not England, not yet.

On September 12, 1941, Buzz was near the front lines, waiting in his Hurricane at Mamaia airfield near the Black Sea. He was on alert, ready to scramble in the event of a Russian air raid, when his squadron leader climbed up on the wing and handed Buzz a folded note. The squadron leader looked a bit alarmed.

Buzz scanned the note. His eyes widened.

Grounded. Immediately. Ordered to leave the front on the next available transport and return to his home in Bucharest.

Now, of all times.

It didn't make sense. Attrition had drained the squadron, leaving them short on pilots. They were outnumbered by "three to five" Soviet pilots for every Romanian, even in those early days. And already he'd flown fifty-six combat missions and scored four victories. He was needed *here.*

But orders were orders. Buzz had been, in his words, "pulled out of the plane between battles."

Back at home, he learned why. Antonescu's secret police, the notorious Special Service of Intelligence, the Siguranța—Romania's equivalent of the Gestapo—had done some investigating of Nadia. Her real name was Nadejdea Kujnir, and her family had fled Russia during the Bolshevik revolution. They'd wanted to escape the political instability and violence, and because the Bolsheviks were cracking down on religious institutions. The facts were as plain as day.

Nadia was Jewish.

Buzz was incensed. As if heritage or bloodline should matter! But in the eyes of Antonescu's regime, it did.

Ever since the dictator's rise to power, Romania's Jews had been second-class citizens. Across the country, the fascists made it difficult for Jews to work, live, and prosper. To "Romanian-ize" society, authorities barred Jews from owning farmland or businesses and excluded them from public life, journalism, and the arts.

Nadia's dreams of a career in theater were canceled before they began. She couldn't drive any of Buzz's cars, because she couldn't obtain a driver's license. When she shopped in a grocery store, she couldn't buy as much sugar or wheat as an ethnic Romanian. When it came time to check out, a Jew had to pay twice as much for bread. And she couldn't legally marry her beloved, even when he asked.*

It could have been worse, and the couple knew it. At least the secret police didn't hand her over to their German "protectors."

What was the dictatorship to do with the troublesome couple?

The Siguranța deemed Nadia to be "dangerous to our institution, because she maintains intimate relations with Reserve Lieutenant Cantacuzino." In their eyes, the prince's loyalty as an officer was irreparably compromised. The nation couldn't have a man like that in uniform. So the dictatorship relegated Buzz back to flying for the state airlines. From then on, he'd fly the ministerial plane, among other odd jobs.

As for Nadia, the director general of the Siguranța instructed his subordinates to deliver a message: "Kindly instruct NADIA KUJNIR that she is not allowed to leave the Capital, and if she fails to comply, she will be interned in a labor camp."

Nevertheless, in Antonescu's wartime Romania, the couple had basically got away with a slap on the wrist. Yet their situation was far from ideal. Facing the shame of losing his military wings, Buzz wrote to the upper brass of his fighter group:

> I felt both very discouraged and deeply saddened. Regarding the accusation against me, I believe that each person is the master of their private life, as long as they do not break any laws, regulations, or receive verbal warnings. This is especially true when fulfilling their duty and contributing to the country, as I have done.

* For Jews in the newly liberated Romanian territories and conquered Soviet lands, their experience was a vastly different story than in Romania itself. Alongside German forces, Romanian troops committed numerous "horrific acts of mass butchery" under the banner of their "holy war" against "Judeo-Bolshevism." Scholar Larry Watts described the dichotomy: "If you were a Jew within Antonescu's Romania proper, you were more likely to survive World War II than if you had been living virtually anywhere else in Axis-occupied Europe. On the other hand, if you were a Jew in the areas that Antonescu's troops recaptured from the Soviet Union, there were few places worse."

> Regarding the "suspect" person, I specify that I have known her perfectly for three years. If she hadn't initially refused politely not to cause harm to me, and later if the law concerning marriages hadn't appeared, she would be my wife today.
>
> I declare that I renounce any kind of decorations or publicity, but I request to be sent back to the squadron, so I can fulfill my duty to the end.

Despite his royal blood—and the public humiliation it would bring him, far worse than for any ordinary pilot—the reply from his fighter group came back negative. Their hands were tied.

FOR THE NEXT TWO years, Buzz bit his lip and flew for the state airlines. They kept him busy ferrying war supplies back and forth and shuttling cabinet ministers to Hermann Goering's headquarters in Berlin. When they needed someone to fly "unannounced mock attacks" over Ploesti, they sent up Buzz and made him carve patterns in the darkness in a Ju-52, so anti-aircraft crews could have something to aim their searchlight at.

All the while, the dictatorship kept Buzz under constant surveillance. Everywhere he went, he was tailed by dark cars. Plainclothes Siguranța agents slithered through the door behind him in any restaurant or shop. When he grabbed a drink at Dragomir Niculescu's wine bar, they were there. When he dropped by Apostolescu's caviar shop to place an order, they were there.

Buzz never let them get under his skin. Whenever he spotted agents, he just nodded politely to them.

Nadia and Buzz kept seeing each other. They kept a low profile and avoided their old friends. And during the two years that Buzz flew for the airline, he tracked the news from the front where his veteran fighter pilot friends were dropping like flies. Soon, it looked as if no one would be left but a new crop of rookies.

Buzz couldn't keep quiet any longer. He did the unthinkable. He personally wrote to Antonescu, requesting to return to the front lines as a fighter pilot. This was highly contrary to protocol, but Buzz had little to lose. As it turned out, even Antonescu could be a realist. The situation at the front had grown dire, and the dictator knew what his country was up against. A fighter pilot with Buzz's skill was simply too valuable to have flying searchlight drills.

That was how the regime went from punishing Buzz to giving him his own squadron. That was how he became the fighter pilot–prince again.

Nadia understood. This was who he was, ever since day one. This was the pilot she'd fallen in love with.

BUZZ STEPPED OUT THE front door of his apartment building, slapped on his cap, and draped his black leather jacket over his arm. It was time to go to work. His blue uniform pants were already tucked into his heavy black fleece-topped boots. It was cold where he was heading, and Buzz moved with a calm demeanor, firm in his purpose. A black limousine idled at the curb, its driver ready to take him to the airfield north of the city, a distance too far to pedal on his bicycle.

Romania's second-highest-scoring ace had a squadron to lead. Whenever the American bombers thundered back over the city, Buzz and his pilots would be waiting. Someone had to stop the bombs from falling. The inevitable clashes would turn the skies into the deadliest battleground yet faced by Romania's fighter pilots. America's technical edge, the training of her pilots, not to mention the sheer number of aircraft, were unmatched.

The remaining Romanian pilots could sense the raised stakes. Captain Alexandru Șerbănescu, leader of the 9th Fighter Group, stated plainly: "I don't understand how an enemy, no matter how big and powerful they might be, can enter my country as if it were an undefended village and devastate it. It cannot be said that in Romania, no Romanian stood up against the Americans, even if we lose the battle."

And none felt this more keenly than Buzz. The mission now wasn't about protecting a handful of German grenadiers in a frontline trench, or risking his neck for Antonescu's crusade.

It was about defending the Romania he loved.

Buzz's loyalty rested unshakably with the king and crown, the people, his city, his family, and *her*. He would have fought to the death to protect Nadia. When the American bombs fell on the Bucharest North rail yard, the war came home. Now, in his heart and mind, he was flying for everything that ever mattered.

Buzz stepped into his car and closed the door behind him.

Fate was waiting.

CHAPTER 39

THE WONDER WEAPON

A WEEK LATER, APRIL 21, 1944
Ploesti

SLOUCHED IN A CHAIR IN THE SMALL POLICE STATION ON THE EDGE of Ploesti, the young American pilot looked the worse for wear. His white scarf and hat were gone, his green rayon jacket was singed at the cuffs, and his RAF-style leather boots with their sheepskin tops were charred by fire. With his left hand, he cradled his injured right elbow, wincing whenever he tried to move.

Tall and athletic, Second Lieutenant Jack Williams filled most of the chair he was slouched in. At twenty-one, he had a boyish, all-American face—brown hair, friendly eyes, and a chin that tapered to a V. In high school, he'd done it all: tumbling team, glee club, pep club, hobby club, the *Scribblers* newspaper staff—you name it.

Jack Williams

Now he tried to smile through the pain, though the expression came out more like a grimace. Across the room, a squad of Romanian gendarmes studied him warily.

Several peasants had found the lieutenant beneath a tree in a field with his parachute blossomed around him. They'd given him morphine from his escape kit and a bit of fruit juice, but he hadn't said much. Whoever he was, he and his fellow fliers had just bombed Ploesti's rail yard. Outside the police station, smoke from the attack still hung in the afternoon sky. Another American high-altitude raid had occurred, this time aimed at the city's train lines.

Bucharest. Ploesti. Brasov. Ploesti again. The Americans were smashing rail yards across Romania one after another. This had been the fifth raid since April 4. Soon there wouldn't be a train left to catch anywhere in the country.

And everyone knew what came next. The Americans would turn their attention to a familiar target—the refineries of Ploesti.

Hitler's Gas Station, it turned out, hadn't completely closed shop.

In the days after Tidal Wave, the Germans proved as relentless as ever. Hitler's civilian engineers rolled up their sleeves. Russian POWs were forced into slave labor, clearing rubble by hand. Piece by piece, the Germans brought some of the refineries back to life.

Pipelines were rerouted to carry oil from damaged plants to those still standing. Machinery was cannibalized, swapped, and rebuilt. "Throughout Hitler's Reich," one account noted, "first priority for parts and expertise was given to the effort."

The surviving plants ran overtime. Even "old, small, inefficient" refineries—long past their prime—were pressed back into service.

Production rebounded. But there was a catch.

Ploesti's *product mix* had changed. Not all oil output was created equal. The thick, tar-like bunker fuel that powered battleships wasn't the same as the fine high-octane gasoline needed for fighter planes. And Ploesti, once the pride of Europe's petroleum industry, could now produce only low-grade products.

Still, it was naïve of the American brass to ever believe they could silence Ploesti with one mission, one blow. The complex was simply too vast, too vital, too well defended.

Now the 15th Air Force, and their British allies, were determined to finish what Tidal Wave had started. They'd bring Romania to its knees, however long it took.

IT WAS TIME TO talk. The Romanian military was here to interrogate the flier. A sergeant entered the room and sat across the table from Williams. He spoke to the POW in superb English, explaining he would serve as the translator. The sergeant indicated he'd once lived in Pittsburgh and wanted to return after the war.

Williams was amazed. "Some world we live in?" he later wrote.

The sergeant leaned closer and whispered that his superior, a major, was about to walk through the door. He would make threats, the sergeant warned, but "not to worry—he won't hurt you."

Just then the Romanian major strode in, huffed in impatience, and slapped his boot with a riding crop—just like his sergeant said he would. The Romanians looked less favorably on this "unmannerly" new bunch of 15th Air Force POWs, whom they'd taken to calling the "Italians" because they'd flown from bases in Italy. Their bombing raids weren't as kind to civilians as the dashing low-level raid of the African Knights. During the April 5 attack on Ploesti's rail yard, American bombs had killed 262 Romanian civilians—more than three times the entire non-military death toll of Tidal Wave. Speaking through the interpreter, the major conducted his interrogation.

Williams had a forthright manner about him. He told them his name, rank, and serial number, but that was all the Geneva Conventions required him to say.

And how had he been injured? the major wanted to know.

Williams figured he could answer this question. It was no military secret. His aircraft had been hit by flak over Ploesti and set afire. He had to bail out. When he jumped, he smacked the tail of his own plane. He cringed at the memory—that was how he'd been injured.

"They say God takes care of drunks, fools, and children," wrote Williams in his memoirs. "I don't think I was any of them, so there was formed that morning a new category."

And what kind of plane were you flying? the Romanian major asked, his tone casual but his eyes sharp. He was fishing for information: Was Williams's plane one of the new kind, perhaps? Rumors had spread of a mysterious American fighter, sleek and fast, spotted for the first time over Romania escorting the bombers. If there was such a plane, that spelled trouble for the country's already outnumbered fighter pilots.

Here Williams drew the line. He shut his mouth and shook his head. They could figure that one out on their own.

His refusal to speak made the Romanian major hopping mad. This was life and death. His country was being pummeled by the bombers, and he needed any information that could help Romania fight back.

And this American wouldn't even tell them what kind of plane he flew.

ANOTHER AMERICAN PILOT, Major James Beane, found himself in a similar situation. Beane was shot down about two weeks earlier over Ploesti, too. A B-24 squadron leader, he soon found himself being interrogated by a Romanian colonel, who told him gloatingly that Beane's group had missed the target entirely, which wasn't true.

Beane gave it back to him, saying, "Well, if they missed, they will be back tomorrow or the next day."

The remark shook the colonel. He snapped back, reminding Beane of the Romanian civilians his bombing had killed. "It's a custom of Romania for a murderer to be required to be at the funeral of his victim if the murderer is known," he said. "Will you select the men who will attend the funeral or shall we?"

It was a low blow. "It's your funeral, you invite the guests," Beane muttered.

The colonel kept needling him, trying to heap guilt upon the POW in an attempt to soften him into admitting secrets.

Finally, Beane had heard enough and retorted: "If you don't want to be bombed, get the Goddamn hell out of the war!"

The colonel shooed out everyone but his interpreter. He paused, then in a low voice asked Beane the one question on every Romanian's mind: "How, how do we get out of the war?"

Beane was baffled by the question. He'd meant his statement to be angry rhetoric, but it seemed now that the colonel was serious. Beane was at a loss: As if he would know how to get Romania out of the war!

"You have ambassadors in Turkey, and so do we," Beane said. *Try there?*

THE ROMANIAN MAJOR ACROSS from Williams had lesser ambitions. He kept asking questions about what kind of plane the American flew.

Frustrated by Williams's refusal to talk further, the major was so busy pacing back and forth, slapping his boot, that he failed to detect someone entering the small police station. Williams did notice: "A tall, good-looking young man walked in."

It was King Michael.

He'd been visiting the victims of the latest raid, just as he had in Bucharest, offering all he could to comfort and reassure his people, and had decided to visit the POW too. As he entered, his secretary and two aides-de-camp followed, their presence a reminder of the weight he carried.

Noticing the king, the major quickly fired off a panicky salute. In return, Michael said he wanted to speak alone with the American pilot.

But the American might be dangerous, the major warned.

Williams caught the gist and could have laughed. In his painful condition, "I couldn't have hurt a pillow," he recalled.

The king dismissed the major and the others, but for the sake of decorum kept a police officer in the room. Michael sat across from the young American, who simply stared at him. Finally, Williams asked, "Are you the king?"

"Yes, I am."

"I thought I recognized you," Williams said. He'd seen Michael's picture in *Life* magazine.

They swapped stories. Michael was just a year older than the POW. Williams told the king that he was from Pontiac, Illinois, and had worked at an aircraft factory on the south side of Chicago before deciding to become a military pilot.

The king volunteered that he was a pilot, too, and had soloed that past September. He'd visited the recovering Tidal Wave men numerous times and enjoyed their conversations about flying. They'd inspired him to take a leap: He'd flown a B-24. In a stroke of ingenuity, his military had managed to repair the B-24 *Boilermaker II,* which had been shot down during Tidal Wave. Using parts scavenged from other wrecks, they'd pieced her back together—their own Frankenstein B-24—and gotten her flying again. As for Michael's impression, he "thought it was a great ship."

Williams was amazed, although a part of him remained skeptical. What kind of interrogation tactic was this? Using the king to get him to give up secrets? What the American didn't know was that the young Romanian king was a mechanic at heart. This was not a trick. He simply wanted to talk airplanes, one pilot to another.

Michael asked Williams what he flew—bombers or fighters?

Williams didn't know how to respond. What exactly was a military secret, and what wasn't? Not bombers, he offered, content to let the matter drop.

The opposite took place. The king's eyes lit up with boyish enthusiasm. That meant Williams was a fighter pilot, maybe the first downed in Romania.

Had Williams been flying the Mustang?

Everyone had heard about the P-51 Mustang, the newest hot rod in the American arsenal. Michael and his fellow Romanians regarded the machine with a mixture of fear and fascination. Reportedly, it could reach Berlin, battle anything the Luftwaffe had, and still make it back to England with gas to spare. The Germans had their *Wunderwaffen,* "wonder weapons." The Americans had this.

But what's it like to fly a Mustang? That was what the king was angling at.

Williams tensed at the mention of the plane making aces over Berlin. He put on his best poker face and looked away: *Sorry, can't talk about that.*

An awkward silence followed. The king wasn't about to press for answers. Besides, Williams was clearly wounded and in no mood to discuss flying any further. His health was the priority now. Although the king noticed something odd. Williams kept glancing at his Colt 1911 pistol, resting on a table just out of reach.

"Why are you worrying about your gun?" Michael asked.

Williams looked up and said something about "his girl's picture" being on there. He hated having to give it up.

The king rose and stepped toward the weapon. He picked up the pistol, turning it in his hand. The grips were Plexiglas, translucent, "and underneath was a photo of a pretty girl." The American fliers referred to such adornments as "sweetheart grips"; they were made with Plexiglas salvaged from the turrets of wrecked bombers.

Quickly, the king popped out the magazine and checked the chamber. He was as good with guns as he was with cars. The pistol wasn't loaded. The king fished in his pocket, took out his pocketknife, and used the screwdriver component to unscrew the grip. He lifted the Plexiglas cover, removed the photograph, and handed it to Williams.

"Thank you." Williams's eyes fixed themselves on the photo.

Michael turned to the gendarme. *Let's get this man to a doctor immediately.*

As the king was leaving, a report came into the station. Locals had found the wreckage of not one, but two, crashed American fighter planes nearby. And these weren't the usual P-38s. These were something unknown.

Michael raised an eyebrow.

THE NEXT MORNING, WILLIAMS was recovering in a clinic in Ploesti when the king visited him again. Doctors confirmed the American pilot's back was broken and his elbow was fractured. At least now that he was getting medical care he was feeling better.

But Williams's guard was still up: *They weren't talking about his plane!*

The king wasn't here to pry. "Your plane was a P-51," Michael said.

Williams's eyes went wide.

The king held out his hand. In his palm was the data plate from Williams's aircraft. It listed the plane's manufacturer, serial number, and more. Michael revealed that he'd visited Williams's crash site himself and located the placard in the wreckage.

Williams was astounded that the king had pieced the facts together. A king snooping around the wreckage with a pocketknife? Who was this guy?

Williams softened. "She was a lovely machine," he admitted. He'd been escorting bombers in his P-51 before the flak got him. The Mustang had only just arrived in the Mediterranean, and Williams's unit, the 31st Fighter Group, was the first to get them. He'd flown his first mission in his P-51 five days earlier. This was the fighter the Allies had been waiting for: a machine that could escort bombers to their targets and back. For all he knew, the plane was still top secret—or at least it had been.

There was a second crashed P-51, Michael announced with a solemn tone, found a half mile from the first wreck site, and he'd gone there as well.

Michael handed Williams an American class ring. It had belonged to Second Lieutenant Roland Jackson, he explained; the police had recovered it from his body.

P-51 Mustangs

Had Williams known him?

Williams nodded sadly. He and Jackson were in the same squadron, although Williams hadn't known him well. Jackson was newer.

"Would you send it to his wife or parents when you're freed after the war?" Michael asked.

Gulp. This was an important task. Williams said he'd see it through.

The king lingered for a while, steering clear of any questions about the military. The two men seemed to enjoy each other's company. When it came time to go, Michael mentioned he was having Williams transferred to his private hospital, several steps up from the local facility. Williams smiled. The king was all right.

OUTSIDE THE CLINIC, the king settled into his car while his driver fired up the engine. Even then, when Michael fished the P-51's data plate from his pocket for another glance, his expression shifted, for what it said gave cause for concern:

"North American Aviation Inc., P-51B."

The Mustang was here. And that meant trouble for his country, inevitably more bombing runs, more destruction, more deaths. Michael felt the pressure settle on his shoulders. He had to find a way to pull Romania out of the war, to break Antonescu's grip. But how?

Every day he hesitated cost good men their lives. His mind went straight to his pilots, the ones who flew into battle wearing his emblem, the Michael's Cross, on their wings.

If the rumors were true, and if the Mustang could truly do what the Americans claimed, then this was a machine that could wipe any other plane from the sky.

God help our air force.

CHAPTER 40

THE SPORTSMEN

AROUND A MONTH LATER, JUNE 6, 1944
Eastern Romania

THE SKIES WERE BRIGHT AND COLD AT NINETEEN THOUSAND FEET AS the squadron of Romanian fighter planes climbed toward the American bombers. It was about 10 A.M. Buzz peered through the bulletproof windscreen, his goggle-covered eyes locked on a distant target. His oxygen mask made his breath sound raspy. Crisp frost clung to the canopy glass, refracting the sunlight in a dazzling glare. He wore his black leather jacket and a fabric helmet against the bitter temperature.

Around Buzz and his wingman, a dozen Romanian Me-109s flew upward in tight formation. The prince was flying in the 9th Fighter Group now, an outfit formed from the best of the nation's remaining pilots and known as "the spearhead" of the air force. Buzz and about thirty other old hands had been drawn together into one group in a final attempt to stave off the nation's slow, inevitable defeat.

The silver bombers, about a hundred in all, were still four thousand feet above, flying away from the Romanians. Their contrails raked a white path across the sky, leading the eye straight to them. They were B-17s, the Liberator's more rugged cousin, streamlined, with a single tail and a reputation for taking punishment.

And this was only a fraction of the American fleet in the air. On the same day the Allies were storming the beaches of Normandy, the 15th Air Force was unleashing its own invasion on Romania. Five bomber streams—B-17s and B-24s, nearly five hundred planes in all—were making an all-out blitz, sending a message to Antonescu: Your days are numbered.

Buzz spotted something between him and the bombers. Tiny glimmers, a series of silver specks sparkling like tinsel, drifted in a downward slope in his direction.

Escort fighters.

"Motociclişti!" a Romanian pilot called. Motociclişti—motorcyclists—was their code word for American escort fighters.

The glimmers were larger now, and beginning to look like airplanes. Buzz estimated as many as thirty enemy escort fighters were roaring down toward him and his comrades. Bold and fearless, the unpainted, bare metal planes made no attempt at camouflage. If Buzz could have heard the American radio channel, he would have heard a voice coursing through the airwaves: "Burglar to Ripple 2, we're engaging bandits." The two formations were on a collision course.

Buzz's breathing quickened and he nudged the power forward. His fighter's Daimler-Benz motor surged. Buzz lowered his chin and held his climb. The lift was effortless—once again the '109 climbed "like an elevator." The Romanians' only hope was to hold formation and stay the course. Maybe, just maybe, they could joust through the American escorts and reach the bombers before the fighters peeled back around for another go.

Four-plane flights of Americans came at him. Their combined closing speed topped seven hundred miles per hour. Guns blazed. Silver fighters ripped past Buzz, wave after wave, as Axis and Allied fighters clashed at more than twenty thousand feet above the earth. Buzz tracked them over his shoulders as they went by, each a silver streak smeared in brash warpaint, red noses and black-and-yellow checkerboard tails. He'd never seen such colorful planes. Spotting their distinctive belly scoops, Buzz realized what kind of escorts these were: P-51 Mustangs. No wonder they weren't camouflaged. This was the machine with nothing to hide from.

There'd be no pursuing the bombers now. Romanian '109s peeled off in every direction, "forced to engage" the escorts. A massive dogfight began. Buzz broke from his climb to join the fight. Mustangs filled the sky wherever he looked, slicing this way and that, crisscrossing. Faster, more maneuverable, two Mustangs chased every Romanian fighter. Every gun on their wings fired. The Mustangs of the 325th Fighter Group, the "Checkertail Clan," were out for blood and Buzz's earphones were alive with calls from one Romanian to another, pilots urging, "Check your tail!"

Taking evasive action, Buzz racked his fighter one way, then another, always looking for a target while trying not to become one. His Messer groaned under heavy Gs. In the violent maneuvering, Buzz lost track of his wingman. His Revi gunsight flickered, then died—of all the times! Any unit cohesion was gone. The small Romanian force was outnumbered by more than two to one, and this wasn't even taking account of all the Mustangs in the dogfight. The Americans had so many planes that a dozen Mustangs remained over the bombers as top cover.

The Romanians couldn't win. More than one pilot sensed it now. Buzz saw other Me-109s running for their lives. To stay was suicide. As one Romanian put it: "We were compelled to disengage." It was every man for himself.

Buzz turned to the tactic he used whenever he was cornered. He racked the stick sidelong, threw the Messer on its back, and then dove. His plane plunged, its frame shuddering under the pressure. Buzz knifed through the sky at a ferocious speed. The altimeter needle spun backward: Nineteen thousand feet. Eighteen thousand. Seventeen thousand. His fighter groaned, the controls turned heavy. At 466 miles per hour, his airspeed indicator crossed the red line. But Buzz knew there was more to give. 480. 490. The aircraft screamed in protest. It was no comfort knowing that each wing was held on by large bolts, a Messerschmitt design feature. Somewhere around 530, the plane would come apart.

Reaching his limit, Buzz pulled back on the stick. The Messer trembled violently, then began to level out around sixteen thousand feet, about four thousand feet below the mêlée. He gave his gunsight a slap, hoping to bring it back to life. No luck. A roar of engines shattered Buzz's respite. A quick glance around told him everything. Messerschmitts and Mustangs were cutting through the sky around him. The dogfight was spiraling downward. He broke hard, trying to latch on to a Mustang, anything to throw off their pursuit of a comrade. But before he could line up a shot, orange tracer bullets slanted down from above, slicing past his canopy. He glanced over his shoulder, above and behind. More Mustangs, guns blazing. They dove, targeting him with dogged persistence. Their pilots' fearlessness and apparent bloodlust concerned him.

This was just not his day.

Buzz peeled over into another dive. He spotted a wide patch of cumulus clouds at 6,500 feet and steered toward them. Again, the altimeter needle spun backward as the Messer threatened to shake itself apart. He punched through the cloud layer and emerged into a hot, hazy summer morning. As he leveled off at six thousand feet, the cockpit became thick with heat, steamy air from outside. Buzz tore off his oxygen mask. He saw fields stretching in every direction, plus some roads and villages. The clouds above his head hid his whereabouts for now.

It was discouraging to think how quickly his squadron had been overwhelmed. They hadn't even been able to put up much of a fight.

Then he saw it: a lone Mustang, off to the side and a little ahead. A glint of bare metal gave it away. The pilot hadn't seen him yet. He looked lost.

Buzz's eyes locked on the threat. His instincts, carefully honed since 1941, kicked in, and he broke violently in the Mustang's direction. There was only one rule that mattered: Shoot him before he shoots you.

Buzz went in for the kill.

AT THE CONTROLS OF the Mustang was a man Buzz would have had something in common with. First Lieutenant Donald "Mac" MacDonald, twenty-four, was a sportsman too. His narrow face, brown hair, and blue eyes matched his lanky frame, all arms and legs, perfect for his life back home. In Wayzata, an upscale suburb of Minneapolis, MacDonald had been the tennis pro at Woodhill Country Club, teaching lessons to kids, seniors, and everyone in between. His picture hung on the wall there, his personality captured in a wide grin.

Donald "Mac" MacDonald

A veteran pilot with forty-five missions under his belt, MacDonald wasn't smiling now. He leaned side to side in his cockpit, scanning the skies above and below. He had been separated from his wingman, Second Lieutenant John Mumford, twenty-two, of St. Petersburg, Florida. They had chased two Me-109s in a spiraling dogfight, and MacDonald had shot one down. But something had happened to Mumford. The last time MacDonald saw him, he was diving into the clouds at a steep angle. Maybe his radio had gone out, maybe his wounded plane was limping around somewhere, or maybe, God forbid, smoke was already rising from a crash site.

MacDonald was so focused on searching for his wingman that he didn't notice the gray shadow slipping in behind him. Another sportsman, but this one played for the opposing team. MacDonald glanced over his shoulder. It was like seeing a ghost.

BUZZ HAD THE MUSTANG right where he wanted him. As he closed the gap, his Messer bucked in the wake of the enemy fighter, jolted by turbulence. He had him dead to rights.

Stalking from the tail like a predator, Buzz got a closer look at the P-51. He knew the shape by now, the long, streamlined nose, narrow tail, and muscular fuselage perched atop sharp, square wings built for speed. A machine of deceptive beauty, the Mustang was crafted for one purpose: to destroy other airplanes.

Buzz's gunsight was dark, only a blank pane of glass where an illuminated aiming circle and cross hairs should be. He would need to fire by feel. He aimed the nose at the Mustang's vitals, the belly scoop beneath the cockpit, where the radiator sucked in air to cool its powerful engine. With his thumb, Buzz pressed the trigger.

The cannon in the nose hammered and belched flame. Brass shell casings poured down in a rain of spent ammunition. Fragments of metal skin flew off the Mustang and flung themselves back in a slipstream. Buzz's 20mm shells found their mark. The belly scoop ruptured, and the Mustang's coolant system vented a hissing white cloud. It was a mortal blow to a liquid-cooled engine. The engine would soon overheat, and the machine would seize up.

The American was going down.

INSIDE THE P-51, MACDONALD shook off the shock of being hit, forcing himself to focus on survival. A 20mm shell exploded behind his armored seatback. Fragments and the force of the blast punched forward, grazing his head and knee. He had been lightly wounded. His plane was not so lucky.

One glance at his instruments told him everything. Temperature was rising fast. His engine was melting into a solid block. He had to jump.

MacDonald pulled the emergency canopy release on the right side of the cockpit. Nothing. He yanked it again. Still nothing. Frantic, he tried the manual hand crank, hoping for the best, but the canopy was jammed shut by enemy shellfire.

He was trapped.

The Messerschmitt loomed behind him. There was nothing to do now but tuck into his shoulders, pray, and wait for the death blow.

BUZZ HELD HIS THUMB over the trigger of the 20mm cannon. One pound of pressure, one more burst, and the Mustang would be finished. He could shear off a wing, send it tumbling in a helpless spiral, or walk the shells into the fuel tank for a fiery explosion.

But why?

This fight was over. His opponent was clearly defeated. Buzz lifted his finger from the trigger, letting the moment settle. Now that the other pilot could no longer hurt him, he saw the plane in a different light. Up close, it was beautiful. The red nose, the checkerboard tail—it looked more like a race car than a fighter plane. And it was fresh from the factory, barely worn in. The 325th had taken their Mustangs into combat just the week before. Buzz couldn't help but admire it. The undisputed hot rod of the skies.

What would it be like to fly that machine?

A realization hit him. They were about sixty miles behind the front lines. If the American pilot didn't bail out, that Mustang was coming down in Romanian territory. Could this be true? He had a chance to capture the American wonder weapon. Not to study it—what would that accomplish at this stage in the war? Buzz wanted to fly it. His mind worked fast. They could fix it, like the B-24 they'd patched up, and bring it back to the air. If he could get behind the controls of a Mustang and take it up for a spin, just once, it would be a career-defining move for a man who loved airplanes more than almost anything else.

Buzz slipped out from behind the tail and edged forward, almost parallel with the Mustang. Staying behind the wing, he flew with it "as if providing cover" from anyone who'd think to harm it.

Don't jump! he urged the Mustang pilot. That would ruin everything.

The American pilot lowered his nose toward the ground: He was bringing the plane in. Three thousand feet. Two thousand. One thousand. The two planes descended in tandem. The Mustang pilot steered for a freshly plowed field. Buzz was delighted. There was no flatter place to land wheels-up.

But at five hundred feet, the Mustang's propeller suddenly came to a stop. The engine seized. All four blades froze. At any moment, the P-51 would lose speed, stop flying, and fall like a rock.

Put her down! Buzz urged.

The American had no choice. Quickly he forced the plane down. The Mustang was still doing more than two hundred miles per hour when it hit the soil. The plane skipped and wobbled, flew again, launched over a hedgerow, then bellied in and skidded to a quick stop. A good crash landing. Pilot and plane were intact.

Buzz banked around for a closer look. His relief turned to alarm. Smoke was rising from the Mustang. *No, no, no!* His prize was catching fire, and worse, the canopy was still shut. Smoke poured from every seam. Buzz was horrorstruck. The plane was on fire and the pilot was still inside. *Get out!*

IN THE SMOKE-FILLED COCKPIT, MacDonald groggily lifted his head. Blood seeped from his forehead where he'd smacked against the gunsight. He coughed, then looked around. The plane was on fire. Heat rose from the floor and behind his seat. He struggled to unlatch his seatbelt, but the clip wouldn't give. He tried to wrestle his way out, but the seatbelt held fast. He pulled and tugged, but the clip would not release.

Burning to death was every pilot's worst fear.

Desperately, MacDonald reached down with both hands to where the seatbelt was secured to the seat. He pulled with his arms, pushed with his legs, and stood with all his might, until the seatbelt tore free. The engineers at North American Aviation would have been amazed. It was "actually an inhuman feat."

MacDonald pried at the canopy with both hands until it gave way, and then his boots hit the soil. He staggered away from his burning plane, half walking, half limping toward the nearest tree line. He had made it about seventy-five yards into a field when a sound from the sky stopped him in his tracks: the smooth purr of a Daimler-Benz engine. The Messerschmitt that had shot him down was circling back around, most likely positioning for a strafing run.

And he was the target.

MacDonald saw no sense in running. He'd only die more exhausted than he already was. There was nowhere to hide, not in the middle of a field. Everything he'd overcome—the jammed canopy, the crash landing, the seatbelt—had it all led to this? MacDonald turned to face death head on.

At the far end of the field, the Me-109 leveled its wings in his direction. As the plane bore down on him, the flickering disc of its props looked like a buzzsaw. Over the engine roar came the scream of fast-moving air over intakes. MacDonald saw the dark gray aircraft had yellow markings on its wings. Romanian. He braced himself.

Then, much to his surprise, the flaps dropped from the 109's wings. The enemy pilot slowed, and the fighter's right wing dipped in his direction. It was as if the Romanian was making an air-show pass for an audience of one.

As the '109 flew past him, MacDonald looked up. The Romanian pilot looked down and made the simplest of human gestures.

He waved.

MacDonald was dumbstruck. Should he wave back? They didn't give instructions for this in the officer's manual.

The fighter flew past without firing. The sounds faded, and the plane entered a graceful left turn. Whoever he was, the pilot wasn't out to kill him.

Now that MacDonald had been shaken from his stupor, his thoughts turned again to his survival. He was still behind enemy lines. He resumed running toward the distant patch of woods. But as the downed American crossed the field, the '109 made several protective orbits overhead before it departed and flew west. When MacDonald reached the woods, he looked back and questioned what he'd just lived through.

They would never believe this at the Woodhill Country Club.

A SHORT TIME LATER, a Fieseler Storch observation plane landed in the field near the smoldering P-51. The German-built plane with its high-set wings and long, spindly landing gear looked more like an insect than a flying machine, but it made easy work of the bumpy terrain. Already the local police chief, some gendarmes, and a few curious locals had gathered at the wreckage. The Mustang had burned to the ground in its center.

Out from the observation plane stepped Buzz, followed by the pilot, and a Romanian public relations officer with a camera. The locals were surprised. Romania's fighter pilot prince himself, here?

Buzz looked around. Where was the American pilot?

The police chief said the American had last been seen moving east toward the Dniester River on the Romanian border, trying to reach the Russians.

Buzz was crestfallen. Didn't he know being a Romanian prisoner was far better than being a German prisoner?* That was why Buzz had hitched a ride back to the wreckage. There was no salvaging the Mustang, but Buzz hoped to meet the pilot, if only to talk. He'd always had an affinity for Americans, dating to before the war, back when he'd faced them on the ice, as the captain of the Romanian national hockey team.

At the 1931 World Ice Hockey Championships in the mountain resort town of Krynica, Poland, Romania suffered a brutal thrashing, 15–0, at the hands of the Americans.

When the final whistle blew and the teams skated toward their locker rooms, Buzz did not follow his teammates. Instead, the prince glided to the bench where the coaches were packing up and asked for the score sheet. On the back, he wrote a short note in English, then skated it over to the referee.

Inside the American locker room, the celebration was loud, boisterous, unfiltered. The referee entered, brushing ice from his jodhpurs, and handed the note to the American captain.

He read it aloud.

The laughter ebbed. A strange silence settled over the room as the players absorbed the note's deeper meaning. It offered neither surrender nor excuse for the defeat. Instead, it marked something higher, a gesture of true nobility.

* History shows MacDonald made it six hours on the run before being captured by German troops and taken to a POW camp in Germany. In spring 1945, he would come home and tell his mother and older brother, Norman, the story of the chivalrous pilot who spared his life. MacDonald died in 2005. During the writing of *Tidal Wave,* his son, Mike, wrote the author: "I regret my father died at age 86 before I was able to discover all this information [about Cantacuzino]. I would have loved to tell him: 'Don't feel bad, you got shot down by one of the best.'"

"We thank you sincerely," the prince had written, "for giving us the opportunity to learn something [from this game]—and to play with America."

"Let's get a photo!" The PR officer of the Military Propaganda Section had ridden along for this moment. Buzz approached the Mustang. He stood near the cowling and studied the melted cockpit. Smoke was still rising, and the metal was so hot he could only linger a moment.

Click.

Buzz examines MacDonald's downed P-51

Buzz stepped out of frame and stood alone, lamenting the loss of the Mustang and everything the war had come to stand for. The Romanian side had lost five planes that day, and destroyed two Mustangs. For what? They never even touched the bombers. To Buzz, all the violence felt foolish, immoral, and even criminal. Antonescu and his acolytes were intent on ushering Romania to its doom. They wanted to drag out the combat to the last day, hour, and man. And it was happening. The Royal Romanian Air Force was being ground down to nothing. When the Americans had first shown up over Bucharest on April 4, 1944, Romania had 115 fighters in service. By the end of the present month—June 1944—they would have fewer than fifty, and this was not to mention the thirty-three pilots put in the ground. Romania was fighting to the bitter end, but for what? They soon wouldn't have any pilots left. Buzz's conscience couldn't take it much longer.

Seeing the burned-out Mustang, Buzz wondered about the man who got away. The prince had always told himself he had no choice but to "fight who's in front of me." But being enemies was a choice. He'd never been a friend of the Axis powers, and he was certainly no friend of Antonescu and the fascists. They'd put Nadia and him through hell. Romania had joined forces with the Germans only as a survival tactic. At the time, it had seemed better than being flattened by the Soviets. But now, standing next to a smoldering P-51, fighting Americans, the unpleasant truth ate at him.

Romania was playing for the wrong team.

But what could one man possibly do about it?

CHAPTER 41

ANYWHERE BUT HERE

TWO MONTHS LATER, EARLY AUGUST 1944

Lagărul No. 2

THE OFFICERS IN THE LODGE IN TIMISUL HEARD THE TRAIN LONG BEFORE it came into view. Windowpanes rattled, floorboards vibrated, the whole building seemed to tremble. Ernie and his friends quickly made their way through the jam of fellow POWs to the front porch where they could get a better look. Outside, the sun blazed down on a steamy summer morning. The summer heat clung to the skin. The sound of the train swelled to fill the valley. Every head turned south.

A German locomotive appeared, puffing smoke as if it was breathing hard. It thundered by the camp, the noise deafening. Car after car blurred past "only a few feet from our barbed wire." The passenger coaches leaned and swayed, creating a rhythmic clatter as the wheels crossed the rail joints.

It was a hospital train. Each coach was crowded with wounded German soldiers. Gray-clad men leaned from windows, eager for air. Other soldiers filled the covered platforms at the ends of each car. Every man was bandaged, splinted, or bound in plaster casts. Through the windows, Ernie could see wounded men in stretchers stacked three high.

He and his fellow officers exchanged uneasy glances: Another one. They had seen plenty of trains before. Most were freight trains loaded with munitions heading into Romania. But this was different. Now the trains were coming back full of the wounded. Several times a day, the hospital trains clattered past the camp, headed north. The American officers didn't need it spelled out. The German retreat from Romania had already begun.

In the east, the Soviet Red Army was preparing for its final push into the country. Any day now, the great offensive would begin. The collapse of the German-Romanian front was inevitable.

The POWs should have been elated. They were not. The men had come to a terrifying realization while watching the troop movement outside Lagărul No. 2: Their camp lay smack on the war's main thoroughfare between Romania and the Reich.

Currently, the POWs were seeing only the hospital trains. The Germans were evacuating their wounded first. But what would happen when the main German army retreated, stinging with defeat? Did anybody truly believe they would just nod and wave at the Allied POWs as they passed?

At best, the Americans would be herded up and carted away to Germany. At worst, the Germans would take out their rifles and make quick work of the POWs.

The possibility of execution had once seemed impossible. The Germans had signed the Geneva Convention. They were obligated to treat POWs humanely. But a troubling bit of news had wafted in over the radio from the BBC that spring.

During a routine Red Cross inspection of Stalag III, a German POW camp near Berlin, in May, the ranking British POW had slipped the Swiss representative a list of names. A few weeks earlier, seventy-six Allied POWs, mostly British airmen, had tunneled out of the camp in an event that would come to be known as the Great Escape. The attempt fell short. All but three were recaptured.

Furious, Hitler ordered all seventy-three recaptured men shot. But his generals intervened. If word got out, what would that mean for German POWs in British hands?

So Hitler settled on a compromise: "more than half." On his orders, the Gestapo gunned down fifty men, executing them singly and in pairs. Those were the names passed to the Swiss.

"We knew all about the fifty Allied fliers who had been shot in Germany," a Timisul POW later wrote. "And we certainly sweated it out thinking about it."

In response, the Red Cross tacked posters to the walls of POW camps across Europe, a quiet yet urgent reminder: "Escape is no longer a sport."

LONG AFTER THE HOSPITAL train's caboose had grown small in the distance, and only the sharp scent of coal hung in the air, the POWs lingered on the porch. They banded together in solidarity, speaking in low voices, discussing their mutual sense of concern. No one needed to say it outright: The officers were spooked. Ernie included.

Clearly, the Romanians who ran the camp didn't know the future. And the POWs didn't have Major Moruzi to turn to for a military perspective. The affable moon-faced commandant had been sacked that summer. A POW recalled: "Almost every evening he dropped in to talk for a while in our dining room." Sometimes he'd stay to listen to the war updates on the radio, and his daughter even baked pastries for the men. The commandant had chosen "to cultivate personal friendships with his prisoners." And it cost him. One day, he was telling a POW that "he hoped to have my address so that we might correspond after the war." The next he came in with his head hanging, his own guards at his side, to say goodbye. His parting words were "I am sorry."

The Germans had caught wind of his leniency and replaced him with his deputy, Major Matiescu, who harbored pro-Axis sympathies.

And for good measure, the Germans had the POWs' radio confiscated.

OVERALL, THE POWS' FUTURE didn't look promising. With Moruzi gone—and the radios with him—they were cut off from the outside world.

If only Princess Catherine had been here.

Her visits had fallen off sharply, though not for lack of trying. She had troubles of her own. The American high-level raids had upended daily life for ordinary Romanians as much as for their military. "My trips to Timisul were curtailed," Catherine admitted. "Each day I had more difficulty getting supplies and never had enough time for the children. I was busier than ever trying to keep the schools going in the villages and worrying about the babies in Bucharest."

The prisoners had lost a crucial ally at the worst possible time.

The more Ernie thought about their tenuous situation, the more he felt an urge to run. Anywhere. As fast as his feet would carry him. Every glance reminded him of the razor wire on all four sides of the camp. He was caged in, which spurred a greater feeling of panic. And as hospital train after hospital train rattled past the camp, it was only a matter of time until the main German army came for them. He became convinced it was not a matter of if but when. He could almost hear the Germans' hobnail boots.

After everything the Americans had survived, was that how it would end? Would they be shoved into a boxcar to Germany, or gunned down?

The princess had always told them, "It's safer to stay put." And maybe that had once been true. But those days were gone. No one was coming to their rescue. The more Ernie studied the situation, the more certain he became. There was only one solution, and he knew one person would certainly understand.

Bob O'Reilly.

THROUGH ONE OF THE camp guards, Ernie and Bob summoned Sandy. The friendly Romanian lieutenant came through the gate and into the lodge, his narrow face marked with his usual grin.

"What do you need, gentlemen?" he asked.

Sandy had been promoted to captain of the guard, which made him the second-highest-ranking officer in camp. And his Allied sympathies were firmly cemented. On June 6, when news broke of the D-Day landings, he and other Romanian officers came into camp cheering: "The British and Americans have landed in France!"

One POW quipped, "They're as happy as we are."

The pilots of *Chattanooga Choo Choo* led Sandy aside, away from the windows so his own guards wouldn't see them conspiring. This was delicate business. Ernie and Bob voiced their concerns about the deteriorating situation outside the wire. They hinted, not so subtly, to the very man who was supposed to keep them inside, about breaking out.

"We need to get the heck out of here," Ernie whispered.

Sandy listened and nodded; something in his face told them they could speak freely. Ernie and Bob outlined a plan: What if they were to take to the woods, using the chaos of the German collapse as a distraction, find a place to lie low, and wait for the enemy to be chased out? Late summer was the ideal season to be on the run. The weather was mild, and they could forage from farms. This wouldn't be a handful of officers skipping out on their own. They were talking about all of them—Americans, Brits—every POW in the camp.

The kicker was that they wanted Sandy to come with them.

Ernie and Bob half expected the Romanian lieutenant to laugh. Instead, Sandy pulled Ernie and Bob farther away from the others and said in a low voice, "It's not a terrible idea."

He expressed his own fears about how the Germans would behave in retreat, and confessed he'd been already thinking about his next moves.

"Do you know what they did in Italy?" he asked.

They had all heard the dispatches: When Italy quit the Axis the previous autumn, the Germans were furious. Infighting erupted on the Greek isles between the former allies. The Italians wanted to go home after the capitulation. They were finished with fighting Hitler's war. But the Germans had other ideas.

After quashing the brief rebellion, the German 1st Mountain Division went on a rampage. On Corfu and Kos they shot all the Italian officers. On Cephalonia, in what history would call the Cephalonia Massacre, they murdered five thousand Italian officers and enlisted men, bringing them to a beach in small groups and machine-gunning them, before pushing their bodies out to sea.

And the rest? The 600,000 remaining Italian soldiers were rounded up across the Mediterranean and disarmed by their former allies, then shipped to the Reich as slave labor, where forty thousand would eventually perish.

What would the Germans do to Sandy and his men if Romania folded—or worse, followed the Italians and switched sides?

When the German army came by, Sandy didn't want to be here to find out. And he already had a destination in mind.

"Pietroșița," he said.

It was a remote village on the southern slope of the Transylvanian Alps, near Sinaia, about thirty miles south of their camp. Sandy had friends there—loyal Romanians. He believed they would harbor the POWs if the men could reach the town. And there was another plus to Pietroșița. It was about halfway to Bucharest, where the other American POWs were being held. By now, according to reports from the capital, upwards of a thousand men from the 15th Air Force had fallen during the high-altitude raids and wound up in Romanian captivity.

That was good enough for Ernie and Bob. They were ready to tell the others to start preparing to slip the wire.

Sandy urged patience. It was too soon. The German retreat had only just begun. Besides, they couldn't just show up at Pietroșița, unannounced. The villagers would need to feed 110 men, but food was scarce with wartime shortages. It was a lot of men to house, as well—not the easiest thing to do in a small village. And they'd need to have a plan in place to keep anyone with a big mouth from running to the Germans.

Therein lay the problem. Sandy couldn't just phone up the townspeople to explain the plan—you never knew who was monitoring the phone circuits. Besides, the villagers wouldn't believe a voice on the other end of a phone line. Someone needed to go to Pietroșița to ask for their help in person. And that presented another problem. Sandy couldn't go. He was the captain of the guard now; he couldn't leave his post. Commandant Matiescu was no Moruzi. He wouldn't be a party to this plot.

But, Sandy mused, if a single POW could escape, it wouldn't raise many eyebrows. A single POW could deliver the message to the village.

The job wouldn't be easy. Because there was increased German traffic in the valley, the escapee would need to travel overland through the Alps, a couple of days' journey. He would need to be experienced in the outdoors; that ruled out city slickers, who made up half the men in camp. Even Bob admitted he wouldn't last a day alone in those mountains—his experience in the great outdoors began and ended in his usual seat by the flagpole in Sportsman's Park, home of the Cardinals.

It needed to be someone else.

One POW fit the bill. He was careful, steady, forward-thinking—and the last man anyone would suspect of planning an escape. Oh, and he'd spent his boyhood hunting mountain lions.

Sandy and Bob both turned to Ernie.

"Me?" Ernie asked.

Bob grinned. "It was your idea!"

ERNIE WANDERED THROUGHOUT THE LODGE, doing "some considerable soul-searching" as he pondered a journey beyond the wire. Bob wasn't wrong. The escape was Ernie's idea, but in his head it had looked different. Everybody would slip away together and hide in the woods. Not just him, alone.

Could he really do it? Break through the wire and traverse hostile territory during the chaos of the last days of the war in Romania?

Doubt plagued his mind. He'd only joined in the previous escape attempt out of loyalty to his friends. The woods weren't safe. Romania's forests were home to Europe's largest populations of bears and wolves. There were many ways a person could get hurt out there, or simply vanish without a trace.

What would they tell his parents, Lester and Ada, after the war? "He was killed while trying to escape." And a risky, desperate escape attempt would go against the one promise Ernie had made before taking off for Romania: He'd come home alive.

Slowly, his uncertainty gave way to clarity. If the escape had been only on his own behalf, he wouldn't have risked it. The danger was too great, the odds of success too small. But inactivity wasn't an option either. If he stayed put, he was in danger, and so were all his friends.

Ernie faced a choice familiar from his youth: Accept his circumstances, or set out to change them. There were a hundred reasons *not* to step outside that wire. But there was one reason that mattered more. If Ernie succeeded, they might all make it home.

It was like that time with the sheep.

Roll up your sleeves, get the job done.

AT DUSK ON THE evening of August 15, 1944, the prisoners at Lagărul No. 2 strolled around the yard behind the lodge as if nothing were amiss. Men smoked and chatted among themselves, doing their best to look nonchalant.

Lately, as a small grace, the Romanian guards had been allowing the POWs to stay outside longer. Everybody sensed that their time together was coming to an end. Even the guards. "Grata razboi, merga la casa," they'd been heard saying joyfully. Sometimes they said it in English: "War finish, return home."

That night, the camp was bathed in the deep shadows of the mountain. The sky was pale blue. A few stars had already begun to show. At the exact moment when the Romanian sentry drifted to the front of the building, the POW lookouts nodded to the other men at the back door of the lodge.

"Now!"

Ernie and another POW barreled out the back door and made a beeline to the northwest corner of the yard, where the stream that fed the pond flowed into the camp. They carried their belongings in sacks.

The two prisoners dove into the streambed. Hearts pounding, they lay flat on the ground next to the cold, bubbling water. They didn't speak or move. Not yet. They just blended seamlessly into the shadows.

At the last minute, Ernie had decided to bring a fellow copilot, Second Lieutenant Bob Snyder, as backup. Snyder would be an extra set of eyes and ears—and someone to deliver the message if the worst happened to Ernie. The senior American officers had fully blessed the plan. They were hanging their hopes on the outcome, too.

At twenty-five, Snyder had wavy brown hair, blue eyes, and a quiet, pleasant demeanor that made men trust him quickly. Before his days in the cockpit, he'd been a skilled woodworker who knew his way around the forests of northern California.

Soon, the Romanian guards came back to the yard. Nothing looked out of place. They began ushering the other POWs into the lodge for the night. The prisoners stamped out their cigarettes without a fuss and headed inside. It would be a while yet before the guards took the head count.

An hour later, it was fully dark. The perimeter guard stepped into his sentry box at the front of the building. The coast was clear.

Ernie rolled out of the streambed and crawled toward the fence, pushing his bag in front of him. Inside was some food, primarily bread and cheese, and a letter from Sandy to present to the villagers if he reached his destination. Sandy had told him simply, "They'll know what to do."

And there was Ernie's diary, wrapped in wax paper. His last entry read: "I am living for the day I get home."

Using wire cutters that someone had scrounged, Ernie began clipping a hole in the fence. He hoped the sound didn't travel far. He wondered whether the perimeter here was mined, as the Romanians had said when the POWs first rolled off the buses.

There was only one way to find out.

Ernie tested the dirt outside the wire with his hand, then crawled through. Snyder was right on his heels. Rising to their feet, the two POWs darted into the nearest line of trees. In a blink, they escaped into the darkness.

CHAPTER 42

PERIL ON ALL SIDES

THE NEXT MORNING
Lagărul No. 2

THE ROMANIAN GUARDS GAZED UP TOWARD THE STEEP RIDGELINE BEhind the camp. The mountains stood motionless, their slopes thick with trees and secrets. The big farm boys looked at the birds lazily crisscrossing the pale blue sky above. Nothing moved on the ground. There was no sound except the occasional creak of tree limbs. One guard glanced at another. A shrug.

No Americans.

Oh well.

"The imminent end of the war no doubt had something to do with their lack of enthusiasm for an all-out search effort," wrote a POW.

Escape now? When the war was almost over? Who in their right mind would do that?

INSIDE THE LODGE AT Timisul, the mood had shifted. An air of hope and urgency permeated the camp, spurred on by widespread realization of the danger the prisoners were in and the fact that they might just make it out alive. The mood was felt in the quickened pace of footsteps across the floorboards, in the way shoulders squared with new purpose.

Ernie and Snyder had done it.

The message was on its way.

Everyone now pitched in, collecting food and supplies for the impending breakout. Someone had had the idea to make knapsacks to hold those provisions. The prisoners happily surrendered their Romanian-issued uniforms, which made sturdy backpacks complete with buttons.

"Getting out became an obsessive thought," recalled a POW.

A FEW DAYS LATER, on August 20, a surprise visitor flew through the front door and was immediately embraced by Britt, Bob, and Al.

Princess Catherine.

"It was a doozy getting here," she told them. She'd hit multiple checkpoints and explained that the Germans were fortifying Predeal Pass, the entrance to the Transylvanian Alps behind Sinaia. It was a miracle they'd let her through. And she was worried that this might be her last visit to her boys for some time.

In the east, the Soviets' final offensive had begun. After they'd polished off the Axis forces, the Red Army would be "poised for a sweep" into Romania, "and a shiver of fear spread through the land."

As it did most Romanians, the prospect of a Soviet invasion had made the princess despondent about the future. She and others had been "praying for an Anglo-American invasion" that was not to be. The Yanks and Brits were bogged down climbing the Italian boot. Rome had been liberated, but the Germans were clinging to the northern third of the country. And in northern France, the Allies were only now approaching Paris, after two and a half months of bloody hedgerow fighting.

Now there was nothing to do but wait for the "Red invasion," as Catherine called it. The dark cloud that had loomed over Romania in 1939 was back. The USSR had taken Romanian territories then. And now, the enemy that had pulled the country into war was coming for vengeance.

Princess Catherine was already looking down the road. An occupation by the Bolsheviks would mean "the end of her class, the royalty," and with it, everything she had built. One POW noted: "The political and money class dread their coming."

What would become of her orphanage and her three thousand orphans? Princess Catherine kept a stiff upper lip, but the men could tell she was deeply concerned about the ones she called "her children."

She wished more Americans could understand the truth about the Soviets. The USSR might have been an ally, but the Red Army was not coming to liberate. They were coming to subjugate and indoctrinate.

Already, the princess had spoken with the other American POWs in Bucharest. She'd befriended them and done what she could to help. But her warning was "difficult for her to put over." The 15th Air Force men could not bring themselves to see the Soviets for what they truly were. They still thought of Stalin's boys as the good guys.

The Tidal Wave survivors didn't have that problem. They had no love for the USSR, and they didn't need Princess Catherine's speeches to tell them why.

Before their Great Raid, American diplomats had approached the Soviets with a request. After the B-24s hit Ploesti, could they land in Soviet-held territory? The plan made a lot of sense. It would shorten the raiders' return leg since they wouldn't have to fly all the way back to Benghazi. And the B-24s could carry "twice the bomb load and half the gas," instead of using that space for spare fuel tanks. Besides, the mission stood to benefit the Soviet war effort as much as anyone's. They were the ones getting steamrolled by Hitler's Panzers. The Western Allies hadn't even invaded mainland Europe yet.

The Soviets hemmed, hawed, and obfuscated. Stalin claimed that "the issue required further study." Further study didn't make a difference. No matter how closely it was examined, the answer remained unspoken but unmistakable.

No.

When the crews going to Ploesti were briefed, the men were told they "couldn't under any circumstances fly a crippled bomber to Russia." Stalin wouldn't permit them to land. The American mission planners were emphatic: "If you are forced to crash land, do so in enemy territory—not Russia."

"Strange, as Russia supposedly is our ally," wrote a gunner in his diary.

So the five groups filled their planes' bomb bays not with extra bombs, but with fuel: 450 sloshing extra gallons that would keep their planes airborne, but that would also cost many young Americans their lives in crashes.

"We simply did not trust the Russians," wrote one prisoner at Timisul, "and were worried about them bombing our camp or otherwise taking us back to Russia for some later repatriation."

THE OFFICERS OF *Chattanooga Choo Choo* didn't have the words to console or reassure the princess. What could they say or do? They weren't free men. Not only was their time together coming to an end, but they were all suddenly facing the same bleak future: No one in Romania was safe anymore.

Princess Catherine pulled herself together with her usual motherly resolve. Enough talking about her woes; it was time to talk about her boys. She glanced around, checked over her shoulders, and noticed something amiss.

"Where's Ernie?"

Britt, Bob, and Al exchanged sheepish "About that . . ." looks.

Britt suddenly remembered: His roommate, Ernie, had left something with him. He dug in his pocket, then pressed a $20 bill into her hand. It was the same bill that Ernie had been secreting here and there since they were shot down.

"He said to give you this," Britt said, "for the foundation."

The princess's face dropped. The gift could mean only one thing.

Oh, no.

SOON AFTER, THE ALPS

FROM WITHIN THE SHADOWY woods, Ernie peered into the valley and studied the flow of German traffic below. Beside him, Snyder crouched low, watching too. The movement was picking up. In addition to the usual retreating hospital trains, other kinds of German vehicles could be seen—a truck here, a Kübelwagen there. All of the traffic was heading north, out of Romania.

The two men sank lower into the underbrush, keeping out of sight. They were assuming that every vehicle carried soldiers whose eyes were scanning the terrain, searching for them.

It had been five days since Ernie and Snyder escaped from Lagărul No. 2, and one thing never changed. "The element of fear was a constant reality," Ernie later wrote.

On the positive side, they were about halfway through the journey and still undetected. But the terrain was rugged, making for slower going than hoped. They'd covered a mile that first night, no small feat in the dark. Since then, they had moved by day, slowly, carefully, always keeping the road in sight. They'd seen villagers from a distance but avoided contact.

Shaking off the spell of the German traffic, Ernie and Snyder pressed onward. The men followed the rugged terrain through the spooky forest of centuries-old trees, clambering over fallen trunks, skirting upheaved boulders. At times, they felt as if the wilderness was working against them, trying to hold them back. But they knew they had to keep moving. More than a hundred men were counting on them.

The two pushed south, hiking past misty waterfalls and shadowy caves, pausing now and then to gaze up at alpine peaks shrouded with fog. But the beauty of the landscape could be a dangerous distraction in such treacherous terrain. Every step needed to be watched. One wrong move, and even a twisted ankle could spell disaster.

The men kept their ears tuned to every forest sound. The mountain wind threading through the trees whispered caution. Ernie would stop and look around, glancing over his shoulder, always feeling like they were being watched or pursued. And whenever the forest fell silent, their instincts went on high alert.

The previous autumn, the British escapees had observed the same phenomenon. "To be alone in them [the woods] is to watch the silence and to see how the Ancient Greek and American Indian feared them and acknowledged the spirits that lived in them."

Ernie and Snyder felt an instinctive tug, drawing them closer to the valley, the road, farms, and inhabitants. The uncertainty of what they were attempting was terrifying. But neither man ever spoke about turning back or giving up.

Snyder carried his own private sense of duty. During the Ploesti raid his bomber, one of the Eight Balls, had taken a heavy hit. He and his pilot managed to put it down, but flames tore through the fuselage, and Snyder barely escaped the cockpit.

Not everyone was so lucky.

His top turret gunner was trapped, and Snyder couldn't get to him before fire consumed the crashed bomber. Standing fifty yards from the inferno, he and the rest of his crew were forced to listen to their friend being burned alive.

"I'll never forget his screams," Snyder would later write. "There's hardly a day that goes by that I don't relive that moment."

For Snyder, the trek through the wilderness with Ernie was more than an escape attempt. Making it to Pietroșița and whisking the POWs out from under the noses of the Germans? This would be payback.

THEIR DINNERS CAME FROM whatever they could forage from the farms below—usually squash or potatoes, and always raw: They couldn't risk a fire. Now and then, they saw the distant glint of headlights winding through the valley. Anybody could be an enemy.

When it came time to sleep, they stretched out on beds of leaves, using their packs as pillows. Ernie would lie there in the dark, hunkered beneath the canopy of old-growth trees, in the mountains of Transylvania, fully aware "that these very peaks were the legendary haunt of Dracula and the werewolves."

Every sound would seem magnified in the stillness. The soft crack of twigs. The pad of unseen paws. It was the hour when bears and wolves were on the move.

In the early morning light they would awaken, damp from dew, bellies rumbling. But no hot shower or breakfast would be waiting for them. This wasn't the lodge. They would have to get back on the trail. Each new morning, one question still troubled Ernie, a weight he couldn't shake: Even if they made it to Pietroșița, and even if the villagers agreed to help, and even if Bob and Sandy could steer all the prisoners there, they had no answer yet to the biggest question of all:

How were they going to get out of Romania?

They were still POWs stranded in a foreign land, about to be caught up in the chaos of the Axis collapse. And the nearest American lines were more than five hundred miles away, on the other side of the Adriatic Sea.

For their American Great Escape to succeed, it was going to take something special. Something beyond grit, luck, or effort. They were facing peril on all sides, with Hitler, Antonescu, and Stalin all having a hand in their fate.

For them to make it home? It would take a miracle.

CHAPTER 43

YOU WILL ALL HANG

THREE DAYS LATER, AUGUST 23, 1944
Bucharest

IT WAS A SCORCHING SUMMER AFTERNOON IN ROMANIA'S CAPITAL CITY, still a hundred degrees by four P.M., and every window in the Royal Palace remained shut against the heat.

When the ornate black wrought-iron gates swung open, a string of four black cars swept into the courtyard. A limousine rode at the center, flanked by government escort cars in front and behind. The polished cars shimmered in the blazing sun.

The caravan braked to a halt beside several government cars already parked at the palace. A pack of men in long, loose coats and fedoras, with "hats low over eyes, hands in pockets," flew into action, forming a security perimeter. They were preparing for the man who clung to supremacy in Romania using "bloodshed and assassination" as his "macabre ingredients of power."

"This was the ruthless personage who had sought to emulate Hitler," the man who proclaimed himself the Conductor.

Antonescu had arrived.

INSIDE THE PALACE, the royal butlers stood aside as Marshal Ion Antonescu stormed through the corridors, his hat tucked beneath one arm. The Romanian dictator was sixty-two but still cut a sharp figure in a gray cavalry uniform. He was short and trim, with receding gray hair and black bushy eyebrows above blue eyes. A hero of the Great War, he had risen to the rank of general in the Romanian army, although these days he looked more like a

Antonescu and Hitler in Munich, June 1941

German. His uniform was adorned with Nazi decorations, and hanging from his neck was the Knight's Cross personally given to him by Hitler in August 1941 for joining his invasion of the East.

Antonescu was hot, tired, and impatient as he followed Colonel Ionescu, King Michael's adjutant, through the palace. The battle for Romania was already under way, and now the Boy King insisted on seeing him.

Antonescu had bigger concerns. The situation in the East was desperate. The front was collapsing, and 900,000 Axis troops were in peril. The Soviet offensive had already decimated two Romanian armies and now had the German Sixth Army surrounded again. That same army had been shattered at Stalingrad, then painstakingly rebuilt. The dictator "had nothing but bad news for the King, and he certainly did not need his advice." If anything, Antonescu needed to be at the front, not here.

Antonescu's foreign minister, "a slick-looking operator, the image of a melodrama villain," was already waiting by the door that led to the garden. Antonescu frowned in his direction, visibly perturbed. What did the Boy King want, a council of war?

The foreign minister was at a loss. Who knew?

BEHIND THE PALACE THE windows stood open in the Casa Nouă, the royal family's garden retreat. Inside, in a yellow drawing room "thick with cigarette smoke," King Michael waited, sweating through the heat beside his loyal confidant, General Sănătescu, the Marshal of the Palace.

The king burned through cigarette after cigarette. He wore a polo shirt and gray flannel pants, the same outfit he'd thrown on before driving down from Sinaia. General Sănătescu wore civilian attire, too. Neither man was looking forward to the meeting ahead.

Vain and elitist, Antonescu was "forever talking about honor," mostly because he believed he alone possessed it. Michael had once characterized him as a man with "an unhappy nature, a suspicious man who sees enemies everywhere." When Antonescu met with one of the new POWs the day after Tidal Wave, he made no effort to build bridges. Instead, with a blasé glance, he said, " 'So, you're an American, eh?' "

"Which it was pretty plain I was," the POW recalled, "what with the uniform and all."

Now Michael spotted his adjutant leading the dictator and his minister across the lawn. Uncertainty hung in the sweltering summer air, as if the meeting would cause everything to tip, either toward triumph or toward disaster.

Antonescu greeted the king and Sănătescu coldly and noticed their casual attire. "That, in itself, would have annoyed the Marshal," wrote a witness to the events. The men took seats around a circular coffee table.

"I have heard the news of the Russian breakthrough," King Michael said with concern. How would Romania respond?

The dictator conceded that the Red Army was gaining ground. "But it was anticipated," Antonescu said. "At the right time and place, it will be halted."

Michael was not reassured. "The situation is very critical," he said, before urging a dramatically different course of action.

It was time for an armistice with the Allies. Romania still had more than a million men under arms, counting those not at the front, and Michael wanted them all out of the war. Even if that meant leaving 250,000 German troops high and dry.

Antonescu bristled at the thought. He might have been pompous, but he wasn't blind; he knew an armistice wouldn't halt the Russians' advance. Besides, there was only one life he seemed intent on preserving—his own.

"I should seek an armistice only on [certain] conditions," he said stiffly. He wanted guarantees that all Romanian territory would remain intact, including even the disputed provinces.

Michael shook his head. The Soviets would never agree: They already had boots on Romanian soil. "We can't start bargaining at this late hour and in this situation," the king said.

But Antonescu wouldn't budge. "Without guarantees, I shall go on fighting," he vowed. He said his plan was to pull the army back to the Alps, "and, with German help, form a citadel of resistance that the Russians will never break."

Michael was dismayed. The Red Army was rolling over the Romanian troops in the east. The American 15th Air Force was a regular visitor overhead. And yet Antonescu was still standing by Hitler?

The whole country would be ruined.

"You must seek an armistice," Michael said. Failing that, there was another course. "If you won't give way, the right thing to do is to resign, and make way for somebody who is prepared to approach the Allies."

"For several moments Antonescu sat in incredulous silence," wrote a witness. "Then the blood rushed to his face in a spasm of rage."

"I shall not resign!" Antonescu snapped. "Who can take Antonescu's place? Do you think I shall hand the country to you—into the hands of a child!?"

The king let the insult hang in the air.

There was no swaying the dictator. "[Antonescu] had determined that if he were to be destroyed, Romania should also be destroyed."

The king stood and muttered something about needing a drink. He'd be back. He left the room.

Antonescu had won.

But in the hallway, the king's men were ready. Michael's adjutant Colonel Ionescu waited with four of the Royal Guards, dressed in their stone-gray tunics. All were armed, and looking to their king for orders.

Michael eyed them carefully. "The moment has come," he said.

He ducked into his study across the hall from the drawing room, poured a glass of water, and took a drink.

A year ago, when he'd first learned to fly, his conversations with the American pilots had nudged him to pursue the skill. But there had been practical reasons, too. He'd been planning an escape—to fly his mother and staff to safety before Antonescu dragged them to their doom. Just take the Ju-52 and go. Now, if ever, would be the time. He could save himself, his mother, the household.

But what about his country? If he didn't pull Romania out of the war now, there might be nothing left to save.

King Michael set down his water glass. He knew what his next move needed to be. Still, a nervous energy ran through him. Like that time he'd flown the patched-together "Frankenstein" B-24 rebuilt from Tidal Wave wrecks. But this time, he was about to risk far more than his own neck. The lives of millions were on the line.

The king returned to the drawing room and looked Antonescu directly in the eye. Reminding him he was acting on "the wishes of my people," to save Romania from destruction, Michael told Antonescu there was nothing left to discuss. The dictator had made his intentions clear.

"You are dismissed," the king said.

He didn't mean that Antonescu should leave. Michael stepped back into the hallway and gave the order: Arrest him.

The royal guards surged into the room. After saluting Antonescu, they seized him.

"Antonescu was taken completely by surprise," a witness reported. "He looked, puzzled, toward Sănătescu, who simply shrugged."

General Sănătescu was in on the plot. The Marshal of the Palace and the king had been planning this "operation," as they called it, for weeks.

"Follow me," the captain of the guards said, leading the dictator by the arm. Antonescu turned to Sănătescu, his colleague as a general officer. "You can't treat me like a bandit!"

Sănătescu's composure began to slip. This was the Conductor, after all, and the general was used to obeying the dictator's orders. Even the royal guards began to exchange nervous glances, suddenly gripped with indecision.

Antonescu could be very persuasive. But before the dictator could exert any more sway, the king's adjutant, Colonel Ionescu, issued a firm command: "Carry out your orders!"

The captain of the guards nodded and began to lead the dictator away. Antonescu scoffed and spat in his face. Two more guards grabbed the dictator by the arms. A third seized Antonescu's foreign minister, who was "looking pale as a sheet."

The guards steered the dictator and his minister into the hallway, now full of the king's staff, who had been drawn by the commotion. Many of the staff were "holding pistols behind their backs, in case the business degenerated into a shootout."

Starting up the staircase to the second floor, Antonescu looked back at the king and his numerous accomplices. His eyes blazed with wrath. "You'll live to regret this!" he shouted. "Tomorrow you will all hang in Palace Square!"

UPSTAIRS, ON THE SECOND floor, the guards steered their prisoners to a room that held a massive safe. Michael's father, King Carol II, had once stored his stamp collection there. The safe was eight feet deep and already had a table and chairs set up inside. It was to be the dictator's cell.

The king had seen to every detail. He'd left a pen and paper on the table as a courtesy, should Antonescu wish to pen a letter to his wife.

Or a last will and testament.

Antonescu was filled with fury—*that royal brat!*

DOWNSTAIRS, MICHAEL AND HIS accomplices "heard a dull thud upstairs and knew the safe door had been shut."

It was 5 P.M. Antonescu was no longer running the show. But the mission to take back Romania was far from over. Between Antonescu's escort and the foreign minister's, there were at least twenty armed men in the courtyard in front of the palace. It was only a matter of time before they came in to check on their bosses.

To arrest that many well-armed men would be no easy task.

Across the street from the palace stood the Ministry of the Interior, its offices teeming with Gestapo and the Siguranța secret police.

This made the next steps even more challenging. The king knew that "the firing of a single shot could [bring] hundreds of police and soldiers, Romanian and German, tumbling into the palace within a matter of minutes."

The king needed the twenty armed men arrested quietly. And everything would need to happen in plain sight of any civilians beyond the palace gates.

A plan was in motion, but it was tenuous. One wrong move, and Michael and his men would end up hanging in Palace Square, just as Antonescu predicted.

A lone officer of the royal guards entered the courtyard in front of the palace and approached the dictator's retinue. The hard, suspicious men, mostly bodyguards and drivers, stood in clusters around the cars, smoking cigarettes in the summer heat. They were "a perfect caricature of gangsterdom," recalled a witness. "Al Capone would have been proud."

At the sight of the officer, the men stiffened. They knew their bosses' endless disdain for the Boy King, and there was heavy tension between the two factions. "Their hands were on their hips, or in their pockets, or nestling gently across their chests, where at least one enormous holster could be seen strapped under the armpit."

"Want to come in for coffee while you wait?" the king's officer asked simply. It was cooler in the palace.

The dictator's men glanced around at one another. They weren't expecting a friendly gesture. But it made sense. All of them wore long coats to hide their weapons. They mopped their brows as sweat ran from their fedoras. Their scowls melted. A drink would be good. The bodyguards headed inside.

But a problem surfaced.

The drivers didn't move. Their orders were clear—they had to stay with the cars.

Moments later, the bodyguards entered the waiting room of the aides-de-camp, just inside the front door of the palace. They were assured their coffee would arrive soon. Some men sat. Others stood. Most began "chatting animatedly."

Out in the hallway, the officers of the royal guards conferred in whispers about their next moves. The man who had invited the bodyguards inside was worried. Eight armed drivers remained outside. There'd be no luring them in. And dealing with the bodyguards alone was a risky move. If one of the bodyguards called for help, it would draw in the drivers. The arrests needed to be flawless, or the king's whole operation would come undone.

The officers concluded to act in waves, banking on surprise. They'd take the bodyguards first. The drivers second.

"I will do it," one brave officer volunteered.

He opened his holster, drew his revolver, and strode into the room, sweeping his pistol in front of the dictator's bodyguards. "I will shoot whoever moves!" he said in a low voice.

The hardened gangsters "were too dumbfounded to stir."

Other royal guards rushed in and quickly disarmed them.

Now, to deal with the drivers. As long as men loyal to Antonescu were out in the courtyard, the dictator still had a chance.

Outside, the drivers chatted and smoked around the cars. Some sat behind the wheel, on the alert.

An officer and five royal guards marched out from a covered entrance, bound for the sentry post at the front gate. The drivers saw the royal guards and apparently thought nothing of it. The king's men wore shiny silver helmets with white plumes and carried their rifles on their shoulders. They high-stepped across the courtyard, just as they would at the usual changing of the guard.

Had the drivers checked their watches, they'd have noticed it wasn't the correct time for the ceremony.

The king's men passed by the cars, then suddenly stopped, turned ninety degrees to face the dictator's men, "and leveled their rifles at the stupefied drivers."

"Keep quiet!" the officer hissed. "Drop your guns or you are dead men."

The drivers' submachine guns were within arm's reach, on the passenger seats next to them. But no one wanted to be a hero.

Hands came up. "Tamely, the drivers stepped from their cars," leaving behind the submachine guns. Their pistols fell to the gravel.

And leave the keys!

The royal guardsmen swiftly steered the last of Antonescu's men inside the palace, where they joined their friends under lock and key.

Quietly, when the coast was clear, the royal chauffeurs emerged from the palace and fired up the engines of the dictator's limousine and the other government cars and whisked away the cars into the palace's subterranean garage. On the avenue in front of the palace, pedestrians kept passing by.

No one noticed a thing.

THAT NIGHT, THE KING readied the palace for battle.

The garrison of fifty-two royal guards took up their posts. Windows were locked; doors were barred.

The immediate threats had been defused, but they were far from safe. Countless steps still had to unfold—each one requiring precision, forethought, and no small measure of luck.

The administrator of the royal estates, Dimitrie Negel, fifty-four, reported to the palace in darkness. All exterior lights had been extinguished. He was met at the front door by "an officer and soldiers armed with automatic rifles and hand grenades."

Negel stated his business. He had been summoned to become the new secretary of agriculture. King Michael was forming a new government to return the country to democracy.

After admittance, and being searched inside, Negel followed "a babel of voices" to a wing of the palace where he was met by an astounding sight. There was King Michael "in the center of a large, animated group." To Negel, "the scene appeared to be one of feverish confusion, with people coming and going in an unbroken stream. At a desk sat Sănătescu, masses of papers before him, people all round him, his [now] high-pitched voice rising above the general hubbub. At another desk was a Signal Corps colonel with a battery of telephones, passing orders in the King's name to army commanders, civil governors, the police. At side tables clerks clattered busily at typewriters. People moved around talking clamorously, smoking incessantly."

"In the midst of all the excitement," noted Negel, "the King stood head and shoulders above the others, courageous and in good spirit."

There was reason to be optimistic. Their mission to take back Romania was working. Encouraging reports were already coming in.

General Sănătescu had gone to Romanian army headquarters and returned with good news: They had the loyalty of the army. Every last unit. Even the Axis-leaning generals "were surprised" by the coup d'état, "but firm in their loyalty to the King." Already, the army was disengaging from the battle with the Russians.

And the Germans were none the wiser.

At the central telephone exchange, dispatchers had broken the circuits to any German offices. The Germans could still use their radios to call Berlin, but they couldn't place a phone call anywhere in the city.

Having bought themselves some time, the king and his accomplices "insisted on a return to proper constitutional procedure." Michael appointed his level-headed confidant, Sănătescu, as the nation's prime minister, then replaced every member of Antonescu's cabinet. With swipes of a pen, the king began signing decrees, undoing Antonescu's damage. He pardoned the dictator's political foes, rescinded anti-Semitic measures, and shuttered all the forced-labor camps.

Soon the manager of the Bucharest radio station and his technicians arrived at the palace and set up their equipment to record the king's proclamation to the nation.

"Michael was for the first time exercising the full prerogatives of a head of state," wrote one observer in the king's inner circle.

The king was quick to remind anyone who congratulated him that this wasn't actually a coup d'état. By law, there was nothing underhanded about what he and his supporters had just done. Under Antonescu, the king had been reduced to a figurehead, but technically he had been the head of state during the dictator's entire reign. Antonescu had maintained such an iron grip on Romania through violence and intimidation that getting rid of him hadn't been possible before now.

"It was perfectly on my prerogative to dismiss him," the king said.

Meanwhile in the cell behind the palace, Antonescu penned "notes to his wife and made a will. But then tore everything up and threw the pieces on the floor."

THE MOST STAGGERING DEVELOPMENT was what *hadn't* happened. Nearly five hours had passed since the king arrested the dictator, but there'd been no response from the Germans in Bucharest yet.

"So little was the possibility of an uprising in the local Nazi reckoning, that during the evening, German officers dining at their hotels, still unaware of the day's events, handed their revolvers to the cloakroom attendants in the usual routine," remembered an observer.

Still, it was only a matter of time before the Germans awakened to the reversal in their situation.

While they waited to find out how the Germans would respond, the Romanians mobilized all the forces they could to defend the capital. They summoned flak gunners in from the fields, called the Royal Horse Regiment out from the stables, and barricaded the streets around the palace. They even summoned the "half-trained boy cadets of the military school."

Full mobilization, however, would take at least forty-eight hours. The nearest Romanian infantry were billeted thirty miles outside the capital, and "the military could not be sure of holding the Germans until frontline troops had reached Bucharest."

In contrast, the Germans were strong. Thirty thousand enemy troops and flak gunners stood on alert across the region, most just a short drive from the palace at their stronghold in Ploesti. "Should either the King or the Queen be captured, Hitler's hand would be immensely strengthened."

One of Michael's supporters recalled, "The next forty-eight hours until Romanian troops could return from the front would be critical. Until then, the Germans could still turn the tables."

Now, the king had to turn his mind to other priorities.

His new duty was simply to stay alive.

The miracle he'd set in motion—the damage done to Antonescu, to the fascists, and to their Nazi allies—could all be undone in an instant if they got their hands on him.

His escort was ready. The royal guards had changed into plain clothes. The king's car, a Lincoln, was waiting in the garage.

It was time to disappear.

Before King Michael departed the palace, bound for a safe house in the countryside, he gave special instructions to his staff. He wasn't the only one the Germans would be looking to kidnap. "In the turmoil of that evening he appears to have been the only one to remember [them]," remarked a witness.

The prisoners in Timisul.

He'd opened a hospital for them. He admired them as peers, even as friends, and worried for their safety. Now, by their association with him, they were in grave danger.

One of King Michael's last commands? "Send for the Americans."

It was imperative. His army had to get them to Bucharest before it was too late.

The side gate of the palace opened. In the darkness, a small four-car convoy slipped out. King Michael was behind the wheel of his Lincoln. His guards rode in other cars. Their taillights faded into the ink of the night.

AT SINAIA, THE ATMOSPHERE inside Peleș Castle was tense. Queen Helen and her staff clustered around the radio, fingers trembling as they tuned in to the 10 P.M. news. It was going to be a long night.

Her bodyguards stood close by, including the commander of the royal guard, Colonel Negulescu. The king had dispatched him to Sinaia to tell his mother what he'd done—and to prepare her evacuation to somewhere safe.

First, they had to hear the king's prerecorded proclamation. History was about to turn a page.

"Attention, attention," the broadcaster announced. "Leave your wirelesses on after this bulletin. We will broadcast a communiqué of importance to the country."

At 10:15, once the news had ended, an official-sounding chime rang out. Then came the calm, measured voice of King Michael.

"Romanians, in this most difficult hour of our history, I have decided, in full understanding with my people, that there is only one way to save the country from total catastrophe: our withdrawal from the alliance with the Axis powers and the immediate cessation of the war with the United Nations [the Allies]."

Gasps of surprise—and relief—swept through the halls of Peleș.

Michael continued, explaining that the new government marked "the beginning of a new era in which the rights and liberties of all citizens of the country are guaranteed and will be respected."

At last, he concluded with words that offered no illusions: "Romanians, the fate of our country rests on the courage with which we shall defend, weapons in hand, our independence and our right to decide our destiny for ourselves."

The broadcast ended. Silence settled over the castle.

"The BBC monitoring service heard it [the broadcast]," noted a witness of that chaotic night, "and within half an hour had made it world news."

Queen Helen "felt a mixture of anxiety and pride." Her son had taken Romania back from Antonescu. But she feared for him, for the people of the capital, for Romanians everywhere—and just as much for the Americans in their care—because she knew what would come next. For the first time in four years, Romania had made the right move.

Now, it was Hitler's turn.

CHAPTER 44

BROTHERS-IN-ARMS

THAT SAME NIGHT, AUGUST 23, 1944
Timisul

BY 10 P.M., MOST OF THE PRISONERS AT LAGĂRUL NO. 2 WERE ALREADY in bed except for Bob, Al, and a few others who played poker in the dining room of the lodge. They were fidgety and couldn't sleep. Outside, rain drummed against the windows, a sound that didn't soothe as much as provoke, like the buildup before a storm. Any day now, the men expected to rouse the others, slink out the back door, and hightail it for the village of Pietroșița.

Between hands of poker, the POWs tried to predict what would happen next. Their whispered voices were tinged with concern. They'd made the preparations for their exodus, but what were they forgetting? What else might they need?

"Razboiul e gata!" From outside the window, the shout of a Romanian sentry cut through the murk. "Razboiul e gata!"

The men set down their cards, alarmed at the commotion.

What was he shouting?

The front door of the lodge burst open. Sandy ran in, soaked and trembling. "The war is over!" he cried.

The men leapt to their feet. How did he know? Sandy said he'd heard it on the radio. The king himself made the declaration. He'd gone over to the Allies. Romania's alliance with Hitler was over. And that meant one more glorious thing:

The prisoners were free.

Word spread quickly throughout the lodge. Britt and other officers stumbled into the dining room, wiping the sleep from their eyes. A group of men gathered, talking fast, filling the room with a hubbub of voices.

"The war is over in Romania," explained one man to his friend. "The country's quit."

The war over? thought the friend. *No longer a prisoner?*

It seemed too good to be true until more guards "came running in, more and more of them." The guards embraced the Americans, saying "Bune comrade." Good comrade. Brothers-in-arms.

The Americans laughed, bewildered, and hugged them back. "A few minutes before, they were our guards," Britt recalled. "Now they were calling us friends."

One Romanian soldier spoke for many, with sadness and relief: "At last! Romania is on the right side."

But what now?

All thirty-seven officers gathered in the dining room, along with many of the guard staff. Britt found Bob and Al in the commotion. But Commandant Matiescu, the German sympathizer, was noticeably absent. He'd bet on the enemy, against his own people, and bet wrong. Who knew where he'd scooted off to.

All attention turned to Sandy. As captain of the guard, he was next in line. Sandy relayed what he knew: A delegation from the Romanian army's HQ was coming from Bucharest with a plan. In the meantime, they'd need to sit tight.*

It all seemed like good news. But a concern had begun to stir among the Americans and their new Romanian allies. How would the Germans respond?

THAT SAME NIGHT, the gates to the camp were thrown open. The POWs could go anywhere they wanted. Oh, and that fence line the POWs had been told was mined, back when they first rolled off the buses? That had been a bluff. There were never any mines.

A few men, like Britt, set a cautious toe outside the wire, then headed back in. His plan was to stay close to the lodge, waiting for more news.

One of the more senior POWs, Captain Taylor, who'd lost his entire crew, urged the men to "try to get some sleep."

* "Michael's courage in acting at this time, when everyone else on his side only talked, stands out justly," a Timisul POW would later write.

"The uncertainty was pressing in." Who knew what tomorrow would hold?

Sleep would prove impossible.

AT DAYBREAK, A STRING of Romanian military cars drove through the front gate, their windshield wipers brushing away a light rain. The delegation was here.

Inside the lodge, the core American officers gathered again. "Several generals and colonels came in, smiling and shaking hands with one and all." The Romanians "seemed to be asking our forgiveness," Britt recalled.

Medeiros translated as a general laid out the situation. The news was not promising.

Hoping "to delay hostilities for as long as possible," King Michael had offered the Germans a truce: They could have twenty-four hours to leave the country, with the promise of no provocation from Romanian forces as they withdrew.

But any hope for peace was already hanging by a thread.

Street fights were breaking out in the capital, the general said, as the Germans, staggered by Romania's exit from the war, were now reacting to their situation. Instead of withdrawing peacefully, the enemy were marshaling their forces about six miles north of the capital. Retaliation was coming, and King Michael believed the Americans were prime targets. The general said that he had heard the Germans "are either going to take you to a German camp or shoot you."

"We didn't like either option," recalled a copilot.

The delegation had been ordered by the king to transport the Americans to Bucharest. But that wasn't possible yet, not with Germans holding the capital hostage. The Americans would need to wait for the arrival of frontline Romanian troops. For the moment, the general concluded, the camp would be the safest place for them.

A wave of protest rose from the ranks. The Americans didn't like the sound of doing nothing.

Off to one side, Sandy and Bob compared notes. The escape plan to Pietroșița was still riddled with unknowns. Was the village ready to receive the Americans? Ernie and Snyder had set out nine days ago. Had they made it?

Sandy and Bob made the game call. Pietroșița still looked like the best option. It was time to go public. No one could get in trouble now.

"We know a place," Sandy told the general. He described Ernie's escape and the remote mountain village that could potentially harbor the POWs.

The general listened intently, then broke into a grin. Brilliant! The king wanted the Americans somewhere safe. This was the solution.

Sandy and Bob asked whether the general could provide trucks. It would be better than going to Pietroșița on foot.

The general said that trucks wouldn't be easy to find in the ongoing upheaval, but he'd try. Then a realization flashed across his face. He had brought something for the POWs "in case the Germans attack you." The general led the men outside. The Romanians hauled wooden crates out of the cars, set them on the porch, and pried them open.

Inside lay a gleaming cache of German Mauser bolt-action rifles, along with a few MP 40 submachine guns. The general beamed. He'd been stockpiling for this day.

The POWs passed out the weapons. All but a few squeamish navigators armed themselves. The American sergeants, in particular, showed no hesitancy. They were trained gunners and this was their forte.

Then, as quickly as they'd arrived, the Romanian brass sped off, leaving Sandy and the Americans with a single directive: Stay alive.

IT WAS STILL EARLY morning when Sandy called the American leaders back together to formulate a plan. The Romanians were preparing to defend the camp. If the Germans arrived before the Americans could leave for Pietroșița, he advised the Americans to "head for the woods."

Both parties began preparation in earnest. The defense force of forty Romanian guards locked the front gate, then took axes and cut openings in the back fence to make escape paths for the Americans. "We thought we could expect the Germans to arrive at any minute," recalled a POW. "We dressed and packed kitbags, ready to scamper off at a second's notice."

As the preparations unfolded, the Americans and Romanians worked side by side, the former POWs and the former guards. They both had rifles now, and the humor wasn't lost on them.

As for the prospect of duking it out with the Germans, their former allies, the Romanians felt not the slightest "twinge of scruples." They were with the good guys now.

"Well, if we don't know how to win a war, we should at least know how to lose it," remarked one.

For the finishing touch, the Romanians set up two machine guns aimed at the roadside in front of the camp.

"It was peculiarly pleasing to see these guns facing outward," remembered one POW. "But would we be helped to get away to a more remote spot until the situation was clear?"

AROUND 8 A.M., BRITT and several other POWs were outside discussing further plans with the Romanians when Sandy darted into the compound. It was still drizzling. The lieutenant was breathless, alarmed.

"They're coming!" Sandy said. "Germans!" He'd just received a call from a Romanian agent claiming that "the Germans were coming our way with a tank and were going to blow the Americans to hell."

"A tank?" Britt and the others were shocked.

Reportedly, the Germans had sent troops from the Predeal Pass, where they set up a field headquarters, only fifteen minutes' drive away.

If the report was true, there'd be no way a hodgepodge of American and Romanian soldiers could stop a tank.

No one wanted to wait around to find out. Sandy triggered the escape plan. Everyone needed to head to the mountain, *now.* They were evacuating Lagărul No. 2 until the danger had passed.

Britt and the other Americans bolted into the lodge to alert their friends.

"Get your backpacks and get out of here!" an American captain shouted.

The Americans double-timed it out the back door of the lodge, following several Romanian guards serving as guides. The former prisoners looked like a partisan band in their mismatched attire. Some wore Romanian fatigues. Others had on suntans. A few sported a jumble of clothing from the Red Cross. Most wore leather bandoliers around the waist or tossed over a shoulder.

The good news was that the officers of *Chattanooga Choo Choo* were at last reunited with their sergeants: Rurak, Medeiros, Riffle, Bowker, and McCrary. They hiked along together.

"The guards stood in stunned silence as we marched past with our packs," Britt recalled. The role reversal was complete. Armed Americans headed out like soldiers, filing through the holes in the fence. "We laughed at their reaction, and they joined in."

But the Americans had been out of training for a while. Some hadn't recovered from their injuries. Bob, Britt, Al, and their fellow POWs' breathing was labored as they ascended an alpine footpath behind the camp. The persistent drizzle made it tough to see. Behind them, a long human chain of men snaked up the mountain away from the lodge. The mountain was steeper than Britt had imagined, "but the fear of being shot by the Germans kept us climbing," he recalled.

Reaching a safe enough height, the men hunkered down on the densely forested slope and hid. The evergreen boughs blocked some of the rain. The men could see the camp but were safely hidden in the trees.

As the morning wore on, the mountain weather swung on a dime. The rain stopped. Steam rose. Low, wispy clouds floated through the Alps.

The guards and POWs nervously clutched their rifles, searching for the enemy and its tank. More than one man wondered aloud what the vengeful Germans might do to them if they were caught.

Second Lieutenant Charles Cavit, twenty-two, a good-natured 389th copilot known for his jug ears and wide grin, had a theory. Shot down on Tidal Wave, he'd staggered into a German medical tent with his pilot propped up on one shoulder. Cavit's hands were burned, and his fingers curled like claws. His pilot, First Lieutenant John McGraw, a fine man who "flew the hell out of that plane," was in bad shape. He'd tried to wriggle out through the small side window to escape the fiery cockpit but got stuck and was burned below the waist. Cavit circled around the wreck and somehow dragged him free.

A German doctor, a major, tended to them. As he applied a salve to Cavit's scorched skin he spoke to him in German. Both pilots' uniforms were so blackened by the fire he didn't realize they were Americans.

Until Cavit thanked him—in English.

The doctor flew into a rage. *Americans!* Those damn "Luft gangsters" had "bombed his home in Germany and killed his wife and daughter." He would treat Cavit's burned hands, all right. He made a sawing motion, intent upon cutting them off.

His tirade was suddenly interrupted when German troops hauled in

John McGraw and Charles Cavit

Cavit's tail gunner, Sergeant Jack Ross, a lanky kid from Philadelphia who was the only other survivor of their crew. The other seven were dead. Ross's hands were burned too. Not knowing better, he held them out to the doctor. The major drew a knife.

Ross pulled his hands back sharply and shoved them behind his back. "What have we gotten into?" he asked Cavit.

When the doctor turned to bark orders at his orderly, Cavit positioned himself in front of the jar of salve the doctor had left on the table. He gripped the jar with the backs of his hands, shielding it from view. The doctor snarled one last command: No treatment for the Americans! Then he stomped off.

Cavit and Ross quietly covered their wounds with the salve. They didn't know what to do for McGraw, so they did the only logical thing: They slathered his legs, what was left of them, with the same salve.

Exhausted and in brutal pain, the three Americans lay on the tent floor, shaking, shock setting in. Hour after hour passed.

Sometime that night, McGraw died.

Cavit and Ross went a full thirty hours before receiving medical care.

The doctor had murdered his pilot. Failure to provide medical care contravened the Geneva Convention, a war crime. And Cavit and his fellow crewmen weren't the only ones mistreated and abused on August 1.

Some men hypothesized that a slaughter of American POWs would be the ultimate retaliation against Romania for changing sides.

Cavit's theory was that the Germans would kill them to cover their crimes.

THEY WERE HERE. Two truckloads of soldiers pulled up outside the lodge. They broke the lock and threw open the front gate. Some forty German troops poured from the trucks. With weapons leveled, the enemy entered the lodge, searching for the POWs. Others ran around to the back, spotted the holes in the wire, and scanned the misty hills.

The Americans kept hidden. They could feel the eyes of their enemy. Cavit pictured the face of the German doctor.

But a new thought began circulating among the men. There was no tank.

"Let's go get 'em."

"About half" of the Americans wanted to charge down the hill and shoot it out.

The other half looked at them as if they were crazy. As one POW observed, they'd been out of the fight for a while, and no one was "in a condition" to do it. Besides, the Americans hadn't been spotted yet.

"We have to stay together in one group!" a major insisted.

Cooler heads prevailed.

AFTER ONE LAST LONG gaze at the mountainside, the Germans climbed into their trucks and drove away. Only then did a cold weight settle on the Americans: There had been no space for them in the German trucks.

The Germans had access to prisoner records. They knew there'd be 110 POWs at Timisul—yet they'd brought only two trucks.

The Americans had possibly come within an inch of execution. "We were glad we were not home," Cavit would later quip.

Thoroughly soaked, chilled to the bone, and miserable, the men climbed down the mountain to face an uncertain future. They had dodged a bullet, at least for now. But the enemy would be back, undoubtedly with more men. If not tonight, then tomorrow.

The German troops had seen the holes in the wire.

The Americans couldn't hide forever.

CHAPTER 45

FOR ALL THE MARBLES

THAT NIGHT, AROUND 11 P.M.
Lagărul No. 2

DARKNESS SAT HEAVY IN THE VALLEY, AND "RAIN POUNDED THE pavement." Inside the lodge, every light had been deliberately snuffed out and the dining room was cloaked in a thick collective silence. The room was packed with POWs, most still clutching their packs and rifles. Across the way, the Romanian guards huddled in their own clusters. The men waited and watched but did not speak.

Sandy and Bob crouched at the front window, trying to peer into the driving rain. Every so often a flash of lightning cut the sky. Heavily armed convoys of German trucks drove by the lodge with their headlights on, casting yellowish beams into the gloom. All rolled past without stopping. All were heading north.

An hour passed. And then another. More and more trucks passed. The Germans were leaving Romania as King Michael had hoped, but the Americans knew they would retaliate if given the chance. The POWs kept a nervous watch on the traffic.

Five gray trucks rumbled up the road, then slowed in front of the lodge and pulled in to the gravel driveway. Sandy and Bob shushed the men. Safeties were snapped off. Rifles were readied. No one made a sound.

The trucks were hulking military-grade Opels, made in Germany. Their flatbeds, framed on three sides with wooden panels no taller than a man's knees, were open topped and filled with black canvas tarps. Bob and Sandy strained to see the drivers' shadowy uniforms in the darkness.

Bob gave a little start. There was something different about the way the drivers climbed out of the trucks. And they'd come from the north, against the flow of heavy traffic. Then it clicked.

The drivers were Romanian, soldiers sent from the 5th Army. The trucks just happened to be German-built, like most of their equipment.

"They're ours," Sandy said at last, relief in his voice.

The Americans' ride to Pietroşiţa had arrived.

THE MEN SILENTLY FILED outside the lodge and slipped into the flatbeds of the trucks, packs and weapons still gripped tight. They moved as quickly as they dared. Technically, Germany and Romania were still under a truce, but that hadn't stopped the previous truckloads of enemy soldiers who had come hunting for them. Besides, as of midnight the truce would finish. All bets then were off.

The Romanian drivers hoped the truce could help them slip the Americans through German lines.

After the POWs got into the truck beds, the Romanians slid the canvas over their heads to hide them. "That's the plan?" one American said, incredulous. More than one hundred Allied POWs were trying to escape by hiding under tarps in the back of trucks, "traveling through retreating Germans?"

Someone suggested the alternative: "Want to stay?"

Sandy and Bob wished each other luck. It was time to put the final stage of their plan in motion.

This was for all the marbles.

Bob slid into the bed of the last truck in line along with Britt and Al, ducking beneath the tarp. Several guards would ride with the convoy, although up front in the cabs. With everyone aboard, Sandy took his seat in the lead truck and slammed the door.

The convoy set out. "The dirty tarp was warm and kept off the cold misty rain," Britt recalled. As they rolled through the front gate, Britt raised the lip of the canvas. He and Bob and Al sneaked one last look at the lodge where some of them had spent nearly a year. Through the glow from the taillights, the lodge seemed a fortress.

"We were leaving what had been, at the least, security for us," Britt would write.

Part of him was hesitant to go.

THE TRUCKS FOLLOWED THE highway south through the mountains. Every mile felt tense. The trucks were conspicuous, the only vehicles heading that direction. After their close call earlier in the day, each man knew the stakes. If they were discovered, they were dead.

In the cab of the lead truck, the driver next to Sandy let off the gas and began downshifting as they reached a stretch where the valley became narrow and squeezed the road ahead.

They'd come to the Predeal Pass.

Ahead, the lights of a hamlet winked from the darkness, its ramshackle buildings standing guard along the only route into and out of the Alps. Beyond the pass lay the road to Pietroșița—but it wouldn't be easy getting there.

Up ahead, Sandy could see the opposite lane jammed with an "endless" column of military vehicles stopped at a German checkpoint. Headlights stretched deep into the rainy darkness—every German who could was trying to get out of Romania.

This was the most dangerous stretch. The pass, a natural chokepoint, was crawling with enemy activity. The Germans had established their field headquarters here to manage their embittered retreat. And there were tanks. Two of them flanked both sides of the road, their big guns aimed south.

The lead driver slowed the American convoy to a crawl as they approached the checkpoint. German MPs, Feldgendarmes, were stopping each vehicle in the dark and checking papers. The Feldgendarmes wore long rubberized raincoats; their motorcycle goggles were perched atop their helmets, brass gorgets indicating their authority hung from their necks, glinting in the headlights.

The narrow road was passable for cars but a tight squeeze for trucks. Ahead on the driver's side, a German MP signaled for the Americans' convoy to stop and wait while he continued to check vehicles coming the other direction. The Romanian driver edged his truck to the side of the road and stopped. German military trucks in the oncoming lane crept past.

The convoy of five open-topped trucks idled by the roadside, their headlights illuminating the falling rain. Everywhere Sandy looked, there were enemy troops.

One POW would describe the checkpoint: "High-ranking officers stood at the sides of the road consulting maps, as smart as if they had been in Berlin," while soldiers with machine pistols "sat quietly on the flanks of tanks, alert for trouble."

"The Germans in defeat were as good as they had been in victory," he noted. "Disciplined and organized, they moved with purpose."

And this wasn't even the full retreat—not yet. The Germans in the vehicles heading north were the lucky ones, permitted to retreat before the fighting was over. Reports were that only essential traffic was being allowed to leave the country.

Under the tarp, the officers of *Chattanooga Choo Choo* stayed perfectly still as the truck idled beneath them and the rain pattered down. From the other lane came the rumble of trucks, the sputter of Kübelwagen jeeps, the snarl of motorcycles. And the blood-chilling sound of voices.

"We heard them speaking German as the trucks passed close to each other on the narrow road," Britt recalled.

The Americans gripped their rifles and "stood in readiness to fight for their lives." But if it came to a shootout, they were vastly outnumbered and outgunned.

They would lose.

The German MP turned his attention back to the Americans' convoy. He held a small box flashlight and had a machine pistol slung over one shoulder. Rain poured off his helmet. He looked miserable.

The MP held up his traffic wand, red side forward, and kept it there. The wand had a disc on top, one side colored red, the other green. The MP would twist it as a signal. Red meant stay put. Green meant go. The convoy sat.

Slowly the MP scrutinized the trucks. What were these vehicles doing together? Why were they heading south when everyone else is fleeing north? What kind of cargo were they carrying?

Sandy tensed as seconds ticked by. The opposing headlights lit up his cab like a Christmas tree. A simple twist of the wrist would decide their fate.

For another long moment, the MP stared in the direction of the convoy. Then, as if guided by some unseen benevolent force, he twirled the disc to green.

Testily, he waved the lead truck forward.

The lead driver released the brake and got them rolling. The whole convoy passed through unhindered. Sandy could have melted into his seat with relief.

Had the MP detected that the drivers were Romanian? Maybe, maybe not. One American attributed their good fortune to humanity. "It takes time for allies to become enemies."

Another thought they'd benefited from dumb luck: "They were too busy to stop us."

TWENTY MINUTES LATER, THE convoy arrived at the entrance to Pietroșița. Raincoated villagers with rifles stood guard. It was midnight. The rain was lighter now, just a drizzle falling on the hillside town. A sentry sounded the alarm.

The Americans were here.

From the center of town, Ernie and Snyder came running, taking their place with several armed locals, the mayor of Pietroșița, and Sandy's friend, a soldier sent home from the front with a wound. The village was threaded with winding cobblestone streets and anchored by an ancient Roman bathhouse. A charming day-trip getaway for the rich in Sinaia, Pietroșița was known for the special qualities of its water.

Ernie frowned, disappointed to see the trucks carrying nothing but tarps. But then the convoy stopped, the men in the cabs climbed out, and the tarps were pushed back. Americans began to disentangle themselves from the beds of the trucks. Ernie spotted Sandy stepping down from the lead cab and felt a wave of relief. "Our good lieutenant was in charge, and his cargo was our whole POW camp."

"What took you so long?" Ernie asked Sandy with a grin.

The two friends embraced.

BOB AND THE REST of the crew of *Chattanooga Choo Choo* quickly found Ernie and Sandy among the crowd of Americans and Romanians. After riding under a tarp for seemingly half the night, it was good to stand in the fresh air on the cobblestone streets. A few of the Americans were wobbly on their legs, and a few were still shaken from their "harrowing experience." But overall, the men were exuberant: Their wild scheme had actually worked.

Ernie reported that everything was in place for the new tenants. The villagers had rooms and food for everyone, and the guards would keep watch all night. Seeing that the POWs were armed, Ernie "felt more secure and hopeful now."

The mayor assigned the men to their accommodations. Teenage boys with flashlights began leading the airmen, two at a time, to their lodgings. Some would sleep in the attic over the bowling lanes. Others were billeted in a hillside villa owned by a wealthy family. The father, a colonel, was away at the front. Most would stay in the village's typical small, single-story stucco homes, many of which had an atrium in the center.

To the POWs, what kind of home they stayed in didn't matter. The men were amazed by the display of hospitality.

The next day, the officers and sergeants, eager to repay the debt, would form a home guard to help defend the town. And they would set up their base of operations in an inn with a hand-painted sign out front: "Headquarters, USAAF Pictroșița."

But that was to come.

Tonight, for the first time in a year, they were "tired, but happy, free men."

BRITT AND AL CAUGHT up with Ernie, Bob, and Sandy. They wanted to hear all about Ernie's journey. But Ernie wasn't one for patting himself on the back. "We got here," he said simply. The rest of the story could wait. Although Ernie felt relieved, he sensed it was too soon to celebrate. He led his friends to the hillside overlooking the valley. There was something troubling they needed to see.

Far in the distance "a spectral glow lighted the sky in the direction of Bucharest." As their eyes adjusted, they could see flashes of explosions from bombs and flak in the sky.

The capital was under aerial attack.

The truce was officially over. The Germans weren't giving up Romania without a fight after all. "Hitler's boys didn't like the peace idea," a POW noted.

It had turned out that instead of devoting his energies to stemming the tide of the advancing Russians, Hitler had ordered a blitz of Bucharest—a "revenge attack." He wanted King Michael arrested and a "pro-German regime" restored within forty-eight hours. But Romania was fighting back with everything it had. The following day, the country would officially declare war on Nazi Germany.

For Ernie and his friends, it was a sobering sight. The thousand other American POWs—men shot down in the high-altitude raids—were now under attack in Bucharest. And by order of the king who had freed them, Bucharest was exactly where the Tidal Wave survivors still had to go.

"Well, we've got the trucks," Ernie said to Sandy. It was a start.

Who knew how many well-armed German troops were still roaming the countryside? At the very least, the Americans would need to wait for the fighting to die down in the capital before they could try for the city. From there? No one knew how they were going to get home.

Flashes on the horizon ended the night on an ominous note. An uneasy shiver went down Ernie's spine. He had carried the message through the countryside, alerted and convinced the villagers, and secured a temporary refuge for his fellow airmen. But whatever happened next was beyond his control. At any rate, the Americans wouldn't be going anywhere tonight. There was only one last thing to do.

"Let's get out of this rain."

CHAPTER 46

THE DAMNED HUNCHBACK

TWO DAYS LATER, AUGUST 26, 1944
Near Bucharest

ON A GRASS AIRFIELD FIVE MILES SOUTHEAST OF THE CAPITAL, A Romanian bomber waited, ready to roll. Its crew was already aboard, its fuel tanks full. All that remained was to fire up the engines. Still, the plane sat idle—waiting.

The bomber was a Savoia-Marchetti SM.79, an obsolete prewar Italian design, license-built in Romania as the IAR 79. Its nose was glassed on three sides, and its two inline engines looked too small for the aircraft's girth. Behind the cockpit, a large dorsal hump rose from the top of the fuselage, housing the gunner and earning the aircraft its unflattering nickname: *il gobbo maledetto,* "the damned hunchback."

The Savoia-Marchetti 79/IAR 79

It was 1 P.M. on a Saturday, "quite cool" for August. Despite the solitary bomber waiting by the runway, urgency could be felt everywhere at the Popești-Leordeni aerodrome. With the Transylvanian Alps faint in the dis tance, ground crews crisscrossed the tarmac while Romanian fighter pilots took to the skies in their Me-109s. Romanian military aircraft, dispersed around the airfield, were being rearmed and refueled in the lull between German raids. Today, it was every hand on deck.

The airfield looked almost rustic, more like a flying club than a military base, with wood-sided buildings and sharply pitched roofs. Once home to civilian flight schools, it was now the last airfield in Bucharest still under Romanian control. Fortunately, reinforcements had arrived. The last battered remnants of the Royal Romanian Air Force had gathered at Popești to make one final stand, defending the capital.

Still, one bomber remained on the ground waiting for its passenger. It was tasked with a special mission all its own.

A NEWLY FREED AMERICAN POW dashed toward the waiting bomber. Lieutenant Colonel James Gunn III was the only American on a field full of Romanians. An energetic Californian with an easy grin, he was tall and slender, though his receding blond hair made him look older than his age. The younger airmen called him Pop. *Good grief!* He was only thirty-two.

Lt. Colonel James Gunn III

Back in Italy, Gunn had commanded the 454th Bomb Group, a B-24 outfit with the 15th Air Force. Nine days earlier, during a high-altitude raid on Ploesti, he had been shot down and imprisoned in the main POW camp in Bucharest. He was still dressed in the same long-sleeve suntans he'd been wearing when he parachuted down. Today, he was being brought to Popești on a new mission of vital importance.

To the north, smoke rose into the sky above Bucharest, fresh signs of the latest German bombings. For two full days before the Romanian reinforcements arrived, the city had endured Hitler's "revenge attack." Waves of Luftwaffe He 111 and Stuka dive-bombers had "worked the town over" as "the Germans savagely unloaded their remaining bomb stocks on the helpless Romanian capital." The Royal Palace was now a shell, pummeled by seventy bombs that Hitler had intended for King Michael. "Eighteen poor little soldiers of our guard killed," Queen Helen noted when word reached her. "Lots wounded."* Across the city, the Romanian army were clashing with "small groups of diehard Nazis holed up in buildings," and there were "snipers in the streets." The Germans would compare the blow dealt by the king's coup—and Romania's sudden break with the Axis—to nothing less than a second Stalingrad.

Meanwhile, a thousand newly freed American fliers were trapped amid the chaos, staring up as German bombs rained down. Only one American airman had been killed so far. But danger lay everywhere, and it was only a matter of time before the He 111s and Stukas returned. Did the brass in Italy even know what was happening?

Someone had to alert the American high command.

Gunn and the other senior POWs had asked the Romanians if there was a radio they could use to send a message to the 15th Air Force. But their new allies had bad news: "All radio stations had been destroyed or were in German hands." Not even the Romanians could get a message out. So, Gunn and the POW leadership raised an audacious question, born of desperation.

If they couldn't call Italy for help, couldn't someone just fly a message there?

HIS FLIGHT WAS WAITING.

Gunn climbed aboard the waiting Romanian bomber at Popești, pausing

* The Romanian populace who once shook their fists at the American planes experienced a change of heart after enduring the German "revenge attack." Explained one POW: "The difference between stray bombs from formations aiming at legitimate targets and a deliberate attempt to level the most beautiful parts of the capital was evident. Many apologized when given an example of true frightfulness." One Romanian man went further. He told a POW "he was glad that it was the Germans [bombing them] this time instead of the Allies, because he was mad at the Germans and just couldn't get around to being mad at the Allies."

only to stare at the oddly shaped plane. From the outside, he "did not like the looks" of the Savoia-Marchetti. It appeared dated, awkward, and slow. He went aboard anyway.

The entire plane was for him. Romania's new government, just four days old, had arranged his flight. They couldn't just hand over a plane for Gunn to fly on his own—there simply weren't enough to go around. But they could give him a lift. If the enemy's aerial assault was blunted long enough, perhaps one plane could make it out?

Gunn was the logical choice for a messenger to go to Italy for help. As the highest-ranking American POW in Romania, he carried the weight of experience and credibility; if anyone could make the brass listen, it was he.

The American colonel took a seat in the waist, and looked around. The interior of the plane was no more welcoming than the exterior. It was "of a poor type," woefully outdated. Before the war, the Italians had used these as airliners before converting them into bombers. But Gunn was optimistic and eager. If this was the best they had, he'd make do. A lot of guys were counting on him—both the thousand Americans in the city, and the Tidal Wave survivors stuck in the Alps. His message had to get through.

The pilot and four crewmen of the Romanian 2nd Bombing Fleet were already on board. As the bombers' Jumo engines spooled up, the Romanian gunners eyed their passenger with suspicion. They might be allies now, but they were still leery of the newly freed Americans. What if the ex-POW harbored a grudge?

Gunn later discovered that the crew, who had pistols strapped to their waists, "had been put on board to guard me. Everyone seemed to be suspicious of me and feared that I might attempt to murder the pilot and take over the aircraft. I had no such thought."

The Romanians took gun positions in the nose, dorsal, and the waist. They needed to leave immediately. Their window of opportunity between German raids was closing fast. The enemy's airfields were just fifteen miles away on the other side of the city. Another raid could come at any moment.

The ugly bomber taxied to the runway and lumbered into the skies. Gunn's spirits soared. They were on their way.

THIRTY MINUTES INTO THE flight, the bomber turned in the air and began heading back to Bucharest. Alarmed, Gunn asked what was wrong. No one spoke English. Finally, on the ground at Popești, he received an answer. The pilot pointed to the right wing and insisted "the right engine was acting up." Gunn shook his head, disappointed. He knew engines, and nothing had appeared wrong to him. He suspected the pilot was afraid they'd never make it to Italy, so he'd invented an excuse to turn around.

The bomber crew could not be convinced to fly again, and it was no use arguing with a brick wall. Gunn loitered in the shadows of the flight school's hangar, crestfallen, watching Romanian fighters take off and land. There was nothing else for him to do except wait for a ride back to the capital. Only one plane had been authorized for his use by the Romanian government. The grounded bomber wasn't merely a setback. It was the end of the road.

Gunn waited in uneasy silence, fiddling with a cigarette, until a Romanian pilot spotted him, approached, and struck up a conversation "in excellent English." Tall and rugged, he wore the Romanian summer uniform: a tan short-sleeved shirt with epaulets, blue slacks, and a blue tent-shaped cap. He'd just returned from flying a mission. An affable fellow, he introduced himself as "Captain Cantacuzino."

It was the prince. Gunn knew the name. "I had been told about this officer since he was considered the number one pilot of Romania."

Buzz was tired but in good spirits. It had been a tumultuous couple of days. His unit, the 9th Fighter Group, was now flying out of Popești. And he was now the commander. Just a week earlier, he'd been promoted to lead Romania's spearhead unit after his predecessor and friend, Captain Șerbănescu, was killed in combat against American fighters. When Buzz heard the king's broadcast he immediately led what remained of his group—about fifteen planes—back from the Eastern Front and joined the last remnants of the air force defending the capital. His old unit, the 7th Fighter Group, was there as well, equally depleted. The Royal Romanian Air Force was in sorry shape. All told, the country had only twenty-nine Me-109s still flying.

Buzz and the 9th had gone straight to work anyway, using the Germans' own plane against them. Already the prince was leaving his mark. The day before, his group had shot down six of eleven attacking German He 111 bombers. And Buzz had personally shot down three, bringing his victory tally to forty-five, and making him Romania's top living ace.

As for fighting the Germans, his former allies, "this troubled him not a whit."

The prince knew all about Gunn's aborted flight. He told Gunn "how foolish he thought it was to try to fly to Italy in a Savoia-Marchetti." It was a terrible plane. If the German fighters didn't intercept them on the way there, the American fighters would surely blast them out of the sky when they showed up in an unknown bomber.

But Buzz sympathized with Gunn's predicament. The prince knew that many Americans were trapped in his country, now caught in a perilous crossfire, and when he'd heard the king's proclamation on the radio, "an image came to mind" of the American aviators confined in Timisul, although he'd never had the opportunity to meet them.

Buzz indicated there was another option for Gunn.

"Colonel," he said, "if you will ride in the belly of a Messerschmitt, I will take you to Italy."

Gunn blinked once, twice, like the words hadn't landed right. In the belly of a '109? What belly? Everyone knew the airplane was a single-seater.

Buzz led the American over to his Messerschmitt. He showed him what he had in mind. If they removed the radio from the fuselage, there would be just enough space for Gunn to fit inside. The trip wouldn't be easy. Although the flight would be quick overall, perhaps two hours in the air, Italy lay at the far limit of the Messer's range. They'd need an external drop tank to stand a chance of reaching their destination.

Gunn wrestled with the decision. Riding in a rickety bomber was one thing. But riding in the belly of a '109 like a stowaway presented an entirely new level of danger. Once he went inside, there'd be no way for him to get out on his own. If anything happened—a fiery crash, a ditching at sea—the plane would become his coffin.

Could he trust his life to a Romanian pilot he'd just met? Why would this man volunteer to help him? Four days ago, he was the enemy. In the recesses of Gunn's mind, the prince was still a lethal ace who'd shot down forty-five planes—Russians, Germans, and Americans. Loyalties didn't flip that fast, did they?

The American remembered the nearly eleven hundred POWs who were depending on him. He figured he owed it to them to give it a try. And there was something else. "The man's personality in itself was a selling point," Gunn notcd.

Gunn looked Buzz in the eye.

"I'll ride inside the fuselage."

TIME WAS AGAINST THEM. Buzz and Gunn alerted the Air Ministry about the change of plans, then set about preparing for their flight. They needed to leave tomorrow at the latest, and a lot needed to be done.

Buzz inquired with his pilots, seeking their best-maintained '109. He told them the full plan, that he was heading to Italy "to convey a message," and that he couldn't afford engine trouble with an American locked inside with no parachute.

Jaws hit the floor.

It was "a beautiful mission," scribbled one of Buzz's pilots in his diary. They'd be "on the brink of running out of fuel, with hundreds of kilometers in enemy-controlled territory, full of risks and responsibilities. A mission very suitable for him."

Mechanics set about removing the radio from the group's best '109, making room for Gunn to fit inside.

Buzz turned his attention to the next challenge: How would they get there? He had never flown to Italy before. Gunn knew the route to his home base, San Giovanni, a field on the ankle of the Italian boot shared by his group and another—but he wouldn't be much help from inside the fuselage.

They tore apart the map room of the civilian flight school, but came up empty; there was not a single map of Italy. So Gunn made one. On a piece of cardboard, he sketched the 550-mile route by memory, showing the American air defenses—barrage balloons and flak zones—they'd need to avoid. Still, the biggest hurdle remained.

Without a radio, they'd be showing up in an unknown Messerschmitt with no way to tell American fighters or anti-aircraft gunners to hold their fire.

The American colonel suggested they fly low, skimming the waves to slip into Italy undetected. But Buzz saw a potentially fatal flaw in the plan. If intercepted by fighters, German or American, he'd have no space to maneuver.

Conversely, the Romanian proposed taking the plane up to twenty thousand feet, the very limit that Gunn could survive without oxygen, then diving at top speed into Italy. By doing so, the prince figured they'd be "picked up by radar for [a] minimum length of time," giving Allied fighters little window to make an intercept.

Gunn saw the logic and was pretty sure he could hold up at twenty thousand feet, even without oxygen. He was a straight shooter, and so was Buzz; together they made a good team. Both had been professional aviators before the war, and they "spoke the same language" of flying.

Even so, one huge and deadly problem remained. Even if the German fighters didn't catch them, and even if they slipped past the American fighters and flak, and even if they made it all the way to San Giovanni, they still needed to get past the airfield's defenses.

They might make the whole 550-mile gamble only to get shot down at the finish line.

Both men were stumped.

Without a radio, how do you land on a heavily guarded American bomber base in an enemy aircraft?

CHAPTER 47

THE AMERICAN MESSERSCHMITT

THAT SAME NIGHT, AUGUST 26, 1944

WHILE GUNN RETURNED TO BUCHAREST TO SCRAPE TOGETHER A few hours' sleep, Buzz worked late into the darkness at the Popeşti aerodrome. For "approximately three hours," the prince mentally rehearsed their plan, hunching over Gunn's map, studying it, searching for an answer, his eyes burning a hole in the cardboard map.

How could they land on the bomber base without being shot down?

He had logged six thousand hours of flight time, with more than five hundred in combat, but he'd never faced a problem like this. Every possible approach into San Giovanni carried grave danger. It was like flying into a firing squad. The prince wasn't afraid of death, but he knew that if he got himself killed now, with the war on Romanian soil nearing an end, the people around him would suffer. Nadia most of all.

Some might have argued the mission was unnecessary. But although Buzz would gain nothing personally, he had unfinished business with the war. Romania was "finally on the right side," yet Buzz still carried the weight of what he'd done. As he'd admitted to Gunn, he'd shot down American planes "on many occasions." He had only been doing his duty, yet he felt no pride. Some of the very POWs now in danger were there because of him. Forced to defend his homeland, the prince had been pitted against the Americans, flying against a nation he had long admired.

King Michael's brave act had changed everything.

Now, Buzz was finally free to follow his conscience. The POWs in the city and in the Alps were counting on this flight. They were no longer enemies. They were brothers-in-arms. If he could help return them to their families, perhaps something good could come from his role in this war. The more he thought about it, the more he believed that this flight was far more than a high-stakes courier run across the sea.

It was a shot at redemption.

And as he kept studying the map, desperate for a solution, finally, mercifully, deep into that long stretch of a dark night, a flicker of light broke through. Buzz had a revelation. The plan that unfolded in his mind was imperfect and dangerous.

But maybe, just maybe, it could bring them into Italy without getting killed.

EARLY THE NEXT MORNING, August 27, Buzz led Gunn and his Romanian ground crew out to a Messerschmitt 109 at Popești.

The men carried paint cans.

She was a gray, sinister-looking machine, with wavy dark camouflage on her spine and a bold red number 31 on her flanks. This machine was the group's best aircraft, a new Me-109G-6 delivered to them by the Germans just before the king's coup. She'd logged just seven and a half hours of flight time.

Crewmen climbed on her wings while men on the ground passed up cans of blue paint. Others slathered a base coat of white over the numbers, while still others worked on the nose with red paint to cover the black German-style spinner with its white corkscrew. Buzz and Gunn rolled up their sleeves and pitched in, slapping paint wherever it needed to go.

A crowd of curious Romanian servicemen formed around the plane, watching the Messerschmitt's transformation. For secrecy's sake, Buzz didn't advertise where they were going or reveal the takeoff time. After all, it would take only one enemy spy or fascist sympathizer to slip word to the Germans, and enemy fighters would be waiting to ambush Buzz and his American stowaway the moment they were in the skies. What greater target could there be than a Romanian prince and an American colonel trying to bring an important message to the Allies?

But the bystanders began to connect the dots.

THE TIME HAD COME.

At 4:30 P.M., Buzz and Gunn met in a hangar for the final few checks before their flight. As Buzz's fellow Romanian pilots looked on, the prince lashed on his pistol belt and armed himself with a German MP 40 submachine gun. They'd be flying their longest stretch over Yugoslavia, a region teeming with both Germans and Communist partisans. If his Messer went down, either group would love to get its hands on him.

Gunn removed his watch and anything metal that could throw off the aircraft's compass. A Romanian group commander, Captain Dan Vizanty, saw that Gunn was wearing only the same khaki suntans he had on when he was shot down. At twenty thousand feet, he would be freezing. Vizanty disappeared, then the cheerful, balding Romanian returned carrying his personal leather jacket with a fur collar. He handed it to Gunn—Vei dori asta! (You'll want this!)

Gunn smiled his thanks. He and Buzz bid goodbye to their fellow pilots, then headed out to the Messerschmitt.

The menacing gray Romanian fighter had taken on a new life, now dressed in red, white, and blue. Large American flags covered both flanks of the fighter, while U.S. stars adorned the tops and undersides of the wings. The ground crews had gone with the old prewar insignia—with red circles in the center—for extra visibility. And they'd painted over the black spinner and its corkscrew, turning it red, the same color the P-51s in Italy wore for identification.

The only thing the ground crew hadn't touched was the 9th Fighter Group crest on the nose. That was a point of Romanian pride.

A crewman was still applying the finishing touches, painting the last of forty-eight stars on one of the flags. He looked up, dismayed by the interruption, as if his unfinished work was due to be judged by a jury of their new American allies. The painter "could not understand why we were in such a hurry," Gunn would recount.

It was time to fly.

Buzz opened the hatch for his new friend to climb aboard. Gunn would be sealed inside the cramped, dark compartment for the next two hours. The prince looked to his passenger, giving him one last chance to back out. It wasn't too late—not yet. Once Gunn was inside, there would be no room for second thoughts. If he changed his mind, Buzz wouldn't hear him over the roar of the engine. In the event of a crash on takeoff, Gunn wouldn't be able to free himself. On top of everything, Gunn had told the prince he had a "wife and 2-year-old son, James," who were staying with his mother-in-law in San Antonio.

"Colonel," Buzz said, the hatch still open. "I promise you one thing—we won't be shot down." If they ran into fighters, he explained, instead of dogfighting, he'd put the plane down in the nearest field and do his best to get Gunn out. "If the Americans don't shoot us on the ground, we'll be all right."

Buzz's promise was assurance enough for Gunn. The colonel managed an uneasy grin, then turned his shoulders and crawled headfirst into the narrow compartment.

Without another word, Buzz shut the hatch, secured it tight with a screwdriver, and climbed into the cockpit.

IT WAS 5:20 P.M. when Buzz at last fired up the Daimler-Benz engine. It crackled and popped, sputtered to life, and settled into a steady roar. The violent propwash began streaking the wet paint. The painter's forty-eight white stars bled like melted ice cream.

The Messer's regular 105-gallon fuel tank had been topped off. Beneath her belly, mounted on a centerline rack, an extra drop tank brimmed with 79 additional gallons.

Drawn by the engine sounds, Romanian pilots and ground crew poured from hangars and gathered on the flight line, marveling at the sight of the American Messerschmitt taxiing to the end of the grass runway. We can imagine their conversation:

"Who's that?"

"The prince!"

"He's going to the Allies?"

"Apparently!"

"Only an American and 'Bâzu' were capable of doing something like this!" wrote one of Buzz's pilots, Lieutenant Ion Dobran, in his diary. "To go enclosed in the uncomfortable fuselage of [Messerschmitt] 31, among the control cables, without seeing anything . . . and to risk crossing the Adriatic without being able, in case of an accident, to even stick a hand out. Pure sportsmanship, adventurous spirit, or more likely, recklessness!"

As Buzz lined up at the end of the grass runway, nervous tension filled his body. He knew Gunn was sealed in the plane, helpless, and the potential pitfalls of this mission were great. A young father's life was entirely in his hands.

"Ace though Captain Cantacuzino was," wrote a war reporter, "his route was new to him, he had no adequate maps, no radio to tell the Americans he wasn't a German, no recognition signals, and, because of his passenger back there without oxygen, no chance to climb if attacked."

This would be the most difficult flight of Buzz's life, and one he wouldn't trust to anyone else. He'd been waiting the entire war for this moment. His days of fighting "who's in front of me" were behind him. He was flying for the good guys now. Sticking your neck out for someone else? That was what teammates did.

Buzz pushed the throttle forward. The engine surged, and the Messerschmitt raced down the runway. The prince was careful not to feed the engine too much power, too fast. The '109's rudder was notoriously too small for the fourteen hundred pound-feet of torque generated by the engine, so the aircraft had the tendency to swing left on takeoff. Sure enough, as the speed picked up and the tail left the ground, the Messer began veering left. Buzz skillfully corrected with the rudder and coaxed her upward.

They were airborne.

Ever mindful of his cargo, Buzz eased into the skies over Popești. His fighter was not alone. Two other Romanian Me-109s circled the field at a distance like watchful hawks. The pair of friendly fighters banked sharply toward Buzz's plane and took up protective positions around the American Messerschmitt. One escort pilot was Lieutenant Hariton "Toni" Dusescu, an ace with nine victories to his name. The other was Lieutenant Ioan "Sim" Simionescu, with four. Both belonged to Buzz's group.

The prince had arranged an added precaution in case German fighters were lurking. His pilots would escort them only until they were out of Romanian airspace, then return to Popești. Romania still needed every plane to defend Bucharest.

The wingmen nodded to Buzz.

Together, the small three-ship flight steered into the sun, heading west in the direction of Italy.

AN HOUR AND A half later, the American Messerschmitt was flying alone at twenty thousand feet, high above the sea. It was just the colonel and the prince now.

In the dark fuselage compartment, Gunn lay flat on his back, staring at the ceiling, concentrating on every breath. The cold metal walls pressed in around him, so tight he couldn't sit up or turn over. The temperature was well below freezing. He could hear the engine roaring through the thin walls. Control cables stretched past him on both sides, tugging pulleys each time Buzz worked the elevators or rudder. The American's lungs felt small, squeezed in the thin oxygen-starved air. He was riding at the human limit of survival without an oxygen mask. No matter how much air he drew in, it was never enough. Without enough oxygen, his mind felt drowsy and dull, but he knew not to close his eyes and doze "because of the danger of sleeping under such conditions." Without his wristwatch, he'd lost track of time. As the plane bounced through the turbulence, he could only guess at how much longer they had until they reached their destination. He shivered. The cold seemed endless.

Gunn tried to occupy his mind by calculating the odds they were facing. "He figured them one way, then another, then another. Over and over again."

The American's shoulder brushed against a dark square along the port sidewall. He recognized it as "a small kickplate used as a stirrup by the pilot to enter the cockpit." Desperate for light, he pulled the internal spring. The kickplate retracted, revealing a small slit, open to the outside world. He peeked through the opening and looked down.

Outside, it wasn't yet dusk. He could see the evening rays of the summer sun shimmering on the sea beneath them.

The Adriatic.

Gunn let out a sigh of relief. That meant Nazi-occupied Albania, Yugoslavia, and Bulgaria were behind them. It also meant that Italy, and their moment of truth, were close.

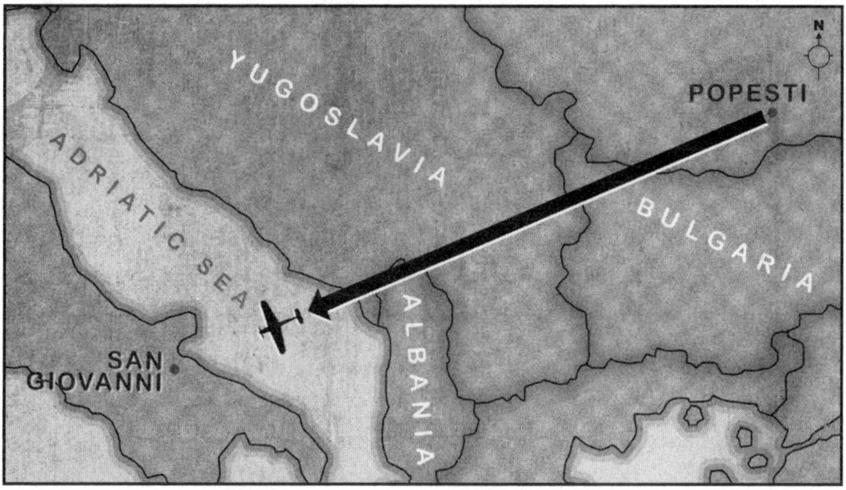

Just then the engine sputtered.

Gunn heard it. He felt the vibration change in the floor. His eyes darted toward the source of the sound. Engine trouble? Now? Over water? In a water landing, even if Buzz could successfully belly-in, the Romanian ace would never get him out in time. The plane would sink with him trapped inside.

"Clunk!" A loud noise jostled the front of the plane.

"Hit by a 20 mm?!"

But that couldn't be it: Buzz wasn't taking any evasive maneuvers, and as quickly as the Daimler-Benz started skipping, the engine regulated itself and returned to normal.

Gunn tried to think. When nothing more happened with the engine, it dawned on him. The sputtering was Buzz switching to the main tank after draining every drop of fuel from the drop tank. And the clunk was the spare tank being jettisoned.

For some time longer, the '109 continued in level flight.

Then, without warning, the plane sharply nosed downward, into a 45-degree dive. Gunn felt himself sliding forward. He knew what was happening outside his tight compartment.

The hazardous descent into Italy had begun.

IN THE COCKPIT, BUZZ held the Messer in the high-speed dive. Nineteen thousand feet. Eighteen thousand. Seventeen. The '109 shuddered under the strain, its frame quivering as the wind tore at the wings.

The prince ripped off his oxygen mask. Through his whirling propeller, he could see the southern Italian coastline taking shape in front of him, still about fifty miles away. In one hand, he held Gunn's map, flipped to the more detailed side. It showed various landmarks in Italy, including a river to follow inland, and the monastery where he'd turn to find the base.

Once they penetrated American airspace, Gunn estimated they would have five minutes, maybe less, before the Allies could vector fighter patrols to them. But if the '109 went fast enough, they just might slip past them and get onto the ground first.

Buzz edged the throttle forward. The engine's roar deepened, and the Messer leapt ahead, slicing faster through the sky in a headlong dive. Gunn could not help but notice that "the speed of the aircraft was now terrific." They were hurtling down at more than 450 miles per hour.

Buzz's heart hammered in his chest. He scanned the skies around him. No silhouettes. No contrails. No Allied patrols, not yet. So far, so good.

If they made it to San Giovanni, Buzz knew what he needed to do. Gunn had coached him to slowly rock his wings, the surrender signal used in rare situations by damaged bombers.

But would that and a splash of fresh paint be enough to keep them from getting killed?

All bets were off.

NEAR 7 P.M., OPERATIONS were winding down at the San Giovanni air base, a hot, dusty strip hastily built on an old olive farm. Here, just as in the desert, British anti-aircraft gunners manned the perimeter defenses of the American base.

The British troops were the first to see Buzz's plane coming. Beyond the end of the long, pierced-steel plank runway, an unidentified fighter was dropping fast, passing low over the Italian farmland south of the base. The gunners, some in khaki, others shirtless, tipped back their flat-brimmed helmets and squinted into the fading evening light.

Whoever was flying that plane, he looked to be in some trouble. The landing gear was down, the wings rocking steadily as if the pilot were wounded, the controls damaged, or he was wrestling a wildcat in the cockpit. Sleek and razorbacked, the incoming plane had the look of a P-51 from one of the neighboring bases. But something didn't add up.

A Mustang's landing gear dropped straight down. This one's angled outward, forming a V. Only one fighter had a profile like that.

It was a Messerschmitt.

For a moment, the men stood "stunned," their feet "frozen to the ground." Then their training kicked in. They scrambled to their guns, shooting glances at the control tower, a spindly framework of steel and crisscrossed stairs. Where was the air raid alarm!? Why was no one calling on the field phone? Were the radar boys asleep?

The Brits swung their 40mm Bofors guns toward the aircraft and set it squarely in their gunsights. It was still rocking its wings, but that wouldn't throw them off. Flying at almost eye level, it would be an easy kill.

Pulses quickened; feet were poised over the guns' foot-activated triggers. Standing orders were clear: Shoot down any potential threat. Gunners spun handles, traversing their 40mms, tracking the moving target. Loaders hustled forward with heavy magazines, ready to feed fresh shells into the breech.

The enemy fighter crossed the perimeter track; then it roared over the edge of the runway. He was coming straight down the strip. The gunners were ready to cut loose.

Wait.

The aircraft's gear was still down, and the plane kept wagging its wings as it flew down the pierced-steel runway.

That was no way to make an attack run.

The gunners held their fire, letting the Messerschmitt make an air-show-style pass. In a colorful blur, the '109 streaked past B-24s parked on dirt hardstands, past the Quonset huts, and past the tents where aircrews lived.

The gunners followed the intruder with their gun barrels, ready for anything. Then they saw it. The red spinner. U.S. stars on the wings. And along the flank of the fighter—something unmistakable.

An American flag.

"Don't shoot!"

Feet moved away from triggers. The gunners stepped back, wide-eyed, as the Messerschmitt "made a pass over the airstrip," before it broke off to the west and began circling the field to land.

ON THE WESTERN FRINGE of the base, American aircrews from the 455th Bomb Group—Gunn's sister unit—were playing baseball in the warm summer night. A small crowd of their fellow fliers cheered from the sidelines. Then a sound from the sky cut through the evening, freezing their play.

"Everybody looked up," recalled a B-24 pilot who was spectating.

The next thing they knew, a fighter with its gear down "buzzed" over the ballfield, rocking its wings like some jokester trying to make the pitcher balk.

"That's a funny looking P-51," one man remarked.

"That's not a P-51!" another shouted. That's "a German Me-109!"

The plane was lining up on the runway.

The fliers dropped their mitts and bats and sprinted for the strip.

WITH A CHIRP OF tires, the American Messerschmitt kissed the tarmac at ninety miles per hour and rolled down the runway.

A jeep full of MPs roared up alongside, keeping their machine gun trained on the pilot as they followed him onto a taxiway.

Did he know he had the wrong field?

The MPs were truly baffled when the Messerschmitt taxied straight up to a former olive warehouse—now the HQ of the 454th Bomb Group, Gunn's former unit—and cut its engine.

That was odd. Whoever this enemy pilot was, he knew right where to park.

A "curious throng" of American airmen and British gunners gathered around the enemy fighter. The MPs kept their carbines at the ready.

Buzz's Me-109, San Giovanni

The canopy slid open. The prince raised his hands and stood in the cockpit. "Gentlemen!" he shouted. "Will someone get me a screwdriver? I have somebody here you'll be glad to see." Buzz climbed down from the wing and helped an American corporal open the compartment in the fuselage.

"Look at those GI shoes sticking out!" someone yelled. Surprise rippled the ranks, spreading from one astonished airman to the next.

Buzz urged the bystanders to give Gunn a hand. "When two sergeants pulled the colonel out, they dropped him [in their hurry] to salute," recalled an officer. "He was unhurt, but stiff from the long, cramped 550 mile ride."

Dizzy from the lack of oxygen, Gunn stood. The crowd recognized him immediately and broke into wild applause. Ten days had passed since he'd been shot down over Romania, and now, miraculously, he was back. A grin spread across Gunn's face as he scanned the cheering throng. He recognized "a great many of the crowd."

The prince was physically and mentally taxed from the journey, but relieved it had all worked out. "The reaction was enormous, indescribable," Buzz later recounted. The cheers rolled on, endless, and he marveled at the "shouts of 'bravo!'" "These were purely American expressions of joy," he'd amusedly note.

Buzz's methodical yet daring approach had worked. The Romanian ace hadn't just crossed into Allied airspace—he'd flown straight into the heart of it.

"Their flight also caused some embarrassment in high places," recalled a P-51 pilot, "since their approach and landing went undetected by whatever air-defense system was supposed to be functioning."

The American colonel turned to the prince. Beaming a toothy grin, Gunn extended a hand to the Romanian ace who had brought him home.

"I had great faith in Cantacuzino, and the faith was justified," Gunn would later tell a reporter, before he gave the highest compliment between aviators: "He's a great pilot. He came in and landed as if he lived here."

AFTER SHAKING FREE FROM the crowd, Gunn slipped inside the group HQ to place a call to the 15th Air Force headquarters, an hour's drive down the coast at Bari, to tell the higher-ups that he and the prince would be arriving soon.

But first, the two men were starving. "After all the hurrahs and cheers," they made a beeline to the nearest taverna, where they toasted their success with glasses of water. Wine would have to wait—there was still a message to deliver to the upper brass.

"We ate, drank, and in the end, Gunn had to firmly and authoritatively intervene for people to understand that this was an important and urgent mission," Buzz recounted.

Gunn and Buzz immediately after their arrival in Italy

Gunn threw on a fresh set of suntans, a car pulled up, and the unlikely duo were "hustled off" to Bari. That night they would meet with General Charles Born, the operations officer of the 15th Air Force, the first in a string of top brass eager to hear what they had to say. In Born's picturesque seaside headquarters, Gunn and Buzz would brief him and the assembled officers, explaining the situation in Romania and asking "that a plan of evacuation for our POWs should be started as soon as possible."

Gunn would propose an airlift: They could fly a fleet of heavy bombers into Romania to extract the eleven hundred American POWs. Buzz would pledge Romania's full support.

An airlift?

It was an ambitious request, one that would require extraordinary coordination to make it happen. But after the gutsy flight they'd just made in a single-seat aircraft, through hostile airspace, braving the cold and lack of oxygen, all the way from Romania, all while facing the very real risk of being shot at their destination—for men such as this, the brass would be all ears.

CHAPTER 48

REUNION

FOUR DAYS LATER, AUGUST 31, 1944
Popești aerodrome

POPEȘTI WAS "A CIRCUS."

When Ernie and the Tidal Wave survivors stepped onto the airfield that morning, carrying their packs and bundles, they were surprised by what was waiting.

All the POWs in Romania were in one place.

"Well, they weren't kidding around," Ernie quipped to his friends.

A sea of POWs, mostly 15th Air Force men from the main camp in Bucharest, crowded the grass of the rustic-looking flight school at Popești. The full array of the downed airmen was staggering. Bomber crewmen and fighter pilots milled around, smoking cigarettes, talking loudly, and mingling with their new Romanian allies. The "Romanian pilots were dressed in their best uniforms, smiling and shaking hands, happy to be on our [the Allies'] side. Romanian dignitaries were all over the place." Joining the 1,127 Americans were thirty-one British airmen, two Dutch naval officers, and a lonely French sergeant.

It was 9 A.M. on a warm late-summer morning with haze in the air up to fourteen thousand feet. Everyone waited on a massive airlift. Supposedly, the 15th Air Force was sending planes to fly all the POWs out. Meanwhile, Me-109s from the Royal Romanian Air Force patrolled overhead, providing air cover.

The 110 Tidal Wave survivors took their place on the edge of the crowd. A day earlier, they'd been in Pietroșița when word from the main camp reached them, telling them to get to the capital at any cost. The situation at Bucharest had stabilized. Romanian armies had returned from the front and pushed out the Germans. In the last week alone, Romanian fighters had shot down twenty-two Luftwaffe aircraft.

Sandy and his guards from Lagărul No. 2, as well as the protective citizens of Pietroșița, hated to see their American friends go, but understood. The POWs were still in danger and far from home.

Ernie and the other POWs piled into trucks and hightailed it south. They skirted the fighting northwest of Ploesti, where the Romanians were encircling the remaining Germans, including their top brass. Now they were here at Popești, the destination they'd envisioned when they hatched their escape from Lagărul No 2.

Dressed in their mix of threadbare year-old suntans and Romanian fatigues, the Tidal Wave survivors stood out from the crowd. They were welcomed into the fold as celebrities.

"You guys were crazy to come in at low level in four-engine bombers," a 15th Air Force man said.

"The more I think about it," wrote Lieutenant Cavit in his diary later, "I expect maybe 'insane' was the right answer."

The 15th Air Force had flown in an OSS team, led by a colonel, to coordinate the evacuation. (The OSS was the forerunner of the CIA.) The team brought radio gear to establish a communications link with Italy, and even a cameraman to record what was shaping up to be the largest POW rescue ever attempted. Just a day earlier, Paris had been liberated. Could the Allies pull off another victory here, in the Mediterranean?

There was just one problem. Whether because of atmospheric distortion or mechanical failure, none of the OSS radios worked. There was no way to reach Italy. The result was a worst-case scenario: Every POW was here for extraction, but the OSS couldn't trigger the airlift. No one knew when—or if—the planes were coming.

It was as if the gods of Olympus were trying to foil them again, plotting to keep them held fast to the earth. Desperately, Ernie wanted to leave. This was the last crucial step in the men's journey from Lagărul No. 2. They had survived the wilderness, dodged a potential German death squad, and smuggled themselves under tarps through a hostile checkpoint.

They were so close.

But now they were stranded on an airfield with every POW in Romania, presenting the Germans with a golden opportunity to target them.

"Who knew what reserves the Germans might hurl into the battle from

Hungary or from the northern Mediterranean seaboard?" worried one Timisul POW. Here they were, caught in "the jigsaw of war."

"Would the pieces close around us before there was time to get out?"

IT STARTED WITH A glance. An American POW admired a Romanian pilot's fancy dress uniform, navy blue and crisply tailored, with ornate metal wings on his chest in the shape of an eagle. By contrast, American wings were plain pewter.

"Wanna trade?"

A memento from an American? The Romanian pilot didn't hesitate.

The idea spread like wildfire. Across the lawn in front of the flight school, American and Romanian fliers swapped wings, patches, and rank insignia. Romanian paratroopers stationed on the field saw what was happening and disappeared. They returned with arms full of war loot seized from the Germans. Thus "they started a great fair," a Romanian observer noted, "a kind of exchange in nature of insignia, caps, guns, belts, in a word, everything we can imagine."

Britt murmured aloud that he wanted a souvenir from Romania.

Ernie volunteered to go with him.

Britt was surprised. Ernie was not normally the nostalgic type. But Ernie was curious to see what all the fuss was about. Bob and Al tagged along.

All around them, POWs bartered for Wehrmacht helmets, Lugers, MP 40s, Luftwaffe caps, SS caps, and even a Kriegsmarine admiral's hat with a black brim.

A Romanian fighter pilot in full dress uniform, with a wide crush cap tilted just so, proudly crossed paths with the officers of *Chattanooga Choo Choo.* Ernie had lost his wings and rank insignia when he was first captured, but he had Romanian currency. Fistfuls of it. The smiling Romanian peeled the crush cap off his head and sold it to Ernie on the spot.

Britt came back to his friends dangling a German Iron Cross with a swastika in the center. It was for his little brother, Teddy.

Bob approved. Kid's gonna love it.

Crush cap in hand, Ernie looked at the exchange. All around him, American fliers bartered with Romanian fliers, both sides smiling and backslapping like old friends. Just two weeks ago, the same guys were trying to kill each other.

Being enemies is a choice.

AS THE MINUTES DRAGGED on, all eyes turned to the sky. The sun grew hot, so some of the Timisul POWs sought shelter in the shade beneath the wing of a derelict German Heinkel bomber.

"Had something gone wrong?" one of the Brits wondered as he took a seat. "Were the planes still coming?"

The OSS men wondered the same. Stepping out from their command post in the flight school hangar, they craned their necks to the sky, trying to project confidence, but their eyes betrayed unease. Not only were their radios down, but word had also reached them that the Soviet Red Army, closing in from the east, had arrived sooner than expected. Their advance elements were already rolling into the northern outskirts of Bucharest. This raised another concern in the OSS ranks. If the Soviets could get their hands on the POWs, they might try to intern them under the guise of "offering protection," but then take them back to the USSR to use as bargaining chips after the war.

The POWs didn't know the full extent of the danger they were in. The OSS wasn't about to inform them and spread fear unless absolutely necessary.

The OSS commander had notified his Soviet counterpart "and told him about the US evacuation plans." The Red Army officer had "agreed to inform the Red Air Force."

But that was no guarantee Moscow wouldn't interfere.

AROUND 9:45 A.M., an unmistakable growl shook the sky, signifying the arrival of approaching aircraft. Ernie and the other POWs looked west. The sound built, rising like a wave.

Suddenly, in a silver blur, a lone P-51 Mustang burst into sight at treetop level. Coming from the direction of Italy, it streaked across the field with a whistling whine, rocking its wings in greeting. Its nose was red. On the tail, a high-visibility black and yellow checkerboard gleamed, the markings of the 325th Fighter Group. A 15th Air Force plane! As it reached the midpoint of the runway, the pilot executed a "daring low-altitude" victory roll at just fifty feet above the ground.

The downed fighter pilots among the POWs were astounded. Who was this pilot? He could fly the hell out of that thing.

Ernie was intrigued and excited. Something was happening. Maybe something big.

But the show wasn't over. Hot on the Mustang's heels came more P-51s, flying in four-ship flights.

"Within moments, formation after formation of P-51s made low, high-speed passes across the field—as knights of the air charging with the unique violence that only great speed can impart," recalled a POW. The crowd of airmen erupted in celebration. "The roar of engines was all but lost in the sound of voices cheering, driven beyond exhilaration by the thrilling sight."

The additional American fighters had red noses, gleaming silver bodies, and vibrant red candy-striped tails. They were from the 31st Fighter Group—the same unit as Lieutenant Jack Williams, who stood on the ground, waving at his fellow flyboys and carrying the ring the king had entrusted to him.

Mustangs kept ripping past, one flight after another with a throaty growl, making high-speed passes.*

"What a feeling to see those planes!" remembered one POW.

Another swore that "all the fighter planes in Italy" were here.

Their presence in the airspace was no accident. This lethal fighting force was here to provide cover for the impending airlift. Meanwhile, the pilot of the checker-tail Mustang pulled into a climbing left turn, then "dropped his gear, held a tight pattern, and greased the ship onto the grass field."

But there was something odd about it all.

Why was that checker-tail Mustang leading P-51s from a different fighter group?

ON THE GROUND AT Popești, the checker-tail Mustang taxied past Ernie and the POWs, while other P-51s formed a circuit and made thrilling high-speed runs over the field. The fighter's name, *Sweet Clara II,* was scrolled along the engine cowling. Just behind it stood the nose art of a yawning blond pinup girl, set in a pale blue circle. The engine sputtered softly, almost idling, as the pilot looked left and right, checking his path.

* High above the field, more P-51s of the 31st Fighter Group joined up on the patrolling Romanian '109s. "I pulled up next to some and waggled my wings," a Mustang squadron commander remembered. "They waggled back. A few days ago there would have been a bang-up scrap instead." The two sides had something in common: They were part of a war none of them asked for. The new allies began hunting for German aircraft together.

Ernie noticed something curious. At the controls sat a pilot with a simple headset over black hair slicked back from the V of a widow's peak. He was calm, intensely focused, dressed in a beige uniform shirt, not American, with epaulets. He looked foreign, too, with deeply tanned skin.

A Romanian in a P-51?

At the time, it didn't register to Ernie who he was seeing.

THE CHECKER-TAIL MUSTANG TAXIED up and stopped in front of an astonished Romanian ground crew.

One American POW's eyes strayed from the spectacle of the Mustangs' passes. Lieutenant William Cubbins, a B-24 pilot, looked over his shoulder just in time. "I almost missed seeing the pilot of the ship that made the daring low-altitude roll kill his engine and climb out," he recalled.

It was him, the Romanian pilot everyone was talking about. "It was Cantacuzino."

Standing on the wing, with sleeves rolled up, Buzz reached into the cockpit and removed his MP 40 submachine gun, then climbed down. He had

Buzz exits the cockpit of *Sweet Clara II*

returned to Romania in the hot rod of the skies, the same aircraft he had yearned to fly since his battle with the Mustangs in June. His reserved nature hid his pure delight.

The Romanian ground crewmen and dignitaries were amazed to see him at the controls of the Allies' best fighter. They converged around him and welcomed him back from Italy.

"In my life, I've never seen so many generals in one place," Buzz told a comrade.

His transformation was complete. He'd gone from shooting down Americans to flying for them. But how?

Luck—good or bad, depending on one's perspective—had played a part in how he wound up in a Mustang. Back in Italy, while Buzz and Gunn were briefing the American brass, the base commanders at San Giovanni had to rope off the American Messerschmitt because too many curious men, fliers and non-fliers alike, were crowding around for "their first close-up view of an Me109."

"What a tiny little airplane it is!" one man exclaimed.

When Buzz returned, the young bomber pilots bombarded the prince with requests to fly it. Buzz had reservations. He still needed the Messerschmitt to get back to Romania for the airlift. But he also was their guest, and wanted to avoid reproach. So, at last, he said yes.

But Buzz had forgotten one thing. These men flew bombers, not fighters. The first one crashed the '109 on takeoff. He had to be carried away. The plane was nearly totaled.

"I felt crushed, seeing that some kids were damaging my plane, seeing my mission rendered futile," Buzz later told a fellow pilot.

How was he going to return for the airlift?

Embarrassed by the mishap, the American brass offered a potential solution: What if we loan him a P-51?

But could the prince handle the hot rod of the skies?

A pair of Mustangs were flown in, and the prince was given a checkout. When Buzz first sat in the cockpit, Lieutenant Walter Goehausen, an American double ace, gave Buzz an overview of his new ride. "What do you know about the Mustang?" Goehausen asked.

"I've shot down two of them," Buzz said.

Goehausen's eyes went wide.

When the American told Buzz the landing approach airspeed he'd need to use, Buzz surprised him again. "One hundred twenty miles per hour?" he mused. "Hmm, that is one-ninety kilometers." He had converted the speed from imperial to metric in his head.

When it was time to take off, Colonel Gunn and a flock of pilots gathered at the end of the runway to see Buzz fly. He was supposed to make one lap of the field and land, safe and easy.

Instead, Buzz gave a flying display that "rolled their socks down." Launching down the runway, he lifted off, rolled the Mustang on its back with the wheels still down, then pushed forward on the stick, making an inverted climb out, before finally completing the roll and leveling out.

He "wrung it out briefly," recalled Lieutenant Robert Goebel, a P-51 pilot, "and then landed the Mustang as if he had flown it all his life."

Buzz opened the canopy and called to the astonished Americans: "No wonder you shoot down so many German planes in a swell ship like this!"

The brass was sold. Orders were cut, and to Buzz's "great joy," they loaned him a Mustang.

"As for Capt. Cantacuzino," Gunn later wrote, "he gave up his Me-109, and we sent him home again happy in a P-51."

The twist?

The plane he'd been assigned belonged to the 325th Fighter Group, the same unit he had battled earlier when he'd shot down—and spared—pilot "Mac" MacDonald.

AT POPEȘTI, THERE WAS no time for Buzz to enjoy the acclaim. While his new American comrades and his old friends from the 9th Fighter Group provided an aerial umbrella overhead, Buzz made his way to the OSS team by the hangar. His arrival had triggered the airlift, code-named Operation Reunion, a mission that would span the entire Mediterranean.

Right at that moment, 252 American fighters were aloft, all part of the plan to bring the POWs home. While the 31st Fighter Group held the airspace above Popești, another forty-four Mustangs strafed the nearest German airfield, clearing the way for the extraction. A further ninety-seven American fighters were hammering Luftwaffe bases in neighboring Hungary, keeping the enemy distracted there.

As a result, the skies over Bucharest were empty, at least for now. Time was of the essence.

The OSS men were glad to see Buzz, who greeted them with a handshake before telling them to fire flares, the signal to begin the next stage of the operation. The OSS men were thankful. They hadn't come all this way for nothing.

Buzz couldn't linger. There was still work to be done, and the war wasn't waiting. He had a fighter group to lead. If the Americans needed him, they knew where to find him. With a final wave to the men at Popești, he turned and walked away.

Behind him, the OSS colonel stepped forward, raised a flare gun, and fired two bright streaks into the morning sky, setting the next phase of Operation Reunion in motion.

MOMENTS LATER, A LOUD droning sound from the sky announced the arrival of more American planes.

Ernie, Bob, and the others shielded their eyes and looked up to five thousand feet as the first of thirty-six silver B-17s of the 2nd and 97th Bomb Groups thundered overhead. Known as the Flying Fortress, the streamlined, four-engine B-17 was born of the art deco era, designed with an eye for beauty as much as it was for taking punishment. And these were the latest G models, with chin turrets. Beneath the roar of engines, an old debate resurfaced. There'd always been a rivalry between B-24 pilots and B-17 pilots over which plane was truly the better ship.

Bob liked to insist B-17s were "overrated." And B-17 pilots were known to joke that "they didn't care whether they had friendly fighter support on missions, as long as the B-24s went along. If the B-24s went, they would draw all the Nazi fighter attacks."

"But that day," Britt recalled, "the B-17s looked great to us."

The bombers would serve as transports. They were here to bring the men home. POWs began celebrating, "laughing and congratulating each other as only men who have found release from imminent danger can."

"Childishly I repeated to myself, 'I made it! I made it!'" remembered one airman, Sergeant Bill Fili.

In a rapid-fire sequence, bombers peeled off and began landing on the bumpy strip. Sunlight sparkled from their wide wings. Balloon tires bounced. It took a moment to sink in for Ernie. *We're actually going home.*

After more than a year of constant worry, fear, and outright danger, Ernie felt the weight begin to lift. Thirteen months in captivity, and now, finally, it was happening. They were leaving Romania.

Ernie and the crew knew their success didn't rest solely on the wings of American aircraft. As they watched the planes land, they remembered how thirteen months earlier, on August 1, 1943, Ernie, Al, and Medeiros had been imprisoned in a moldy cistern. Britt was trapped in the metal coffin of his smashed-up plane. Bob was already in German hands.

Now they were on the verge of freedom. Not by ingenuity. Not by the favor of Olympus.

They had Princess Catherine to thank.

She rescued them. Adopted them. Steadied them through the toughest year of their lives. They wouldn't have been standing there without her, or without a few unlikely allies from the other side: a twenty-two-year-old king who'd set them free, and a daring Romanian ace.

Now they were going home, back to their mothers and fathers and sisters and brothers, just as the princess had always intended.

Sporadically, their eyes swept the crowd; they longed to see her come bounding forward with that energetic step, to hear her voice again: "Hello, boys!" Periodically, they glanced toward the airport entrance, half expecting her Chevy to roar through the gate. Earlier, Britt had "rushed around asking questions" of the high-altitude boys—had anyone seen her?

But the princess had bigger worries: She couldn't leave her orphans, not with the Red Army closing in.

The men were heading home with only one regret. They never got to say goodbye or thank her for all she'd done for them. None of them had imagined it would end like this—yet it had. That was war, Ernie had to remind himself. Life didn't always have a storybook ending, even when it involved a princess.

THE OSS COLONEL WAVED the POWs forward to the grass airstrip and shouted, "Soon as your plane lands, climb aboard on the double. Don't sit on the ground waiting for Jerry!"

The Tidal Wave survivors, who'd been prisoners the longest, had been selected to go out in the early plane loads. Ernie and others hustled to prearranged spots along the perimeter of the track. They formed into twenty-man groups spaced a hundred feet apart. The planes would be loaded rapidly. No delays. The first bombers pulled up, taxiing on two engines to keep the dust down. Ernie's group would load after these.

"And here they were, beautiful sun-washed birds that rolled up through the dancing haze to where we were waiting," wrote one of the Timisul men. "This was the magic carpet of our dreams."

The first groups sprinted out and scrambled aboard. A flight engineer in his white parachute harness stood by the rear door in the tail section of each plane. He shook hands with as many men as he could, quickly welcoming the Americans, Englishmen, "and one Romanian stowaway with a dubious lean on an American citizenship."

The former prisoners were packed in like happy sardines. There were no parachutes. But the 15th Air Force planners had made sure the POWs wouldn't need them. They'd positioned more fighter groups—including the 325th Checkertail Clan and 332nd Red Tails, the Tuskegee Airmen—along the route to provide fighter cover all the way to Italy.

The first pilots fired up the engines and taxied out to their takeoff positions, while other planes quickly landed to take their place.

"The Americans weren't messing around," noted one of the Brits.

"You guys better get in fast," a senior POW shouted to the Timisul POWs over the idling engines. "You never know when some Kraut might pop up and put you in the bag again."

He didn't have to remind them twice.

The crew of *Chattanooga Choo Choo* grabbed their gear and dashed for the plane. Ernie and Bob were the last to leave. Their men were already ahead, and the sight of them moving toward the B-17 as one brought a quiet surge of relief and accomplishment. They knew one shadow lingered, laid to rest in the princess's family plot, his name etched in their minds. Every survivor of the crash on August 1, 1943—except one—was going home.

Frank Kees remained behind.

Now, on the crowded Romanian airfield, Ernie tucked his small bundle under his arm. In his threadbare suntan shirt and Romanian fatigue trousers, still streaked and torn from his wilderness escape, Ernie—the guy who had once prided himself on never having a hair out of place—looked like a vagabond. But he also wasn't the same Ernie Poulson who had taken off from Benghazi. He slapped his newly acquired Romanian fighter pilot's crush cap onto his blond hair and dashed toward the bomber with Bob.

The engines were already coughing to life as the pilot fired them up for takeoff. The propellers turned, caught, and settled into a steady roar. Waiting at the tail door, the flight engineer beamed with pride as he counted each POW, "ready to call the pilot and tell him we were aboard."

When he reached the door, Ernie gave the sergeant a grateful nod before he ducked and stepped aboard.

AFTER A THREE-HOUR AND forty-five-minute flight, the B-17 was finally back on solid ground. Ernie, Britt, and Al crowded around one of the bomber's waist windows. They stooped, straining to see out the window, squinting into the steamy Italian sunlight as the bomber taxied across Bari airfield, a sunbaked American base ringed by groves of olive trees. Behind them, a few of their crew members leaned in for a glimpse.

On the floor, Bob reclined with a copy of *Stars and Stripes* spread across his knees, devouring the pages as if someone might snatch the paper away from him. He looked like a professor in the sweater vest he'd picked up in Pietroșița. The B-17 crews had brought back issues of *Stars and Stripes, Yank,* and other magazines—a small gift for the men who'd missed more than a year of news from the home front.

Ernie pointed out the window and waved Bob over, shouting above the roar of the engines: "Take a look!"

Bob pressed in beside him. "Oh boy," he murmured.

As the plane pulled up parallel to the base headquarters, the men could see an unexpected crowd. Across the pierced-steel taxiway, a hero's welcome awaited. A throng of "equally excited news photographers, war correspondents, interrogators, high-ranking officers, and surprised bystanders" packed the edge of the tarmac. Among the officers in tent-shaped caps and green-lensed sunglasses stood Colonel Gunn, grinning alongside General Nathan Twining, the pensive, square-jawed commander of the 15th Air Force. A movie crew waited, nearby with a camera perched in the back of a weapons carrier and a boom mic dangling overhead.

They were a sensation—the largest group of rescued POWs yet. And the PR men were especially keen to spotlight the 110 survivors of the daring low-level raid that had captured America's imagination: the flyboys who had struck Hitler's Gas Station.*

In the background, trucks idled, ready to carry the freed airmen to a tent city nestled among the olive trees and enclosed by low stone walls. Waiting for the returnees were hot showers with strong soap, crisp new suntan uniforms, "swell" beds, plates piled high with "fantastic" American food—and

* To view the actual WWII film footage of Operation Reunion—including Buzz's P-51 flyby over Popești, the arrival of the B-17s, and even cameos by Colonel Gunn and Bob O'Reilly—visit my website, AdamMakos.com.

the best news of all: After a brief return to their units in Italy or England, they'd be heading home.

The bomber swung right, brakes squealing, came to a stop, and parked. The engines revved hard for a moment, then wound down, conked, and fell silent.

The rear door opened by the tail, and Ernie and the crew made the short leap down onto the dirt apron. Ernie blinked against the glare. Bob, Britt, and Al scanned their surroundings, wide-eyed and disbelieving. They'd made it. They were really here.

On either side of them, a neat line of gleaming B-17s stood wingtip to wingtip, each disgorging its human cargo.

Newly repatriated POWs stream onto Bari airfield

Under the wing, Medeiros, Rurak, Riffle, and the rest of the crew laughed, shouted, and stumbled forward, merging with the waves of jubilant POWs streaming by on the taxiway, many still wearing their souvenir German caps and helmets, all sharing the same wide, grateful grin as they were "immediately swept into a whirl" of the waiting reception.

Ernie headed the other direction. There was something he wanted to do. He broke from his friends and walked to the quiet space behind the tail. There, he dropped his bundle and sank to his knees. Before the raid, Ernie had vowed to Britt, "If only one plane makes it back, we'll be on it." He'd never imagined it would take this long, but now, they were finally here. Ernie bent forward and kissed the dry, dusty soil. It felt like something straight out of a movie, but he didn't care. He was overcome by the magnitude of the airlift, by the courage of the pilots who had made it possible, and by the sheer, humbling feeling of freedom.

Ernie's friends saw him and traded quiet grins. Emotional? Ernie? Now, they'd seen everything. When he came back to join them, the officers of the *Chattanooga Choo Choo* were pretending not to have noticed.

"Now, where were we?" Ernie said.

Bob threw an arm around his shoulder. Together, they walked out from under the wing and into the celebration.

"How sweet it was," Ernie would later write, "to kiss the ground in Allied-held Italy."

After thirteen months in captivity, they were back.

CHAPTER 49

THE RED INVASION

AROUND THE SAME TIME
South of Ploesti

SHE HAD TO GET TO BUCHAREST.

In the front passenger seat of her sleek 1939 Chevrolet business coupe, Princess Catherine leaned close to the windscreen and searched the sunlit sky for airplanes. At the wheel beside her, the chauffeur kept his foot on the gas as they sped down the two-lane highway toward the capital.

She'd learned of the airlift—"her boys" were leaving from Popești. Now she needed to reach the airfield, see them off, wish them well, and close the book on the unforgettable chapter they shared.

But could she reach the airfield in time?

Her friends in the capital had warned her to be careful. The Soviets were already here, on the northern outskirts, possibly between her and the airfield. And they were moving fast.

The Red Army's speed was new. When Stalin had first learned of King Michael's revolt and his new government, "hellbent on preparing for free elections," he'd deliberately slowed the Red Army's march into Romania. Stalin figured the Germans would crush the democratic uprising, saving him the trouble.

But this was no ordinary uprising. Michael believed the success of the coup had "God's hand" in it. By all logic, the uprising should have failed before it began. "Only, we had the luck to finish them [the Germans] ourselves, without them," King Michael recalled. "And that disturbed them very much."

Now the Red Army was racing forward, eager to make up for lost time. The USSR had its sights set on Bucharest "with a directive to eliminate Romanian nationalists, and to forestall Anglo-American intervention."

That was exactly what the princess had feared all along. She told her friends: "When they get here, we'll pray that we are back under the [Americans'] bombs again."*

THE CHAUFFEUR LET OFF the gas. Princess Catherine glanced ahead. The highway was blocked by armed soldiers clad in mustard brown uniforms and oddly shaped green helmets.

The rumors were true. The Red Army was here.

The princess instructed her chauffeur to keep driving. Slowly. Maybe the soldiers would move aside. Instead, a Soviet officer suddenly stepped into view and flagged them down. He approached the driver's side, and the chauffeur rolled down his window.

Speaking Romanian, "the officer instructed her chauffeur to drive to his command post." He circled the car, opened the passenger door, and took a seat next to the princess. Scarily close.

Drive.

When they arrived at the command post, a Romanian estate, a Red Army colonel came out "beaming" at the sight of the shining American car. "With him was a booted Red Army woman," her "grimy campaign uniform" half concealed beneath a looted civilian blouse. The Soviets had bragged they were "bringing in a million troops." These were just the early arrivals. The Romanian-speaking officer presented the prize to his superior.

In Bucharest, a wave of looting would soon be under way, and the Romanians would learn a new word: "Davai," Russian for "Give me." "Davai ceas. Davai palton": "Give me the watch. Give me the coat."

The demand was clear: Davai masina. *Give me the car.*

The colonel motioned for the princess and her chauffeur to exit the car and leave the keys. The princess turned to the Romanian-speaking officer who could translate. She wasn't going to surrender without a fight.

"Tell him this car is used on vital social services!"

* For the time being, many Romanians clung to a fragile hope that somehow, a Communist occupation might be kept at bay. "The Romanians do not want the Russians to take over their country and, as a preventative to such a move, strongly desire that either America—or British forces—preferably American, maintain a commission or even a standing army in Romania," noted the Operation Reunion after-action report.

The Russian colonel "reflected on the term, 'social services,' undecided what to do." He offered a compromise: a trade.

The colonel instructed his troops to give her "a rusty 1926 Chrysler sitting in the courtyard." "The car had no hood, the radiator was held on by a wire," wrote a reporter. "Princess Caradja's chauffeur was more upset to see the Chevrolet go than she was."

"My car!" he wailed. "My whitewall tires!"

"Shut up and make it run," the princess hissed.

The Soviets were the law in Romania now. Two years later, in 1946, they would shoot Antonescu just to prove the point.

Catherine retrieved her driving papers from the Chevrolet's glove box, then opened the trunk. Inside were several parcels of clothing intended for orphans. She transferred them to the antiquated wreck, then went back for her spare tire components. Most important was the inner tube. Due to wartime rubber shortages, inner tubes were hard to come by.

"She was fishing in the trunk for an inner tube when the Russian colonel noticed it and cuffed her across the face."

The princess reeled from the blow, then steadied herself. She turned toward him, her voice calm but steely. "No harm in trying."

The old car had no starter. What was she supposed to do now? The Romanian-speaking officer had the answer: "The Russian Army will start it for you."

The princess nodded to her shaken driver and said, "Get in."

Russian soldiers gathered behind the Chrysler and tried to push-start it, but the motor wouldn't catch. After a pause, the Russian colonel gave them permission to use his new Chevrolet to jumpstart the old car. The old Chrysler rumbled to life with a cough of exhaust.

The princess and her chauffeur climbed in and pulled away.

THE OLD CAR LURCHED and rattled down the road, but every minute brought them closer to Popești and her boys. Ahead, a Russian tank column loomed into view.

This was bad news.

The princess thought fast. Even if they bypassed the enemy vehicles, more Reds would follow. She had a car for now. On the other side, she and the chauffeur would probably be walking.

There was no clear passage to the capital. Too many Soviet soldiers lay between her and the Americans. It was too dangerous. The princess made a gut-wrenching decision and told her chauffeur to exit the highway. There would be no reaching Popești now.

After driving "through the backwoods and cornfields," the old Chrysler pulled up at the nearest village. The chauffeur brought the wreck to a halt, and Catherine stepped out. They could take refuge here until the dust had settled.

A SOUND CAUGHT HER ears. A droning noise filtering down to earth. The princess looked up. High above, formations of silver B-17s were climbing in the direction of Italy, leaving the capital behind.

"I watched with tears in my eyes as the American planes flew overhead, taking my boys to their homes and freedom," she recalled.

She was solaced by knowing that her boys would be safe, but her joy was tempered by sadness. On one hand, the airlift would be a rousing victory for the Americans. Over the course of three days, 401 aircraft would fly them all out, whisking 1,162 POWs to safety "from under the noses of the Russians."

But she "did not get to say goodbye to even one of the Americans."

Back when she had nursed Britt to health after his crash, they'd talked of the future.

"He told me of his family, his friends, his ambitions and plans. What plans!" Catherine recalled. "After the war was over, he was going to arrange for me to visit his family. He told me while I was in America, he would present me to the president!"

Now that dream had vanished with the dissipating vapor trails of the American planes. As for her boys, she had no hope "to see any of them again."

For the princess, Romania's new reality was particularly chilling. A glance at the old wreck, sitting in place of her cherished car, spoke volumes.

Her royal title, once used to protect the POWs, now placed her squarely in the Communists' crosshairs. Their new "liberators" had labeled the nobility and anyone with means as persons "of unhealthy social origin." This designation gave them grounds to dismantle the aristocracy, usually through violence.

It didn't matter that Romania was now allied with the United States, or that the country was also technically allied with the USSR. The "Red Invasion" was here, and that could mean only one thing for a person of noble birth.

She was the prisoner now.

CHAPTER 50

NOTHING LEFT TO LOSE

EIGHT YEARS LATER, DECEMBER 1951

The Danube waterfront

ON A COLD WINTER DAY, PRINCESS CATHERINE, DRESSED IN A WORN-OUT coat, made her way to the seedy waterfront south of Bucharest at Giurgiu, where barges were docked along the Danube River. By all appearances, it was business as usual in the Soviet bloc.

She carried a bag and moved quickly, hugging herself against the cold. Now fifty-nine, the princess was tired and thin, and the bounce was missing from her step. The ensuing years had taken a heavy toll.

The theft of her cherished car had been only the start.

The Soviets moved quickly, expelling the western Allies and silencing dissent, until only one man still stood in the way of Stalin's complete take-over of Romania.

King Michael.

But in November 1947, the Communists found their opening. Michael had traveled to England for the wedding of Princess Elizabeth. There, at his hotel, he met Princess Anne of Bourbon-Parma—a vivacious twenty-four-year-old brunette who, some said, resembled Judy Garland. She wasn't your typical royal. During the war, when her family had taken refuge in the United States, Anne had done the unexpected: She returned to war-torn Europe and in 1943 enlisted "as an ambulance driver in the Free French army." Her service carried her from North Africa to Italy, and then onward, "following the Allied advance" into Germany. She was decorated, too—a holder of the Croix de Guerre.

After the wedding, Michael flew his aunt and mother back to Switzerland in his Beechcraft. He invited Anne to come along with them. There, "within days," he proposed. She said yes.

Michael returned to Romania, newly engaged. And the Communists didn't like that one bit. The Soviet-backed prime minister, Petru Groza—who held power only thanks to a rigged election—summoned the young king to the palace to discuss a "family problem." Using Michael's new fiancée as a pretext, Groza put it plainly: "You have to abdicate." The last thing the Communists wanted was a royal dynasty. On Michael's desk lay the papers of abdication and a pen. He was told to sign them "and leave the country."

If he refused? Groza said he would "order the execution of about 1,000 pro-monarchy supporters, most of them students," already under arrest for having attended anti-Communist rallies.

"What are you supposed to do in a situation like that?" Michael later said.

In the swipe of a pen, he surrendered his crown and went into exile, leaving behind millions of Romanians "grieving and unable to recover from the shock."

With King Michael—the very face of Romanian nobility—gone, no one was safe.

As Princess Catherine had feared, the Communists took everything from her. First, it was her charitable foundation. They seized the buildings, the land, even the children, declaring everything "property of the state." St. Catherine's Crib was redesignated Children's House Number One.

Next, they claimed her home and land at Nedelea, cutting off her regular sources of income. "I was sent packing from my estate with only what I had on my back," she recalled. After moving to Bucharest, Catherine barely subsisted. "I sold my watch, then my gold fountain pen. I sold until there was no more to sell. Then I sold English lessons."

Finally, the limited diet and constant stress took their toll on her health. She lost half her weight, withering to ninety-five pounds. In time, her marriage formally ended, and her only daughter fled to France in 1948. She was hopelessly alone.

"What did I have to lose—or live for?" Catherine remembered thinking. "I had to find a reason."

Her friends, the ones who dared to stay in touch, urged her to escape.

The Communists were at war with her class, and it was only a matter of time before they would make her disappear, too.

"Get out and tell people what is happening here," they pleaded with her.

If anyone could survive outside Romania, it was Princess Catherine. She spoke English. She had helped the Allies during the war. And besides, her cousin Buzz had already fled the country.

The Communists had taken everything from him, too. Stripped of his five estates and allowed to keep just "100 hectares" of land, he was left with only one "stable source of income": the state airline, where he found work again.

Before long, the regime pressed him into service as chief pilot for Ana Pauker, the dreaded Communist foreign minister. Between his regular routes, Buzz dutifully flew the minister to Moscow and back.

Then, in August 1947, a scandal swept Bucharest.

Buzz had left his apartment—the one he shared with Nadia, whom he'd married in 1945—and was now living out of the Athénée Palace Hotel. "Offended and humiliated" by the prince, Nadia applied for a travel permit to Paris, where her mother lived. The permit was granted.

Nadia left Romania a woman who had been "abandoned" by her husband.

Except it was all an act—events, as one account put it, "worthy of a crime film." There had been no feud. Working quietly behind the scenes, Buzz had helped Nadia defect. And before the secret police could dig deeper into his loyalties, he beat them to the punch.

Because he was deemed a flight risk, the prince was barred from flying international routes except on orders of the Communists; but in January 1948 "an opportunity arose." The airline needed a pilot to fly to Milan; no one else was available.

The Communists turned to Buzz. *Be on your best behavior.*

On the night of January 21, 1948, Buzz landed in Milan. At 11:25 P.M., he sent a telegram to the state airline:

"In response to the treatment you have applied to me, please consider me resigning —Constantin Cantacuzino."

Before catching a train to Paris and his long-awaited reunion with Nadia, he left a note on the hotel nightstand for his copilot: The plane is all yours.

Princess Catherine's cousin had made it out—and that meant something.

PRINCESS CATHERINE FOUND HERSELF facing the same dilemma as the American POWs had all those years ago. Catherine had always discouraged Ernie, Bob, Britt, and their friends from escaping, insisting, "It's safer to stay put." But had she been wrong to think that? Life had come full circle, and she finally understood their hunger for freedom.

Catherine had never considered fleeing, not with her three thousand orphans to care for—"I was not going to run out on the children," she recalled. But after the orphanage was seized, she had "no intention of succumbing to a hopeless situation."

So she contacted her daughter in France, who steered her to the French secret service operation in the Soviet bloc. Working through the underground, the princess set a plan in motion to escape.

ON THIS COLD WINTER'S day, Catherine asked around at the waterfront for ship #6198. The rough-and-tumble Romanian dockworkers were surprised. A woman, here, alone? But they shrugged and pointed to a long, squat tow barge with an enclosed helm, the control station where the captain steered the ship. A line of seven barges stretched behind the tow vessel, each carrying gasoline tanks the size of small trucks.

She located Florea Ardeleanu, the captain, a smuggler working clandestinely for the French secret service. Already they had contacted him and tasked him with getting her out of Romania. The usual border crossings were heavily patrolled, so he would attempt to smuggle her out on the Danube using his barge.

Although the French had agreed to help the princess, nothing came for free. Catherine needed to gather a selection of the latest identity papers issued by the Romanian Communists to former military officers, rural farmers, and even fallen members of the nobility. The French intended to use the documents as templates for forgeries.

The barge captain asked if she had what the French required. Catherine confirmed that she did.

Satisfied, the captain laid out his plan. It would be freezing on the river, and the journey could take five weeks or longer. But the barge had a small cabin where she could hide, and if he could get her to Vienna alive, the French would take over from there.

Catherine nodded, she knew the danger.

There was one more particularly sensitive topic the captain needed to address. Capture by the Communists meant a fate worse than death.

"Madame," he said. "I do not like the way the Russians question people. If we are caught, I am going to shoot myself. Would you like me to shoot you first?"

It was her last chance to retreat, but Princess Catherine wasn't running from fear. She leaned in close and whispered in a low voice: "I would be most grateful to you if you would."

The barge captain admired her fighting spirit.

Well, then. Welcome aboard.

CHAPTER 51

ESCAPEES

NEARLY FOUR YEARS LATER, AUTUMN 1955

Paris

WEARING THE CRISP BLUE UNIFORM OF THE U.S. AIR FORCE, ERNIE walked out the front door of NATO headquarters in Paris, just a few blocks away from the Eiffel Tower. It was lunchtime, and his stride was hurried as he rushed across the street.

Ernie was a lieutenant colonel now and held a prestigious assignment in post-war Europe as chief of the budget branch for all of NATO. That shimmering destiny he'd imagined during his hardscrabble youth had become his reality. Ernie had come a long way since he kissed the ground in Italy.

After rejoining the 389th in England, Ernie was one of two men selected to brief the 8th Air Force leadership "on the low level raid, conditions in prison camp, and conditions of escape."* Once his duty was complete, he, Bob, Britt, and Al returned to the United States.

The first thing Ernie did was call his girlfriend, Helen. They'd only gone on about nine dates, but Ernie knew she was the one. He proposed over the phone. She said yes.

Ever since, they'd traveled the world together, following the arc of Ernie's rising career in the Air Force. From base to base and city to city, he soon reached one of the most trusted posts of the era, running his own office at

* When asked to rate the effectiveness of the low-level attack method employed during Tidal Wave, the air intelligence unit reported Ernie's response: "In the returnee's opinion, very successful. Although the loss rate was high, he feels the number of planes lost in the subsequent high-altitude bombings of Ploesti, considered with the comparative destructiveness of the two methods indicates the soundness of the low-level methods."

NATO. With Europe locked in the Cold War, it was arguably the most important organization of the time.

Overall, he liked his new assignment very much. He was picking up French quickly, enough to bond with the locals, and he still smoked cigarettes, a habit he didn't kick until the 1960s.

From time to time, he thought about the not-so-distant past. Ernie looked back with quiet pride at his World War II service. He had concluded that Tidal Wave "was the single most important raid of World War II." But he didn't talk about it at work. He led a team from eight different nations, but none of his staff knew that he'd been shot down at Ploesti or that he'd helped smuggle more than a hundred POWs out of a camp in Transylvania.

For his role in getting the Tidal Wave men to safety, Ernie had earned a special distinction, a title, a place in history, though he was the last person to seek it. A notation in his file under his POW timeline read: "Escapee." He and Lieutenant Snyder stood alone in that regard—the only American or British POWs to successfully escape from a Romanian POW camp in World War II, while the country still fought on the side of the Axis.

If the war ever came up in conversation, Ernie downplayed his contributions. The war belonged to a past chapter in a former life. But like it or not, his past was about to come rushing back.

AS ERNIE WALKED THROUGH the leaf-strewn streets of Paris, the scenery grew rougher and grimy. He wasn't spending his lunch break with Helen and their three children today. Instead, his path led him into one of the city's impoverished districts.

Inside a dingy apartment building, Ernie searched the numbers on the doors before finding the one he was looking for. He knocked. After a moment, the door opened.

There stood Princess Catherine.

She was sixty-two now, gaunt, with silver streaking her hair. But it was unmistakably her. She stared in disbelief. For one long beat, she simply looked at the man, as if trying to reconcile the present with the past. They hadn't seen each other in more than a decade.

Finally she said, "If you've come for your twenty dollars, I don't have it."

Ernie laughed. Her memory—and wit—hadn't dulled a bit.

The princess was overjoyed to see him. She embraced Ernie and invited him inside.

After V-J Day in 1945, Ernie and the officers of *Chattanooga Choo Choo* had received postcards from the princess, but she asked them not to write back. She was living under Communist rule by then, and it was too dangerous to have contact with anyone in the West. So Ernie kept silent, never putting her at risk, but he thought of her often. Years passed. When the Parisian press reported something about a princess-turned-refugee who'd escaped Romania and come to France, making it out with only her wedding ring, Ernie followed every lead until he finally tracked her down.

Now he was troubled to find Catherine living in a "rather destitute state," surviving on small fees from translation work. She downplayed her troubles, reminding him that even the roughest district of Paris was safer than where she'd come from. As for her new, trim appearance, "she joked about the Reds slimming her down." If only he had seen her back in Romania! "I was half and half," she said with a laugh. "Half here, and half gone."

Ernie was eager to learn about her flight to freedom. How had she slipped through the iron grip of the Soviet bloc? They had something in common that neither had asked for nor anticipated. They were escapees.

The princess told Ernie about her secret barge journey up the Danube. She had spent most of the icy voyage hiding in a small sleeping compartment in the bow of the ship. The space was just big enough for her to lie down, and there were only two small portholes. The barge captain—whom she'd nicknamed St. Peter, because "he opened the gates of Paradise for me"—covered the entrance with a locker, so agents of the regime making a snap inspection wouldn't know it was there.

For her, there was no turning back. After the Romanian Communists realized she fled, her name was added to the weekly fugitive list published in *România Liberă,* Bucharest's daily newspaper. Officially, she was not just a stowaway.

She was an enemy of the state.

She spent the journey huddled in an old sheepskin to keep warm. A deck of cards was all she had for company. And the most dangerous aspect of the trip was that the barge had to pass through three border crossings: into Hungary, then Czechoslovakia, and finally into Austria. At each checkpoint, Communist border guards came aboard and searched the vessel. She would need a better hiding place.

As they neared the first crossing, into Hungary, St. Peter came to her.

"Time to hide," he said in a hushed voice.

She followed him outside into the cold air and back to the large tanks of gasoline. One was half full of water, not fuel. The captain pried it open and motioned for her to climb inside, swiftly. Princess Catherine hesitated at the hatch. It was dark inside. The metal tank smelled of rust and gas. She couldn't believe she'd agreed to this.

The captain gave her a hand "and put her in the water tank." The princess found herself standing in frigid water above her waist. At the top of the chamber, a small, spongy shelf hung from the ceiling, with just a tiny space between the shelf and the top.

"It's an old sofa back," the captain said. "Close quarters but not too uncomfortable."

The princess waded over to the platform, hoisted herself up, and wriggled around until she lay flat on her back, her nose inches from the metal top. There was no room to sit upright; she was too close to the ceiling. Then came the truly terrifying part.

The captain opened a valve and pumped more water into the tank.

Breathless, the princess mentioned she couldn't swim. He assured her she wouldn't have to.

The water rose, inch by inch, until it nearly touched the platform. St. Peter wished her luck and closed the hatch. Everything turned pitch black. Princess Catherine was gripped by claustrophobia and panic. As the barge rocked on the river, the water in the tank sloshed, just beneath her. With her face near the tank's ceiling, and water just below, she fought the urge to move or scream. The platform swayed with every wave. If she fell off, she wouldn't be able to touch the bottom. She'd drown.

To steady her nerves, Princess Catherine began reciting a list of comforting words, familiar remembrances etched in her mind. They were the only solace she could still recall, the fragile thread that kept her from unraveling. She whispered these words "like a rosary to herself. Over and over."

When the barge pulled to the riverbank, she could hear the border guards clamber aboard. They shouted orders in Hungarian, inspecting the manifest. Then they began to shift about on the deck, intent in their search. She could hear them working their way along the tanks of gasoline, pounding each one with their fists. If ever they heard a hollow sound, they'd order the tank opened so they could inspect inside.

The pounding sounds came closer to the tank where the princess hid. They were just outside now. A fist pounded the steel wall. Moments ticked by. The princess's heart thudded so violently it felt like it might burst out of her chest. Would she be shot on sight or interrogated first? She remembered the captain's dark question. Did she want him to shoot her?

But the water swallowed the sound. The border guards kept going.

Soon, she could hear them scrape and shuffle off the boat. More orders were shouted in Hungarian. The barge pulled away from its mooring.

After a short while down the river, the hatch opened, releasing a flood of light over the princess. St. Peter, wearing a swimsuit, climbed into the tank and swam to her. She climbed onto his back, and he paddled her to the opening.

As the days passed and the barge traveled farther north, the winter weather grew colder. Twice more she climbed into the water tank to hide. Twice more she stared at the steel ceiling in terror, reciting the same thread of comforting words.

Finally, mercifully, after fifty-six "terrifying, uncomfortable, and cold" days on the Danube, the reassuring sight of the Vienna skyline appeared through the porthole of her cramped compartment under the bow. It was January 1952. She had made it. An open city, Vienna still had zones controlled by the Allies, including the French.

When she landed, the French secret service took over from the captain. The princess provided the agents with the identity papers she'd smuggled out for them. In return, they gave the princess fake papers and put her on a night train to the West.

ERNIE WAS STUNNED BY Catherine's account. Here she was, by some miracle, standing in front of him on her own two feet. The princess was still the same woman he remembered—"proud, intelligent, and energetic"—but it was difficult to see her alone and barely scraping by.

She deserved better. That was one of the reasons Ernie had sought her out. He wanted to repay her "in some small measure" for all she'd done for him. So he proposed an idea.

What if he could use his contacts at NATO to secure her residency with her boys in America?

Ernie had three years left in his current assignment. He couldn't leave

Paris to help her with the journey, but he knew Britt, Bob, and Al would take her in and help her get established. She'd have a new home in America and loyal friends wherever an ex-POW could be found. Would she consider relocating?

Princess Catherine could see it in Ernie's eyes. He wasn't just testing the waters. His offer was real. The reversal in roles wasn't lost on her, either.

And it all felt daunting. Just when she'd found some stability in France, he was asking her to uproot herself again, to give up everything for something unknown—a new country, a foreign culture, a life she hadn't imagined. It was the same dilemma she faced before her flight to freedom: Was it safer just to stay put?

It was a lot to take in, but Princess Catherine promised Ernie she'd think it over.

Now, how about a cup of tea?

CHAPTER 52

THE ANGEL OF PLOESTI

SEVERAL MONTHS LATER, EARLY DECEMBER 1955
***Aboard the SS* Nieuw Amsterdam**

THE PRINCESS SAT ALONE IN A WINDOWLESS CABIN ABOARD AN OCEAN liner, its hull groaning and pitching as it crossed the Atlantic. Rough December swells churned against the ship, making the ride dizzying and uncomfortable. But she had made the leap and taken Ernie up on his offer.

She was going to America.

Ernie had secured a one-year visitor's permit for Catherine. That would give her time to apply for permanent residency, if she chose to stay. First, she would try life in the new country and see what it felt like.

A glance at her surroundings on the ocean liner made it clear: This was not the degree of comfort one would expect for a princess's voyage. She had refused Ernie's offer to book her a first-class ticket to New York. After all, she still had her pride and she'd had enough of charity. Instead, she had booked passage in steerage, third class, the lowest of passenger accommodations. Her conditions were cramped. The air was stale, the lighting dim. But compared to her ride on the Danube, it felt like heaven. Albeit a bumpy one.

The princess would recall, "In the rough sea I was uncomfortable. Each time I mentioned the weather to the steward, his reply was, 'Madame, the sea is moderate.' I dreaded his estimate of a rough sea—it would be a hurricane!"

Before the princess left Paris, she granted an interview to "the most persistent" reporter from the International News Service. He'd been begging for the story of her escape from Romania, but she wouldn't talk about that—

not while the barge captain she'd nicknamed St. Peter was still working the waterways, smuggling others to freedom. "I wouldn't dare endanger somebody else's chance," she explained. Instead, she spoke about her upcoming journey to America to see "her boys." She was going on a mission, she said, to "call on as many as possible of the 110 fliers shot down during attacks on the Ploesti oil fields." She was particularly interested in visiting Texas, to see her "adopted son," Britt.

Catherine during her travel to New York

"How will you get there?" the reporter asked.

"On a Greyhound bus, of course," the princess said.

The reporter chuckled. He knew he had his story. But neither he nor the princess could imagine how much that one offhand comment would change.

MIDWAY ACROSS THE ATLANTIC, a steward located the princess in her steerage cabin and told her she was wanted on the bridge. A call had come through on the ship's radio for her. The princess tensed. A wireless transmission was serious. Was something wrong with her visa? Was someone in trouble? The steward couldn't say.

She arrived on the bridge of the sleek two-tone ship, its hull a blinding white above the black waterline. Two smokestacks rose like sentinels. Massive yet swift, the SS *Nieuw Amsterdam* was the pride of the Holland America line, their answer to England's *Queen Mary*.

The princess donned a radio headset and took the microphone. On the other end, a voice identified itself as that of a producer from NBC News.

Her interview in Paris, and the story that followed—"Princess to Turn Dream Into Reality"—had hit the news wires. The NBC producer had caught wind of it. A princess riding on a Greyhound bus? It was too good to make up.

That was why he was calling. He wanted her to appear on the *Today* show in New York. At the time, *Today* was America's most-watched morning program, drawing as many as five million viewers each day. Television was still new in 1955, but already more than half of all American households had a set glowing in their living room.

The princess wrinkled her brow. "I can't be there today," she said. "I'm still at sea."

The producer chuckled. He explained that *Today* was the name of the show. Filming could be done whenever she arrived in New York.

In that case, the princess agreed to appear. The NBC producer was overjoyed. He asked to speak to the captain of the ship. He had one more arrangement to make.

And just like that, the princess was upgraded to premier class, courtesy of the network. When she entered her new stateroom, sunlight streamed in the windows. The air was fresh and clear. A bouquet of flowers greeted her on the coffee table.

For the penniless refugee from Romania, things were looking up.

SEVERAL DAYS LATER, DECEMBER 13, 1955

WHEN THE PRINCESS STEPPED off the ship in New York harbor, NBC News had taken care of everything. A chauffeured limousine waited to whisk her away to a fancy hotel.

But the princess couldn't accept another gift; the network had already been so generous. Enough charity! She made her own arrangements and instructed the chauffeur to take her to 610 Lexington Avenue.

When they arrived, the chauffeur couldn't believe his eyes. A utilitarian nine-story building stood on the corner. Plain, practical, and unassuming.

The princess was staying at the YWCA.

Early the next morning, Princess Catherine took her seat on the set of the *Today* show at NBC Studios in Rockefeller Plaza. Large cameras rolled. Behind the scenes, voices dropped to a whisper. The "Quiet!" sign lit up.

On live television, against a backdrop of a map of the United States marked with time zones, she spoke with the host, Dave Garroway. They discussed her escape from Romania, although she left out the confidential details, and her vital wartime role in protecting American POWs. Ever since the ex-POWs had returned to Allied lines, they'd given her a new name: "The Angel of Ploesti."

"I'm eager to see my American boys," Catherine said. "As many of them as I can . . . they were all such really good boys."

Garroway smiled. He wore a suit with a bow tie and round glasses; his hair was thinning slightly at the temples. He spoke in the classic tone of the era, intelligent, emphatic, and reassuring. He "asked good questions to put me at ease," Catherine recalled.

The day before the broadcast, the show had aired archival footage taken from bombers during the actual Ploesti raid. It served as a sneak preview in the run-up to the princess's appearance, and it had an unexpected side effect: "This had alerted the ex-POWs to watch the program the next day."

As the cameras kept rolling, Garroway and Princess Catherine talked about what would be next for her. She said she hoped to do some speaking engagements in the United States to "tell of life today behind the Iron Curtain." She hadn't forgotten her responsibility to her friends back in Romania, who'd urged her to "get out and tell people what is happening here."

"I am lucky to be one of the few who made it," she explained.

Garroway glanced at his printed notes. "I understand you're heading for Houston to meet Richard Britt," he said.

It was true. Catherine said she was looking forward to spending Christmas with her "adopted son," the one she'd pulled from the wreckage of his plane during the war.

"It's been twelve years since he left your country," Garroway added. "Do you think you'll recognize him?"

"Oh, yes," the princess said. In fact, she kept a photo of him with her. As she searched her purse for Britt's photo, a door on the set opened.

Right on cue, a familiar figure walked out.

Britt.

He wore a smart charcoal suit with a black tie. In the past twelve years, he'd grayed around the ears. The once athletic young man now carried a bit of weight in his face, a softness earned over time.

The princess whirled in her seat. The sight of Britt brought a tear to her eye. "What a wonderful surprise!" she cried. She rose and embraced him. His eyes were wet, too.

Britt was a family man these days, with a wife and two daughters, and had built a quiet career as a salesman for a lumber importer in Houston, selling "hardwoods from around the world."

He was in Houston when the call came from NBC, inviting him to appear on the same program as the princess.

Catherine and Britt on *Today*

After they regained their composure, Catherine and Britt took their seats and shared the fuller story with Garroway.

Britt cut in with some news. "I am going to take her to Texas," he said proudly. His grand plans were coming true. "Texas folk are friendly folk, just as she was to me."

During the segment break, the phones at NBC started ringing off the hook. Producers scribbled notes as calls poured in. After the episode ended, they rushed to Britt and the princess with more news.

Ex-servicemen who'd been POWs in Romania were calling from all across the country. They were inviting Catherine to visit their towns, meet their families, and stay in their homes. Audiences would be lined up to hear her speak, promising work and a sense of purpose. The outpouring of support brought tears to her eyes once again. Upon arriving at America's sea-washed sunset gates, she had received kindness, acclaim, and a job.

"It was a marvelous introduction to this great country."

AS THEY LEFT NBC and stepped into Rockefeller Plaza on a crisp winter morning, the city sparkled with holiday decorations. People of all ages were ice skating on an outdoor rink beneath a towering Christmas tree. Catherine felt on top of the world. Britt was all smiles.

The network had arranged for three nights' lodging for Britt and the princess, so they could explore the city. It had also booked flights for them to Texas.

There would be no Greyhound bus for this princess.

Their visit would be big news before the day was out. The story hit the wire, and soon, bold front-page headlines appeared in papers across the country:

PRINCESS AND TEXAN
MEET IN NEW YORK

ROMANIAN PRINCESS COMES TO SEE
'MY AMERICAN BOYS'

'MOTHER' TO 100 FLIERS
IN U.S. FOR REUNION

Catherine eagerly looked forward to her ready-made speaking tour and to meeting the many ex-POWs and their families who had invited her into their towns and homes. It was a dream come true, and her American adventure was only beginning.

Her original boys, the crew of *Chattanooga Choo Choo,* were waiting to see her.

At first, Catherine would stay with Britt and his wife, Dorothy, and their two daughters in Texas. Soon, she would visit them all. The whole crew. There would be road trips, family dinners, and lots of reminiscing. Ernie would join them when he returned to the United States in 1958.

Sure enough, Princess Catherine would stay in America. She had found her new home, just as her boys had hoped.

AS BRITT AND THE princess walked past the skating rink on their way to a day of sightseeing in New York, they wondered aloud: Where should we go from here?

The question made them laugh. For the first time since they'd met, there was no danger, no urgency, no war. No place they had to be.

They'd come a long way from the dry banks of the Prahova River.

When they first met, Britt was pinned in the wreckage of his plane, soaked in gasoline, waiting for the deadly spark that would end his life.

Then she had appeared, confident, smiling, and calm. "Don't worry," she said. "We'll have you out in a jiffy."

That day, she had saved him. And in a strange twist of fate, almost a decade later, her boys saved her.

During her flight from Communism, it was their names she whispered, "over and over" again, like beads on a rosary. Those names steadied her when she was locked in the dark confines of the barge on the Danube. Those names kept her hope alive.

Ernie Poulson, Richard Britt, Al Romano, Bob O'Reilly . . .

Now, for the first time since that fateful August day in wartime, they were together and free. Free to stay. Free to go. Free to choose.

As they set out on the sidewalk, arm in arm, to catch a cab, Britt couldn't stop smiling at the thought. Whatever came next, the princess and her boys had a future together.

AFTERWORD

THE FUTURE TOGETHER THAT BEGAN IN NEW YORK CITY WOULD SPAN more than three decades.

Catherine and Britt had "hardly put down the suitcases" at Britt's home in Houston when the phone began to ring. Her boys were eager to see her.

"The holidays were filled with parties," Britt recalled.

After that, the princess hit the road.

She already had a visit with **Bob O'Reilly** on the books, even before she'd left Paris. So first, she traveled to St. Louis and stayed with Bob "at the home of his parents," where he lived with his daughter, Margaret. Following the war, he'd had a short marriage with the wrong woman. Now he was raising Margaret as a single dad. Bob was a steel salesman, a manufacturer's representative, and traveled every week on business.

The job was a perfect fit for him. After he'd been caged up as a POW, it was "hard for him to be in one place. He just needed to move and explore and visit friends." Margaret often went with him and found the trips "fun and adventuresome." She ended up seeing "most of the US before [she] was 10."

FROM ST. LOUIS, CATHERINE and Bob set out on a road trip to Kentucky, bound for the farm of **Frank Kees's** parents. It was a somber journey, but one they wanted to make, to pay their respects to the family of *Chattanooga Choo Choo*'s fallen flight engineer.

In the farmhouse kitchen, the princess and Mrs. Kees stood together, gazing at a framed photograph of Frank while a reporter lingered nearby, keeping a respectful distance. He would recount the quiet exchange that followed. After burying Frank in the family plot at Nedelea, Catherine had written to Mrs. Kees, offering sympathies and sharing the news. Since then,

Frank's remains had been brought home and reburied. Mrs. Kees never forgot the princess's kindness.

"Only a mother could realize how grateful we are for what you did," Mrs. Kees said.

"Any woman would have done the same," the princess said. "I have been a mother myself."

SOON AFTERWARD, THE PRINCESS headed to the Bay State to visit **Al Romano**. Once a bombardier, Al now built things. He worked as a land surveyor and civil engineer for the state of Massachusetts. The man who had once dropped bombs for a living now built roads and even helped lay the foundation of Logan Airport.

The newspaper recounted Catherine's visit with the "35-year-old veteran."

"'He hasn't changed much,' said the princess as she sat beside Romano at his Revere home last night. 'Of course he's not as slim as he was in those days. But none of my 'boys' are as slim as they used to be.'"

Louis Medeiros came by to see the princess during this visit. He had assumed his role in the family printing business down the coast in New Bedford and was married to Lorraine, who operated her own stationery shop.

From there, Catherine visited **Jack Bowker** in Phoenix. The burly former waist gunner cracked jokes and sprinkled comic book idioms into his speech, as always.

The crew's Polish-American replacement gunner, **Phil Rurak**, was married. He and the other sergeants would get a Christmas card from the princess every year.

One newspaper headline summarized Catherine's feelings about her exciting new life in America: "For Romanian Princess Catherine, Life in the West Is 'Paradise.'"

IT WASN'T ALL FUN and games in her new country. Ever service-oriented, the princess knew she had work to do. She set out on a speaking tour "to acquaint Americans with a firsthand knowledge of the evils of Communism." The woman who had once thought "It's safer to stay put" became a road warrior for democracy.

Britt arranged her first speech at nearby Bryan Air Force Base. As luck would have it, the base commander was an old friend of theirs: **Colonel James Gunn.** He never talked much about the war—you "had to pull it out of him"—but five decades later, Gunn would be posthumously awarded a Silver Star for his actions in Romania.

From there, the princess went from town to town by Greyhound bus, speaking at churches, civic groups, schools, and veterans' clubs. Her "favorite groups were those organized by [her] ex-POWs."

"What you have here is frankly, marvelous," she said during one of her speeches. She had seen communism snatch away freedom, and she "urged Americans to preserve theirs."

One talk led to the next. Princess Catherine kept touring the country by bus, living out of a suitcase, funding the trips by honorariums and donations. In the summer, she went north. In the winter, she went south.

And the invitations kept coming faster than she could accept them.

AS SHE TOLD HER story to rapt audiences, one figure was never far from the princess's mind: her cousin, **Constantin Cantacuzino—Buzz.**

After leaving behind everything he'd known, Buzz reunited with Nadia in Paris. She was living with her mother and trying to get her acting career off the ground. It would take a decade, but she would succeed, making her breakout in Federico Fellini's *La Dolce Vita* under the stage name Nadia Gray. But that was still years away.

Meanwhile, Buzz tried to find work for himself. He quickly discovered that prospects for a former Romanian pilot were bleak. He sought advice from a colleague from the state airline who had fled the country earlier. The man, also a pilot, had managed to find work with Air France—but only "as a ground attendant."

Postwar Europe was awash with ex-military flyers, and something else was working against the former ace. Even though Romania had switched sides and joined the Allies before the war's end, the country was still viewed with suspicion through much of Europe. "The policy of repression against those who had collaborated with the German armies continued."

Nadia, at least, was where she needed to be. But Buzz couldn't stay. There was no future in Paris for him.

In the summer of 1949, he moved to Spain, penniless. By then the couple had separated, although they refused to divorce. They were still best friends.

In southern Spain, the prince—hair silvering at the temples—found work as a crop duster, flying worn-down Boeing Stearman biplanes, "spraying the vast olive fields in Andalusia." He wasn't ideally suited for the job, it was noted, because he was always flipping the biplane inverted.

Between flights, Buzz entertained a dream: What if he could move to America? Surely, he could find a job as a pilot there.

He reached out to an old friend, Colonel Gunn, who was then stationed at Wiesbaden Air Base in Germany. Would he help him get a visa? Gunn agreed to try. He contacted his former boss, General Twining, now the U.S. Air Force chief of staff, who in turn placed Buzz's case before the newly elected President Eisenhower.

But that created a dilemma. Ike had campaigned on an anti-Communist message, and Buzz—once a pilot for the Romanian Communist government, even for Ana Pauker—was a political liability. It was the 1950s, the McCarthy era. "I cannot sponsor this individual," Eisenhower told Twining. "I'll be roasted for that."

Buzz was refused entry.

The prince made the best of his situation. Between long days fumigating fields, he scraped together enough money to buy a Bücker Bu 133 Jungmeister, the same type of aerobatic biplane he'd owned before the war. Soon, he was back in his element, performing in air shows—first city-to-city across Spain, then at international expos in Paris and London before crowds of men in suits and women in summer dresses.*

The papers raved about his "spectacular" performances and "the most daring acrobatics," claiming he "completely overshadowed other pilots." One maneuver in particular thrilled the crowds: "a terrifying inverted flight, only one meter above the ground."

Nadia wasn't a bit surprised. "Prince Cantacuzino was an exceptional man—who cared only about planes," she later told a reporter with a wry smile.

Then illness struck. In May 1958, Buzz was rushed into emergency surgery in Madrid for a perforated stomach ulcer. He'd first detected the ailment during the war, but it had been aggravated by the life of a crop duster, which included "irregular and sometimes inadequate meals, often consumed

* To view the incredibly rare film of Buzz performing an air-show routine in 1950s Spain, visit my website at AdamMakos.com.

in the field during various agricultural operations with different insecticides."

Complications followed. He was hemorrhaging internally. "The entire aviation community in Spain mobilized to help him," one historian recalled. Spanish aviators lined up to donate blood.

But it was too late for Buzz. No amount of care could save him.

On May 26, 1958, Constantin Cantacuzino—Romania's top ace, the fighter pilot prince—died at age fifty-two.

He was buried in Madrid, far from the country he once defended from the skies. His coffin was draped with a Romanian flag.

PRINCESS CATHERINE TOOK THE news hard. Her dear cousin had died "still hoping to come to America." She resolved to make the most of her time in the States, so she kept up with her speaking engagements and made another vow.

To find all of her boys.

It was a mission of tribute. She wanted to honor every former POW who had been imprisoned in her country during the war.

The quest wouldn't be easy. Though her courage had helped many, she didn't know them all by name. "Aiding in her search for her 'boys' [was] a little black notebook containing the names of some 400 Ploesti survivors," a reporter noted. She'd smuggled it out during her barge escape from Romania. But she knew her list was incomplete. As she continued to traverse the country, the princess sought out each man in her notebook.

By 1965, her friend Colonel Gunn had heard of her quest. Moved by her devotion, he contacted her with a gift. He'd pulled some strings at the Pentagon and secured for her a list of all 1,127 Americans who were POWs in Romania during World War II, a list that included "the towns from which they enlisted."

Catherine was filled with new hope. As she continued, every ex-POW invariably knew others, and "she contacted radio and TV stations asking for help in locating the men."

"Each day in this country I hear from another of my boys," she wrote. "I am so happy they have not forgotten their friendly enemy."

The headlines tracked her progress. In Akron, Ohio, when she reconnected with Clell Riffle, the top turret gunner of *Chattanooga Choo Choo,* and four others, the papers announced: "'Angel of Ploesti' Finds Five of Her 'Boys' Here." After the war, Riffle had become a "Goodyear tire builder," and he remembered the princess fondly.

"She helped me a lot," Riffle told a reporter. "She was a classy lady."

"It was obvious he still thinks so," the reporter penned.

And there was someone else Riffle remembered, the man who turned a hotel into a hospital for him and the other wounded raiders.

Whatever had become of King Michael?

AFTER HIS FORCED ABDICATION in early 1948, **King Michael** and his wife began life anew in England. The British press greeted his arrival with an unusual headline: "Ex-King Michael of Romania Becomes Market Gardener."

Newsreel footage showed the former monarch and his family making a morning inspection of a farm. It was true. He and Princess Anne—now the queen of Romania—had moved into an old manor house with their two young daughters. There, in the quaint countryside of Hertfordshire, they ran a small farm, tending "chickens and vegetables" as they scraped by through the "lean years in exile."

The tall young king who had once inspected armies behind Antonescu was now seen following his gardener, Mr. Hobbs, through the greenhouses, inspecting rows of squash and tomatoes. For the loyalists who remembered his wartime stature, the shift required some adjustment.

"When you have to leave the way I had to leave [Romania]," Michael admitted, "it is human nature. But when such a thing happens, all of a sudden, nobody knows you anymore."

He struggled with the change and drifted into melancholia. To his young daughters, he became "a silent, sad, serious man" during those difficult years.

The former king found solace alone in his garage. The man who was "as much mechanic as chauffeur" began restoring World War II jeeps. In time, he would completely rebuild nine, including one that had once carried General Patton himself.

In 1956, a glimmer of opportunity appeared. Bill Lear, the inventor of the Learjet, went to Switzerland to launch the Swiss American Aviation Company. His goal was to develop a new, innovative small business jet. Michael, who had friends at the company, paid him a visit. The king who had once flown the royal Ju-52, and a B-24 rebuilt from wrecks of Tidal Wave, still loved to fly.

He asked for a job.

Lear welcomed him aboard. Michael moved his family to Switzerland and became a test pilot for the company. Each morning, he reported to work in a suit, slipped on his sunglasses, and for the rest of the day piloted prop aircraft over Lake Geneva. He tested everything from "radio compasses to automatic pilots." Then he drove home in his humble Volkswagen Beetle.

STARTING IN 1953, THE Tidal Wave veterans began holding annual reunions. At first, "about 25" men and their families converged on Kansas City. Bob and Al attended, and **Ernie Poulson** flew there in a B-25 from his post at the Pentagon. Britt was tied up on business and couldn't join.

As the years went on, the former POWs found themselves drawn closer by the reunions. These gatherings served a deeper purpose, something they'd put off in captivity. The men still needed to talk and heal.

During her first summer in America, Princess Catherine traveled with Britt and his wife to the 1956 reunion at the Air Force Academy. Even after she got her own apartment, the princess and her adopted son, Britt, were always joined at the hip.

And there were other notable appearances that year: The famous British escape artists, Collins and Lancaster, joined the Americans. It became a party for escapees, a shared wink among men who had all, in one way or another, slipped through the wire.

As the decades passed and the survivors aged, the gatherings continued. The 1985 reunion in St. Louis marked a milestone for the crew of *Chattanooga Choo Choo.* For the first time since 1944, all four officers and their princess stood together in one place. One of their gunners, Jack Bowker, joined them too.

Catherine was ninety-two then. Her boys were all in their mid-sixties. As they traded stories around the table, the lives they'd lived, apart and together, came into focus.

Britt had gone full Texan, hanging his hat in Comfort, Texas. The navigator who once persuaded the princess to give them tunnel-building materials—lights, wood, and costumes—had ventured into showmanship. In 1960, he and his wife purchased the Pot o' Gold Ranch in Comfort, "which they made into a square-dancing ranch." After selling that, they bought the Comfort Theater, "one of the oldest stage and screen theaters operating in the United States." They renamed it the Hill Country Opry. Between stage shows during the week, it operated "as a dinner theater on weekends." The man who once plotted a transatlantic crossing in a B-24 now choreographed curtain calls.

As for Al, he was still happily entrenched in Revere, the same neighborhood where everyone knew his name. He was still working, now running his own engineering firm. He and his wife lived next door to his parents, and just across the street from the former site of Romano's Market.

"He would never pass a lilac, without pulling over and picking one to bring home to Nana, no matter whose lawn he was trespassing on," a granddaughter recalled.

Al had taken up ice skating. In his senior years, he kept a pair of ice skates in the trunk of his car everywhere he went . . . just in case he needed them. And he never lost his boyish love of roller coasters: He would ride them with his grandkids "into his late 80s."

Bob, in his postwar life, was still always on the go. He often visited Ernie or Al and their fellow POWs. Ernie recalled that whenever Bob was in town he would begin every morning by going to Catholic Mass.

The man "who'd never met a stranger" had another tradition. "Every year he sent out St. Patrick's Day cards to his friends and business associates," his daughter recalled. "He would take them to St. Patrick, Missouri, where they would be mailed with a large shamrock postmark." At the peak of this tradition "he was sending out over three thousand cards every year."

And he still loved to play poker.

AFTER A PROUD MILITARY career, Ernie had retired in 1961 as a full colonel. His last role was equally significant in the atomic age: helming the Atlas missile program.

Throughout the 1960s and 70s, Ernie and Helen hosted Princess Catherine multiple times at their home, first in Torrance, California, and then in Utah, where Ernie returned to his roots. He followed his mother's example and earned a PhD, embarking on a second career as a business professor at the University of Utah. After Ernie's mother died, he took in his ailing father, who lived with him until his death at age seventy-two, from emphysema brought on by sixty years of smoking. He and Ernie "joked many times" about the time when Ernie was eight and homesick—and his dad sent him home alone on his horse, through eighteen miles of frightening wilderness.

The older Ernie grew, the more he reflected on what they'd lived through during the war. In June 1985, Ernie, once reluctant to embrace his role as a POW, traveled with Helen back to Timisul. He wanted to see, one last time, the place where he'd been confined.

The fence was gone. Lagărul No. 2 had become an apartment building. He gazed up at his old bedroom window and remembered his time spent there with his friends.

At the 1985 reunion in St. Louis, when Ernie sat around the table with Bob, Britt, Al, and Princess Catherine, he pulled out the photos from his trip.

Any disdain they'd once felt for the camp had long since faded. In its place was the warmth of friendship and nostalgia. As they passed around the snapshots, they laughed about the tunnel and the absurdity of the disguises the princess had brought them. They could only imagine what it would've looked like if they tried to slip through the Romanian countryside in flapper dresses and tuxedos.

When it came time for the group photo, "her boys" insisted the princess join them. To the event staff, it may have looked unusual—a woman standing at the center of so many men who had flown and fought together. But what bound them was something only they could understand." To the former flyboys, the princess wasn't just a wartime acquaintance. She was one of them.

AT AGE NINETY-FOUR, PRINCESS Catherine was still spending six months of the year on the road.

Then came December 1989. The Romanian people rose against communism. After a bloody revolution, the dictator fell, and with him a big slice of the Iron Curtain.

As she watched the events unfold on TV, Catherine had something to consider that gave her pause. There was no longer a fugitive list. The nobility and countless other exiles could finally return.

"For the first time in forty-five years," she wrote, "I could go home again."

ON EASTER SUNDAY, 1992, in Bucharest, nearly a million Romanians flooded the streets as a silver Mercedes rolled through with a police escort.

King Michael was back.

Now seventy years old, he'd returned for his first visit since his exile. In a scene "befitting a conquering hero," the king's motorcade "halted repeatedly along the crowded route from Otopeni Airport," noted a reporter, "so that the twice-dethroned king could wave to the masses or venture out to shake a few hands."

People of all ages crowded along the streets, hoping to glimpse or meet their adored national icon, the last king of Romania. In one plaza, where Michael spoke, a "crowd that swelled beyond 100,000" chanted: "King in, Communists out!" And "Stay with us!" And then, a single, rising chorus, simple and unrelenting:

"King Michael! King Michael! King Michael!"

But Michael hadn't come home to reclaim his birthright. He sensed that Romania would find its new footing without him.

"My interest is not in the throne, but in the good of my country," Michael told journalists. "I want to try to help Romania explain to the world the difficulties through which it is passing."

But even he hadn't expected such an "affectionate outpouring."

With tears in his eyes, he told the crowd simply: "I am happy you remember me."

IT WAS TIME FOR Princess Catherine to make her last audacious journey.

Romania's new, democratic government chose to "return to Catherine more than twenty acres of her estate." And she was granted "a small pension."

"Her eyes sparkled a little brighter with the thoughts of going home," an ex-POW recalled.

Her granddaughter, Brianna, twenty-nine, came to Texas to escort her homeward to Europe. And Catherine left behind a note.

Dear X-POWs and Friends:

I came to America thirty-five years ago to speak to you of the worth of freedom and to find the "boys" who fell in Romania in World War II. I did not run away, but came to alert you to the danger of your losing your freedom in this great land. I am now returning to Europe, but there is still danger. Yugoslavia is breaking up, my poor Romania is in the throes of reform, and alas, so is big and dangerous Russia. Until there is real relaxation and common justice everywhere, the world is not yet safe.

I have loved every minute of my stay here, talking in all the fifty states and enjoying your great hospitality. With your help I have found nearly all the boys. It hurts to know I will not return, but age finally caught up with me. My message now is "Keep your Hopes High, but keep your Powder Dry!" I love you ALL and perhaps you can visit me back there.

May the Lord keep you in His kind care.

Good-bye and God speed!
Catherine Caradja

BACK IN BUCHAREST, PRINCESS Catherine returned to lodgings that seemed plucked from a storybook ending—the attic above her beloved orphanage, St. Catherine's Crib.

"Of course, another place could have been rented," her granddaughter would recall, "but for my grandmother, The Cradle was her life."

She returned to a happy welcome. A few of the doctors and nurses still serving there had remained at their posts since the day the princess left in 1951. When word of her return spread, they were overjoyed and "eager to see her again."

A quiet tribute remained. Something the Communist regime had neglected to tear down. Near the entrance, a marble plaque still hung on the wall, "engraved with the images of the exiled princess and her mother."

Catherine celebrated her one hundredth birthday in January 1993. Four months later, peacefully, "in the attic of her former Cradle," she died.

Her most precious gift was time. She gave it freely, to orphans and those in need, like the boys who fell from the sky, who'd been imprisoned far from home.

After Operation Reunion, the airlift to bring the prisoners back from Romania, officers at the Army Air Forces concluded:

> It was pointed out that of all the people in Bucharest that helped the American prisoners of war, the one who did the most, and who made life bearable for them in the prison camps, was a lady by the name of Ecatarina Caraja [Princess Catherine]. She visited the camps weekly, took athletic equipment, food, et cetera, to the men.
>
> Being well known and, apparently, feared by certain Romanian officials, [she bridged the cultural divide], and it was pointed out by a large number of the evacuated airmen that her efforts alone did more for their morale than any other one thing.

Before Princess Catherine left America to return home, she had accomplished an extraordinary feat. Of the 1,127 Americans held prisoner in Romania during World War II, she found and visited more than eight hundred.

IN 2018, AT THE beginning of the writing of this book, there was one last known survivor of Tidal Wave.

Ernie.

He knew the raid had changed him forever. His time as a POW marked the defining chapter of his life. The lessons he carried from captivity stayed with him all his days—proof that good can come from even the hardest seasons.

"I know the names of every officer in that camp," Ernie said. "I can still recount them. I just recite those names when I can't go to sleep at night. I can name all forty prisoners, can outline them, and tell you the name of every guy in every room. Some of them were my friends forever."

Most people today are unaware there was a campaign in Romania that took the lives of some one thousand American fliers during World War II. Or that a princess, a fighter-pilot prince, and a twenty-two-year-old king helped the survivors reach freedom.

But Ernie knew. He was there for all of it. A pilot in Operation Tidal Wave, the most death-defying low-level attack of the war. Thirteen months as a POW. An escapee on the run.

In looking back, at the end of his life, Ernie wouldn't have had it any other way.

Princess Without Crown

No crown was necessary Friday for Linda Kees, right, to recognize a princess. Left to right, George Kees Jr., Linda's father, ex-pilot Robert O'Reilly, St. Louis, Mo., and Romanian Princess Catherine Caradja, explain to Linda that the crown had to be left behind when the princess escaped from the Communist-controlled country. Princess Catherine was visiting with Mr. Kees and his parents, Mr. and

Buzz, 1952

Princess And Her 'Boys'

ROMANIAN PRINCESS Catherine Caradja greets two of her "boys," Louis C. Medeiros of New Bedford (left) and Albert A. Romano at his home in Revere. The men are two of 110 American fliers the princess helped when they were shot down in her country during World War II. The princess has visited 34 of the 110 men and hopes to visit all during her tour of the country.

Buzz flying his Jungmeister

Michael & Anne, 1953

The princess and her boys

Bowker, Ernie, Al, Bob, and Britt, 1985

ACKNOWLEDGMENTS

I'D LIKE TO EXTEND MY DEEP THANKS TO THE FOLLOWING PEOPLE for their help with *Tidal Wave:*

To the veteran at the heart of this story, Ernie Poulson: You gave us your time and energy, your memories and writings, so that I might retrace the great adventure you lived. Thank you for entrusting me with your story.

To the World War II flyboys whose technical advice and supplemental interviews brought poignancy and depth to this book: Ploesti veterans R. D. Lawrence and Andy Pendleton and P-51 pilots of the Tuskegee Airmen, General Charles McGee and Colonel George Hardy.

To Princess Brianna Caradja, for the valuable insights into your remarkable grandmother, Princess Catherine, whose work now lives on through you and the Caradja Cantacuzino nonprofit. Your effort to build a museum to the Ploesti raiders at Princess Catherine's former estate (https://ongcc.ro/muzeul-tidal-wave) is a cause worthy of our support.

To historian Dénes Bérnad, distinguished author of *Rumanian Aces of World War 2,* whose research and consultation helped illuminate the life of Buzz Cantacuzino and the fighter pilots of Romania for us. Your work honors their memory.

To the family of our "cast of characters," you unearthed priceless wartime letters, fielded our countless questions, and opened the doors to your family histories for us: Cindy Driggs (Poulson family); Margaret Culver (O'Reilly family); Harriet Kirchhoff (Britt family); and from the Romano family, Courtney Doucette (Al's youngest sister), Diane Falite, Kristal Markiewicz, Denise Ratti, and Janet Prochilo; Danielle Rurak (Rurak family); Mike MacDonald (son of Donald "Mac" MacDonald); David Snyder (son of Bob Snyder); Colonel (ret.) Dennis Cavit (son of Charles Cavit); and Major (ret.) William Gunn (son of James Gunn III). Thank you for entrusting us with your stories.

To my editor, Mary Reynics, who believed in this book from the beginning and whose impeccable sense of "story" helped shape the manuscript into its final form—your insight and experience, hard earned at the top of one of the world's most demanding fields, made this a far better book. *Tidal Wave* was a team effort, and I'm grateful to have had you on ours.

To the president and publisher of Random House, Sanyu Dillon, and the publishing team at Ballantine Bantam Dell, including Scott Shannon, Jennifer Hershey, Kara Cesare, Kim Hovey, Ivanka Perez, Sarah Breivogel, Alex Peterson, Evan Camfield, Barbara Bachman, Angela McNally, and Jolanta Benal: Thank you all for bringing *Tidal Wave* to the world.

To this book's aviation advisor, Rob Collings, CEO of the Collings Foundation, a modern-day warbird pilot—it was Rob who I turned to for details about flying the B-24, the P-51, and everything in between. Thank you all for lending your expertise to this, our fourth book in a row.

To our "boots on the ground" in Romania, researchers Filip and Alessandra Twarowski, who ventured into Transylvania so I could visit Lagărul No. 2 from afar; Lucian Dobrovicescu, Dan Melinte, and Colonel Marius Trifan, who provided essential archival research; Constantin Stanescu, who returned to Pietroșița on our behalf; our translator, Larisa Giubega; and our overseas agent, Włodzimierz Twarowski, and his wife, Aura: Thank you for always being on call and ready to help.

To the historians who helped bring these forgotten chapters of history to life for us: Chris Gregg, who runs the 389th Bombardment Group page on Facebook; Erik Goldstein of the 454th Bomb Group; Dave Blake of the 461st Bomb Group; Ed Clendenin of the 376th Bomb Group; distinguished World War II historian Steven Zaloga; Patrick Houda, a former Swedish hockey player and historian who guided us through Buzz's sporting days; archivist Patricia Thomasson, who helped us unearth the writings of Bob O'Reilly; and Pam Ives and Matt Scales, who dug deep into the Air Force archives to aid our quest.

To the dedicated archivists, experts, and researchers who provided vital data, photos, and artwork: Alan Armitage, Beth Ciullo, Debbie Conroy, Jenna Grindberg, Kristin Hagaman, Megan Harris, Gareth Hector, Jason Hill—son of Michael Hill, the esteemed author of *Black Sunday*—Kim Hobb, Kristin Holzhauer, Elaine Johns, and Darren Neeley.

To my writing mentor, Marcus Brotherton, the veteran author and coauthor of multiple *New York Times* bestsellers, who has advised nearly every project I've undertaken—thank you for sharing the tips and tricks born from your decades of experience. Marcus offers an online course, *The Book Captain,* where he teaches writers how to craft, structure, and position a book for success, a service I heartily endorse. I'm lucky to count you as a friend.

To the early readers who lent a discerning eye to this manuscript: Noah, Phoebe, and Samuel Clewley, Joe Gohrs, Matt Hoover, Tricia Hoover, Karin Kurtz, Chris Kurtz, and Pete Semanoff.

To my friend, the late Mr. Fred Smith, and his daughters Molly Smith and Rachel Smith of Black Label Media—it was the Smith family who first discovered this epic story decades ago. You introduced me to this grand adventure and urged me to pursue it. Finally, when I met Ernie, I came to realize why this story meant so much to you.

To my closest "story advisors"—my sisters, Erica Schoo and Elizabeth Makos; my sister-in-law, Agata Makos; and my mother, Karen Makos—who read every first draft: Your feedback steered this book in a wonderful way.

To my dad, Robert Makos, who spearheaded our interviews for this book: Your lifetime of experience in the psychology field proved priceless once again. To my brother, Bryan Makos, *Tidal Wave*'s research director and co-creator: Your talents made this a one-in-a-million book.

Lastly, thank you, dear reader, for journeying along with us through the pages of *Tidal Wave.* I hope the memory of the young Americans who flew over Ploesti, and of their unlikely Romanian allies, stays with you long after you close the final page.

If you're hungry to go "beyond the book," head over to my website for bonus features—including wartime footage of *Chattanooga Choo Choo,* film of Operation Reunion and Buzz Cantacuzino, and more—all at AdamMakos.com.

On behalf of Ernie, and the heroes of *Tidal Wave,* I pass the torch to you. The legacy of great men and women lies in your hands. Spread the word.

NOTES

A NOTE ON SOURCES

Tidal Wave DRAWS ON A WIDE RANGE OF HISTORICAL SOURCES. AT ITS core is Ernie Poulson's firsthand account of his World War II experience, as told to us directly and drawn from his diary and memoir, supplemented by written accounts from members of his crew.

From there, we examined period reports of aerial combat; operational records; personnel files; newspapers and magazines from the war years; personal letters; interviews with descendants; contemporary lectures; and the works of distinguished historians and veterans.

We combined records, memories, and firsthand testimony to reconstruct this story as faithfully and accurately as possible. If every fact were cited, the notes section might exceed the length of the book; instead, attributions are provided for direct quotations drawn from outside sources.

Any book written eight decades after the events it describes may contain minor errors. *Tidal Wave* is a living document. If you spot a mistake, please contact my research team through my website so it can be corrected in a future printing.

1. THE NEW ARRIVALS

3 **"shimmering in the clear, dry air":** Philip Ardery, *Bomber Pilot: A Memoir of World War II* (University Press of Kentucky, 1978), 75.

4 **"quiet, unassuming, pleasant":** Ernest Poulson, Official Military Personnel File, National Archives and Records Administration (henceforth to be abbreviated NARA).

5 **"Liberators are needed in the Middle East":** *History of the 389th Bombardment Group (H) AAF: Part II,* Air Force Historical Research Agency, Maxwell AFB, Alabama.

5 **"never met a stranger":** Margaret Culver, daughter of Robert O'Reilly II, interviewed by Bryan Makos, April 2024.

5 **"on the verge of falling apart":** Richard Britt, *The Princess and the P.O.W.* (Gabriel Publishing, 1988), 14.

6 **"enviable" record at his high school:** Richard Britt, Official Military Personnel File, NARA.

8 **boundless "Iron Treasure":** Jack Preble, *Written in the Sand: A Personalized History of the*

376th Bombardment Group (H), AAF, Air Force Historical Research Agency, Maxwell AFB, Alabama, 37.

8 **The radio popped with static:** Andy Opsata, "Flight over Ploesti: Part 1," *389th Bomb Group Newsletter,* vol. 6, no. 2 (spring 1993), 6.

9 **"blew up on takeoff":** Richard Byers, *Attack* (Litho Printers, 1992), 135.

9 **no hand in the artwork:** Robert O'Reilly II, letter to his father, June 16, 1943.

9 **"hotter than the hinges of hell":** Preble, *Written in the Sand,* 44.

9 **Ernie identified some familiar nose art:** Opsata, "Flight over Ploesti: Part 1," 6.

10 **word reached them of a significant development:** *History of the 389th.*

10 **"a great raid":** Ardery, *Bomber Pilot,* 96.

10 **"medal raid":** Byers, *Attack,* 164.

10 **"anyone who participated":** Ardery, *Bomber Pilot,* 96.

10 **"It was funny how great the percentage":** Ardery, *Bomber Pilot,* 96.

11 **"dances and debut parties":** Margaret Culver, daughter of Robert O'Reilly II, interviewed by Bryan Makos, April 2024.

11 **"to avoid use of vulgar and irreverent language":** Ernest Poulson, *A Personal History* (self-published, 1985), 9.

11 **"But then I had a horse and saddle":** Poulson, *Personal History,* 7.

12 **"the most bombed and shelled":** Ardery, *Bomber Pilot,* 75.

2. UNDER A DESERT SUN

13 **"all-pervasive" red dust:** Poulson, *Personal History,* 26.

14 **"at best, like a very primitive Boy Scout camp":** Michael Hill, *Black Sunday: Ploesti* (Schiffer Publishing, 1993), 28.

14 **"a few" venomous snakes:** Ardery, *Bomber Pilot,* 75.

14 **"One quickly develops a healthy respect":** Byers, *Attack,* 69.

14 **studied architecture in college:** Richard Britt, Official Military Personnel File, NARA.

15 **"hundreds of hours":** Poulson, *Personal History,* 13.

15 **"an over-population of rabbits":** Poulson, *Personal History,* 8.

16 **"Heading for the beach":** Gene Hartley, "389th Green Dragon Flares," *2nd Air Division Association Journal,* vol. 32, no. 2 (summer 1993), 25.

16 **"delicious-looking" waves:** Ardery, *Bomber Pilot,* 77.

17 **"covered with bathers":** Ardery, *Bomber Pilot,* 77.

18 **"Liberators are needed in the Middle East":** *History of the 389th.*

19 **"barreling down the beach":** Ardery, *Bomber Pilot,* 77.

19 **Pink Pigs:** Earl Zimmerman, *Recollections of Earl L. Zimmerman: 389th Bomb Group, 565th Squadron, 2nd Division* (self-published, 1983), 3.

19 **had slow control responses:** Information about flying the B-24 was drawn from my interviews with the book's aviation advisor, Rob Collings, CEO of the Collings Foundation and a modern-day pilot of the B-24 and other warbirds.

19 **"Maybe this was just the natural thing":** Ardery, *Bomber Pilot,* 77.

20 **"every few minutes":** Ardery, *Bomber Pilot,* 77.

3. THE MILK RUN

22 **a series of "break-in" raids:** Ardery, *Bomber Pilot,* 84.

22 **left the group "greatly affected":** H. H. "Chris" Christensen, "[389th BG B-24 Co-Pilot Memoir]," lipper.cc/8th_AF/Chris/Chris_Chapt2.html.

23 **"milk run":** George Neilson, *A Bomber Pilot's Story: The George H. Neilson World War II Memoirs* (AuthorHouse, 2016).

23 **Messerschmitt Me-109s:** During World War II, the Luftwaffe referred to the Messerschmitt 109 in official manuals as both "Me-109" and "Bf-109." For consistency, we have chosen Me-109. See Mark Postlethwaite, "Me109 or Bf109—Which One Is Correct?," posted September 6, 2023, 4:03, youtube.com/watch?v=XtJT14InwF0.

23 **"rather ordinary" mission:** Poulson, *Personal History,* 26.

24 **"filled with blurred voices":** O'Reilly Crew, Sortie Report, July 9, 1943, 389th Bomb Group, Air Force Historical Research Agency, Maxwell AFB, Alabama.

26 **"Don't worry if you get word":** "Lt. Arthur J. Scates, Bomber Pilot, Missing in Action, Since July 9 Was Serving in the Middle East," *The Commercial* (Union City, Tenn.), July 1943. findagrave.com/memorial/56250173/arthur-jesse-scates.

26 **"did not seem invincible":** Christensen, "[389th BG B-24 Co-Pilot Memoir]."

4. THE OLD HANDS

27 **Royal Romanian Air Force:** For the sake of clarity and consistency, I have updated the World War II–era spelling of "Rumanian" to its present-day form, "Romanian," throughout this book.

27 **Bâzu, as he was known:** Mircea Dumitru, *Aviatorul Erou. Constantin M. Cantacuzino Bazu si Lumea in Care a Trait* [The Hero Aviator Constantin M. Cantacuzino "Bâzu" and the World He Lived In] (Editgraph, 2016), 19.

29 **"Anyone who knows him, loves him":** Dobran, Dobrovicescu, and Grecea, "Regretatul general-locotenent (r) Ion Dobran vorbind despre prințul aviator Constantin 'Bâzu' Cantacuzino [The Late Lieutenant General (r) Ion Dobran Speaking About the Aviator Prince Constantin "Bâzu" Cantacuzino]," posted September 24, 2021, Facebook video, 14:45, facebook.com/share/v/1Bfdn9ZvVU/.

29 **"the warmest behavior":** Vasile Tudor, *Constantin "Bâzu" Cantacuzino, Prințul Aşilor* [Constantin "Bâzu" Cantacuzino, Prince of Aces] (Editura Modelism, 2000), 63.

29 **"The prince was one of the few":** Tudor, *Cantacuzino,* 63.

29 **"He couldn't bear sitting behind a desk":** Marian Christy, "Nadia Gray's No Longer Blue: Banker's Wife Enters Limelight," *Mansfield* (Ohio) *News Journal,* May 12, 1976, 18.

31 **"Experienced, modest, and brave":** Tudor, *Cantacuzino,* 117.

33 **"three to five" enemy fighters:** Constantin Cantacuzino Siguranța file, September 16, 1941 entry, Consiliul Național Pentru Studierea Arhivelor Securității [National Council for the Study of Securitate Archives], Bucharest, Romania.

33 **"in abandoned rooms, destroyed and dirty":** Tudor, *Cantacuzino,* 76.

33 **"were now angry and bitter":** Tom W. Murrey, Jr., "Romania's Disaster at Stalingrad," *WWII History,* January 2011, warfarehistorynetwork.com/article/romanias-disaster-at-stalingrad.

33 **"increased the unpopularity of the war":** Murrey, "Romania's Disaster."

33 **"that his troops despised Antonescu":** Murrey, "Romania's Disaster."

5. THE JOUST

36 **"continuous undulating maneuvers":** Tudor, *Cantacuzino,*7.

36 **"from the thinning clouds":** "Lt. Aviator Bâzu Cantacuzino Luptă Singur Cu Unsprezece Avioane Inamice, Doboară Două si Aterizează in Liniile Noastre [Lt. Aviator Bâzu Cantacuzino Fights Alone Against 11 Enemy Planes, Shoots Down Two of Them, And Lands Behind Our Lines]," *Universul* (Bucharest), July 21, 1943.

36 **heavy-G "turning combat":** Otso Leskinen (Finnish fighter pilot), quoted in Hannu Valtonen, *Me 109 Ja Saksan Sotatalous* [Messerschmitt Bf 109 and the German War Economy] (Keski-Suomen Ilmailumuseo, 1999), virtualpilots.fi/feature/articles/109myths.

37 **"projected" through the sky:** Constantin Cantacuzino Combat Report, 7th Fighter Group, June 29, 1943, collection of Dénes Bernád.

37 **"Lieutenant, I've been hit":** "Lt. Aviator Bâzu Cantacuzino Luptă Singur Cu Unsprezece Avioane Inamice."

37 **"Please allow me to leave the fight":** "Lt. Aviator Bâzu Cantacuzino Luptă Singur Cu Unsprezece Avioane Inamice."

37 **"I don't think he intended to kill people":** Dobran, Dobrovicescu, and Grecea, Facebook video.

38 **The wings were elliptical. *Spitfires!:*** Cantacuzino, Combat Report. Buzz maintained that the aircraft he fought were Spitfires, though some present-day historians question whether the Russians had them at that location, suggesting a possible misidentification. With the answer locked away in the archives of the Russian Federation, I defer to Buzz—who was there that day.

39 **Buzz's mind turned "feverishly":** "Lt. Aviator Bâzu Cantacuzino Luptă Singur Cu Unsprezece Avioane Inamice."

39 **firing "almost simultaneously":** Cantacuzino, Combat Report.

39 **"Strike and (get) out!":** Leskinen quoted in Valtonen, *Me 109 Ja Saksan Sotatalous.*

40 **it "rose like an elevator":** Mauno Fräntilä (Finnish fighter pilot) quoted in Valtonen, *Me 109 Ja Saksan Sotatalous.*

41 **"gently, surrounded by strips of blue clouds":** "Lt. Aviator Bâzu Cantacuzino Luptă Singur Cu Unsprezece Avioane Inamice."

41 **"I breathe a sigh of relief":** Ion Dobran, *Doi Ani de Foc pe Messerschmitt: Jurnal de Front 1943–1945* [Two Years Under Fire in a Messerschmitt: Battlefield Journal 1943–1945] (Editura Favorit, 2018), 186.

41 **"I declare on my word of honor":** Cantacuzino, Combat Report.

42 **"Hauptmann Schultz":** "Lt. Aviator Bâzu Cantacuzino Luptă Singur Cu Unsprezece Avioane Inamice."

6. IT MUST BE DONE

43 **Known informally as the Green Hut:** Hill, *Black Sunday,* 28–29.

43 **five more break-in missions:** *History of the 389th.*

44 **"We felt this experience [was] enough":** Philip Ardery, *Bomber Pilot: A Memoir of World War II* (University Press of Kentucky, 1978), 87.

44 **"against a military objective":** *History of the 389th.*

44 **"greatest strategic import to the future":** Ardery, *Bomber Pilot,* 98.

44 **the "lifeblood of war":** James Dugan and Carroll Stewart, *Ploesti: The Great Ground-Air Battle of 1 August 1943* (Potomac Books, 1998), 105.

45 **the Transylvanian Alps:** The mountains nearest Ploesti are technically the Prahova Sub-Carpathians. Romanians today refer to them as the Carpathians, or "the Romanian Alps," while to the Americans who flew Tidal Wave they were "the Transylvanian Alps." For consistency, this book uses the 1943 American term.

45 **"Several expressed doubt":** Hill, *Black Sunday,* 28–29.

45 **"This thing can't work":** Jim Fausone, "When Heroes Filled the Sky: Addison Baker, Lloyd Hughes, John Jerstead, Leon Johnson, and John Kane," Home of Heroes, homeofheroes .com/heroes-stories/world-war-ii/when-heroes-filled-the-sky.

7. SOMETHING IS UP

46 **"Security around the base":** Richard Byers, *Attack* (Cassville, MO: Litho Printers, 1992), 164.

46 **"Don't get in their way":** William H. Yaeger, Jr., War Discharge Review Board Interview, Official Military Personnel File, 1946, NARA.

46 **it was "just as well":** Poulson, *Personal History,* 26.

47 **Desert Quickstep:** Hill, *Black Sunday,* 34.

8. BOMBS CAN FLY

48 **they called suntans:** Poulson, *Personal History,* 25.

49 **"Something new is in the air":** Lewis Ellis, "Ploesti: A Pilot's Diary," *American Heritage* (October/November 1983), americanheritage.com/ploesti-pilots-diary.

49 **"This mission is the reason":** Ellis, "Ploesti."

49 **"We're all getting a few gray hairs":** Byers, *Attack,* 168.

49 **was going to be a "suicide run":** Byers, *Attack,* 164.

50 **"Now we knew they weren't kidding":** Ellis, "Ploesti."

51 **called it buzz-bombing:** "New Technique Proves Deadly in Combat," *Life,* November 15, 1943, 93.

51 **both branches was "skip bombing":** Christensen, "[389th BG B-24 Co-Pilot Memoir]."

51 **"I'll put one right through the middle":** Ardery, *Bomber Pilot,* 98.

52 **"right through the center of the frame":** Ardery, *Bomber Pilot,* 98.

52 **"The blueprint boys would have":** Preble, *Written in the Sand,* 83.

9. RAMPING UP

54 **buzzing had been "legalized":** Dugan and Stewart, *Ploesti,* 45.
54 **"How low?" one nervous pilot:** Sternfels, "Flying Through Hell to Bomb Hitler's Oil: 'Ploesti' the Documentary," youtube.com/watch?v=g3vpX98-5u4.
54 **"hard, hot work":** Poulson, *Personal History,* 26.
54 **"a snoot full of sand":** Hill, *Black Sunday,* 31.
55 **"along the desert for quite a distance":** Hill, *Black Sunday,* 32.
56 **"almost burst your eardrums":** Byers, *Attack,* 159.
56 **"Something big is in the making":** Byers, *Attack,* 137.
56 **"Just to say you've been here":** Byers, *Attack,* 171.

10. THE TEST

58 **the continent's "soft underbelly":** *The New Yorker,* vol. 28, nos. 1–10 (1952), 64.
58 **"a priority second only to":** Byers, *Attack,* 173.
59 **"Don't worry," Wood said:** Dugan and Stewart, *Ploesti,* 63–64.
61 **"dodging the skipping bombs":** Dugan and Stewart, *Ploesti,* 64.
61 **"Well, Colonel, you knew our ETA":** Dugan and Stewart, *Ploesti,* 64.

11. THE EXPEDITION

62 **July 26, 1943:** Owing to the mission's extreme secrecy, the exact date of this briefing remains uncertain. Logbooks and diaries confirm that the men flew a second dress rehearsal on July 27 with Ploesti in mind as the target. The briefing, therefore, had to have taken place on July 26, when logbooks show the group was grounded.
63 **"The 389th Bomb Group has been":** Christensen, "[389th BG B-24 Co-Pilot Memoir]."
63 **"plenty of money changed hands":** Kenton McFarland, Arturo Gonzalez, Jr., "Hell at Fifty Feet," *Argosy* (February 1960), 33.
64 **"wishing to avoid the fate of":** Kevin McDermott and Matthew Stibbe, eds., *Stalinist Terror in Eastern Europe: Elite Purges and Mass Repression* (Manchester University Press, 2012), 40.
64 **heir to a "powerless throne":** Dugan and Stewart, *Ploesti,* 26.
64 **"as both head of state":** Ivor Porter, *Michael of Romania: The King and the Country* (Sutton, 2005), 63.
65 **labeled their arrangement a protectorate:** Zoltán Pálfy, *National Controversy in the Transylvanian Academe: The Cluj/Kolozsvár University in the First Half of the Twentieth Century* (Akadémiai Kiadó, 2005), 215.
65 **"Hitler's Gas Station":** Carroll Stewart, *Ted's Traveling Circus: 93rd Bombardment Group (H), United States Army Air Force, World War II* (Sun/World Communications, 1996), 153.
65 **"the horrible position of owning the oil":** "Romania Has Oil Trouble," *Life,* February 19, 1940, 66.
66 **"Any plane that's flyable will go":** Byers, *Attack,* 169.
66 **"biggest low-level mass raid":** "St. Louisan, Who Bombed Rome, Missing in Action," *St. Louis Globe-Democrat,* August 16, 1943.
66 **"pleasure loving" Romanian gunners:** Preble, *Written in the Sand,* 118.
68 **Theirs was "Red Target":** Steven Zaloga, *Ploesti 1943: The Great Raid on Hitler's Romanian Oil Refineries* (Osprey, 2019), 30.
69 **"the number one air target":** Poulson, *Personal History,* 27.
69 **"Though the defenses at Ploesti may":** Leon Wolff, author of *Low Level Mission,* quoted by Ernest Poulson in an interview with Bob Makos, 2018.
71 **"This will be a history making mission":** Byers, *Attack,* 169.

12. FINAL PREPARATIONS

72 **"You'd think it was a prisoner-of-war camp":** Byers, *Attack,* 174.
72 **"The strain of waiting for The Day was terrific":** *History of the 389th.*
72 **"There was little else to do":** Preble, *Written in the Sand,* 117.
72 **"There are no nonbelievers":** Byers, *Attack,* 168.

74 **"happy-go-lucky":** Britt, *The Princess and the P.O.W.*, 57.
74 **"well known about the city":** "Lt. A. Romano Is Missing in African Area," 1943, Romano family newspaper clipping.
74 **"Give my regards to the whole neighborhood":** Al Romano, letter to his parents, January 10, 1942.
75 **even christening him Bambino:** Robert O'Reilly II, letter to Al Romano, February 27, 1946.

13. IF ONLY ONE COMES BACK

77 **"The days of gloom and doubt were done":** Dugan and Stewart, *Ploesti*, 69.
78 **round glasses on a "dead-pan" face:** Clare Boothe, "Brereton," *Life*, June 1, 1942, 76.
79 **Hitler was now "almost entirely dependent":** "Attack on Ploesti," *Air Force*, November 1943, 9.
79 **"The sudden, complete, and permanent":** "Attack on Ploesti," *Air Force*, 9.
79 **"Now that makes a lump":** Russell Hayes, "Recorded Memoir of Russell Hayes," Second Air Division Digital Archive, 1985. digitalarchive.2ndair.org.uk/digitalarchive/ImageBrowser?catNum=mc_371-882-1-1#NRO_MC371-882-1_i1_s1_f1_v1.
79 **"He talked about getting to the target":** Hill, *Black Sunday*, 35.
80 **a shockwave had "hit the planners":** Hill, *Black Sunday*, 34.
80 **what they called Festung Ploesti:** Dugan and Stewart, *Ploesti*, 29.
80 **"the tough, hard-boiled general":** Boothe, "Brereton," 71.
81 **"intended to be inspirational":** Glen Underwood, "Northern Star over Ploesti," *Friends Bulletin*, vol. 11, no. 2 (summer 1988), 35.
81 **wandered over to the cheerful "Limey Gunners":** Hill, *Black Sunday*, 36.
81 **a sudden "thunderous roar of B-24 engines":** Preble, *Written in the Sand*, 41.
82 **"red-eyed" ground crews:** Britt, *The Princess and the P.O.W.*, 35.
82 **"there was a quietness":** Dugan and Stewart, *Ploesti*, 78.
82 **"A great morale builder":** Byers, *Attack*, 175.
82 **"some crews were quietly giving away":** Dugan and Stewart, *Ploesti*, 78.
82 **"Well, don't take your fancy shoes":** Walter Stewart, interviewed by Elizabeth Searles, "Utah WWII Stories" (Benjamin, Utah), April 29, 2005.
82 **"I had a feeling that there was":** Hill, *Black Sunday*, 38.
82 **"Time is running out":** Byers, *Attack*, 174.
82 **their sacrifices would be "justified":** Britt, *The Princess and the P.O.W.*, 35.

14. OFF WE GO

85 **"men in jeeps tore around":** Ardery, *Bomber Pilot*, 101.
85 **"rubber pancakes":** Byers, *Attack*, 101.
85 **"with a good deal of dust scrambled":** Ardery, *Bomber Pilot*, 76.
86 **"One might have thought":** James McClain, "My Most Memorable Combat Mission," *Heritage Herald*, issue 52 (June 2013), 3.
86 **"Most of us have already determined":** Byers, *Attack*, 175.
86 **"Gloom" settled over Ernie:** Britt, *The Princess and the P.O.W.*, 42.
86 **trade "a damn good wingman for":** John McCormick, quoted in Lyndon Shubert, "World War II: Eyewitness to the Raid on Ploesti," *Aviation History* (March 2000), historynet.com/world-war-ii-eyewitness-to-the-raid-on-ploesti.
87 **"One cannot help but wonder":** Byers, *Attack*, 172.
87 **"It was a good crew," wrote Britt:** Britt, *The Princess and the P.O.W.*, 58.
88 **"Our first look at the plane":** Britt, *The Princess and the P.O.W.*, 42.
88 **"should be named 'Borrowed Time'":** Hill, *Black Sunday*, 45.
90 **"raw metal and zinc-oxide paint":** William Cubbins, *The War of the Cottontails* (Algonquin Books, 1989), 257.
90 **"a good day for a picnic":** Paul Wilson and Ron Mackay, *The Sky Scorpions: The Story of the 389th Bomb Group in World War II* (Schiffer Publishing, 2006), 31.
91 **"The Flying Coffin," they'd scrawled:** Britt, *The Princess and the P.O.W.*, 42.
91 **"You'll never get back in this crate":** "World War II Bombardier Al Romano," *Primo*, vol. 9, no. 4 (November/December 2008).

91 **"Starters whined as the props":** Hill, *Black Sunday,* 45.
91 **"nervous bark of engines":** McFarland and Gonzalez, "Hell at Fifty Feet," 34.
92 **the next day would be "a full day for us":** Ronald Helder, letter to family, July 31, 1943, rajordan.com/pete/19430731-letter.html.
93 **leaving a "rooster tail":** Christensen, "[389th BG B-24 Co-Pilot Memoir]."
94 **"groaned into the air":** Hill, *Black Sunday,* 45.
94 **"We looked to our engines":** McCormick, quoted in Shubert, "World War II: Eyewitness to the Raid on Ploesti."
95 **"The target must be destroyed":** Dugan and Stewart, *Ploesti,* 79.
95 **"Either we hit Ploesti":** John Young, "Over the Target," *Air Force,* November 1943, 11.

15. THE WRATH OF OLYMPUS

96 **would dub the Ploesti Express:** Hill, *Black Sunday,* 54.
96 **"the bluest Mediterranean you can imagine":** McCormick, quoted in Shubert, "World War II: Eyewitness to the Raid on Ploesti."
97 **decided to "play Combat Correspondent":** McFarland and Gonzalez,"Hell at Fifty Feet," 92.
97 **"a morning when one would rather":** McClain, "My Most Memorable Combat Mission," 3.
97 **lifted their noses, "painfully, sluggishly":** McFarland and Gonzalez,"Hell at Fifty Feet," 92.
98 **was "not a pilot's airplane":** Underwood, "Northern Star over Ploesti," 33.
99 **"a fiery temper when provoked":** "Uzal Girard Ent: Commanding General Second Air Force Wendover, UT," Atomic Heritage Foundation, ahf.nuclearmuseum.org/ahf/profile/uzal-girard-ent.
99 **but "like it or not":** Hill, *Black Sunday,* 24.
103 **"What's burning up there, Al?":** Britt, *The Princess and the P.O.W.,* 45.
103 **a fast descent to "duck in":** McFarland and Gonzalez, "Hell at Fifty Feet," 92.

16. THE HAND OF FATE

106 **"Others ignored us completely":** Ellis, "Ploesti."
106 **"nevertheless, they smiled and waved":** Ellis, "Ploesti."
106 **almost pulled "the entire outfit off course":** McFarland and Gonzalez, Jr., "Hell at Fifty Feet," 92.
106 **"This is where I bail out!":** Dugan and Stewart, *Ploesti,* 102.
106 **"We thought this was going to be heaven":** Dugan and Stewart, *Ploesti,* 103.
107 **"there was now no hope of all five groups":** Wilson and Mackay, *The Sky Scorpions,* 32.
107 **twenty-six, "older and wiser":** Britt, *The Princess and the P.O.W.,* 24.
109 **"Has the Luftwaffe taken the day off?":** Hill, *Black Sunday,* 51.
110 **"talking and joking nervously":** McFarland and Gonzalez, "Hell at Fifty Feet," 92.
111 **faced their lot with "grim determination":** *History of the 389th.*

17. BENDING THE POPLARS

113 **"a handsome, robust, blue-eyed woman":** Dugan and Stewart, *Ploesti,* 189.
113 **"the most awful roaring noise":** Catherine Caradja, "Plane Crash Sends Rumanian on Mercy Mission for American Fliers," *The Birmingham* (Alabama) *News,* January 08, 1956, 16.
113 **"a dozen trains were bearing down":** Catherine Caradja, *Princess Catherine* (Gabriel Publishing, 1991), 116.
113 **"They're touching the tops of the poplars":** Caradja, "Plane Crash," 16.
113 **"were nearly bowled over by air blasts":** Dugan and Stewart, *Ploesti,* 189.
114 **"lowest-flying planes":** Helen Waterhouse, "'Angel of Ploesti' Finds Five of Her 'Boys' Here," *Akron* (Ohio) *Beacon Journal,* April 22, 1965, 1.
114 **"The planes were so low that":** Caradja, "Plane Crash," 16.
114 **The little girl was "clinging" to her:** Caradja, "Plane Crash," 16.
115 **"We stood and watched the huge columns":** Caradja, "Plane Crash," 16.
115 **"looked like a fishing net woven of":** Dugan and Stewart, *Ploesti,* 118.

115 **"the closest thing to Dante's Inferno":** Byers, *Attack,* 201.

115 **"the loud explosion of bombs":** Caradja, "Plane Crash," 16.

18. RED TARGET

117 **lending a "typically romantic" charm:** Richard Britt, "The Crew Diary," February 1944.

118 **"reflected the bright sunlight":** Ellis, "Ploesti: A Pilot's Diary."

118 **"We were so low you could":** Hill, *Black Sunday,* 112.

119 **"Maybe we were actually going to":** Hill, *Black Sunday,* 54.

119 **"attended by women in embroidered skirts":** Dugan and Stewart, *Ploesti,* 70.

119 **"an unnatural noise," remembered one:** Dumitru, *Aviatorul Erou,* 117.

120 **"hurtling down the valley":** Dugan and Stewart, *Ploesti,* 182.

121 **"Gunners, keep your eyes open for fighters":** McCormick, quoted in Shubert, "World War II: Eyewitness to the Raid on Ploesti."

121 **bursts of sporadic "orange blips":** Hill, *Black Sunday,* 143.

121 **"That was us looking down the barrels":** Hill, *Black Sunday,* 143.

122 **"Lead, they're shooting at us":** James Salter, *The Hunters* (Counterpoint, 1997), 148.

122 **"You can't fight back":** Byers, *Attack,* 92.

122 **"running in all directions desperately":** Dumitru, *Aviatorul Erou,*118.

122 **"Farm couples down in the streets fall":** McFarland and Gonzalez, "Hell at Fifty Feet," 92.

123 **flying "so low that I could discern":** Dumitru, *Aviatorul Erou,* 117.

123 **"helplessly looking" at the rooftop guns:** Dugan and Stewart, *Ploesti,* 182.

124 **"flinging up a fountain of debris":** Dugan and Stewart, *Ploesti,* 184.

124 **"Explosive flames were leaping high":** Preble, *Written in the Sand,* 121.

125 **from a "small wooded area":** Britt, *The Princess and the P.O.W.,* 46.

125 **a "ball of fire" came at him:** Hayes, "Recorded Memoir of Russell Hayes."

125 **better than being a "sitting duck":** Britt, *The Princess and the P.O.W.,* 46.

125 **just "interrupted his Sunday dinner":** Hayes, "Recorded Memoir of Russell Hayes."

127 **first you'd hear "chunk!":** James Beane, *James B. Beane, US Air Force, retired: AO413562* (self-published, 2000).

127 **"grinding in your ears":** Byers, *Attack,* 162.

127 **"plainly hear" the flak guns:** Phillip Rurak, "The Crew Diary," February 1944.

128 **"really pouring it out":** Rurak, "Crew Diary."

129 **"gently lowered by some invisible arms":** Britt, *The Princess and the P.O.W.,* 47.

129 **"blue-white" sparks onto the ground:** Britt, *The Princess and the P.O.W.,* 47.

129 **"Bombs away!" Al shouted:** Jack Bowker, "The Crew Diary," February 1944.

130 **like "rats, gnawing through building":** Dugan and Stewart, *Ploest,* 118.

130 **careening "down a narrow city street":** Hill, *Black Sunday,* 141.

130 **"It was like stirring up a bee's nest":** Christensen, "[389th BG B-24 Co-Pilot Memoir]."

132 **spot the gun "drift away" from him:** Louis Medeiros, "The Crew Diary," February 1944.

132 **a good burst of "45–50 rounds":** Medeiros, "Crew Diary."

19. EVERY TRICK IN THE BOOK

134 ***Chattanooga Choo Choo* "was acting funny":** Clell Riffle, "The Crew Diary," February 1944.

136 **"Panic may be the equivalent of suicide":** Ardery, *Bomber Pilot,* 90.

140 **the crew could "feel the earth":** Troy McCrary, "The Crew Diary," February 1944.

140 **"horrible sound of metal scraping, screeching":** Poulson, *Personal History,* 31.

140 **The bomber was "tearing apart":** McCrary, "Crew Diary."

140 **"wondering when consciousness would leave":** Poulson, *Personal History,* 31.

20. THE HUNTED

141 **"It seemed incredible that I could still walk":** Ernest Poulson, "Diary—Ernest L. Poulson: Written While a Prisoner of War in Rumania During World War II," August 1, 1943.

143 **"our powerful warbird":** Poulson, *Personal History,* 32.

143 **"I found I could walk by dragging my leg a little":** Riffle, "Crew Diary."
144 **"excited voices," in a foreign tongue:** Poulson, *Personal History,* 32.
144 **"crawled about 5-7 paces away":** Medeiros, "Crew Diary."
145 **"Scores of pistols and rifles were cocked":** Poulson, *Personal History,* 32.
145 **"A puzzled sigh was all I could offer":** Poulson, *Personal History,* 33.
146 **"their hands trembled, and their voices":** Poulson, *Personal History,* 32.
146 **"The military personnel have at least some semblance":** Beane, *James B. Beane.*
146 **come "from nowhere":** Medeiros, "Crew Diary."
146 **A guardsman "pointed his gun at her":** Medeiros, "Crew Diary."
147 **Ernie heard Al "furiously" reciting:** "World War II Bombardier Al Romano."
147 **He "cut loose" with his machine pistol:** Medeiros, "Crew Diary."
147 **"for whom they have a real mortal fear":** Poulson, *Personal History,* 32.
147 **"I think they understood":** Poulson, *Personal History,* 32.

21. BACK TO LIFE

149 **Britt began "coughing and gasping for air":** Richard Britt, "The Crew Diary," February 1944.
150 **"was so great that the turret might just as well":** Britt, "Crew Diary."
150 **a "flaming" bomber as it crashed:** "Princess Visits 'Her Boys' in US," *Austin American Statesman,* April 17, 1963, 34.
150 **"The dead man is moving!":** Caradja, "Plane Crash," 16.
150 **"Now, my dear, you must go inside":** Dugan and Stewart, *Ploesti,* 190.
150 **"The crumpled plane was almost hidden":** Caradja, "Plane Crash," 16.
151 **"Your Honor, the Russians have come":** Dugan and Stewart, *Ploesti,* 190.
151 **"making feeble movements and heard":** Caradja, "Plane Crash," 16.
151 **"You're not a Russian, are you?":** Caradja, "Plane Crash," 16.
151 **"Good! We'll have you out in a jiffy":** Caradja, *Princess Catherine,* 118.
151 **"My legs were quite useless":** Britt, "Crew Diary."
151 **uttered a "loud sigh" of relief:** Britt, *The Princess and the P.O.W.,* 4.
151 **Britt began "shaking violently":** Britt, "Crew Diary."
151 **"freshly drycleaned," but a look underneath:** Britt, *The Princess and the P.O.W.,* 6.
151 **"an angry murmur swept the crowd":** Catherine Caradja, "Jab of Elbow Doubled Up Guard, Freed Flier," *The Birmingham* (Alabama) *News,* January 9, 1956, 13.
152 **"We will take that man, your highness":** Caradja, "Jab of Elbow."
152 **"I had an idea of what would happen":** Caradja, "Jab of Elbow."
152 **"the Nazis followed, demanding that we":** Caradja, "Jab of Elbow."
152 **"We will take him," the officer said:** Caradja, "Jab of Elbow."
152 **in a "tug of war" over:** Dugan and Stewart, *Ploesti,* 191.

22. HELLO, BOYS

153 **"halted by the sight" of a throng:** Caradja, "Jab of Elbow," 13.
153 **"For safety's sake we hid the Americans in a cellar!":** Dugan and Stewart, *Ploesti,* 191.
153 **wanted to slap her forehead":** Dugan and Stewart, *Ploesti,* 191.
154 **"It all seemed almost like a dream":** Poulson, *Personal History,* 33.
154 **A "widely-known" Phoenix girl:** "Wed New Year's Eve," *Arizona Republic,* January 7, 1945, 17.
154 **"old time residents" who owned:** "Wed New Year's Eve."
155 **"regrettably did not include Helen":** Poulson, *Personal History,* 22.
155 **"and a lady of about 50 years greeted us":** Poulson, *Personal History,* 33.
155 **"Boys, there are only friends here":** Dugan and Stewart, *Ploesti,* 191.
155 **"Bring food!" she called:** Caradja, *Princess Catherine,* 119.
156 **"one of the most joyful bits of news":** Poulson, *Personal History,* 34.
156 **for "a peep" at the fliers:** Poulson, *Personal History,* 34.
156 **"gay and vivacious":** John Manley, Executive Director War Prisoners' Aid of the Y.M.C.A., Letter to Next of Kin of American Prisoners in Rumania, November 24, 1943, Al Romano Collection.

156 **"The Romanian army was looted":** Vasile Tudor, *Constantin "Bâzu" Cantacuzino,* 46.
157 **"astounded the Americans":** Caradja, "Jab of Elbow," 13.
157 **"We like Americans very much":** Dugan and Stewart, *Ploesti,* 192.
157 **"I explained to them that Romanians":** Caradja, "Jab of Elbow," 13.
157 **"We're on the wrong side of this war":** Britt, *The Princess and the P.O.W.,* 65.
157 **"While officially Romania is an Axis partner":** Manley, Letter to Next of Kin.
157 **"We began to see that maybe we had":** Ernest Poulson, interviewed by National World War II Museum, Salt Lake City, Utah, October 23, 2013, ww2online.org/view/ernest-poulson.
158 **"clamoring for our custody":** Poulson, *Personal History,* 35.
158 **"No, never in my life":** Caradja, "Jab of Elbow," 13.
159 **"cold declaration":** Poulson, *Personal History,* 34.
159 **"No, we will never see you again":** Caradja, "Jab of Elbow," 13.
160 **"in the main hall, upon a straw-littered floor":** Dugan and Stewart, *Ploesti,* 227.

23. THE AFRICAN KNIGHTS

161 **renamed Piața Adolf Hitler:** Diana Toea, "Piața Charles de Gaulle s-a numit Hitler în '40 şi Stalin în '47, după cum a bătut vântul intereselor" [Charles de Gaulle Square was called Hitler Square in '40 and Stalin Square in '47, depending on which way the wind of interests was blowing], October 4, 2012, adevarul.ro/stiri-locale/bucuresti/piata-charles-de-gaulle-s-a-numit-hitler-in-40-si-1375459.html.
161 **"A plan had been forming":** Caradja, *Princess Catherine,* 123.
162 **among them "several wives of":** Dugan and Stewart, *Ploesti,* 230.
162 **"would have a better chance of being":** Julia Cass, "For American Prisoners, the Princess Let Bars Down," *Philadelphia Inquirer,* August 21, 1981, C11.
162 **"The Americans are trying to help us":** Caradja, *Princess Catherine,* 123.
162 **"What falls in our country is *ours*":** Marion Mitchell, "Romanian Princess Visits 'Her' POWs," *Standard Times* (Mass.), Al Romano Collection.
162 **"I used every argument":** Cass, "For American Prisoners."
162 **"I don't blame the Americans":** Caradja, *Princess Catherine,* 123.
163 **"an understandable military necessity":** Edith Hoad, *The Eagle's Child: The Life and Times of Romanian Princess Catherine Caradja* (self-published, 2011), 161.
163 **"shoplifters, political opponents of Antonescu":** Dugan and Stewart, *Ploesti,* 127.
163 **"had at that time the support":** Ivor Porter, *Michael of Romania: The King and the Country* (Sutton, 2005), 70.
163 **"Romania's natural ally":** Porter, *Michael of Romania,* 71.
163 **"We do not have one Romanian soldier":** Murrey, "Romania's Disaster."
163 **"declare Romania's war goals complete":** Murrey, "Romania's Disaster."
163 **"Romania had no place in Hitler's war":** Porter, *Michael of Romania,* 71.
164 **"They failed to stop him":** Porter, *Michael of Romania,* 71.
164 **"holy war" against "Judeo-Bolshevism":** Jean Ancel, "Antonescu and the Jews," in Michael Berenbaum and Abraham Peck, eds., *The Holocaust and History: The Known, the Unknown, the Disputed and the Reexamined* (Indiana University Press, 1998), 466.
164 **Romania would "continue their advance":** Murrey, "Romania's Disaster."
164 **"What a reversal of concepts":** Tudor, *Constantin "Bâzu" Cantacuzino,* 108.
164 **"Cavaleri Africani":** Hill, *Black Sunday,* 174.
164 **"It wasn't difficult to get their support":** Caradja, *Princess Catherine,* 123.
164 **"Threaten to lock your bedroom door":** Caradja, *Princess Catherine,* 123.

24. ORPHANS

165 **"heavy brown wooden beams":** Britt, *The Princess and the P.O.W.,* 8.
165 **"like an Egyptian mummy":** Britt, *The Princess and the P.O.W.,* 9.
165 **"Why the hurry?" Britt later wrote:** Britt, *The Princess and the P.O.W.,* 21.
166 **His "English-speaking friend"?:** Britt, *The Princess and the P.O.W.,* 21.

167 **"Are you really a princess"?:** Britt, *The Princess and the P.O.W.,* 22.
167 **becoming "a human torch":** Britt, "Crew Diary."
167 **"She looked at the others":** Britt, *The Princess and the P.O.W.,* 24.
167 **"Three thousand." She beamed with pride:** Caradja, "Plane Crash," 16.
167 **Saint Catherine's Crib, an orphanage:** Caradja, "Plane Crash," 16.
167 **"from infancy to young adulthood":** Caradja, "Plane Crash," 16.
168 **"How do you support three thousand":** Britt, *The Princess and the P.O.W.,* 28.
168 **"1,000 of the older boys and girls":** Caradja, "Plane Crash," 16.
168 **"I managed to provide for my children":** Caradja, "Plane Crash," 16.
168 **She called them "my kids":** Cass, "For American Prisoners."
168 **"There aren't enough hours in the day":** Britt, *The Princess and the P.O.W.,* 56.
168 **At last, "the officer stepped out of the group":** Britt, *The Princess and the P.O.W.,* 28.

25. THE ENEMY OF YOUR ENEMY

170 **"worrying about the suffering of":** Tudor, *Constantin "Bâzu" Cantacuzino,* 110.
171 **"amplify the sufferings of the":** Tudor, *Constantin "Bâzu" Cantacuzino,* 110.
171 **a "fervent" Anglophile whose:** Constantin Cantacuzino Siguranța file, March 1, 1943, entry.
171 **"close friendship ties":** Constantin Cantacuzino Siguranța file, December 24, 1939, entry.
172 **"a wealth on the table":** Tudor, *Constantin "Bâzu" Cantacuzino,*102.
172 **"That was really insulting!":** Tudor, *Constantin "Bâzu" Cantacuzino,*102.
172 **"Bâzu stood up," Dobran recalled:** Dobran, Dobrovicescu, and Grecea, Facebook video.

26. EMPLOYEE NO. 158

174 **"shy in the presence of strangers":** "King Carol of Rumania: A Reformed Rake Is Shrewdest Balkan Politician," *Life,* February, 19, 1940, 75.
174 **"There was a certain gentleness":** Porter, *Michael of Romania,* 43.
174 **"Romanians, who all love him":** "King Carol of Rumania: A Reformed Rake," 75.
174 **they decided to "import a king":** Britt, *The Princess and the P.O.W.,* 23.
175 **had "bucked up" Antonescu:** Dugan and Stewart, *Ploesti,* 231.
175 **"I shall hand over all those we have arrested":** Dugan and Stewart, *Ploesti,* 231.
176 **"wanted to see some of the downed":** Caradja, *Princess Catherine,* 123.
176 **"he liked delving into the interior":** Arthur Stanley Gould Lee, *Crown Against the Sickle: The Story of King Michael of Rumania* (Hutchinson, 1950), 19.
176 **"Every Friday morning he went":** Porter, *Michael of Romania,* 42.
176 **He was simply employee "No. 158":** "King Carol of Rumania: A Reformed Rake," 75.
176 **"he became an excellent self-taught engineer":** Porter, *Michael of Romania,* 42.
177 **"He was impressed with the size of the plane":** Caradja, *Princess Catherine,* 124.
178 **"What is this?" Michael asked:** Porter, *Michael of Romania,* 70.
178 **"My country declaring war against":** King Michael I of Romania, interviewed by Paul Shapiro, United States Holocaust Memorial Museum, November 12, 2001.
178 **"He called for Romania to discontinue":** Porter, *Michael of Romania,* 81.
178 **The German ambassador "protested violently":** Porter, *Michael of Romania,* 81.

27. MEET THE NEIGHBORS

180 **"most comfortably furnished" hotels:** Manley, Letter to Next of Kin.
181 **"had a brief encounter with his own mortality":** Thrity Umrigar, "Freedom Contributes to a Rare Friendship," *The Akron* (Ohio) *Beacon Journal,* August 19, 1987, 33.
182 **"It looked like a setting for":** Britt, *The Princess and the P.O.W.,* 94.
182 **"His majesty Mihai the first!":** Dugan and Stewart, *Ploesti,* 236.
182 **Queen Helen, the "pillar" of his life:** Ștefana Totorcea, "Queen Mother Helen of Romania Was Born 125 Years Ago. King Michael: 'She Was Strong Through Prayer,'" May 4, 2021, basilica.ro/en/queen-mother-helen-of-romania-was-born-125-years-ago-king-michael-she-was-strong-through-prayer.

182 **with a "luminous personality":** Totorcea, "Queen Mother Helen."
182 **"The Bible, undoubtedly":** Totorcea, "Queen Mother Helen."
183 **"The kid looks like good college":** Dugan and Stewart, *Ploesti,* 236.
183 **"He might make a good tackle":** John Palm and Kyle Crichton, "A Texan in King Michael's Court," *Collier's,* November 25, 1944, 17.
183 **"made his way across the room":** Porter, *Michael of Romania,* 43.
183 **"men with the lobes of their ears":** Jerome Caminada, *My Purpose Holds* (London: Jonathan Cape, 1952), 183.
183 **"Don't tell him," he whispered:** "King Carol of Rumania: A Reformed Rake," 75.
184 **"well-treated" during their time:** Dugan and Stewart, *Ploesti,* 236.
184 **From "the rear ranks of the crowd":** "Royal Aid Reported for Ploesti Raiders," *New York Times,* August 30, 1943.
184 **"a lot of excitement":** Palm and Crichton, "A Texan in King Michael's Court," 17.
184 **Still "doped up" on painkillers:** Palm and Crichton, "A Texan in King Michael's Court," 17.
184 **"a distinguished-looking lady":** Palm and Crichton, "A Texan in King Michael's Court," 17.
185 **"Hurts like hell, ma'am":** Britt, *The Princess and the P.O.W.,* 212.
185 **"So they know us in America!":** Palm and Crichton, "A Texan in King Michael's Court," 17.
185 **"I don't think the queen wanted":** Palm and Crichton, "A Texan in King Michael's Court," 17.
185 **"people with big ears" everywhere:** King Michael I of Romania, interviewed by Paul Shapiro.
185 **"Do you think the Americans understand":** Palm and Crichton, "A Texan in King Michael's Court," 17.

28. SCENE OF THE CRIME

187 **"inviting her to visit the grave":** "Princess Who Aided US Flyers Visits Here," *The Courier-Journal* (Louisville, Ky.), May 18, 1956, 17.
187 **"Looks like we're home," one man said:** Dugan and Stewart, *Ploesti,* 191.
188 **"he was of great girth":** Caminada, *My Purpose Holds,* 181.
188 **"strutted about importantly":** Caminada, *My Purpose Holds,* 181.
189 **"If we didn't bomb Ploesti on that day":** "Walter Travis Stewart," American Air Museum in Britain, americanairmuseum.com/archive/person/walter-travis-stewart.
189 **"I intend to go over that target":** Hill, *Black Sunday,* 38.
189 **"a pitch-black inferno filled":** Walter Boyne, "Tidal Wave," *Air & Space Forces Magazine,* December 1, 2007, airandspaceforces.com/article/1207wave.
189 **refineries left "in desolate ruin":** Dugan and Stewart, *Ploesti,* 239.
190 **"The fun-loving Americans figured":** Hill, *Black Sunday,* 174.
190 **"There was an approving hum":** Dugan and Stewart, *Ploesti,* 239.
191 **"could not locate or make out":** "Jack Woodrow Dieterle," American Air Museum in Britain, americanairmuseum.com/archive/person/jack-woodrow-dieterle.
191 **"a near perfect strike at Câmpina":** Hill, *Black Sunday,* 145.
191 **"classically executed" performance:** Dugan and Stewart, *Ploesti,* 188.
191 **"the most accurate and successful":** Zaloga, *Ploesti 1943,* 72.
192 **"For in Romania, one could not":** Caminada, *My Purpose Holds,* 186.
192 **"There's the King's Palace":** Caminada, *My Purpose Holds,* 182.
194 **"The scenery is beautiful":** Douglas Collins, *P.O.W.* (New York: W. W. Norton & Company, 1968), 210.
194 **"You are on your way to a hotel":** Caminada, *My Purpose Holds,* 182.
194 **"and on all sides, boxing the location":** Collins, *P.O.W.,* 212.
194 **It was called Lagărul Prizonieri Nr. 2:** Red Cross Report, September 28, 1943. The lodge was initially known as "Lagărul Prizonieri No. 2," before being administratively redesignated by the Romanians during the war to "No. 14," for reasons unknown. For clarity, I have used the original name throughout.
195 **"little tied-up bundles":** Caminada, *My Purpose Holds,* 181.
195 **"but somehow it doesn't seem so bad":** Collins, *P.O.W.,* 211.
197 **"A Romanian regulation has been":** Red Cross Report, September 28, 1943.

197 **"Someone had been priming Ivan":** Caminada, *My Purpose Holds,* 184.
197 **"set with flowers, with cutlery":** Caminada, *My Purpose Holds,* 184.
197 **"Finally, on a large table against":** Caminada, *My Purpose Holds,* 184.

29. THE BRIBE

198 **"our pride and joy":** Poulson, "Diary," November 1, 1943.
198 **"Vera Lynn singing in the rainbow club":** Collins, *P.O.W.,* 214.
199 **"American bomber crews had been recruited":** Beane, *James B. Beane.*
199 **"they had no intention of letting us go":** Caminada, *My Purpose Holds,* 188.
199 **"box-like, the jawbones seemed":** Britt, *The Princess and the P.O.W.,* 190.
199 **"Anyone thinking of escape should":** Caminada, *My Purpose Holds,* 184.
199 **"one fried egg per man, coffee, stewed pears":** Red Cross Report, September 28, 1943.
200 **"In some planes, no more than one or two":** Caminada, *My Purpose Holds,* 181.
200 **"Sounds great," Britt replied:** Britt, *The Princess and the P.O.W.,* 107.
201 **"The lights were to stay on":** Caminada, *My Purpose Holds,* 185.
202 **"It was a great family event when":** Poulson, *Personal History,* 7.
202 **"Good fiery stuff was what":** Caminada, *My Purpose Holds,* 185.
202 **"The first clear sounds were":** Britt, *The Princess and the P.O.W.,* 119.
202 **"sweat out each foot of ground gained":** Poulson, "Diary," November 1, 1943.
202 **"Each and all seemed to bring us":** Poulson, "Diary," September 23, 1943.
202 **"No one spoke during the broadcast":** Britt, *The Princess and the P.O.W.,* 119.

30. THE COLONEL'S CALL

204 **"This is no mail call! This is the colonel's call":** Caminada, *My Purpose Holds,* 190.
205 **"Parade? Parade? No one had ever":** Caminada, *My Purpose Holds,* 190.
205 **"The trees on either side of the road":** Caminada, *My Purpose Holds,* 189.
205 **treat their subordinates like "vassals":** Murrey, "Romania's Disaster."
205 **"Should a momentary swirl of dust":** Caminada, *My Purpose Holds,* 185.
206 **"In their army, the louder you yell":** Beane, *James B. Beane.*
206 **assembled in "a slipshod way":** Lawrence Lancashire, P.O.W. Statement, found within William H. Yaeger, Jr., Official Military Personnel File, NARA.
206 **"pajama pants, vests, shirt-sleeves, slippers":** Caminada, *My Purpose Holds,* 190.
206 **"The Commandant informs [you] that":** Red Cross Report, November 29, 1943.
206 **"To have his face slapped was a normal":** Caminada, *My Purpose Holds,* 189.
207 **"with great conscientiousness, punctuality":** "Peurmele Vitejilor Gorjului—Cavaleri ai ordinului, Mihai Viteazul" [The Ashes of the Brave of Gorj: Knights of the 'Michael the Brave' Order], Gorjeanul.ro.
207 **"I believe he was, or meant to be":** Caminada, *My Purpose Holds,* 190.
207 **"He looked distastefully at us":** Britt, *The Princess and the P.O.W.,* 123.
207 **"I cannot come out in my slippers!":** Lancashire, P.O.W. Statement.
208 **"that prisoners of war and their captors":** Beane, *James B. Beane.*
208 **"The fellows were laughing, and there":** Lancashire, P.O.W. Statement.
208 **"The colonel bounced about, a demon of rage":** Caminada, *My Purpose Holds,* 190.
208 **"I know the American Army does have discipline!":** Charles Wallace, P.O.W. Statement, found within William H. Yaeger, Jr., Official Military Personnel File, NARA.
208 **"He barked an order":** Caminada, *My Purpose Holds,* 190.
208 **on his heels and "stamped off":** William H. Yaeger, Jr., P.O.W. Statement, Official Military Personnel File, NARA.
208 **headed "gloomily" back inside:** Caminada, *My Purpose Holds,* 191.
208 **"This was a pity," remembered:** Caminada, *My Purpose Holds,* 191.

31. EVERY OUNCE OF BATTLE

210 **"remain in the open air all day":** Red Cross Report, September 28, 1943.
210 **demanding a full "apology":** Yaeger, P.O.W. Statement.

211 **"most of the officers had pretty bad nerves":** Norman Adams, P.O.W. Statement, found within William H. Yaeger, Jr., Official Military Personnel File, NARA.
211 **"a giant vise" for four hours:** Frank Owen, "Capt. Wallace, Back Home from Prison Camp, Finds It 'Like Wonderful Dream Come True,'" *Lynchburg* (Va.) *News & Advance,* 1944.
212 **"no disciplinary action was taken":** William H. Yaeger, Jr., Debrief Statement, Escape and Evasion Report, September 1944, NARA.
215 **"the outstanding boy of his class":** "Westwood Bomber Pilot Missing in European Area," *The Cincinnati Post,* August 16, 1943, 11.
215 **Russell Hayes watched the "horrible sight":** Hill, *Black Sunday,* 141.
216 **a "fine, religious, conscientious boy with":** Ardery, *Bomber Pilot,* 104.
216 **"Okay," Hughes replied. "[But first] I":** Wilson and Mackay, *The Sky Scorpions,* 28.
216 **"He stuck right in formation with us":** Ardery, *Bomber Pilot,* 104.
217 **"To the very end, he gave the battle":** Ardery, *Bomber Pilot,* 106.

32. THE PROJECT

218 **the conspirators called it the Project:** Poulson, "Diary," January 12, 1944.
219 **"before beginning to go outwards":** Caminada, *My Purpose Holds,* 196.
219 **"No one on this crew has any intelligence":** Elmer Reinhart, P.O.W. Statement, found within William H. Yaeger, Jr., Official Military Personnel File, NARA.
219 **"I gradually lost my desire to eat":** Poulson, *Personal History,* 9.
221 **"a man would emerge black in the face":** Collins, *P.O.W.,* 219.

33. THE AMBASSADOR OF GOODWILL

222 **as if it were a "living friend":** Collins, *P.O.W.,* 219.
223 **"She likes Americans. She enjoys fighting for":** Britt, *The Princess and the P.O.W.,* 128.
223 **"would she be of help with escape plans?":** Britt, *The Princess and the P.O.W.,* 128.
223 **"We had learned our lesson":** Britt, *The Princess and the P.O.W.,* 130.
224 **"Welcome to Romania," she said to the men:** Britt, *The Princess and the P.O.W.,* 130.
224 **"Just a moment," she said, with a smile:** Britt, *The Princess and the P.O.W.,* 130.
224 **"cut him down with a few sharp phrases":** Beane, *James B. Beane.*
224 **"I know English very well," she told:** Caradja, "Jab of Elbow."
224 **"I want to tell the Americans that":** Cass, "For American Prisoners."
224 **She "made no bones about her opinion":** Caminada, *My Purpose Holds,* 189.
225 **"wet my whistle," "in a jiffy," "scoot":** Hoad, *The Eagle's Child,* 165–166.
225 **"There was a stunned silence at first":** Britt, *The Princess and the P.O.W.,* 131.
225 **"ping pong tournaments, bridge tournaments":** Yaeger, Debrief Statement, Escape and Evasion Report.
225 **particularly "American books":** Red Cross Report.
226 **a hundred pairs of "union suits":** Catherine Caradja, "Romanian Princess Cheers Airmen by Taking Them Clothing, Food," *The Montreal Star,* January 16, 1956, 19.
226 **"Now," she said. "You select your":** Britt, *The Princess and the P.O.W.,* 132.
226 **she referred to Bambino as "My Al":** Richard Connolly, "Princess Visits Revere Man She Aided as PW," July 1956, Al Romano Collection.
226 **"Well," she said, smiling, "I made it":** Britt, *The Princess and the P.O.W.,* 132.
226 **"to know and love this motherly woman":** Bruce Bissonette, "Princess Meets with Her 'Boys' in El Paso Reunion," *The El Paso Times,* July 31, 1975, 5.
226 **"A more well-versed and interesting":** Poulson, "Diary," November 15, 1943.
226 **"doing graceful ballet steps":** Britt, *The Princess and the P.O.W.,* 133.

34. SEPARATION

228 **"To stand in the compound, knowing what was":** Collins, *P.O.W.,* 222.
229 **they needed for their "theatrical":** Britt, *The Princess and the P.O.W.,* 149.
229 **planned to stage "a few theatricals":** Yaeger, Debrief Statement, Escape and Evasion Report.
230 **"The costumes are in the back seat":** Britt, *The Princess and the P.O.W.,* 143.

230 **Britt found flapper dresses and more:** Britt, *The Princess and the P.O.W.*, 143.
230 **He later wrote, "She outfoxed us":** Britt, *The Princess and the P.O.W.*, 144.
231 **"I'm asking you again—do not try to escape":** Britt, *The Princess and the P.O.W.*, 145.
231 **Britt later wrote, "We could not disagree with her":** Britt, *The Princess and the P.O.W.*, 145.
231 **was a "flamboyant playboy":** Steven Aavang, *In Love with Freedom: The True Story of a Remarkable Woman* (AuthorHouse, 2011), 18–19.
232 **her name was Jeanne Bardin:** Caradja, *Princess Catherine*, 1.
232 **"A mother who lost her child, for children":** Cass, "For American Prisoners."
233 **"not many people have a monument":** Britt, *The Princess and the P.O.W.*, 28.

35. THE BIG BREAK

234 **"Each scoop of dirt meant we were a little closer":** Britt, *The Princess and the P.O.W.*, 139.
234 **everything "was ready for the big break":** Collins, *P.O.W.*, 223.
235 **"It was difficult to play that evening":** Britt, *The Princess and the P.O.W.*, 157–158.
235 **"the way the cowboys do it in the movies":** Collins, *P.O.W.*, 226.
236 **From his "worm's eye view":** Collins, *P.O.W.*, 226.
236 **"wading streams and crossing wheat fields":** McCrary, "Crew Diary."
237 **"The bushes, thank Christ!":** Collins, *P.O.W.*, 227.
237 **"Below us the camp is an oasis of light":** Collins, *P.O.W.*, 227.
237 **"the clouds have cleared and the moon is up":** Collins, *P.O.W.*, 228.
237 **"Only one thing for it now. Run like hell":** Collins, *P.O.W.*, 228.
238 **lay still "in a patch of deep shadow":** Collins, *P.O.W.*, 241.
238 **"permanent duty" on the Eastern Front:** William H. Yaeger, Jr., War Discharge Review Board Interview, Official Military Personnel File, 1946, NARA.
238 **He'd fallen "into the gaping tunnel exit":** Collins, *P.O.W.*, 241.
239 **"Merge la sus!" he cried, pointing:** Britt, *The Princess and the P.O.W.*, 158.
239 **"If you want us to 'merge la sus,' get these":** *The Princess and the P.O.W.*, 158.
239 **"Sergeant Rurak's skull was cut open":** Russell Huntley, P.O.W. Statement, found within William H. Yaeger, Jr., Escape and Evasion Report, NARA.
239 **"with very black hair slicked back":** Phillip Rurak, P.O.W. Statement, Escape and Evasion Report, NARA.
240 **Cavaropol had had his "evening's drinking interrupted":** Collins, *P.O.W.*, 241.
240 **"Drunk on both anger and liquor":** Collins, *P.O.W.*, 241–242.
241 **"so narrow that a man's shoulders touch the sides":** Rurak, P.O.W. Statement.
241 **"At least we ain't been shot":** Collins, *P.O.W.*, 242.

36. THE TIPPING POINT

242 **"yelling at the top of his voice":** Britt, *The Princess and the P.O.W.*, 150.
243 **"His anger increased as he [Cavaropol] yelled":** Britt, *The Princess and the P.O.W.*, 150.
243 **"against this barrage of anger":** Britt, *The Princess and the P.O.W.*, 150.
244 **"There was no one to let me enter":** Caradja, *Princess Catherine*, 133.
244 **"I innocently played a part in the plot":** "Romanian Princess Cheers Airmen."
244 **"What has happened?" she asked:** Caradja, *Princess Catherine*, 133.
245 **"an undercurrent of dislike for the man":** Caradja, *Princess Catherine*, 133.
245 **"Not wanting to make any more trouble":** Caradja, *Princess Catherine*, 133.
245 **"A feeling of gloom descended on us":** Britt, *The Princess and the P.O.W.*, 151.
246 **"We are all lucky to be alive after":** Al Romano, letter to his family, August 14, 1943.
246 **"Let me know who is the winner":** Al Romano, letter to his family, September 16, 1943.
246 **she "broke speeding laws":** Caradja, *Princess Catherine*.
246 **"Oh, no, my dear," she corrected him:** Britt, *The Princess and the P.O.W.*, 66.
246 **"white fur on the hills":** Collins, *P.O.W.*, 246.
246 **"One morning, several military vehicles":** Britt, *The Princess and the P.O.W.*, 160.
247 **"relieved of his command because":** Red Cross Report, "Camp for Prisoners at Timisul de Jos and Military Hospital at Brasov: Visited by Mr. Ch. Kolb, on January 5, 1944," NARA.

247 **"who was openly an Allied sympathizer":** Dugan and Stewart, *Ploesti,* 263. Postwar accounts often misname the Romanian commandants of Lagărul Prizonieri No. 2. Using Red Cross documents from the period, we have identified the correct commandants at the correct times.

247 **"At the close of his speech, without a word":** Poulson, "Diary," December 21, 1943.

247 **"I felt like crying when the national anthem":** Clay Ferguson, "World War II diary," December 24, 1943, omaha.com/collection_b31bf02e-49e6-581b-8c14-256703187dc6.html.

248 **"was tall, beautiful, and knew it":** Adina Scorțescu, "Caradja și Cantacuzino Istoria Numelor Care nu se Pierd și a Patrimoniului Care nu e Avere" [Caradja and Cantacuzino: The History of Names That Do Not Get Lost and of the Heritage That Is Not Riches], *Historia,* no. 248 (September 2022), 20.

248 **"bad boys," as she put it:** Britt, *The Princess and the P.O.W.,* 152.

248 **The tunnel was "the talk of Bucharest":** Caradja, *Princess Catherine,* 134.

37. SPRING

249 **"still as slim as a young cavalry officer":** Ivor Porter, *Operation Autonomous* (Bloomsbury, 2012), 299.

250 **"marking their passage like the breath":** Collins, *P.O.W.,* 257.

250 **"used by Nazi Germany to transport troops":** Sorin Marin, "Bucharest Astronomical Observatory in the Blaze of World War II," Astronomical Institute of the Romanian Academy, 154, astro.ro/~roaj/34_3/2024_3_03.pdf.

250 **"At this eleventh hour, unless Romania breaks":** Porter, *Michael of Romania,* 91.

251 **"For the first time German soldiers":** Porter, *Michael of Romania,* 93.

251 **"could hit a barrel from 25,000":** Palm and Crichton, "A Texan in King Michael's Court," 54.

252 **"You hear the terrible explosions all around":** Dumitru, *Aviatorul Erou,* 119.

253 **"leaping from the asphalt":** Lee, *Crown Against the Sickle,* 53–54.

254 **"There was nowhere to step without":** Dumitru, *Aviatorul Erou,* 120.

254 **"his spirit heavy with the knowledge":** Lee, *Crown Against the Sickle,* 53–54.

254 **"That he was there at this ghastly moment":** Lee, *Crown Against the Sickle,* 53–54.

254 **some called "heedless curiosity":** Lee, *Crown Against the Sickle,* 53–54.

38. EVERYTHING THAT EVER MATTERED

255 **carried "the grace of a ballet dancer":** "Role Played by Princess: Kent Epic Stars Rumanian Royalty," *The Windsor Star* (U.K.), October 6, 1951, 17.

255 **Theirs was a "genuine love story":** Constantin Cantacuzino Siguranța file, September 4, 1941 entry.

256 **"personally assured each exiting passenger":** Marian Christy, "Nadia Gray's No Longer Blue: Banker's Wife Enters Limelight," *Mansfield* (Ohio) *News Journal,* May 12, 1976, 18.

256 **captivating, possessing "natural poise":** "Role Played by Princess," 17.

256 **When they "looped the loop":** Ernest Leogrande, "Nadia's 'Dolce Vita' Play Like a Script," *Daily News* (N.Y.), March 22, 1976, 23.

257 **"pulled out of the plane between battles":** Constantin Cantacuzino Siguranța file, September 16, 1941 entry.

257 **To "Romanian-ize" society:** "The Exclusion of Jews from Romanian Society During the Antonescu Governments with and Without the Iron Guard: Antisemitic Legislation, Romanianization, and Expropriation," Jewish Virtual Library, jewishvirtuallibrary.org/jsource/Holocaust/Romania/six.pdf.

258 **"dangerous to our institution":** Constantin Cantacuzino Siguranța file, September 13, 1941 entry.

258 **"Kindly instruct NADIA KUJNIR that she":** Constantin Cantacuzino Siguranța file, September 18, 1941 entry.

258 **"I felt both very discouraged and deeply saddened":** Constantin Cantacuzino Siguranța file, September 16, 1941 entry.

258 **"horrific acts of mass butchery":** Robert Kaplan, "The Antonescu Paradox," *Foreign Policy,* February 5, 2016, foreignpolicy.com/2016/02/05/the-antonescu-paradox-romania-world-war-ii-hitler.

258 **"If you were a Jew within Antonescu's Romania":** Kaplan, "The Antonescu Paradox."
259 **"unannounced mock attacks":** Dugan and Stewart, *Ploesti,* 33.
260 **"I don't understand how an enemy, no matter":** Dumitru, *Aviatorul Erou,* 126.

39. THE WONDER WEAPON

262 **"Throughout Hitler's Reich," one account:** Jay Stout, *Fortress Ploesti: The Campaign to Destroy Hitler's Oil* (Casemate, 2017), 75.
262 **Even "old, small, inefficient" refineries:** David Klaus and Steve Buss, CAF Warbird Tube, "The Ploesti Raid," youtube.com/watch?v=KYYFLijFmIQ.
263 **"Some world we live in?" he later wrote:** John Williams, *Who Taught Us to Fly* (self-published, 1998), 13. Special Collections and Archives, Florida State University Libraries, Tallahassee, Fla.
263 **"not to worry—he won't hurt you":** Williams, *Who Taught Us to Fly,* 13.
263 **"unmannerly" new bunch of:** Dugan and Stewart, *Ploesti,* 269.
263 **"They say God takes care of drunks":** Williams, *Who Taught Us to Fly,* 13.
264 **"Well, if they missed, they will be back":** Beane, *James B. Beane.*
264 **"If you don't want to be bombed":** Beane, *James B. Beane.*
264 **"You have ambassadors in Turkey":** Beane, *James B. Beane.*
265 **"A tall, good-looking young man":** Williams, *Who Taught Us to Fly,* 13.
265 **"I couldn't have hurt a pillow":** Williams, *Who Taught Us to Fly,* 13.
265 **"Are you the king?":** Lee, *Crown Against the Sickle,* 55.
265 **he "thought it was a great ship":** Palm and Crichton, "A Texan in King Michael's Court," 54.
266 **"Why are you worrying about your gun?":** Lee, *Crown Against the Sickle,* 55.
266 **"his girl's picture" being on:** Lee, *Crown Against the Sickle,* 55.
267 **"Your plane was a P-51," Michael said:** Lee, *Crown Against the Sickle,* 55.
267 **"She was a lovely machine," he admitted:** Lee, *Crown Against the Sickle,* 55.
268 **"Would you send it to his wife":** Lee, *Crown Against the Sickle,* 55.

40. THE SPORTSMEN

270 **"the spearhead" of the air force:** Alexandru Arma, Ciprian Stoleru, Historia, "Misiunile Secrete în Care a Fost Implicat Constantin 'Bâzu' Cantacuzino, Asul Aviației Românești" [The Secret Missions in Which Constantin 'Bâzu' Cantacuzino, the Ace of Romanian Aviation, Was Involved], youtube.com/watch?v=P_zg5hgLE6k.
271 **'109 climbed "like an elevator":** Heimo Lampi (Finnish fighter pilot), quoted in Valtonen, *Me 109 Ja Saksan Sotatalous.*
271 **"forced to engage" the escorts:** Constantin Cantacuzino, Combat Report, 9th Fighter Group, June 6, 1944, reprinted in Dumitru, *Aviatorul Erou,* 122–123.
272 **"We were compelled to disengage":** Constantin Cantacuzino, Combat Report, 9th Fighter Group, June 6, 1944, reprinted in Dumitru, *Aviatorul Erou,* 122–123.
273 **At the controls of the Mustang:** Romanian sources have at times incorrectly stated that Cantacuzino shot down 2nd Lt. John Mumford on June 6, 1944. In fact, the aircraft he downed belonged to Mumford's flight leader, 1st Lt. Donald MacDonald—whom Cantacuzino saluted. This was confirmed by an American military recovery team in the summer of 2016, when Mumford's remains were found in the wreckage of his fighter.
276 **"as if providing cover":** Constantin Cantacuzino, Combat Report, 9th Fighter Group, June 6, 1944, reprinted in Dumitru, *Aviatorul Erou,* 122–23.
276 **It was "actually an inhuman feat":** Mike MacDonald, "Dad, Tuesday, June 6, 1944" (self-published).
278 **"I regret my father died at age 86":** Mike MacDonald, interviewed by Bryan Makos, January 2024.
279 **"We thank you sincerely":** "Dojmy z Krynice" [Impressions from Krynica], *Polední List* (Prague), February 7, 1931. Patrick Houda Collection.

41. ANYWHERE BUT HERE

281 **"only a few feet from our barbed wire":** Ferguson, "World War II Diary," April 1, 1944.
282 **a compromise: "more than half":** Paul Brickhill, *The Great Escape* (W. W. Norton & Company, 1950), 179.
282 **"We knew all about the fifty Allied fliers":** Palm and Crichton, "A Texan in King Michael's Court," 54.
282 **"Escape is no longer a sport":** Max Hastings, *Armageddon: The Battle for Germany, 1944–1945* (Vintage Books, 2004), 386.
283 **"Almost every evening he dropped in":** Caminada, *My Purpose Holds,* 197.
283 **"to cultivate personal friendships with":** Caminada, *My Purpose Holds,* 197.
283 **"My trips to Timisul were curtailed":** Caradja, *Princess Catherine,* 136–37.
284 **"The British and Americans have landed":** Dugan and Stewart, *Ploesti,* 267.
286 **"some considerable soul-searching":** Poulson, *Personal History,* 48.
287 **"Grata razboi, merga la casa":** Poulson, "Diary," March 25, 1944.
288 **"I am living for the day I get home":** Poulson, "Diary," July 29, 1944.

42. PERIL ON ALL SIDES

289 **"The imminent end of the war no doubt":** Poulson, *Personal History,* 48.
290 **"poised for a sweep" into Romania:** Collins, *P. O. W.,* 249.
290 **"praying for an Anglo-American invasion":** Poulson, "Diary," March 14, 1944.
290 **"the end of her class, the royalty":** Poulson, "Diary," November, 15, 1943.
291 **"difficult for her to put over":** Lt. Col. James Gunn III, 1944 Debrief, Reel AO601, Air Force Historical Research Agency, Maxwell AFB, Alabama.
291 **"twice the bomb load and half the gas":** Byers, *Attack,* 182.
291 **"the issue required further study":** Joseph Persico, *Roosevelt's Centurions: FDR and the Commanders He Led to Victory in World War II* (Random House, 2014), 375.
291 **"couldn't under any circumstances fly":** Byers, *Attack,* 182.
291 **"We simply did not trust the Russians":** Poulson, *Personal History,* 48.
292 **"The element of fear was a constant reality":** Poulson, *Personal History,* 48.
293 **"To be alone in them [the woods] is":** Collins, *P. O. W.,* 266.
293 **"I'll never forget his screams":** Larry West, "Ploesti Pilots Reunite 60 Years After Mission," *Deseret News* (Utah), August 1, 2003.
294 **"that these very peaks were the":** Collins, *P. O. W.,* 266.

43. YOU WILL ALL HANG

295 **"hats low over eyes, hands in pockets":** Collins, *P. O. W.,* 253.
295 **"bloodshed and assassination":** Caminada, *My Purpose Holds,* 193.
295 **"This was the ruthless personage":** Collins, *P. O. W.,* 253.
296 **"had nothing but bad news for the King":** Porter, *Operation Autonomous,* 298.
296 **"a slick-looking operator, the image":** Britt, *The Princess and the P. O. W.,* 188.
296 **"thick with cigarette smoke":** Porter, *Michael of Romania,* 108.
297 **"forever talking about honor":** Porter, *Michael of Romania,* 64.
297 **"an unhappy nature, a suspicious":** Porter, *Michael of Romania,* 64.
297 **"'So, you're an American, eh?'":** Palm and Crichton, "A Texan in King Michael's Court," 54.
297 **"That, in itself, would have":** Porter, *Operation Autonomous,* 298.
297 **"I have heard the news of the Russian":** Lee, *Crown Against the Sickle,* 69.
297 **"I should seek an armistice only on":** Lee, *Crown Against the Sickle,* 69.
298 **"You must seek an armistice":** Lee, *Crown Against the Sickle,* 69.
298 **"[Antonescu] had determined that":** Lee, *Crown Against the Sickle,* 70.
298 **"The moment has come," he said:** Porter, *Operation Autonomous,* 300.
299 **acting on "the wishes of my people":** Porter, *Operation Autonomous,* 300.
299 **"You are dismissed," the king said:** Porter, *Operation Autonomous,* 300.
299 **"Antonescu was taken completely":** Porter, *Operation Autonomous,* 300.
299 **this "operation," as they called it:** Porter, *Michael of Romania,* 111.

299 **"You can't treat me like a bandit":** Porter, *Operation Autonomous,* 300.
299 **"Carry out your orders!":** Porter, *Michael of Romania,* 111.
299 **who was "looking pale as a sheet":** Porter, *Operation Autonomous,* 300.
300 **"heard a dull thud upstairs":** Porter, *Operation Autonomous,* 300.
300 **"the firing of a single shot could":** Lee, *Crown Against the Sickle,* 72.
301 **"a perfect caricature of gangsterdom":** Caminada, *My Purpose Holds,* 193.
301 **"Al Capone would have been proud":** Britt, *The Princess and the P.O.W.,* 188.
301 **"Their hands were on their hips":** Caminada, *My Purpose Holds,* 193.
301 **Most began "chatting animatedly":** Lee, *Crown Against the Sickle,* 73.
301 **"I will do it," one brave officer:** Lee, *Crown Against the Sickle,* 73.
302 **"and leveled their rifles at":** Lee, *Crown Against the Sickle,* 73.
303 **"an officer and soldiers armed with":** Porter, *Michael of Romania,* 113.
303 **"a babel of voices" to a wing:** Lee, *Crown Against the Sickle,* 77.
303 **"were surprised" by the coup d'état:** Porter, *Michael of Romania,* 111.
303 **"insisted on a return to proper constitutional":** Lee, *Crown Against the Sickle,* 75.
304 **"Michael was for the first time":** Porter, *Michael of Romania,* 114.
304 **"It was perfectly on my prerogative":** King Michael I of Romania, interviewed by Paul Shapiro.
304 **"notes to his wife and made a will":** Lee, *Crown Against the Sickle,* 72.
304 **"So little was the possibility of an uprising":** Lee, *Crown Against the Sickle,* 80.
304 **"half-trained boy cadets of the":** Lee, *Crown Against the Sickle,* 80.
304 **"the military could not be sure of holding":** Porter, *Michael of Romania,* 117.
305 **"The next forty-eight hours until":** Porter, *Operation Autonomous,* 320.
305 **"In the turmoil of that evening he":** Porter, *Michael of Romania,* 114.
306 **"Attention, attention," the broadcaster announced:** Porter, *Operation Autonomous,* 310.
306 **"Romanians, in this most difficult hour":** The term "United Nations" was coined by President Franklin Roosevelt and first appeared in a 1942 declaration of solidarity between twenty-six Allied nations. Porter, *Operation Autonomous,* 310.
306 **"The BBC monitoring service heard":** Porter, *Michael of Romania,* 115.
306 **"felt a mixture of anxiety and pride":** Porter, *Michael of Romania,* 115.

44. BROTHERS-IN-ARMS

307 **"Razboiul e Gata!" From outside the window:** Beane, *James B. Beane.*
308 **"The war is over in Romania":** Caminada, *My Purpose Holds,* 211.
308 **"came running in, more and more of them":** Caminada, *My Purpose Holds,* 211.
308 **saying "Bune Comrade." Good comrade:** Britt, *The Princess and the P.O.W.,* 216.
308 **"At last! Romania is on the right":** James Straubel, ed., *Air Force Diary* (Simon & Schuster, 1947), 103.
308 **"try to get some sleep":** Britt, *The Princess and the P.O.W.,* 215.
308 **"Michael's courage in acting at this time":** Caminada, *My Purpose Holds,* 194.
309 **"Several generals and colonels came in":** Britt, *The Princess and the P.O.W.,* 216.
309 **Hoping "to delay hostilities for as long":** Porter, *Operation Autonomous,* 307.
309 **"are either going to take you to":** Duane Cavit and Dennis Cavit, eds., *Captain Charles Deane Cavit, U.S. Army Air Corps, 1942–1946: His World War II Military History with Notes. A Story Told (Mostly) in His Own Words* (self-published), 18–19.
310 **"in case the Germans attack you":** Britt, *The Princess and the P.O.W.,* 216.
310 **to "head for the woods":** Kerra Fisher, "POW Never Quit Hoping for Freedom," *Hendersonville* (N.C.) *Times-News,* September 4, 2000.
310 **"We thought we could expect the Germans":** Caminada, *My Purpose Holds,* 212.
311 **not the slightest "twinge of scruples":** Caminada, *My Purpose Holds,* 212.
311 **"It was peculiarly pleasing to see these":** Caminada, *My Purpose Holds,* 212.
311 **"the Germans were coming our way with a tank":** Britt, *The Princess and the P.O.W.,* 217.
311 **"Get your backpacks and get out":** Britt, *The Princess and the P.O.W.,* 217.
312 **"The guards stood in stunned silence":** Britt, *The Princess and the P.O.W.,* 217.
312 **"but the fear of being shot":** Britt, *The Princess and the P.O.W.,* 217.

312 **"flew the hell out of that plane":** Hill, *Black Sunday,* 33.
312 **"bombed his home in Germany and killed":** Cavit and Cavit, *Captain Charles Deane Cavit,* 11.
313 **"What have we gotten into?" he asked Cavit:** Cavit and Cavit, *Captain Charles Deane Cavit,* 12.
314 **"About half" of the Americans:** Beane, *James B. Beane.*
314 **"We were glad we were not home":** Cavit and Cavit, *Captain Charles Deane Cavit,* 18.

45. FOR ALL THE MARBLES

315 **"rain pounded the pavement":** Fisher, "POW Never Quit Hoping for Freedom."
316 **"traveling through retreating Germans":** Cavit and Cavit, *Captain Charles Deane Cavit,*19.
316 **"The dirty tarp was warm":** Britt, *The Princess and the P.O.W.,* 218.
316 **"We were leaving what had been":** Britt, *The Princess and the P.O.W.,* 218.
317 **"endless" column of military vehicles:** Collins, *P.O.W.,* 289.
317 **"High-ranking officers stood":** Collins, *P.O.W.,* 287.
318 **"We heard them speaking German":** Britt, *The Princess and the P.O.W.,* 219.
318 **"stood in readiness to fight":** Charles Deane Cavit, "Miscellaneous Data on Personalities, Anecdotes, Etc.," Official Military Personnel File, NARA.
319 **"It takes time for allies to become":** Collins, *P.O.W.,* 289.
319 **"They were too busy to stop us":** Lindley Hussey, quoted in "Flying Yank Colonel Tells Story of Romania Escape," *The Salt Lake Tribune,* September 3, 1944, 18.
319 **"Our good lieutenant was in charge":** Poulson, *A Personal History,* 49.
319 **"harrowing experience":** Charles Deane Cavit, "Miscellaneous Data."
320 **"felt more secure and hopeful now":** Poulson, *Personal History,* 49.
320 **"Headquarters, USAAF Pietroșița":** Collins, *P.O.W.,* 289.
320 **"tired, but happy, free men":** Britt, *The Princess and the P.O.W.,* 220.
320 **"a spectral glow lighted the sky":** Collins, *P.O.W.,* 286.
320 **"Hitler's boys didn't like the":** Sgt. May diary quoted in William Atkinson, *The Jolly Roger: An Airman's Tale of Survival in World War II* (Wise Publications, 2023), 191.
320 **"revenge attack":** "American Bombing of Prisoners" found within "'Operation Reunion,' Sept. 31–Oct. 1 1944, as Handled by Public Relations Section, HQ Fifteenth Air Force," Air Force Historical Research Agency, Maxwell AFB, Alabama.
320 **"pro-German regime" restored:** Porter, *Michael of Romania,* 119.

46. THE DAMNED HUNCHBACK

322 **"quite cool" for August:** Lucien Fugere, "My Diary," in newsletter of the Association of Former Prisoners of War in Romania, no. 15 (February 1984), 2.
323 **airmen called him Pop:** Beane, *James B. Beane.*
324 **"worked the town over":** Sgt. May diary, in Atkinson, *The Jolly Roger,* 191.
324 **"the Germans savagely unloaded":** "Operation Reunion: Rescue of American Airmen from Roumania, 27 August–3 September 1944," Official Report, Air Force Historical Research Agency, Maxwell AFB, Alabama.
324 **"Eighteen poor little soldiers":** Porter, *Michael of Romania,* 120.
324 **"small groups of diehard Nazis holed":** "Lt. Fox Reports," found within "'Operation Reunion," Sept. 31–Oct. 1 1944.
324 **"snipers in the streets":** Caminada, *My Purpose Holds,* 228.
324 **"All radio stations had been destroyed":** William H. Yaeger, Jr., Escape and Evasion Report, NARA.
324 **"The difference between stray bombs":** "American Bombing of Prisoners," found within "'Operation Reunion,' Sept. 31–Oct. 1 1944."
324 **"he was glad that it was the Germans":** "Eyewitness Account of Return," found within "'Operation Reunion,' Sept. 31–Oct. 1 1944."
325 **he "did not like the looks":** Gunn, 1944 Debrief.
325 **It was "of a poor type":** Gunn, 1944 Debrief.
325 **"had been put on board to guard":** James Gunn III, "Escape from Rumania," *Congressional*

Record, vol. 113, part 9 (May 3, 1967), 11,642–11,643, congress.gov/bound-congressional-record/1967/05/03/senate-section.

326 **"the right engine was acting up":** Gunn, 1944 Debrief.

326 **"in excellent English":** Gunn, "Escape from Rumania," 11,642–11,643.

326 **"I had been told about this officer":** Gunn, 1944 Debrief.

326 **"this troubled him not a whit":** "Operation Reunion: Rescue of American Airmen from Roumania, 27 August–3 September 1944."

327 **"how foolish he thought it was":** Gunn, 1944 Debrief.

327 **"an image came to mind":** Dumitru, *Aviatorul Erou,* 139.

327 **"if you will ride in the belly":** Gunn, "Escape from Rumania," 11,642–11,643.

327 **"The man's personality in itself was":** Gunn, 1944 Debrief.

328 **"to convey a message":** Ion Dobran, *Doi Ani De Foc Pe Messerschmitt: Jurnal De Front 1943–1945* [Two Years Under Fire in a Messerschmitt: Battlefield Journal 1943–1945] (Editura Favorit, 2018), 258.

328 **"a beautiful mission," scribbled:** Dobran, *Doi Ani,* 258.

328 **"picked up by radar for [a] minimum":** Gunn, 1944 Debrief.

47. THE AMERICAN MESSERSCHMITT

330 **"approximately three hours":** Gunn, 1944 Debrief.

330 **shot down American planes:** "Operation Reunion: Rescue of American Airmen from Roumania, 27 August–3 September 1944."

332 **"could not understand why":** Gunn, 1944 Debrief.

332 **he had a "wife and 2-year-old son":** "Californian 'Saves' 1126 Yank Fliers," *Oakland* (Cal.) *Tribune,* September 2, 1944, 1.

333 **"Colonel," Buzz said:** James Gunn III, "Flying Yank Colonel Tells Story of Romanian Escape," *The Salt Lake Tribune,* September 3, 1944, 4A.

333 **"If the Americans don't shoot us":** "Flying Yank Colonel."

333 **"Only an American and 'Bâzu'":** Dobran, *Doi Ani,* 261.

333 **"Ace though Captain Cantacuzino was":** Don Wharton, "Operation Reunion," *Air News,* vol. 8, no. 2 (March 1945), 46.

335 **"because of the danger of sleeping":** Gunn, 1944 Debrief.

335 **"He figured them one way":** Wharton, "Operation Reunion," 47.

335 **"a small kickplate used as a stirrup":** Gunn, "Escape from Rumania," 11,642–11,643.

336 **"Clunk!" A loud noise:** Wharton, "Operation Reunion," 47.

337 **stood "stunned," their feet "frozen":** "1996 Recollections of David Mason, Former US Combat Cameraman Assigned to the 15th Air Force, Italy (as told to Matt Poole)," Key Aero Forum, key.aero/forum/historic-aviation/135632-usaaf-colonel-to-get-posthumous-silver-star-for-mission-flown-in-a-bf-109g.

338 **"made a pass over the airstrip":** "1996 Recollections of David Mason."

338 **"Everybody looked up":** Bill Disbrow, *On the Edge* (Winlock Galey, 2005), 125.

338 **"That's a funny looking P-51":** Disbrow, *On the Edge,* 125.

339 **A "curious throng" of American airmen:** "Operation Reunion: Rescue of American Airmen from Roumania, 27 August–3 September 1944."

339 **"Gentlemen!" he shouted:** Duane Schultz, "The Pilot, the Prince, and the Rescue," History Net, July 14, 2017, historynet.com/pilot-prince-rescue.

339 **"I have somebody here":** "Flying Yank Colonel Tells Story of Romanian Escape," 4A.

340 **"Look at those GI shoes sticking out!":** "Flying Yank Colonel Tells Story of Romanian Escape," 4A.

340 **"When two sergeants pulled the colonel":** Britt, *The Princess and the P.O.W.,* 233.

340 **"a great many of the crowd":** Gunn, 1944 Debrief.

340 **"The reaction was enormous, indescribable":** Dumitru, *Aviatorul Erou,* 174.

340 **"Their flight also caused some embarrassment":** Robert Goebel, *Mustang Ace: Memoirs of a P-51 Fighter Pilot* (Zenith Press, 1991), 205.

340 **"I had great faith in Cantacuzino":** George Tucker, "1,126 Yankee and British Fliers Flown from Romania," *The Wilkes-Barre* (Penn.) *Record,* September 2, 1944, 16.

340 **"After all the hurrahs and cheers":** Gunn, 1944 Debrief.
341 **"We ate, drank, and in the end":** Dumitru, *Aviatorul Erou,* 174.
341 **"hustled off" to Bari:** Gunn, "Escape from Rumania," 11,642–11,643.
341 **"that a plan of evacuation":** Gunn, 1944 Debrief.

48. REUNION

342 **"Romanian pilots were dressed":** L.W. Currin, quoted in Jerry Barksdale, *When Duty Called: World War II Remembered* (Magnolia Press, 1998), 243.
343 **"The more I think about it":** Cavit and Cavit, *Captain Charles Deane Cavit,* 16.
343 **"Who knew what reserves":** Collins, *P.O.W.,* 291.
344 **"the jigsaw of war":** Collins, *P.O.W.,* 291.
344 **"Would the pieces close around us":** Collins, *P.O.W.,* 291.
344 **"they started a great fair":** Dobran, *Doi Ani,* 268
345 **"Had something gone wrong?":** Collins, *P.O.W.,* 294.
345 **"and told him about the US evacuation":** "Operation Reunion: Rescue of American Airmen from Roumania, 27 August–3 September 1944."
345 **"daring low-altitude" victory roll:** Cubbins, *The War of the Cottontails,* 257.
346 **"Within moments, formation after formation":** Cubbins, *The War of the Cottontails,* 257.
346 **"The roar of engines was all but lost":** Cubbins, *The War of the Cottontails,* 257.
346 **"What a feeling to see those planes!":** Marshall Samms, "I Was Shot Down Over Rumania," *Sir!,* September 1945, 450thbg.com/real/biographies/samms/samms.shtml.
346 **"all the fighter planes in Italy":** Harley Ross, "Airman Was WWII POW in Romania," *Rutland* (Vt.) *Herald,* March 17, 2008.
346 **"dropped his gear, held a tight pattern":** Cubbins, *The War of the Cottontails,* 257.
346 **"I pulled up next to some":** "Operational Story: September 1, 1944," found within " 'Operation Reunion' Sept. 31–Oct. 1 1944."
347 **"It was Cantacuzino":** Cubbins, *The War of the Cottontails,* 257.
348 **"In my life, I've never seen":** Dobran, *Doi Ani,* 266.
348 **"their first close-up view of an Me109":** "1996 Recollections of David Mason."
348 **"What a tiny little airplane it is!":** "1996 Recollections of David Mason."
348 **"I felt crushed, seeing that some kids":** Dumitru, *Aviatorul Erou,* 177.
348 **"What do you know about the Mustang?":** William Gunn, interviewed by Adam Makos, 2025.
348 **"One hundred twenty miles per hour?":** Goebel, *Mustang Ace,* 206.
349 **"rolled their socks down":** William Gunn, interviewed by Adam Makos, 2025.
349 **"wrung it out briefly":** Goebel, *Mustang Ace,* 206.
349 **"No wonder you shoot down":** "Flying Yank Colonel Tells Story of Romanian Escape," 4A.
349 **to Buzz's "great joy":** Tudor, *Constantin "Bâzu" Cantacuzino,*192.
349 **"As for Capt. Cantacuzino":** "Flying Yank Colonel Tells Story of Romanian Escape," 4A.
350 **"they didn't care whether they":** Ardery, *Bomber Pilot,* 68.
350 **"the B-17s looked great to us":** Richard Britt, *The Princess and the P.O.W.,* 233.
350 **"laughing and congratulating each other":** Cubbins, *The War of the Cottontails,* 258.
350 **"Childishly I repeated to myself":** William Fili, *Passage to Valhalla: The Human Side of Aerial Combat over Nazi Occupied Europe* (Filcon Publishers, 1991), 286.
351 **"rushed around asking questions":** Britt, *The Princess and the P.O.W.,* 231.
351 **"Soon as your plane lands, climb aboard":** *Project Gunn,* Office of Strategic Services, Field Photographic Branch, August/September 1944, film, NARA.
351 **"And here they were, beautiful":** Collins, *P.O.W.,* 294.
352 **"and one Romanian stowaway":** "Operation Reunion: Rescue of American Airmen from Roumania, 27 August–3 September 1944."
352 **"The Americans weren't messing around":** Collins, *P.O.W.,* 294.
352 **"You guys better get in fast":** Collins, *P.O.W.,* 294.
352 **"ready to call the pilot":** Cubbins, *The War of the Cottontails,* 258.
353 **"equally excited news photographers":** "Eyewitness Account of Return," found within " 'Operation Reunion' Sept. 31–Oct. 1 1944."

353 **Hitler's Gas Station:** Carroll Stewart, *Ted's Traveling Circus: 93rd Bombardment Group (H), United States Army Air Force, World War II* (Sun/World Communications, 1996), 153.
353 **suntan uniforms, "swell" beds:** Cavit and Cavit, *Captain Charles Deane Cavit,* 19.
353 **"fantastic" American food:** Caminada, *My Purpose Holds,* 217.
354 **"immediately swept into a whirl":** "Eyewitness Account of Return."
355 **"How sweet it was":** Poulson, *Personal History,* 50.

49. THE RED INVASION

356 **"hellbent on preparing for free elections":** Porter, *Michael of Romania,* 118.
356 **had "God's hand" in it:** King Michael I of Romania, interviewed by Paul Shapiro.
356 **"with a directive to eliminate Romanian":** Porter, *Michael of Romania,* 118.
357 **"When they get here, we'll pray that":** Schacht, "For Rumanian Princess Catherine."
357 **"the officer instructed her chauffeur":** Dugan and Stewart, *Ploesti,* 279.
357 **Red Army colonel came out "beaming":** Dugan and Stewart, *Ploesti,* 279.
357 **"bringing in a million troops":** Britt, *The Princess and the P.O.W.,* 232.
357 **"Davai ceas. Davai palton":** Octavia Constantinescu, "Ambasada Rusiei mistifică istoria: Soldații sovietici n-au comis atrocități în România" [The Russian Embassy Falsifies History: Soviet Soldiers Did Not Commit Atrocities in Romania], *Newsweek Romania,* December 30, 2018, newsweek.ro/politica/ambasada-rusiei-mistifica-istoria-soldatii-sovietici-n-au-comis-atrocitati-in-romania-reactia-mae.
357 **"Tell him this car is used":** Dugan and Stewart, *Ploesti,* 280.
357 **"The Romanians do not want the Russians":** "Operation Reunion: Rescue of American Airmen from Roumania, 27 August–3 September 1944."
358 **"a rusty 1926 Chrysler sitting":** Dugan and Stewart, *Ploesti,* 280.
358 **"The car had no hood":** Cass, "For American Prisoners," 13C.
358 **"My car!" he wailed. "My whitewall tires!":** Cass, "For American Prisoners," 13C.
358 **"She was fishing in the trunk":** Dugan and Stewart, *Ploesti,* 280.
358 **"The Russian Army will start it for you.":** Cass, "For American Prisoners," 13C.
358 **and said, "Get in":** Dugan and Stewart, *Ploesti,* 280.
359 **"through the backwoods and cornfields":** Cass, "For American Prisoners," 13C.
359 **"I watched with tears in my eyes":** "Romanian Princess Cheers Airmen," 19.
359 **"from under the noses of the Russians":** Poulson, *Personal History,* 50.
359 **"did not get to say goodbye to even one":** "Romanian Princess Cheers Airmen," 19.
359 **"He told me of his family, his friends":** "Romanian Princess Cheers Airmen," 19.
359 **"to see any of them again":** "Romanian Princess Cheers Airmen," 19.
359 **"of unhealthy social origin":** Caradja, *Princess Catherine,* 167.

50. NOTHING LEFT TO LOSE

361 **"as an ambulance driver":** "Queen Anne of Romania—Obituary," *The Telegraph* (London), August 1, 2016, telegraph.co.uk/obituaries/2016/08/01/queen-anne-of-romania—obituary.
362 **There, "within days,":** "Queen Anne of Romania—Obituary."
362 **to discuss a "family problem":** Nick Thorpe, "Romania's Ex-King Michael I Defends His Wartime Record," BBC, October 25, 2011, bbc.com/news/world-europe-15448163.
362 **"You have to abdicate":** Thorpe, "Romania's Ex-King."
362 **"and leave the country":** Eugen Tomiuc, "World War II—60 Years After: Former Romanian Monarch Remembers Decision To Switch Sides," Radio Free Europe, May 6, 2005, rferl.org/a/1058760.html.
362 **"order the execution of about 1,000":** Thorpe, "Romania's Ex-King."
362 **"What are you supposed to do":** Thorpe, "Romania's Ex-King."
362 **"grieving and unable to recover":** Lucian Dobrovicescu, "Cum a Evadat Prințul Bâzu Cantacuzino din România Stalinistă" [How Prince Bâzu Cantacuzino Escaped from Stalinist Romania], *Historia,* historia.ro/sectiune/general/cum-a-evadat-printul-bazu-cantacuzino-din-romania-580776.html.
362 **Children's House Number One:** Hoad, *The Eagle's Child,* 253.

362 **"I was sent packing from my estate":** Catherine Caradja, [Autobiography], 1958, CSUF University Archives and Special Collections, Fullerton, Calif.
362 **"I sold my watch, then my gold fountain pen":** Schacht, "For Rumanian Princess Catherine."
362 **"What did I have to lose—or live for?":** Schacht, "For Rumanian Princess Catherine."
362 **"I had to find a reason":** Scorțescu, "Caradja și Cantacuzino," 10.
363 **"Get out and tell people what is happening":** Britt, *The Princess and the P.O.W.*, 270.
363 **"100 hectares" of land:** Dobrovicescu, "Cum a Evadat Prințul Bâzu Cantacuzino."
363 **"Offended and humiliated" by the prince:** Dobrovicescu, "Cum a Evadat Prințul Bâzu Cantacuzino."
363 **January 1948 "an opportunity arose":** Arma and Stoleru,"Misiunile Secrete."
363 **"In response to the treatment":** Dobrovicescu, "Cum a Evadat Prințul Bâzu Cantacuzino."
364 **"I was not going to run":** "Romanian Princess Cheers Airmen," 19.
364 **"no intention of succumbing":** Scorțescu, "Caradja și Cantacuzino," 10.
365 **"Madame," he said. "I do not like the way":** Schacht, "For Rumanian Princess Catherine."
365 **"I would be most grateful":** Schacht, "For Rumanian Princess Catherine."

51. ESCAPEES

366 **"on the low level raid":** Col. Paul Wolf, letter to Air Technical Service Command, May 5, 1945. In Ernest Poulson, Official Military Personnel File, NARA.
366 **"In the returnee's opinion, very successful":** "Air Intelligence Contact Unit—18 January 1945," Ernest Poulson, Official Military Personnel File, NARA.
367 **"was the single most important raid":** Ernest Poulson, interviewed by National World War II Museum, Salt Lake City, Utah, October 23, 2013, ww2online.org/view/ernest-poulson.
368 **living in a "rather destitute state":** Poulson, *Personal History*, 71.
368 **"she joked about the Reds":** Britt, *The Princess and the P.O.W.*, 270.
368 **"I was half and half":** Cass, "For American Prisoners," 13C.
368 **St. Peter, because "he opened":** Schacht, "For Rumanian Princess Catherine."
369 **"Time to hide" he said in a hushed:** Caradja, *Princess Catherine*, 171.
369 **"and put her in the water tank":** "Declaratie Florea Ardeleanu [Florea Ardeleanu Statement]," November 10, 1952, Consiliul Național Pentru Studierea Arhivelor Securității [National Council for the Study of Securitate Archives], Bucharest, Romania.
369 **"It's an old sofa back":** Caradja, *Princess Catherine*, 170.
369 **"like a rosary to herself":** Britt, *The Princess and the P.O.W.*, 272.
370 **"terrifying, uncomfortable, and cold":** Harriet Hawes, "Princess Visiting in Hub Helped Fliers Flee Reds," *Boston Globe*, July 18, 1956, 8.
370 **"proud, intelligent, and energetic":** Poulson, *Personal History*, 71.
370 **"in some small measure":** Poulson, *Personal History*, 71.

52. THE ANGEL OF PLOESTI

372 **"In the rough sea I was uncomfortable":** Caradja, *Princess Catherine*, 184.
373 **"I wouldn't dare endanger":** Bill Porterfield, "The Story of a Princess Charming," *Detroit Free Press*, May 31, 1967, 3–4.
373 **"call on as many as possible of the 110 fliers":** "Princess to Turn Dream into Reality," *The Courier-Gazette* (McKinney, Tex.), November 30, 1955, 7.
373 **to see her "adopted son," Britt:** Britt, *The Princess and the P.O.W.*, 273.
374 **"I'm still at sea":** Caradja, *Princess Catherine*, 184.
375 **"The Angel of Ploesti":** Waterhouse, "'Angel of Ploesti,'" 1.
375 **"As many of them as I can":** "Romanian Princess Comes to See 'My American Boys,'" *Daily Press* (Newport News, Va.), December 15, 1955, 25.
375 **He "asked good questions to put me":** Caradja, *Princess Catherine*, 185.
375 **"This had alerted the ex-POWs":** Ibid.
375 **"tell of life today behind the Iron Curtain":** "Princess to Visit Flyer Here She Met as P.O.W.," *St. Louis Post Dispatch*, November, 30, 1955, 11.

375 **"I am lucky to be one of the few":** Bill Porterfield, "The Story of a Princess Charming," *Detroit Free Press,* May 31, 1967, 3–4.
375 **"I understand you're heading for Houston":** Britt, *The Princess and the P.O.W.,* 258.
375 **"It's been twelve years since he left":** Caradja, *Princess Catherine,* 185.
376 **"What a wonderful surprise!":** "Princess and Texan Meet in New York," *Abilene* (Tex.) *Reporter-News,* December, 15, 1955, 2.
376 **"hardwoods from around the world":** Britt, *The Princess and the P.O.W.,* 257.
376 **"I am going to take her to Texas":** "Princess and Texan Meet in New York," 2.
377 **"It was a marvelous introduction":** Caradja, *Princess Catherine,* 185.

AFTERWORD

379 **"hardly put down the suitcases":** Catherine Caradja, *Princess Catherine* (Gabriel Publishing, 1991), 186.
379 **"The holidays were filled with parties":** Britt, *The Princess and the P.O.W.,* 275.
379 **"at the home of his parents":** "Princess Who Helped War Flyers Arrives for Visit," *St. Louis Post-Dispatch,* December 14, 1955, 20.
379 **"hard for him to be in one place":** Margaret Culver, daughter of Robert O'Reilly ll, interviewed by Bryan Makos, April 2024.
380 **"Only a mother could realize how grateful":** Russell Rice, "Romanian 'Mother' to Yank Airmen Visits in Lexington," *Lexington* (Ky.) *Herald-Leader,* April 5, 1956, 1.
380 **with the "35-year-old veteran":** "Romanian Princess Visits Revere Man She Helped in War," July 19, 1956. Al Romano Collection.
380 **"to acquaint Americans with a firsthand":** Beulah Schacht, "For Rumanian Princess Catherine: Life in the West is 'Paradise,'" *St. Louis Globe-Democrat,* March 15, 1956.
381 **"had to pull it out of him":** Kevin Lilley, "Pilot's Widow Receives his Silver Star 70 Years After Heroic Escape," *Air Force Times,* October 21, 2014 airforcetimes.com/news/your-air-force/2014/10/21/pilot-s-widow-receives-his-silver-star-70-years-after-heroic-escape.
381 **"favorite groups were those organized":** Caradja, *Princess Catherine,* 187.
381 **"What you have here":** Waterhouse, "'Angel of Ploesti,'" 1.
381 **"urged Americans to preserve theirs":** "Britt POW Author, Owned Old Theater," *San Antonio Express-News,* September 17, 1991, 10B.
381 **but only "as a ground attendant":** Julián Oller, *Bâzu, un Príncipe Legendario* [Bâzu, a Legendary Prince] (Fundación Aérea de la Comunidad Valenciana, 2014), 370.
381 **"The policy of repression against":** Ibid.
382 **"spraying the vast olive fields":** Ibid., 273.
382 **"I cannot sponsor this individual":** William Gunn, son of James Gunn III, interviewed by Adam Makos, August 2025.
382 **raved about his "spectacular" performances:** Oller, *Bâzu, un Príncipe Legendario,* 275.
382 **"the most daring acrobatics":** Ibid.
382 **"a terrifying inverted flight":** Ibid.
382 **"Prince Cantacuzino was an exceptional man":** Marian Christy, "Nadia Gray's No Longer Blue: Banker's Wife Enters Limelight," *Mansfield News Journal* (Ohio), May 12, 1976, 18.
382 **"irregular and sometimes inadequate meals":** Oller, *Bâzu, un Príncipe Legendario* [Bâzu, a Legendary Prince], 277.
383 **"The entire aviation community in Spain":** Alexandru Arma, Ciprian Stoleru, Historia, "Misiunile Secrete în Care a Fost Implicat Constantin, Bâzu" Cantacuzino, Asul Aviației Românești" [The Secret Missions in Which Constantin 'Bâzu' Cantacuzino, the Ace of Romanian Aviation, Was Involved], posted July 12, 2019, 39:36, youtube.com/watch?v=P_zg5hgLE6k
383 **"still hoping to come to America":** Caradja, *Princess Catherine,* 194.
383 **"Aiding in her search for her 'boys'":** Waterhouse, "'Angel of Ploesti,'" 1.
383 **"the towns from which they enlisted":** Caradja, *Princess Catherine,* 190–91.
383 **"she contacted radio and TV stations":** Britt, *The Princess and the P.O.W.,* 261.
383 **"Each day in this country I hear from":** "Romanian Princess Cheers Airmen," 19.
384 **"Goodyear tire builder":** Umrigar, "Freedom Contributes," 33.

384 **"Ex-King Michael of Romania Becomes":** British Pathé, "Ex-King Michael of Rumania Becomes Market Gardener," Pathé video, 8:12, 1953, britishpathe.com/asset/197632.

384 **"chickens and vegetables":** Eugen Tomiuc, "Romania's King Michael: WWII-Era Monarch Who Lived to See Country Emerge from Soviet Domination," Radio Free Europe, December 5, 2017, rferl.org/a/romania-king-michael-ww2-era-monarch-exits-limelight/27623319.html.

384 **"When you have to leave":** Tomiuc, "World War II—60 Years After."

384 **"a silent, sad, serious man":** Tessa Dunlop, "Michael 1 of Romania Obituary," *The Guardian* (U.K.), December 5, 2017, theguardian.com/world/2017/dec/05/michael-1-of-romania.

385 **"radio compasses to automatic pilots":** British Pathé, "Rumania: King Michael Now Test Pilot," Pathé video, 4:15, 1957, britishpathe.com/asset/244239.

385 **"about 25" men and their families:** Cavit and Cavit, *Captain Charles Deane Cavit,* 22.

386 **"which they made into a square-dancing":** "Britt POW Author, Owned Old Theater," 10B.

386 **"He would never pass a lilac":** Kristal Markiewicz, granddaughter of Al Romano, "Eulogy for Al Romano," February 24, 2017.

386 **with his grandkids "into his late 80s":** Ibid.

386 **"Every year he sent out St. Patrick's Day cards":** Margaret Culver, daughter of Robert O'Reilly ll, interviewed by Bryan Makos, April 2024.

387 **He and Ernie "joked many times" about:** Poulson, *Personal History,* 9.

388 **"For the first time in forty-five years":** Caradja, *Princess Catherine,* 195.

388 **In a scene "befitting a conquering hero":** Carol Williams, "A King's Visit Stirs Elation—and Unease," *Los Angeles Times,* April 27, 1992, A3.

388 **"crowd that swelled beyond 100,000":** Williams, "A King's Visit," A3.

388 **"King in, Communists out!":** Gabriel Paslaru, "Romanians Cheer Former King," *The Oregonian* (Portland, Ore.), April 27, 1992, P4.

388 **"My interest is not in the throne":** Paslaru, "Romanians Cheer Former King," P4.

388 **such an "affectionate outpouring":** Williams, "A King's Visit," A3.

388 **"I am happy you remember me":** Paslaru, "Romanians Cheer Former King," P4.

388 **"return to Catherine more than twenty acres":** William Fili, *Biography of Princess Catherine Caradja: Romania 1893–1993* (self-published), 4.

388 **she was granted "a small pension":** Garcia, "Romanian Princess," B12.

388 **"Her eyes sparkled a little brighter":** Fili, *Biography of Princess Catherine Caradja,* 4.

388 **to escort her homeward:** James Garcia, "Romanian Princess Heads Homeward," *Austin American Statesman,* June 12, 1991, B1.

389 **"Dear X-POWs and Friends":** Catherine Caradja, farewell message published in newsletter of the Association of Former Prisoners of War in Romania, no. 34 (April 1991), 3.

389 **"Of course, another place could":** Scorțescu, "Caradja și Cantacuzino," 24.

389 **overjoyed and "eager to see her again":** Garcia, "Romanian Princess," B1.

389 **"engraved with the images of the exiled":** Garcia, "Romanian Princess," B1.

389 **"in the attic of her former Cradle," she died:** Scorțescu, "Caradja și Cantacuzino," 24.

390 **"It was pointed out that of all the people":** "Operation Reunion: Rescue of American Airmen from Roumania, 27 August–3 September 1944."

390 **"Some of them were my friends forever":** Poulson, interviewed by National World War II Museum.

PHOTO CREDITS

Page 3: National Archives
4: Poulson family
7: Robert J. O'Reilly II family
15: Poulson family
23: Robert J. O'Reilly II family
28 (left): Dénes Bernád collection
28 (right): Author's collection
30: Dénes Bernád collection
31: Dénes Bernád collection
43: National Archives
55: National Archives
64: Biblioteca Academiei Române
65: Biblioteca Academiei Române
74: Romano family
78: National Archives
87: Robert J. O'Reilly II family
88: Robert J. O'Reilly II family
90: Bryan Makos
93: Bryan Makos
101: Robert J. O'Reilly II family
108: Robert J. O'Reilly II family
109 (left and right): Robert J. O'Reilly II family
112: Robert J. O'Reilly II family
131: National Archives
142: Arhiva Nationala de Filme
146: Arhiva Nationala de Filme
154: Poulson family
175: Author's collection
177: Romano family
181: Biblioteca Academiei Române
182: Author's collection
193: Biblioteca Academiei Române
194: Biblioteca Academiei Române
195: Romano family
205: Robert J. O'Reilly II family
215 (left and right): National Archives
217: Author's collection
249: Biblioteca Academiei Române
253: Biblioteca Academiei Române
256: CNSAS Archives
261: Dwight Township High School #230
268: National Archives
273: MacDonald family
279: Dénes Bernád collection
296: Bundesarchiv
313: Cavit family
322: Dénes Bernád collection
323: National Archives
339: National Archives
341: National Archives
347: Dénes Bernád collection
354: National Archives
373: Caradja family archives
376: Caradja family archives
392, top left: Robert J. O'Reilly II family
392, top right: Caradja family archives

392, center left: Photo by Harry Pot, copyright National Archief (Netherlands)

392, center right: Romano family

392, bottom: Dénes Bernád collection

393, top left: Author's collection

393, top right: Personal Archives of the Royal Family of Romania

393, center: Caradja family archives

393, bottom: Romano family

INSERT

King Carol awards Buzz: Biblioteca Națională

B-24: National Archives

Ernie Poulson: Poulson family

Engineers' Band, Utah: Poulson family

The crew, stateside: Robert J. O'Reilly II family

Al suited up: Romano family

Buzz on the ice: Author's collection

Romanian ground crewman: Biblioteca Academiei Române

Fleet F10G: Dénes Bernád collection

Buzz during his airline days: Biblioteca Națională

Order of Mihai the Brave: Dénes Bernád collection

Parade before banners: Biblioteca Academiei Române

Wongo Wongo: National Archives

The Sandman: National Archives

Campinâ: National Archives

Chattanooga Choo Choo: Arhiva Nationala de Filme

Aeronautical Order banquet: Biblioteca Academiei Române

King Michael with Antonescu: Biblioteca Academiei Române

The lodge: Romano family

Officer POWs: Romano family

Buzz by the rudder: Dénes Bernád collection

Buzz in the cockpit: Dénes Bernád collection

P-51s: National Archives

Bob and Sandy: Robert J. O'Reilly II family

Brothers-in-arms: Robert J. O'Reilly II family

American Messerschmitt: National Archives

Streaked paint: National Archives

In the fuselage: National Archives

Buzz and the Mustang: Dénes Bernád collection

B-17s: National Archives

A B-17 taxis: National Archives

Greeting POWs: National Archives

POWs waiting to board: National Archives

At Bari airfield: National Archives

Repatriated POWs: Robert J. O'Reilly II family

ABOUT THE AUTHOR

Hailed by the Associated Press as "a masterful storyteller," ADAM MAKOS is the *New York Times* bestselling author of *A Higher Call, Spearhead,* and *Devotion*—now a major motion picture starring Glen Powell. Inspired by his grandfathers' service, Makos crafts unforgettable stories of America's veterans, blending raw human drama with vivid close-up military action. The *Los Angeles Times* puts him "in the top ranks of military writers," a title earned through extensive research that has taken him from flying a World War II bomber to embedding on a Special Forces raid in Iraq and even journeying into North Korea in search of a missing American aviator.

Facebook.com/AdamMakosAuthor
Instagram: @AdamMakos
X: @AdamMakos

ABOUT THE TYPE

This book was set in Bulmer, a typeface designed in the late eighteenth century by the London type cutter William Martin (1757–1830). The typeface was created especially for the Shakespeare Press, directed by William Bulmer (1757–1830)—hence the font's name. Bulmer is considered to be a transitional typeface, containing characteristics of old-style and modern designs. It is recognized for its elegantly proportioned letters, with their long ascenders and descenders.